Eschatology and the Technological Future

MW01061934

This book offers an insightful and timely analysis of key theorists and ideas in the intersection between theology and technology. From the religiously inspired technological optimism of Pierre Teilhard de Chardin and Nikolai Fedorov, to the darker technological pessimism of Jacques Ellul, the contributions of Christian theorists to understanding the technological milieu can offer us fresh perspectives on some intractable problems of modern life. As Burdett clearly shows, technological optimism and utopianism have religious roots, and a technological culture that ignores its own roots is in danger not only of environmental devastation, but also existential and spiritual despair. A fine book at a critical time.

—*David Lewin, Liverpool Hope University, UK*

The rapid advancement of technology has led to an explosion of speculative theories about what the future of humankind may look like. These "technological futurisms" from the fields of nanotechnology, biotechnology and information technology are drawing growing scrutiny from the philosophical and theological communities. This text seeks to contextualize the growing literature on the cultural, philosophical and religious implications of technological advancement by considering technological futurisms such as transhumanism in the context of the long historical tradition of technological dreaming. Michael Burdett traces the latent religious sources of our contemporary technological imagination by looking at visionary approaches to technology and the future in seminal technological utopias and science fiction and draws on past theological responses to the technological future with Pierre Teilhard de Chardin and Jacques Ellul. Burdett's argument arrives at a contemporary Christian response to transhumanism based around the themes of possibility and promise by turning to the works of Richard Kearney, Eberhard Jüngel and Jürgen Moltmann. Throughout, the author highlights points of correspondence and divergence between technological futurisms and the Judeo-Christian understanding of the future.

Michael S. Burdett is Postdoctoral Fellow at Wycliffe Hall, University of Oxford, UK and a Visiting Fellow at the University of St Andrews, UK.

Routledge Studies in Religion

For a full list of titles in this series, please visit www.routledge.com

Eschatology and the Technological Future

Michael S. Burdett

Routledge
Taylor & Francis Group

LONDON AND NEW YORK

First published 2015
by Routledge

2 Park Square, Milton Park, Abingdon, Oxon OX14 4RN
711 Third Avenue, New York, NY 10017, USA

*Routledge is an imprint of the Taylor & Francis Group,
an informa business*

First issued in paperback 2017

Library of Congress Cataloging-in-Publication Data

Burdett, Michael S. (Michael Stephen), 1981–
    Eschatology and the technological future / Michael S.
Burdett. — 1 [edition].
        pages cm. — (Routledge studies in religion ; 43)
    Includes bibliographical references and index.
    1. Technology—Religious aspects—Christianity.   2. Technology and
civilization—Forecasting.   3. Future, The.   4. Eschatology.   I. Title.
    BR115.T42B87   2015
    236—dc23
    2014033290

ISBN: 978-1-138-82633-5 (hbk)
ISBN: 978-1-138-05314-4 (pbk)

Typeset in Sabon
by Apex CoVantage, LLC

To Emily

Contents

Figures

Acknowledgements

Any work of scholarship is a product of the thoughtful and generous attention of many. This work is no exception. Many institutions helped to contribute significant resources towards the completion of this text. Regents Park College, Oxford and the Centre for Christianity and Culture provided a stimulating environment that helped nurture this book in its infancy and contributed substantial bursaries whilst completing it. In the final stages the faculty at St Mary's College, University of St Andrews provided the stimulation and space to complete it. Wycliffe Hall, Oxford and its partner Scholarship and Christianity in Oxford have been my academic home in recent years and have provided research opportunities that, without them, this book would never have seen the light of day. Stan Rosenberg deserves special mention for his loyalty and for encouraging this burgeoning academic.

Other colleagues and friends offered important feedback in informal settings and seminars. Thanks are due to Clark Elliston, Stephen Backhouse, Jinhyok Kim, Mathew Kirkpatrick, David K O'hara, Bradley Onishi and Andrew Dunstan. Many conversations about theology and technology helped form germinal ideas found herein and supplied important theological and philosophical scrutiny.

I would also like to extend my appreciation to other scholars in the field that cast a critical eye on various parts of this book during the different stages of its completion. I am grateful to Paul Fiddes, Peter Harrison, John Perry, Joel Rasmussen, Brent Waters, David Lewin and Ronald Cole-Turner for their thoughtful criticisms and advice.

Prof George Pattison supervised the initial project and provided important insights and tutelage, knowing exactly what to provide at just the right time. I originally turned to issues of theology and technology because of his book *Thinking about God in an Age of Technology* and where it might seem his name is not on every page, his guidance and expertise were the driving force behind each one. Indeed, it is often those we are the most indebted to that we don't know how to properly cite.

Finally, I would like to thank my family for their indefatigable support while I pursued a new career in theological higher education. Particular thanks are due to my wife, Emily, who has supported me whilst we both became academics and has challenged my thinking and loved me unconditionally. I could not have done this without her.

1 Introduction
Our Technological Future, Philosophy and Religion

This is a book about the technological future. It is about how technology in the last two centuries has stimulated our speculations, imaginations and hopes for the future. Of course, it might be added that this preoccupation with the future is not unique to the technological future. Concerns about economic stability and the erosion of confidence in our models of economic growth have equally contributed to increased speculation about the future as have the present ecological and energy crises. Alvin Toffler coined the term 'future shock'[1] in the mid-1960s as a way to illustrate this present concern with the exceeding pace of modern life and our general malaise, uneasiness and anxiety felt about the future. This preoccupation with the future, so Toffler tells us, is a direct result of our growing technological environment. Indeed, we find today that issues surrounding technology can't help but influence these other areas which cause us to reflect on the future. For instance, some experts claim that the solution to economic turmoil is greater technological innovation.[2] And the general consensus is that the ecological and energy crises can be aided with increasing green technologies. Where other forces may compel us to obsess about the future, technology is very much a key component to all imagining of that future today.

Of course, more will be said about our public fixation with the technological future, particularly in the next two chapters. This book, however, is also about how the future gets constructed. What exactly is the future from a more philosophical point of view? How does the future relate to the present and to the past? Does appealing to ontology help? Is the future just a product of the past and present? Is it driven from 'behind', or is it something which beckons from 'ahead'? These issues are the topic of the final three chapters.

This text also addresses these questions from the Christian tradition. The latter half asks how Christians, in particular, have thought about the technological future and how they construct the future. Christian scholars have, in the past century, increasingly reflected upon the force of technology on individual lives, the church, and history and the future more generally. While I would suggest that not enough attention has been devoted to technology, there has been a vibrant tradition that has significantly contributed to Christian reflection on technology and the future. Because the focus of this text is on the technological future, most of these Christian reflections will derive from Christian eschatology—the study of the last things.[3]

Whereas these are the general themes of the present work, I also offer a constructive argument. In the first instance, I aim to assess how and to what extent technological futurism, and in particular transhumanism as an extreme version of technological futurism, can be incorporated into the Christian tradition. In so doing, I aim to highlight the relative deficiencies and harmony transhumanism has with the Christian understanding of the future. In the second instance, I argue that Christian eschatology can provide a more robust account of the future than that offered by technological futurism. I argue that Christian eschatology, when it emphasises the themes of possibility and promise, can—at the least—provide a needed corrective to technological futurisms and specifically transhumanist understandings of the future, or—at most—provide a counterreligious narrative which allows for radical hope in the way technological futurisms alone cannot. Christian eschatology does not restrict itself to what is only actual to create its future. Rather, it is open to a God of possibility and promise who is not limited to interpolation and history, but can bring the radically new in the Kingdom of God. The Christian response to technological futurism is that the future is God's future and must be set within the interpersonal nature of a promissory triune God who brings new possibilities to the world.

But why is this book needed specifically? First, as intimated above, society today is concerned about the future and, in particular, there is concern about how technology is 'ramping up' the stakes of our continued existence. As we will come to see in the next few chapters, technology has been the locus of salvation for many when reflecting on the future whilst, for others, it has been the gravest enemy. Generally speaking, this book is required because technologically driven ideologies verging on the religious are becoming ubiquitous today.[4] This makes explicit dialogue with traditional religions absolutely imperative. I offer an account here derived from Christianity and do not presume to speak for other faiths on the matter. But, for Christians, the concerns of the world are important and the technological future is a major concern of the world. Second, this book is critically important because it focuses on a particular technological futurism which is gaining widespread appeal today: transhumanism. This text is not unique in recognising the need and value of Christians to consider transhumanism. Many books and articles have been written in the past two decades on Christianity and transhumanism. But, none have really contextualised it in the long historical tradition of transhumanism and technological dreaming. They either restrict themselves to the present century and contemporary figures who weigh in on the issues or have not sufficiently assessed the future that transhumanists propose or how they go about constructing that future.[5]

1.1 DEFINITION OF TERMS

How is technology treated here? In some ways, this will become clearer throughout the text. But, suffice it to say here that the technological future to which I refer is not exhausted by, say, the future of the computer, the car or the linear accelerator. I do not mean the future of a particular technology, although this is included. I am interested in how technology as a universalising and totalising force on society and humanity is taken up in imagining the future.[6] This book is not overtly concerned with the ethical mandates of growing technologies, but is interested in how humanity perceives that technology often in religious terms. Through study of speculation about the future, tacit convictions and ultimate concerns become much clearer. All of which implies that study of the technological future can be relevant today because it can help illuminate how we think and feel about ourselves and our environment in relation to that technology.

I suggest in this book that there are two possible approaches to the future. These two approaches provide a helpful heuristic in guiding our reflections on the technological future. Following Jürgen Moltmann and Ted Peters, the future can be interpreted as either *futurum* or *adventus*.[7] The English term for future is derived from the Latin term *futurum* whereas the German term for future, *Zukunft*, comes from *adventus*. *Futurum* refers to the future as an outworking of present conditions and forces so that the future is a product of what has preceded it. It is driven from behind. *Adventus*, on the other hand, describes that which is coming. It makes no claims about the future being the sole product of the past and present and instead speaks of arrival. It is driven by what is ahead.[8]

I have been using the term technological futurism. A technological futurism is a future in which technology figures prominently. I use it to describe notably secular notions of the future that give a certain priority to the future as a product of forces inherent in the present: *futurum*. It is often related to our human future in the form of utopia or dystopia but is inclusive of any reflection on the future. The 'technological' qualifier signifies that the content of this future and the catalyst is technology. Not all technological futurisms are equal. I do not intend to imply by this term that the technological future posed by Edward Bellamy is the same as that posed by R. Buckminster Fuller; still less that transhumanism conveys a future that is identical with that of the technocrats. I see technological futurism on a gradient where religious accounts of the future make up the other end of the scale. Some accounts of the technological future are more secular and depend upon *futurum*, making them favour a technological futurist approach, whereas others might appeal to God's action in the world and adhere to the future as *adventus*.[9]

From the fourth chapter, my main focus is on a unique strand of technological futurism: transhumanism. I prefer to use the term transhumanism instead of posthumanism, another term sometimes used, because, first, it is the term used by the organisation formerly called the 'World Transhumanist Association' and now called 'Humanity+'. Second, the term transhumanism better describes its relation to humanity. 'Post' tends to allude to something just after the human and doesn't necessarily provide orientation as to how it relates to the human except that it has moved on from it. I favour transhumanism precisely because it provides more content as to how this movement relates to the human: It is transcending it.[10] These transhumanists say humanity is in the process of being transcended and this will be important for interpreting it along religious lines.[11] Despite focusing my comments to a specific technological futurism, transhumanism, by the end of this book many of the reflections and criticisms levelled at transhumanism may be extended to technological futurism more broadly.

1.2 METHODOLOGY AND OVERVIEW

The methodology of this text, or how I go about addressing the technological future, is visible from its overall structure.[12] The next three chapters, chapters 2 through 4, consist of what I call 'visionary approaches' to the technological future. These chapters chart the ascendency of our public technological imagination and how it arises from religious sources. My aim is to trace the ways in which our imagining of the future has shifted from one instituted by or in conjunction with God to a future more reliant upon human endeavours—from *adventus* to *futurum*. In many ways, these chapters locate the field in which technological futurisms have arisen in our public awareness. They represent the secular phenomenon to which Christians must respond. These chapters also give a history of how something like contemporary transhumanism could have come about. It isn't a history of just transhumanist ideas per se, but a history of dreaming about the technological future of which transhumanism is a product. The second section, chapters 5 and 6, then considers how notable Christian figures in the 20th century have provided a theological response to these ideas of technology and the future. These Christian responses will then contextualise and orient the final chapters which give a constructive appeal. This final section then considers the philosophical and theological issues at play in constructing the future. Issues such as the future's relation to ontology and, from a Christian perspective, how promise and possibility are central to understanding the future as Christians.

The next chapter looks at the history of our contemporary technological imagination in technological utopias. It begins with works by Francis Bacon and N. F. Fedorov and moves into the 19th and 20th century considering several American technological utopias. The third chapter turns toward works of science fiction and assesses three ways technology has been depicted in the future in science fiction: (1) adventurous and transcendent; (2) dystopian and oppressive; and (3) questioning the demarcation between humanity and technology. Chapter 4 then assesses the proposed future of three contemporary transhumanists: Raymond Kurzweil, Martin Rees and Nick Bostrom. It suggests that transhumanism has many religiously motivated elements and depends upon a future that is constructed purely out of the present, *futurum*. Chapter 5 then moves into past theological responses to technology and the future where it assesses the technological eschatology of Pierre Teilhard de Chardin. Teilhard provides a positive account of technology's influence on the ultimate Christian future whereas we find, in Chapter 6, that Jacques Ellul is much more sceptical of technology and provides an apocalyptic account of the future where a transcendent God must save us from technological determinism. Chapter 7 gives a treatment of Heidegger's works on technology and, aside from arguing that technology plays a central role in his understanding of the future, maintains that Heidegger's argument against any ontology which does not give significant weight to possibility over actuality, as with transhumanism, is inadequate. The penultimate chapter, chapter 8, constructs a Christian response to the transhumanist future around the themes of possibility and promise by utilising the work of Richard Kearney, Eberhard Jüngel and Jürgen Moltmann. The last chapter, chapter 9, concludes by offering three areas of discrepancy between Christianity and transhumanism. First, the Christian future is entirely built upon the mechanics of the interpersonal grounded in the triune life of God that is life affirming and safeguards human virtues whereas, despite their efforts, transhumanism is not. Second, Christians uphold the value of limit and creatureliness whereas transhumanists deny any such limitations and instead espouse a dangerous self-transcendence. And, finally, Christianity upholds the value of radical hope in a future that is beyond calculation and possibilities derived from the outworking of the world. The transhumanist future is interpolated from the past and present, which makes the possibility of such radical hope impossible.

NOTES

1. Alvin Toffler, *Future Shock* (New York: Bantam, 1971).
2. Robin Hanson makes very bold claims about infinite economic growth because of technology. But others who are not as ideological have also noted the important connection between technological growth and economic growth. See Robin Hanson, "Economics of the Singularity," *IEEE Spectrum* 45, no. 6 (2008); David C. Mowery and Nathan Rosenberg, *Technology and the Pursuit of Economic Growth* (Cambridge: Cambridge University Press, 1995).
3. Indeed, Christian scholars have become increasingly concerned with 'future talk' in the public sphere. One recalls the important conversation between Marxists and theologians of hope and liberation in the mid-20th century. The 20th century has been a watershed of reflecting on how futurology and utopianism should relate to Christian eschatology more broadly. I am aware of this history which is why Moltmann and others such as Bloch play such significant roles. But, I would argue that the response to Moltmann's question, 'What has

happened to our utopias?', inasmuch as it does signify the uneasy relationship we have had with history, the future and progress after 1945, is that they have become technological futurisms. Our utopias today are technological utopias. See Jürgen Moltmann, "What Has Happened to Our Utopias?," in *God Will Be All in All: The Eschatology of Jürgen Moltmann*, ed., Richard Bauckham (Edinburgh: T. & T. Clark, 1999).

4. A wider-ranging appraisal of the religious and ideological motivations of this technological dreaming is given in the next three chapters.
5. Ted Peters is one of the few contemporary Christian scholars to have published on the disparities and similarities between the approaches to the future described by Christians and transhumanists. See Ted Peters, "Transhumanism and the Posthuman Future: Will Technological Progress Get Us There?," in H+/–: Transhumanism and Its Critics, ed. Gregory R. Hansell and William Grassie (Philadelphia: Metanexus Institute, 2011). Other seminal texts from the Christian tradition are Brent Waters, *From Human to Posthuman: Christian Theology and Technology in a Postmodern World* (Aldershot: Ashgate, 2006); Ronald Cole-Turner, ed., *Transhumanism and Transcendence: Christian Hope in an Age of Technological Enhancement* (Washington, DC: Georgetown University Press, 2011).
6. As we will see, one of the major features of understanding technology in the 20th century is its universalising and totalising quality. Technological utopias and dystopias respond directly to this overwhelming sense that technology has invaded almost every area of our lives.
7. Jürgen Moltmann, *The Coming of God: Christian Eschatology* (London: SCM Press, 1996), 25–26; Peters, "Transhumanism and the Posthuman Future."
8. Chapter 8 will discuss this distinction in more detail.
9. Many will have a mixture of both.
10. Definitions regarding the distinction between posthumanism and transhumanism are still largely in flux. Some use these terms interchangeably, whereas others are much stricter in identifying transhumanism with a certain subset of posthuman discourse that is an heir of Enlightenment humanism and associated with Humanity+. I recognise the growing pluriformity of posthuman discourse therefore the majority of my contentions are levelled at those identified with the modern transhumanism movement and/or by those referenced in chapter 4.
11. This is a major argument of the fourth chapter.
12. Furthermore, justification for particular authors and ideas in this text is dealt with at the beginning of each chapter.

REFERENCES

Arendt, Hannah. *The Human Condition*. Chicago: University of Chicago Press, 1958.
Borgmann, Albert. *Technology and the Character of Contemporary Life: A Philosophical Inquiry*. Chicago: University of Chicago Press, 1984.
———. *Crossing the Postmodern Divide*. Chicago: University of Chicago Press, 1992.
———. *Power Failure: Christianity in the Culture of Technology*. Grand Rapids: Brazos Press, 2003.
Cole-Turner, Ronald, ed. *Transhumanism and Transcendence: Christian Hope in an Age of Technological Enhancement*. Washington, DC: Georgetown University Press, 2011.
Drees, Willem B. "Religion in an Age of Technology." *Zygon* 37, no. 3 (2002): 597–604.

————, ed. *Technology, Trust, and Religion: Roles of Religions in Controversies on Ecology and the Modification of Life*. Leiden: Leiden University Press, 2009.

Fukuyama, Francis. *Our Posthuman Future: Consequences of the Biotechnology Revolution*. New York: Farrar, Straus and Giroux, 2002.

Grote, Jim, and Carl Mitcham, eds. *Theology and Technology: Essays in Christian Analysis and Exegesis*. Lanham: University Press of America, 1984.

Hanson, Robin. "Economics of the Singularity." *IEEE Spectrum* 45, no. 6 (2008): 45–50.

Hayles, N. Katherine. *How We Became Posthuman: Virtual Bodies in Cybernetics, Literature, and Informatics*. Chicago: University of Chicago Press, 1999.

Hefner, Philip. *The Human Factor: Evolution, Culture, and Religion*. Theology and the Sciences. Minneapolis: Fortress Press, 1993.

————. "Technology and Human Becoming." *Zygon* 37, no. 3 (2002): 655–666.

Kelly, Kevin. *What Technology Wants*. New York: Viking, 2010.

Marcel, Gabriel. *Man against Mass Society*. Translated by G. S. Fraser. South Bend: St. Augustine, 2008.

Mitcham, Carl. "Technology as a Theological Problem in the Christian Tradition." In *Theology and Technology: Essays in Christian Analysis and Exegesis*, edited by Jim Grote and Carl Mitcham. Lanham: University Press of America, 1984.

Moltmann, Jürgen. *The Coming of God: Christian Eschatology*. London: SCM Press, 1996.

————. "What Has Happened to Our Utopias?" In *God Will Be All in All: The Eschatology of Jürgen Moltmann*, edited by Richard Bauckham. Edinburgh: T. & T. Clark, 1999.

Mowery, David C., and Nathan Rosenberg. *Technology and the Pursuit of Economic Growth*. Cambridge: Cambridge University Press, 1995.

Noble, David F. *The Religion of Technology: The Divinity of Man and the Spirit of Invention*. London: Penguin, 1999.

Nye, David E. *Technology Matters: Questions to Live With*. London: MIT Press, 2006.

Pattison, George. *Thinking about God in an Age of Technology*. Oxford: Oxford University Press, 2005.

Peters, Ted. *God—the World's Future: Systematic Theology for a Postmodern Era*. Minneapolis: Fortress Press, 1992.

————. "Transhumanism and the Posthuman Future: Will Technological Progress Get Us There?" In *H+/–: Transhumanism and Its Critics*, edited by Gregory R. Hansell and William Grassie. Philadelphia: Metanexus Institute, 2011.

Postman, Neil. *Amusing Ourselves to Death: Public Discourse in the Age of Show Business*. London: Penguin, 1985.

Szerszynski, Bronislaw. "The Religious Roots of Our Technological Condition." In *Technology, Trust, and Religion*, edited by Willem B. Drees. Leiden: Leiden University Press, 2009.

Toffler, Alvin. *Future Shock*. New York: Bantam, 1971.

————, ed. *The Futurists*. New York: Random House, 1972.

Turkle, Sherry. *Alone Together: Why We Expect More from Technology and Less from Each Other*. New York: Basic Books, 2011.

Waters, Brent. *From Human to Posthuman: Christian Theology and Technology in a Postmodern World*. Aldershot: Ashgate, 2006.

————. *Christian Moral Theology in the Emerging Technoculture: From Posthuman Back to Human*. Farnham: Ashgate, 2014.

Part I

Visionary Approaches to Technology and the Future

2 Planning for the Technological Future
Technological Utopianism

This first chapter in visionary approaches to the technological future presents three issues. First, and most broadly, it diagrams the historical landscape of how we have come to think about technology today as heirs of the utopian tradition. Second, it charts the degradation of the technological future oriented from religious concerns with some appeal to an *adventus* future to one which, by the 20th century, appeals largely to *futurum* where religious concerns are only tacit. And, third, this chapter also gives a history of how something like contemporary transhumanism could have come about. It isn't only a history of explicit transhumanist ideas. Nor is this chapter just about how many of these transhumanist ideas have religious origins. Instead, it is primarily a history of dreaming about the technological future of which transhumanism is a product.

2.1 UTOPIA

The term utopia is an invention of Sir Thomas More. Being a play on words in Greek, it is said to be derivative of both *eutopia* and *outopia*. The former is translated 'good place' whereas the latter is translated 'no place'.[1] This inherent ambiguity in More's neologism is important for the consideration of utopia for it provides the form and conditions for a utopia. Utopia is precisely an idealised society, community or state which is virtually unachievable. It is a good place, but also one which is distinct and removed from the present, 'no place'.

The academic study of utopia has been a growing field. Figures such as Ernst Bloch and Fredric Jameson have solidified the field and its importance for critical theory and cultural studies. Both are responsible for moving the focus of utopian studies away from actual literary utopias, although these are considered, to what might be termed the 'utopian hermeneutic'. Jameson states, 'We would therefore do better to posit two distinct lines of descendency from More's inaugural text: the one intent on the realization of the utopian program, the other an obscure yet omnipresent utopian impulse finding its way to the surface in a variety of covert expressions and practices.'[2] The first strand Jameson refers to is the more overt utopia of political planning, revolution and literature. This is the more traditional 'line of descendency'. But, Jameson and Bloch are more interested in the subtle and philosophically rich impulse of the second strand. They are concerned with utopia as a basic human activity which is 'endemic to the human historico-social world'.[3] Bloch's *magnum opus, The Principle of Hope*, begins from this premise and creates a history of the utopian drive which considers both lines. Employing his utopian hermeneutic, he considers any cultural artefact which could possibly be charged with utopian value. For example, he considers not only literary works such as Campanella's *The City of the Sun*, but even the utopian underpinnings of topics ranging 'from games to patent medicines, from myths to mass entertainment, from iconography to technology, from architecture to *eros*, from tourism to jokes and the unconscious.'[4] Both aspects of utopia Jameson speaks of are instructive for our consideration of technological utopianism here.

This chapter considers technological utopias and creates a specific, but brief history of the technological imagination found in these technological utopias. It follows utopian visionary perspectives which consider technology and its influence on the future. In particular, it focuses on the more overt strand of utopias Jameson suggests above. But, it will become evident that these specific utopias become diffused across a greater cultural zeitgeist in unique social and political movements which are more reminiscent of the second strand of utopia. The primary focus of the chapter is on the 19th and 20th centuries in Russia and America. While there are innumerable nations it might have been advantageous to consider, Russia and America were chosen specifically because they were the two great technological and scientific superpowers of the 20th century and are the two models of technological utopianism in the 20th century. As will become apparent, technology figured in a uniquely mystical way for both nations which was unequalled by others.[5] First, however, the origin of technological utopianism will be addressed in Francis Bacon's works which then get passed on to the Royal Society. Next the utopian writings of Russian philosopher N. F. Fedorov will be taken up and his influence on the Russian technological imagination, which was crucial to the Russian Revolution, will be elucidated. Finally, the utopian drive in America will be assessed and it will be asserted that technology came to be the major catalyst in America's utopian heritage in the 19th and 20th centuries.

2.2   FRANCIS BACON

Bacon's relation to technology and utopia might seem to be obliquely related to his more centrally accepted philosophy of science and political agenda. But, it is argued that his notion of technology[6] is integrally linked with his new philosophy. Bacon's new method and the technologies created from it are essential to the task Bacon outlines. Natural philosophy without action is stillborn and technology without discriminatory method is erroneous. Furthermore, this utopian dreaming is instituted and arises out of a religious conviction about the Fall of Man such that Bacon's new method contributes to the ultimate religious future.

2.2.1 Instauratio Magna

Francis Bacon's (1561–1626) *Instauratio Magna* contains the most important texts he wrote and the fulfilment of his millenarian dream undergirds its inception. The text was intended to contain six parts consisting of The Division of Sciences, The New Organon, The Phenomenon of the Universe, The Ladder of the Intellect, The Forerunners and The New Philosophy.[7] The term itself, *Instauratio Magna*, wasn't commonly used during Bacon's time and points to the very specific way in which Bacon utilises it.[8] The term *instauratio*, argues Whitney, is taken from the Vulgate and alludes to the restoration of Solomon's Temple.[9] So, whereas 'establish' and 'restore' might adequately translate the word *instauratio* one must also recognise that it carries a very particular connotation charged with symbolic value. In fact, this religious undertone lies at the basis of the *Instauratio Magna*'s inception. What is being restored or repaired, for Bacon, are man's faculties which have been lost in the Fall of Man. Bacon states:

> Both things can be repaired even in this life to some extent, the former by religion and faith, the latter by the arts and sciences. For the Curse did not make the creation an utter and irrevocable outlaw. In virtue of the sentence 'In the sweat of thy face shalt thou eat bread', man, by manifold labours (and not by disputations, certainly, or by useless magical ceremonies), compels the creation, in time and in part, to provide him with bread, that is to serve the purposes of human life.[10]

The instauration is the process by which humanity can, in a sense, limit the effects of its unredeemed state. The Fall of Man brought with it alienation from God and a marred relation with Creation. Bacon held that the rift between God and man could only be rejoined through supernatural and ecclesial means, but bridging the chasm separating humanity from Creation was within the power of humanity. As Harrison claims, 'In essence, this is how we are to understand Bacon's account of the two distinct ways in which there might be a restoration of what was lost at the Fall. While the loss of *innocence* could be restored only by grace, human *dominion*, made possible by Adamic knowledge, was not a supernatural gift but a natural capacity.'[11] The *Instauratio Magna* is the outline Bacon purports to restore man's sovereignty over nature which is evident in the book of Genesis. This sovereignty over nature is central to Bacon's task as is attested by Bacon's first usage of the term in an unpublished essay entitled 'Time's Masculine Birth, or the Great Instauration of Human Dominion over the Universe'.[12]

Arguably, Bacon's most important work in the *Instauratio Magna* is the *Novum Organum*. In this text Bacon speaks of the specific ways in which humanity's fall from grace limits the reliability of what humanity can actually know about the world. Bacon refers to these imperfections or illusions as the idols. The first is the idol of the tribe. This idol describes the error that is inherent in perception itself and the limited and fallible nature of the human senses in general. The second idol is the idol of the cave. This idol refers to personal prejudice. People have a tendency to project onto the world what they think they ought to see instead of what is actually present. The third idol is the idol of the marketplace. This idol is best characterized and manifested in our common use of language. Language will sometime fail to discriminate between distinctive phenomena. This could be due to the lack of the proper word or the word could imply something that is not intended. Either way it is a hindrance to perception and understanding. The final idol is the idol of the theatre. This idol speaks of a failure in the actual system of belief itself. Idols of the theatre 'are the misleading consequences for human knowledge of the systems of philosophy and rules of demonstration (reliable proof) currently in place.'[13]

The *Novum Organum*, or new instrument, is precisely this new method which limits these idols. Bacon's new method was a qualitative and organised approach which relied upon induction rather than tradition. This method began with an exhaustive formulation of lists of natural as well as experimental histories. The second step involved the organisation of these histories into distinct tables so that access would be quick and cross-referencing would be easy. Once the tables were created and relationships between them noted, certain phenomena could be induced. After a cycle of going through the tables a claim could be made about the items in the table. From this first definition a refining process of countless other experiments would make the tables even more specific and eventually lead to a more solid axiom that might look like our contemporary laws of nature today. It was through this method that reliable knowledge about nature was to be obtained and the effects of the idols and the Fall of Man limited.

Bacon's *Instauratio Magna* centres on this new method which would bring a golden age to humanity. Not only are these tables meant to be used for the extraction of genuine natural knowledge about the world, but they were meant to be used for the improvement of humanity in the construction of new technologies. The frontispiece of the *Instauratio Magna*, seen in Figure 2.1, illustrates the anthropological significance Bacon attributed to his work. The two Pillars of Hercules represent the boundary between the known and unknown in the ancient world. The ship depicted represents two things related to the known and the unknown. The more literal interpretation suggests Bacon was alluding to the great naval explorations of the 15th century. In this way, it represented man's geographical advancement on the unknown. But, more importantly, it contains natural and philosophical significance as well. The columns did not just represent the geographical

Figure 2.1 Frontispiece to *Instauratio Magna*, Courtesy of Library of Congress, LC-USZ62-95150.

distinction between the known and the unknown for man, but signifies 'the concept of the ancient cosmos in which man had a definite place in the order of things. Knowledge in this conception depended on discovery of the boundaries of man's nature so that he did not fall into a tragic life of wanton and animalic behaviour of sin or of sinful pride that caused him to overstep his boundaries and come into conflict with the gods.'[14] What Bacon is alluding to in this image is an absolute transformation of man from one who is confined by the ancient myth to one which broaches upon the divine.[15] For Bacon, humanity stands on the brink of a new epoch and has the opportunity to throw off the shackles of its forebears and enjoy a more complete life in relation to both the world and God.

In fact, it could be said that these pillars also represent the unknown in terms of the future. Bacon's eschatology was informed by Lancelot Andrewes who relied upon Patristic sources and advocated an 'inaugurated eschatology', 'described as the tension between "even now" and "not yet" in the life of the Church during the time between the resurrection and the second coming of Christ'.[16] In the terms of this book, Bacon believed that the ultimate transformation of the human being and all of creation in the future was to be an act of God through religious means. In this way, he upheld an *adventus* notion of the future. But, as his eschatology suggests, humanity takes part in that future redemption through 'labour, as well in inventing as in executing'[17] so that the ultimate future is also a product of our human work today. Bacon clearly introduces a *futurum* element into the ultimate future.

2.2.2 The New Atlantis

Bacon's other highly popularised text, *The New Atlantis*, relates to the frontispiece as well and reflects his contentions about a religious and technological future. If the waters on the horizon of the frontispiece reflect the possibility of humanity to discover and recover, at least in part, its prelapsarian relation with the world then Bacon's utopia, *The New Atlantis*, could be said to reflect what the world might be like at the horizon. Bacon's utopia, written late in his life, projects what the world will be like if it follows Bacon's task and recovers some of its original faculties.

The most important part of *The New Atlantis*, for our purpose, centres on Salomon's House. Salomon's House represents the very core and pinnacle of Bacon's utopia. Saloman's House carries with it connotations of religious perfection and the essence of the Bensalemite people and society. The society of Salomon's House is founded upon 'the knowledge of Causes and secret motions of things; and the enlarging of the bounds of Human Empire, to the effecting of all things possible.'[18] It is a kind of priesthood which has unencumbered access to the book of Creation. It seeks to uncover these hidden natural laws so that humanity might benefit from the knowledge. For example, the sailors that discover this utopian society learn that this order has massive subterranean halls which are used for refrigeration and research into the production of new metals which can be employed for curing diseases and prolonging life.[19] The society seems to be a mixture of scientific researchers and a religious or monastic order—some hermits live in these very caves of research. Furthermore, Salomon's House has several wells and fountains which are used for medical purposes while also maintaining a daily rite of prayer and services.[20] In this utopia the Baconian method, which emphasises the religious as well as the scientific and technological aspects of the future, is at the very heart of society.

The religious and scientific venture of Bacon's utopia would not be complete without the corresponding action which comes from this knowledge in the form of technical invention for the betterment of humanity. The society of Salomon's House does more than experiment for the knowledge of scientific laws: It has 'engine-houses, where are prepared engines and instruments for all sorts of motion'.[21] These houses contain all things mechanical whether they are instruments of war or intricate clocks. These learned men are also well versed in mechanical arts whether it is in the production of paper, linen or silk. In fact, the subdivision of labour in Salomon's House includes a group called Benefactors whose sole purpose is to draw out of experimentation things for the practical use of the society.[22]

Technical craft is the natural outworking of Baconian science. In fact, this was one of the major accomplishments of Bacon's programme: He brought together natural philosophy and the empirical work of artisans. Both had distinct histories prior to Bacon so that whereas natural philosophy drew from abstract form the artisan depended upon the traditions of his guild.

Each was independent of the other. Bacon melded the two together so that natural philosophy would be yoked with empiricism and utility whereas the engineer and craftsmen could be more systematic in their creation which invoked the science behind their inventions.[23] Bacon held the mechanical arts in high esteem for they consistently improved the situation of all of humanity, not just a select few.[24] Furthermore, the history of the mechanical arts seemed to Bacon to be advancing incrementally. He conjectured that a large revolution would occur in technology and the mechanical arts if one worked from the principles discovered through his *Novum Organum*. Here we see in germinal form the beginnings of modern technology because it is the first time that technical invention is seriously reflected upon in a systematic and rigorous way and the mechanical arts are no longer sidelined as inferior study but an important fruit of this new Science.[25]

Religion and technology cannot be separated from Bacon's project and utopian vision. They both play major roles in *The New Atlantis* and in Bacon's work more broadly. Lewis Mumford claims of Bacon:

> . . . it was his 'The New Atlantis' that first canvassed the possibility of a joint series of operations that would combine a new system of scientific investigation with a new technology. At a moment when the bitter struggle within Christianity between contentious doctrines and sects had come to a stalemate, the machine itself seemed to offer an alternative way of reaching Heaven. The promise of material abundance on earth, through exploration, organized conquest, and invention, offered a common objective to all classes.[26]

Through the employment of Baconian Science and technology, the world could be transformed so that man would no longer be at the mercy of nature, but could rise to his proper place over it. The recovery of man's faculties after the Fall and his ascent to becoming lord over nature is entirely dependent upon the recognition of both science and technology in Bacon's works. The future redemption of man is partially within the grasp of man through human work, *futurum*, but is also depends upon God to ultimately bring about that redemption in Christ on the last day, *adventus*.

Bacon's technological and scientific utopianism did not die with him. The same visionary impulse provided the foundation for the institution of the Royal Society. Many of the founding members saw themselves fulfilling the Baconian project and sought to live out Salomon's House in England. Thomas Sprat's *History of the Royal Society of London* makes constant reference to Bacon as a patron of this new science where he is held in high regard. In fact, in the introductory poem to this text Bacon is likened to Moses who has led them out of the wilderness of fruitless natural philosophy into the Promised Land of a new method of learning.[27] Bacon's vision was not carried out without qualification, however. The Christian theological presuppositions of Bacon's task slowly became troubling to the Royal

Society following the English Civil War.[28] Religion was being reevaluated after its entanglement in the Civil War to the point that Sprat's work devotes little attention to specific theological concerns. Instead of a robust theological basis for the scientific task, the Royal Society opted for a more basic public creed which was more inclusive of diverse members.[29] This further secularisation of the Baconian task became more compounded in Enlightenment figures such as Voltaire and Diderot.[30] What remains then is a more secularised natural philosophy, but which still carries with it the scientific and technological visionary and utopian overtones inherent in Bacon.[31]

Bacon was one of the first to recognise the impact technology could make on humanity. He differs from his predecessors who might include invention or technology in their utopias in that he is the first to couple the mechanical arts, technology, with his new method which would become modern science. It was a watershed moment in the history of technology because technological development became a product of the inductive thinking in Baconian science. It wasn't relegated to the traditions of the guild which limited and stifled the growth of technology. Instead modern technology was generated through explicit attention and scrutiny built upon the findings of Bacon's new method. It was a marriage of what would become modern science with modern technology. Indeed, his utopia is the first with distinctly modern technological themes.

Bacon foresaw that this revised method and the developed technologies produced from it would bring a revolution that would alter humanity and society drastically. This utopian vision for science and technology then becomes ubiquitous during the 19th and early 20th centuries and owes much of its foundation to Bacon. Indeed this utopian sentiment is visible in our next figure considered, N. F. Fedorov. It is to Russia in the 19th century that we now turn.

2.3   N. F. FEDOROV AND RUSSIAN TECHNOLOGICAL UTOPIANISM

N. F. Fedorov (1827–1903) had many notable admirers of his work during his own lifetime and exerted a profound influence on Russian intellectual life and beyond despite his relative obscurity today. Because of this some brief biographical details are warranted upfront. Dostoyevsky was a great enthusiast of Fedorov and, in reference to him, wrote to N. P. Peterson, 'First, a question: who is the thinker whose ideas you have transmitted? If you can, please let me know his real name. I have become so interested in him. . . . Secondly, I must say that in essence I completely agree with his ideas. I read them as if they were my own.'[32] Fedorov is said to have inspired the scene at Ilyusha's grave in Dostoyevsky's *The Brothers Karamazov* which is reminiscent of Fedorov's adherence to a complete bodily resurrection—something both Russian thinkers agreed on.[33] Furthermore, Leo Tolstoy, although not agreeing with Fedorov's project entirely, did deeply respect Fedorov's ideas and, more importantly, his devotion to Christian practice. Tolstoy states:

> Do not be afraid, I do not share his views, but I do understand them to such an extent that I feel capable of defending them and of giving them preference over any other views. Most important of all is the fact that, thanks to his belief, he leads a pure Christian life. Whenever I speak of the need of carrying out in real life the teachings of Christ, he says, 'but this is obvious,' and I know that with him it is so.[34]

Amongst others who admired Fedorov's gifted and creative mind were Berdyaev, Solovev and Lossky.

Fedorov was born in 1828 and died in 1903. He was an illegitimate child to Prince Gagarin. As an illegitimate child he didn't receive all the benefits of being of noble birth—he did not even take his father's name—but he received a good education at Tambov Gymnasium and the Richelieu Lyceum of Odessa. Following his schooling he tutored for a time until he secured a job first at the Chertkovsk Library and then the Rumiantsev Library as cataloguer. He worked there for twenty-five years until his retirement, and it was during his many years as a librarian that his interaction with notable Russian scholars led to his increased fame. But, his life was anything but extravagant. He was a very frugal man who gave much of his salary to the poor and the janitors who worked at the library. His meals consisted mostly of food purchased at wholesale price from the shop he lived above. This included near spoiled cheese, bread and herring. It is even alleged that he did not own a bed, but instead slept on a steamer trunk. He never published anything during his lifetime and forced his friends to vow that if his writings were ever published they must be anonymous and given away freely.[35]

For our purposes, Fedorov represents another instance of this increasing reliance upon human work in the form of the technological endeavour to bring about a utopian future. We find in Fedorov, like Bacon, that this belief in a positive future and in humanity's contribution to the ultimate future is a product of a religious belief. Fedorov radicalises Christian eschatology by asserting a strong *futurum* element where 'the awaited day, the day longed for through the ages, will be God's command and man's fulfilment'.[36]

2.3.1 The Philosophy of the Common Task

Fedorov's major work published posthumously, *The Philosophy of the Common Task*, is written in response to the general discord Fedorov found in humanity's affairs. As Fedorov notes, 'Indeed, people have done all possible evil to nature (depletion, destruction, predatory exploitation) and to each other (inventing most abominable arms and implements of mutual extermination).'[37] Specifically, Fedorov cites the unbrotherly attitude people have towards one another manifested in wars, working for profit at the expense of one's fellow man and the general selfishness and individualism rampant during his time. It is the tension between fellow human beings that is most troublesome to Fedorov. *The Philosophy of the Common Task* is a treatise which presupposes this unbrotherly attitude—especially between the learned and the unlearned. As Fedorov notes, 'The hateful division of the world and all calamities that result from this compel us, the unlearned—that is, those who place action (action in common, not in strife) above thought—to submit to the learned this memorandum concerned with lack of kinship feelings and the means of restoring them.'[38] Fedorov complains that the lofty transcendental writings of German philosophy—especially Kant—do not improve the actual conditions of the world for this philosophy cannot break free from the thinking mind to genuine action. It is caught up in the world of the mind without positing the management of the world outside of the mind.[39] The major problem Fedorov proposes is that education is not used for the improvement of all of humankind as a whole, but only serves a select few and exacerbates the gap between human beings. His *Philosophy of the Common Task*, on the other hand, is meant to provide the impetus for action in the world which could benefit all humanity.

Fedorov claimed that most of the problems that exist between humans are directly related to the struggle humanity has with its own bestial nature. Much of the philosophical and ideological underpinnings of Fedorov's *Philosophy of the Common Task* depend upon how humanity has become distinct from animals. This distinction is most evident in man's assumption of a vertical posture. Fedorov pinned great significance to this act. In this action, Fedorov claimed, humanity literally moves himself away from the forces of nature on the ground. It was, according to Fedorov, the first real act of will on behalf of man. Fedorov claimed:

> Creatures who face the earth, which is covered with vegetation and is inhabited by other creatures, have only one aim, namely, to devour vegetation or these other creatures. . . . On the other hand, the vertical posture of man is above all an expression of man's revulsion from this need to devour. Indeed, the vertical posture is man's endeavour to raise himself above the destructiveness which prevails in Nature.[40]

As this is the first act of will of humanity against the stark and inhospitable forces of nature it also marks the beginning of selfhood for humanity. It is precisely in opposition to nature that man then distinguishes himself, becoming an 'I'.[41] It is this cleavage from the animal kingdom, slowly distinguishing itself as a person, which then transforms the animal fear of death into its more robust and abstract equivalent in this now conscious person. Death is now seen as the destruction of man's identity and his freedom from the forces of nature. It is not a biological death that is important for Fedorov's appraisal of primitive man, but the destruction of man's own self-creation in freedom from this harsh nature.

Fedorov then took up this polarity inherent in primitive man—transcendence of humanity in opposition to the forces of nature—as the basis for his common task. Fedorov's main argument was that the discord which exists in the world can be alleviated through unification against the common enemy, death. As Berdyaev states, 'For Nikolai Fedorov the one and the ultimate evil is death. Every evil derives from death and leads to death. The world-wide struggle against death is the problem confronting mankind.'[42] In fact, Fedorov was so opposed to death that he would rarely sleep longer than a few hours at night because it reminded him of death.[43] Death is the ultimate enemy of mankind and 'is not a quality which determines *what a human being is and must be.*'[44]

But, unifying all of humanity against the common enemy of death, as abstract as this sounds, has a very practical element. Fedorov claimed that as humanity has arisen from and in spite of the natural world—indeed is even defined by this will to break free from nature—uniting humanity against death means regulating this blind force of nature. Fedorov sought to alleviate problems of warfare not by avowing pacifism and disbanding standing armies, as his compatriot Tolstoy did, but instead advocated that the resources and energy be redirected towards the scientific study of the earth and regulating it for humanity's ends. Fedorov suggested that the great military weapons could be used to manipulate weather patterns to increase crop yield or to limit certain natural disasters by setting off explosions in the atmosphere.[45] Fedorov was not without grounds for making this assertion at the time. Scientific experiments were being conducted by the Americans to control weather and even today both the Russians and Chinese have put significant funding into cloud seeding.[46] Fedorov also suggested that massive cables be placed around the earth to manipulate its magnetic field and control the amount of solar radiation.[47] Additionally, Fedorov did not want to limit humanity's regulation of nature to just the planet earth, but he foresaw the need to transform the earth from a piece of rock at the mercy of cosmic forces to one harnessed by humanity so that it might be a 'terrestrial craft' where humanity's exploration and management had no bounds.[48]

Fedorov's rejection of death as a necessary condition for humanity moves beyond conquering the cosmos through human reason. More importantly, Fedorov explained, is the absolute cessation of death for the human species and the material resurrection of our ancestors. This imperative, although grounded in the desire for the unification of mankind, ultimately stems from the Christian message as well. It is not only Fedorov's insistence that man continue his primordial harnessing of nature for his own assertion of freedom and personhood, but this is always and everywhere a response to Christianity. This is why the resurrection of one's ancestors is so important for Fedorov—because Christianity is the religion of resurrection. Death and its overcoming in the resurrection lie at the centre of the Christian narrative.

What is distinctive about Fedorov's interpretation of the resurrection of all mankind is that this is both a complete material and bodily resurrection and also a task meant to be carried out by humanity. The resurrection is not relegated to mere spiritual abstraction, nor does it lie in the hands of God alone. Berdyaev states:

> According to Fedorov's doctrine, the resurrection of the dead is achieved not only through action accomplished by Christ, the Redeemer and Saviour, and not only by the spiritual and moral efforts of mankind and the love of human beings for the deceased, but also by the scientific, technical, and physical activity of people. By the joint efforts of religion and science, of priest and learned technician, the dead and buried must experience their resurrection. Fedorov even spoke about the physico-chemical experiments of resurrecting the dead, which produces an almost frightening impression.[49]

Human action in resurrecting the ancestors stems from Fedorov's rejection of Monophysitic Christology and the sacred continuity between creation and God's life in the Trinity. Fedorov saw a doctrinal basis for human work in the ultimate creation and the ultimate future. Christ's glorified body is an image of the glorified and eschatological creation. His two natures signify a human element in the glorified creation. The future is not just divine, *adventus*, but it is also a product of human work, *futurum*.

Fedorov took a distinctly materialistic approach to this transformation and suggested science and technology be the means by which this should occur. In fact, considerable technical speculation was devoted to the actual mechanics involved with resurrecting the dead. Fedorov claimed that unique individual vibrations (similar to resonance frequency) exist for each person even following death. These could be manipulated in such a way that they could be reunited with their 'solid-state molecules on Earth'[50] leading to a complete material and bodily resurrection. Yet, Fedorov was clear that resurrection was much more than just technological manipulation of matter, but was to be rooted in the love which was modelled in the Trinity and which sought to conform this world to the life of God.[51] For this reason, despite many of his ideas bearing much in common with contemporary transhumanism—eradication of death through technological means—they derive from a robust Christian faith grounded in Christ and the Trinity, not from secular sources.

2.3.2   Russian Technological Utopianism

Fedorov's direct influence was felt all across Russian culture, not just in philosophy and theology. But, where his utopian influence was felt in Russia, often these figures imported his utopian ideals which derived from the *futurum* element of his thought leaving aside his religious basis. A number of important figures in literature, besides Dostoyevsky and Tolstoy, were shaped by Fedorov's writings. Certain members of the Russian Futurism movement, including the famous poet Vladimir Mayakovsky, were heavily influenced by Fedorov's writings. Fedorov's theme of universal resurrection is most evident in Mayakovsky's poem *Voina i mir* (War and the Universe).[52] Boris Pasternak is another notable author with Fedorovian connections. Fedorov was friends with Pasternak's father. The only portrait in existence of Fedorov was painted by Leonid Pasternak, Boris's father. Boris Pasternak's discussion that history is based on 'systematic explorations of the riddle of death, with a view to overcoming death'[53] in *Doctor Zhivago* is said to have been inspired by Fedorov.[54]

Fedorov's authority extends to political and social figures and institutions as well. A group of Clamart Eurasians in France sought to blend Marxism and Fedorovism to form a new ideology. Unfortunately, this political group never came to fruition and the editors of the newspaper devoted to the movement, *Evraziia*, were divided on their stance towards the Soviets, leading to the movement's inevitable demise. But, Fedorov's political influence in the Soviet Union had a much more lasting effect. Fedorovism was rampant in the Commission for the Study of the Natural Productive Forces of Russia and the Bureau for Local Studies.[55] Both were set up by the Academy of Sciences. The former was headed by Vladimir Vernadsky in 1915–17 and 1926–30.[56] Vernadsky was a respected scientist who is noted for his idea of the biosphere and Noosphere which would be important for Russian cosmism.[57] Other notable figures who supported Fedorov's ideas were Valerian Nikolaevich Muravev, the son of the Tsarist minister, and Iona Brikhnichev, the Secretary of the Central Committee for the Relief of the Hungry.[58] Fedorov's most devoted follower was Konstantin Eduardovich Tsiolkovsky, the father of Russian rocketry. Fedorov saved Tsiolkovsky from committing suicide and it was through his mentorship that Tsiolkovsky became an outspoken advocate of exploring space and 'the creator of a Utopian scheme for the reorganization of the universe.'[59]

Fedorov's technological utopian impulses were not unique to him in Russia. Indeed, we find a growing field of science fiction and political utopias in Russia where technology is essential. Stites claims:

> Russian science fiction on the eve of the Revolution was a dialogue of fantasy and a duel of dreams. Bright and hopeful Utopias of progress, with strong urban, technical, and socialist elements, generated counter-Utopias of alternate scenarios and dystopias of warning and fear. Their authors were well known names whose ambivalence and talent give their works a mark of literary distinction, political journalists and publicists of the Right, and popular writers who are otherwise almost unknown.[60]

The end of the 19th century and the beginning of the 20th century saw a major influx of science fiction into Russia. Translations of works by H. G. Wells, Jules Verne and Edward Bellamy were consumed by a large number of the populace. This then led to distinctly Russian science fiction during the time of rapid industrialisation in works such as Chikolev's *Electric Tale* (1895), Rodnykh's *St. Petersburg-Moscow Self-Propelled Underground Railway* (1902) and Bakhmetov's *Billionaire Legacy* (1904).[61] Bellamy's *Looking Backward* was the most significant import for the Russian imagination. It sold more than 50,000 copies and had seven translations in Russian by 1918.[62] It was read by intelligentsia, workers and students alike, and some have even claimed it was the most effective piece of propaganda for the Russian Left.[63] These works and others like it helped shape the prominent technical and urban image of the rising Bolsheviks, and it was during this time that the ideal national image shifted from the peasant of the agrarian countryside to the proletariat of the factory and city.[64] This ideal would become a part of the public identity in the Soviet Union where the utopian image,[65] of which technology was central, would become reality in the events of the revolution of 1917. As Stites asserts, 'The Russian Revolution . . . was deepened by the confluence of two remarkable facets of history: the traditions of Utopian dreaming and alternative life experiments that marked its past and the intersection of the moment of revolution (1917) with the swelling of the twentieth century technological revolution.'[66]

Fedorov was not the exception to the rule in Russian society. He was at the dawn of the growing influence of technology on the Russian imagination. What is noteworthy is that Fedorov was representative of this strand and also influenced a number of visionaries who sought a better world which relied upon technology in Russia. But whereas many of his convictions about technology and the future derived from religious origins, many of his utopian followers made no such appeal. Regardless, he should be situated alongside those with a growing awareness of the possibilities that technology could bring to the future.

2.4   THE AMERICAN TECHNOLOGICAL UTOPIANS

The American psyche has become increasingly obsessed with the possibilities technology has offered to initiate in the past two centuries. Nowhere has the technological promise been met with such zeal and persistence as in America. In fact, the very landscape is marked with this avowal. Some of the most advanced skyscrapers define the skylines of New York, Chicago and Los Angeles. These skyscrapers still exhibit, as they did in the 1920s, the claim that America has advanced to great heights on the world stage.[67] Furthermore, still one of the most important areas in the world for computing is Silicon Valley in California.[68] America's pride in innovation is always and everywhere a function of its fervour towards technology. America has had a unique relationship with technology—especially as it relates to our present inquiry into technological utopias.[69]

America's political origins were established on firm utopian grounds. The group of Puritan Separatists who left England for greater religious freedom in the 17th century were led by a utopian ideal. The leader of their expedition, John Winthrop, is fabled to have given a sermon prior to landing in New England which references the visionary nature of the society they were aiming to create. He states, 'For we must consider that we shall be as a city upon a hill. The eyes of all people are upon us. So that if we shall deal falsely with our God in this work we have undertaken, and so cause him to withdraw his present help from us, we shall be made a story and a by-word throughout the world.'[70] In the eyes of many who first immigrated, America represented a gift given them by God to institute a more holy order and society. The very foundation of America's national existence is premised upon an alternative culture and society, a kind of utopia.[71]

Just as the first Separatists uprooted geographically to fulfil their dreams of political and religious progress, this same zeal towards progress gets carried on in what is referred to in American history as Manifest Destiny. Although this term is well known it represents, according to Ernest Lee Tuveson, 'a vast complex of ideas, policies and actions. . . . They are not, as we should expect, all compatible, nor do they all come from one source.'[72] Yet, several themes characterise the idea of Manifest Destiny according to historian William Weeks. First, it encapsulated the sentiment that America's people and institutions were virtuous. Second, America had a duty to spread these institutions and thereby redeem and transform the entirety of the continent. Finally, this mission was ordained by God.[73] It was to be Manifest Destiny and the issue of determining whether the new states were to be free or slave states that would ultimately tear the nation apart and lead to the American Civil War.[74] This zeitgeist of the mid to late 19th century was characterised by this conviction that America was to settle further west and in the process spread democracy, freedom and human progress.

The image in Figure 2.2 depicts the ideology of Manifest Destiny where settlers march into a vast unknown with the intention of taming the expansive and rugged West. In the picture is depicted the old republican symbol Liberty, but with the new name of Progress.[75] She brings with her the light of advancement and carries with her a wire of the telegraph. The telegraph and train in the background became symbols which would bind the edge of American civilisation with those cities east of the Mississippi River.[76] As this picture represents, the idealism of Manifest Destiny would became entwined with America's growing obsession with technological progress. So much so, that whenever progress was invoked technology was its basis. It would be the hope of progress through technology that would take over for Manifest Destiny as the central ideological theme in America in the 19th and 20th centuries.

As depicted in the picture, it was during this time of rapid expansion westward that some of the most transformative inventions were springing up.

Figure 2.2   'American Progress', John Gast, c. 1872, Courtesy of Library of Congress, LC-DIG-ppmsca-09855.

The light bulb, telegraph, steam engine, telephone and electric motor were all invented within half a century of each other. These devices transformed the face of American life and even affected the outcome of the American Civil War. Scholars such as John E. Clark and George Edgar Turner have stressed the importance of the railroad in securing victory for the Union.[77] In fact, it is because of the American Civil War's utilisation of new technologies that it has been deemed the first modern war.[78]

America was at the forefront of technological invention with such figures as Thomas Edison, Alexander Graham Bell and Nikola Tesla.[79] These men and other inventors were lauded amongst the ranks of politicians and celebrities much like today with figures such as Bill Gates and Steve Jobs. They were part of the elite in society even when, as in the case of Tesla,[80] they fell on hard times. It was their ability to embody the central ideal of America's founding, that one could become anything with enough ingenuity and hard work, which caused so many in America to idolise them.

This time of great technological invention became the source for progress in America. Countless books, tracts and journal articles sprung up all over America which utilised technology as the catalyst to a better society. Howard P. Segal identifies some forty works during the period 1883–1933 which would classify as technological utopias.[81] Most of the twenty-five authors of these texts wrote in relative obscurity, but reflected the growing sentiment of most Americans which relied upon the force of technology to overhaul American life. In fact, Segal's research into the personal lives of these writers reveals that they were not outcasts who lived on the fringe of American society, but were upstanding middle-class citizens who wrote their works well past their thirties, so they cannot be accused of writing because of the zeal of youth. Most were male, white and middle-aged who actually worked in technical fields.[82] It can be argued that the vocations of these writers only serve to further lend credit to the practicality of these writings—they would know whether such projections were even techni-cally possible. Segal claims that these technological utopians differed from the other contemporary utopians in their adherence to a belief in an immi-nent realisation of the utopia they proposed. Whereas these other utopians 'yearned forlornly for the ideal society',[83] the technological utopians con-sidered it a scientific, practical and sensible affair. Perhaps it is precisely this sober planning which reflects that, by the late 19th century and early 20th century, all appeals to God's action in a technological future have become attenuated into tacit religious language. For them, the future is about human planning and technological construction. Yet, a secularised religious impulse lies just below the surface betraying its historical origin. Expounding upon two of these utopias will help illustrate this growing zeal towards technology and how it functions ideologically and religiously for American national identity.

2.4.1   Edgar Chambless's *Roadtown*

Edgar Chambless's *Roadtown* (1910) is a good example from this period. Futuristic and technologically enhanced architectural schemes of the 20th cen-tury are abundant. As mentioned, urban planning and the cityscape were undergoing massive revisions during the earlier part of the 20th century. The skyscraper represented the *ethos* of this forward looking vision and even the home did not go unnoticed.[84] Chambless's own proposal, while lying upon the earlier part of this trend, represents the force technological utopianism had upon architecture and city planning which would extend well into the 20th century.

Roadtown is premised upon the notion that the historical layout of cities is incredibly wasteful. One has to transport all the necessary items to sustain those who live in the centre of the city. Often this means the inhabitants must live a relatively urban life with crowded streets, tall buildings and the atmo-sphere of industry. All means of transportation to get goods to their neces-sary location from vans to railways and boat are all coordinated through separate organisations. At each step in the transportation the cost is levied until it finally gets passed along to the consumer. It is transportation which is central to the city and, as Chambless outlines, makes up the majority of one's life.[85] For this reason the city should be constructed with the knowl-edge that transportation should be efficient and at the fore of all decisions in city planning. As Chambless states, 'The Roadtown is a single unified plan for the arrangement of these three functions of civilisation—production, transportation and consumption.'[86]

What Chambless suggests is that a city not be modelled upon a circular plan, but upon the straight line. As seen in Figure 2.3, a rendering of Chambless's vision, the town stretches along a single axis across the rural landscape for miles. At the very heart of his proposed Roadtown is the common mode of transportation. Built into an excavated trench, the railway system which connects the entirety of the town along this single axis is based upon a then innovative design called the Boyes Monorail. The railway is to transport both people and freight to the surrounding locations along the line. The monorail is placed in the basement of Roadtown to minimize sound travelling to the private homes and workshops above. The next level above the space allocated for the rail is the area for the workrooms situated

Figure 2.3 Drawing of Chambless's *Roadtown* (1910).

at ground level. Chambless envisioned bringing the factory closer to the actual workers when possible so that the people of Roadtown merely had to walk down a level to their own personal workroom. A trap door was to be placed between the workroom and monorail shaft so that items produced in the workroom could be easily transported, and without the train stopping, to the necessary location for completion or distribution. Every home is fixed with a workshop and Chambless even suggests that in the evening one can throw a rug over the bolt plates to be converted into a 'children's playroom, a sun parlor, a palm garden, or a living room.'[87] The machines in the workroom were to be rented so that any maintenance required could be the responsibility of the corporation and upgrading to newer and more advanced machines could be done more readily.

Just above the workroom is the main living quarters for those in Roadtown. They were to be fireproof and made of poured concrete, a relatively new invention by Edison in those days. The wires and pipes servicing the home were to be between the workroom and living area. As Roadtown is based upon a linear model this provides the easiest installation of these pipes and wires. A simple intersection at each home along Roadtown would provide them with all the necessities: water, gas, electricity (a burgeoning convenience at that time), sewage and vacuum. Extending Roadtown is done with little cost and great ease, for existing facilities do not need to be torn out but are merely extended along the end of the Roadtown line. Within the home are all the modern conveniences which were innovative at the time. The home included the following: a vacuum fitted to a centralised tube which services all homes in Roadtown, a central public heating system which could be controlled through the push of a button on a thermostat, a buzzer which would alert the inhabitants to approaching trains when switched on, centralised disinfecting gas for the cleaning of linens and clothes, electric lighting, telephones and a Dictograph which could be used to listen to live music or sermons and, alternatively, be recorded by the Telegraphone.[88] Chambless claimed that the homes in Roadtown would revolutionise housekeeping and would alleviate the duties expected of women. Most of the menial tasks filling her day would be centralised. For instance, laundry would be sent to cooperative cleaners. Cooking would also be done by cooperatives with conveyer belts leading to each household which would transport the ordered food and collect the refuse after the meal. On the whole, most centralised services would be done through greater cooperation where more progressive social practices would be in place and work for profit would be a vice.

All families would be given a plot of land perpendicular to the line of Roadtown and adjacent to their place of residence. They could use this for leisure or agricultural purposes. According to Chambless, this could be used to attract farmers to Roadtown as they would not have to compromise the conveniences of modern living in order to have access to large plots of land. Chambless estimates that each family would have access to two and a half acres of land and if one extended agricultural land to a mile from the homes it would be more than enough to sustain the needs of the community.

The roof on Roadtown would be a promenade for walking, skating or cycling. In the summer, the promenade would be shaded and in winter it would be enclosed with glass panels and heated. Along the promenade would be towers which would house the cooperatives, power houses, schools and recreation facilities. It would be a place for socialising with benches lining the street.

Roadtown seems to be an interesting conglomeration between city planning and an actual concrete incarnation of the American ideal of Manifest Destiny. One can almost envision these cities extending in Chambless's day through the Midwest as they wind further westward and enjoy both the rugged landscape often idealised in this plan along with the modern conveniences of city life and the technologies available at that time. Despite Chambless's pragmatic approach in not only outlining, in exhaustive lists,[89] the cost and viability of constructing Roadtown, but even getting the support of engineers, Roadtown did not catch on in America. Nonetheless, it did encapsulate a certain utopian sentiment common during that time which drew on the theme of movement across the expanse of the American landscape and its hope in the progress of technology.

2.4.2   Edward Bellamy's *Looking Backward*

If Chambless's *Roadtown* was written in relative obscurity, but still represented the colliding ideals of technological progress and Manifest Destiny, then Edward Bellamy's *Looking Backward* (1887) more overtly represents the growing awareness of American society to place their hopes in technological progress. Bellamy's popularity is manifest in that his book, *Looking Backward*, was only the second book in America to sell more than a million copies, after *Uncle Tom's Cabin*.[90] Bellamy's novel would go on to inspire political activism in the form of grass-roots groups known as Nationalism that sought to achieve Bellamy's utopian vision. At one time these groups numbered 165 with around five to six thousand members.[91] Bellamy's success acted as a vanguard for other American technological utopian writers and his book sparked several sequels.

Bellamy's novel, *Looking Backward*, is written from the future of Bellamy's then readers and conveys to the younger generation the advances humanity made in the 20th century. The story begins with the protagonist and author, Julian West, in the 19th century introducing to the readers his aristocratic upbringing in Boston and the folly of constant labour strikes which postpone the construction of his new home and, hence, his marriage to Edith Bartlett. Needless to say, Mr. West, as part of the upper class, holds a very disdainful sentiment towards the working class—especially as they interfere with his plans. Upon returning home from a dinner with his fiancée's parents, where they speak of the labour issues, Julian West employs the services of a master hypnotist, Dr Pillsbury, to aid him in sleeping. West has a secret subterranean chamber in his dilapidated house for situations when his insomnia becomes unbearable. No sound is allowed to enter the room where he is shielded from noise from the city. Julian informs his servant, Sawyer, to arouse him from the charmed sleep the following morning, but upon awakening Julian is surrounded by unfamiliar people and discovers that his hypnotised sleep has caused him to be in a kind of temporary stasis for one hundred years. West is found by Dr Leete and his family who now own the land while excavating to put a new cellar in their home. West is taken from his chamber and brought into Dr Leete's home where he discovers that the 20th century is vastly different from his own time. It is in Julian's conversations with Dr Leete that Bellamy's utopia is outlined.

Boston of the proposed 20th century is based upon publicly owned capital rather than private. The nation has assumed control of all areas of production and each worker is given an equal wage. One's financial situation is not dependent upon which post one can secure with white-collar positions paying more than the blue-collar counterparts. One's wage is not even correlated with the actual work one does, but is solely based upon one being a fellow human being. As Dr Leete says, 'Every man, however solitary may seem his occupation, is a member of a vast industrial partnership, as large as the nation, as large as humanity.'[92] This conviction is carried to its conclusion in that even those who are disabled and cannot contribute any tangible benefit to the community are given adequate subsistence. Furthermore, there is no hierarchy of social class depending upon the job one is employed in; rather, everyone in society is appreciative of the work every other is doing. The waiters at restaurants and those working in factories are not treated disrespectfully, but are seen as important members of the common community. Every citizen is given advanced education and is given the freedom to choose which profession one wishes to pursue. Each person employed in the industrial army, as it is called, enters one's vocation at a much later date than in the 19th century, twenty-one, and retires much earlier, forty-five.[93] Each trade in the industrial army has strict guidelines as to how one advances in that particular trade. Generally, more experienced members of the trade enjoy greater responsibility in the leadership of that guild, but one's incentive in promotion is entirely dependent upon pride of one's work.[94]

Not only is one's profession organised in a structured and technical fashion in Bellamy's utopia, but even the city and the home are marked with the influence and efficiency of technology. Most of the household duties are done outside of the home so that all washing is done by public employees and all cooking is done through public kitchens. One can opt to order one's meals into the privacy of one's home or can elect to have the meal in a restaurant which boasts greater quality. Electricity lights the home and replaces the need for gas and candles. Within each house is a room entirely devoted to listening to music which is performed live by a series of orchestras at all times of the day and transmitted through a telephone which fills the room with music. This telephone device could be accessed in any of the rooms and Julian even listens to it while trying to sleep and to comfort him from the stresses of the transition to the new century. Julian and the Leete family also listen to a Sunday sermon over the telephone and Julian is struck by the utter depravity of those in his former life. Julian is also taken to the local market where he views orders for anything needed in the home being taken by clerks who are not concerned about selling out of the desire for profit, but merely transmit the order to the centralised distribution system through pneumatic pipes. His companion uses a credit card which deducts the value of the items and disposes of the need for physical monetary transactions. The items are then shipped to the Leetes' home and arrive even before they return from the store itself. Technology and the efficiency it provides is an important aspect of Bellamy's utopia.

2.4.3   Religion and Idealism in America's Technological Utopias

What is fascinating to note in both of these utopias discussed is the way in which religious hope is attributed to these utopian visions of the future. The foreword to *Roadtown*, written by Julian Hawthorne, refers to Chambless as Moses who is to lead the world from the bondage of contemporary city life into his Eden of Roadtown.[95] Chambless himself even refers to Road-town as a religion: 'The above expresses the principles of the Roadtown religion—a faith which holds that the Kingdom of God can be realized on this earth and points a practical way by which such realization may be attained.'[96] Similarly, in *Looking Backward* Julian West listens to a sermon which has the minister reflecting on the disparities between the 19th and 20th centuries and its religious significance. The minister states:

> It is a pledge of the destiny appointed for us that the Creator has set in our hearts an infinite standard of achievement, judged by which our past attainments seem always insignificant, and the goal never nearer. Had our forefathers conceived a state of society in which men should live together like brethren dwelling in unity, without strifes or envy-ing, violence or overreaching, and where, at the price of a degree of labor not greater than health demands, in their chosen occupations, they should be wholly freed from care for the morrow and left with no more concern for their livelihood than trees which are watered by unfailing streams,—had they conceived such a condition, I say, it would have seemed to them nothing less than paradise. They would have con-founded it with their idea of heaven, nor dreamed that there could pos-sibly lie further beyond anything to be desired or striven for.[97]

What we find both Chambless and Bellamy referencing is a common attitude many of the technological utopians had of their proposed plans. Cloaked in religious language, these utopians sought to convince the populace that technology was to be the panacea which would solve major issues such as labour disputes and poor urban living conditions. This isn't to say that they weren't practical or realistic in their propositions. On the contrary, almost all of these utopians proposed that with mere extension of the present conditions their utopias were to be the future of America.[98] In fact, the greater majority actually set the time of this achievement within a century of their writing.[99] So while their plans were idealistic and often invoked religious imagery they were also very practical and realisable. We see elements of real planning and calculation but also significant reference to religious and visionary imagery.

These technological utopias during the turn of the 20th century reflect the greater confidence America was putting in technology to shape its future in thoroughly ideological ways. They represent a certain realist trend in American public life which engaged intimately with the world through technology. They fall squarely within the utopian strand, but also had a practical vision for transforming this world through real planning.

2.4.4 Further Developments in the 20th Century

Moving from the early 20th century, this same utopian ideology is expressed in many other American movements which extend into the present. The technocracy movement of the early 20th century is a good example. Beginning with the economist Thorstein Veblen, technocrats proposed businessmen and politicians should be expelled from social decisions and instead should be replaced with engineers and scientists. Veblen's text *The Engineers and the Price System* juxtaposes the wasteful habits of businessmen with the calculated and efficient work of engineers.[100] Whereas engineers worked with an astounding communitarian work ethic, politicians and businessmen were greedy and individualistic. The technocracy movement became a much larger movement under the auspices of Howard Scott, a devoted follower of Veblen.[101] Scott was a visionary engineer who created the organisation Technocracy, Inc. which is still in existence today. The technocracy movement was most influential during the 1930s when the masses were disillusioned with the government's ability to solve the economic issues of the Great Depression. The technocrats suggested 'the ills of the economy were traceable not to the machine per se, but to the inefficient adjustment of the social order to modern high-energy technology.'[102] The technocrats' major accomplishment was to suggest that the answer to a growing technological environment was the expansion of technical craft into social engineering. The answer to the ills of technology, therefore, could be alleviated through greater technologisation.

For a time, technocracy seemed to be a viable alternative for America. But several factors confounded their ascendency. First, the technocrats were ambivalent in breaking significantly into politics. Their key leaders agreed that awareness of the social problems which plagued America as being predominantly technical in nature was the only item they advocated. They were not interested in a 'political theory of action'.[103] Second, Howard Scott's crucial radio address to the nation on 13 January 1933 in New York utterly failed. Charged with apocalyptic language which asserted America's impending doom, Scott's unsavoury speech led members to claim he had been drugged.[104] Finally, scholars contend Franklin Delano Roosevelt's successful New Deal significantly preempted many of the technocrats' suggestions.[105] Indeed, the spirit of technocracy can be found in the policies of the New Deal and would have lasting effect on the national government's intervention in matters related to economics and society.[106] This last issue serves to elucidate the importance of the technocrats to the American technological zeal. Despite their failure, the technocrats left a large mark on America and ingrained the value of technical solutions to economic and social concerns.

The same idealism regarding technology can be found in the writings of R. Buckminster Fuller (1895–1983).[107] Fuller is most known for his futuristic pieces of architecture such as the geodesic dome and the Dymaxion House.[108] He was the grandnephew of the American Transcendentalist author Margaret Fuller. She is said to be the inspiration for his vast visionary perspective on contemporary issues which plagued humanity.[109] In fact, the major thrust of his life was devoted to addressing the rapidly changing social and environmental climate and other significant issues facing humanity as a whole such as war, overpopulation and famine.[110] Fuller held, like many before him, that with the proper scientific study of the issues coupled with elegant and technological solutions, humanity would flourish in the years to come. This conviction drove his development of often bizarre futuristic technologies which were meant to transform ordinary life. For instance, the Dymaxion House and Dymaxion Car boasted radical and innovative designs which could be mass produced and were very advanced technically for their time. The homes were structured around a single mast in the middle and could be delivered and stacked on top of each other. Fuller even proposed they be delivered by Zeppelin.[111] The Dymaxion Car was meant to be a stepping stone to a more general transport vehicle which could fly as well. It had a three-wheeled design with front-wheel drive for tighter cornering and could carry eleven people. It was very lightweight and streamlined and had a top speed of 120 miles per hour and got as much as 30 miles per gallon.[112] Fuller had an unwavering belief that humanity had within its grasp the ability to realise its utopian potential. All generations prior who sought to achieve utopia could only bring local changes, but with the advances of technology it was possible to bring utopia on a global scale.[113] For Fuller, humanity was on the brink of either utopia or oblivion.

R. Buckminster Fuller's legacy is extensive. During the end of his life he devoted himself to a rigorous lecturing schedule which numbered close to 100 a year, with the most being 150 in 1974.[114] He visited 544 different colleges and universities around the world and claimed to have gone around the world 57 times for invited presentations.[115] He was awarded 47 honorary degrees, held 25 academic posts and was on the cover of *Time* magazine in 1964.[116] Being obsessed with documenting his life in what he termed the Chronofile, Fuller calculated that his work by 1974 had come in contact with a quarter billion people.[117] His lasting effect in architecture is still visible through such famous geodesic domes in Florida's Disney World, Japan's Fantasy Entertainment Complex and England's Eden Project in Cornwall. He is considered a founding father of the collection of social critics, scientists and philosophers whom Alvin Toffler has coined 'The Futurists'.[118] He has had a lasting influence on the American psyche and landscape.

It is evident that technological utopianism has functioned largely in both American history and the American national identity in the 19th and 20th centuries. From Bellamy's *Looking Backward* to R. Buckminster Fuller, a distinct strand is identifiable within American history. These utopias both propagate a growing religious hope in technology and also reflect the crystallisation of the already existing sentiment present in American society which lie at the basis of the American identity even today.

2.5   CONCLUSION: TECHNOLOGICAL UTOPIANISM TODAY

These technological utopias disclose something much deeper than a general optimistic attitude toward the future. Howard Segal gives an enlightening response to this utopian strand in America's history:

> The popularity of Fuller and his high-tech successors reveals much about Americans' and others' apparent obsession with the future. Despite professional forecasting's mediocre record, so many still feel compelled to try to uncover the future. That compulsion in turn reflects a deeper anxiety more than a superficial optimism, a profound uncertainty about the future that even our unprecedented access to information and to communications cannot overcome. The unceasing hype over our allegedly unique pace and extent of technological change has, I suspect, made many persons increasingly eager to figure out what comes next.[119]

Much of the uneasiness Segal perceives could be due, in large part, to the quickly changing social and geographical landscape into a highly technical environment. As suggested, the last two centuries in the Western world are marked with such rapid industrialisation and remarkable invention that, as one critic suggests, humanity has had difficulty keeping up.[120] Technological leaders seem to be obsessed with what will come next[121] and the impact technology has had and will have on our individual lives and the future of humanity. Indeed, this utopian drive suggests a much deeper uneasiness with the future which necessitates such prediction in the face of growing technology. So, while these 19th- and 20th-century utopias can be taken as legitimate predictions, they often reveal more about the present worries and hopes of the societies and peoples who create them.

With this in mind, it is evident that societies and nations in the last two centuries have become increasingly obsessed with technology and the future. This time saw a major influx of visions of the future where technology figured largely. We have seen how much of our technological dreaming in the form of utopias and real planning began with religious sources as with Bacon and Fedorov. But, by the mid-20th century, the only expressed appeal to religion in the technological future in these utopias is in charged religious/ideological language. There is no mention of a God who comes and the future is a product of our technological creations today.[122]

It is easy to see that technological utopianism is alive and well and it seems to continue to be a significant thread influencing all of us in developed societies today. We hear it implicitly if not explicitly in today's smartphone commercials, quoted by technological entrepreneurs and even from our own children. If one were to 'virtually attend' the latest TED talk online[123] they might hear how new information technologies are rapidly changing the very fabric of modern society around the world. Indeed, the rapid introduction of new technologies in the last half century and the social and personal changes it has made is reminiscent of the explosive growth of technology and corresponding social changes in the 19th century. As we have seen, this led to a massive influx of technological utopias and speculation about the future at that time. We are seeing this again today, only instead of being fuelled by rapid mechanisation and by such technologies as the steam engine and electric light bulb, it is information technology and the rise of the Internet which has led to our speculations today.

Information technology utopias are ubiquitous at present. They can be found emblazoned across the pages of such periodicals as *Wired* and *Popular Mechanics* and in the heart of Silicon Valley, California, amidst a group of technologists often referred to as 'cyberlibertarians'. These cyberlibertarians adhere to what has been termed 'The Californian Ideology', the belief in a soft technological determinism along with libertarian economic ideals.[124] High-tech industry meets Ayn Rand philosophy in the belief that exploitation of information networks would yield economic growth in a postindustrial age and would likewise weaken political power in favour of virtual self-organised communities. For these technological bohemians, information technology promises a radical transformation of society where old political and economic structures become superfluous because the information network provides the backbone in connecting individuals and the 'invisible hand' of democracy will guarantee freedom and economic progress.[125] Information technology is merely the latest catalyst to technological dreaming visible in centuries past. As one philosopher of technology has said about the utopian dreams generated by groundbreaking technology: 'The basic conceit is always the same: new technology will bring universal wealth, enhanced freedom, revitalized politics, satisfying community, and personal fulfilment.'[126]

Not only is technological utopianism visible today, but it seems to be on the rise. This is in spite of considerable erosion and attack on all utopian dreaming in the early to mid-20th century. It is surprising that even after the events of the world wars where many saw firsthand the might of modern mechanised military technology and the utter decimation of entire nations and people-groups (the Holocaust), some half a century later these memories have been forgotten. And, in our own time it is clear that the current ecological crisis and global warming are themselves products of two centuries of manufacturing and the Industrial Revolution. In spite of all this, technological utopianism has still taken root in our modern consciousness. Perhaps it reveals just how easily and quickly we can become bedazzled with technology as human beings. Our survival and growth as a species has been and continues to be entirely dependent upon these artefacts we create. Our history is a history entwined with our technologies that pervade our hopes and dreams and lead us to planning for the future.

However, the perspectives represented in this chapter only see the benefits of technology and its role in bringing about a desirable future. The technological imagination of the last two hundred years has a richer and more nuanced landscape. Indeed, the subject of the next chapter, science fiction, has done more to influence our conception of the technological future than anything else and it is with it that we see a more complex and multifaceted appraisal of it. It is to science fiction that we now turn.

NOTES

1. Mishtooni Bose, "Introduction," in *Utopia* (Ware: Wordsworth Editions Ltd., 1997), vii.
2. Fredric Jameson, *Archaeologies of the Future: The Desire Called Utopia and Other Science Fictions* (London: Verso, 2005), 3.
3. Wayne Hudson, *The Reform of Utopia* (Burlington: Ashgate, 2003), 21.
4. Jameson, *Archaeologies of the Future*, 2. Bloch considers technological utopias in Ernst Bloch, *The Principle of Hope*, trans., Neville Plaice et al., vol. 2 (Oxford: Basil Blackwell, 1986), 625–699.
5. Clearly Japan and perhaps China and Korea would have to be added to this list for the 21st century. However, space is limited and both America and Russia were vanguards contributing to the ascension of technological utopianism in the 19th and 20th centuries.
6. Bacon does not use the term technology but instead 'mechanical arts', 'operative philosophy' or even 'inventions useful to man'. I do not intend to use the term 'technology' anachronistically but the reader should be wary of importing our contemporary notion without qualification.
7. Markku Peltonen, "Introduction," in *The Cambridge Companion to Francis Bacon*, ed., Markku Peltonen (Cambridge: Cambridge University Press, 1996), 15.
8. Charles Whitney, "Francis Bacon's Instauratio: Dominion of and over Humanity," *Journal of the History of Ideas* 50, no. 3 (1989), 371.
9. Ibid.
10. Francis Bacon, *The New Organon*, ed., Lisa Jardine and Michael Silverthorne (Cambridge: Cambridge University Press, 2000), 221.

11. Peter Harrison, *The Fall of Man and the Foundations of Science* (Cambridge: Cambridge University Press, 2007), 158.
12. Whitney, 371.
13. Lisa Jardine, "Introduction," in *The New Organon*, ed., Lisa Jardine and Michael Silverthorne (Cambridge: Cambridge University Press, 2000), xix–xx. This final idol is the most important for it signifies Bacon's issue with his predecessors such as Aristotelianism. He was critical of their reliance upon tradition to arrive at conclusions instead of correct observation and experimentation which guided the entire method. For the role of experimentation in Bacon and his predecessors see Thomas S. Kuhn, *The Essential Tension: Selected Studies in Scientific Tradition and Change* (Chicago: University of Chicago Press, 1977), 54–55.
14. Stephen A. McKnight, ed., *Science, Pseudo-Science, and Utopianism in Early Modern Thought* (London: University of Missouri Press, 1992), 111.
15. This is precisely where Bacon gets entangled in the transhumanist narrative. For, as we shall see, human redemption is, in part, a work of human scientific and technological work.
16. Steven Matthews, *Theology and Science in the Thought of Francis Bacon* (Aldershot: Ashgate, 2008), 101.
17. Bacon quoted in ibid., 103.
18. Francis Bacon, *The Advancement of Learning and the New Atlantis* (Oxford: Oxford University Press, 1974), 239.
19. Ibid.
20. Ibid., 247.
21. Ibid., 244.
22. Ibid., 246.
23. For a more detailed explanation of Bacon's coupling of the artisan's task with the natural philosopher's work see Jürgen Klein, "Francis Bacon's *Scientia Operativa*, the Tradition of the Workshops, and the Secrets of Nature," in *Philosophies of Technology: Francis Bacon and His Contemporaries*, ed., Claus Zittel (Leiden: Brill, 2008); Paolo Rossi, *Francis Bacon: From Magic to Science*, trans., Sacha Rabinovitch (London: Routledge & Kegan Paul, 1968), 8–10.
24. Bacon, *The New Organon*, 69.
25. Romano Nanni, "Technical Knowledge and the Advancement of Learning: Some Questions About 'Perfectability' and 'Invention'," in *Philosophies of Technology: Francis Bacon and His Contemporaries*, ed., Claus Zittel (Leiden: Brill, 2008), 53–56; Sophie Weeks, "The Role of Mechanics in Francis Bacon's Great Instauration," in *Philosophies of Technology: Francis Bacon and His Contemporaries*, ed., Claus Zittel (Leiden: Brill, 2008).
26. Lewis Mumford, *The Myth of the Machine* (London: Secker & Warburg, 1967), 283.
27. Matthews, *Theology and Science*, 135.
28. Ibid., 136.
29. Thomas Sprat, *The History of the Royal Society of London* (London: 1667), 63–64.
30. Matthews, *Theology and Science*, 137–138.
31. For a more complete appraisal of Bacon's legacy see ibid., 117ff.
32. Fyodor Dostoyevsky, "Appendix I," in *What Was Man Created For? The Philosophy of the Common Task: Selected Works* (London: Honeyglen, 1990), 227.
33. Elisabeth Koutaissoff, "Introduction," in *What Was Man Created For? The Philosophy of the Common Task: Selected Works* (London: Honeyglen, 1990), 15.

34. See Stephen Lukashevich, *N. F. Fedorov (1828–1903): A Study of Russian Eupsychian and Utopian Thought* (Newark: University of Delaware Press, 1977), 22, for a partial translation of Tolstoy's letter to A. I. Alexeev.

35. Ibid., 16–20.

36. Fedorov quoted in George M. Young, *Nikolai F. Fedorov: An Introduction* (Belmont: Nordland, 1979), 107.

37. Nikolai Fedorovich Fedorov, *What Was Man Created For? The Philosophy of the Common Task: Selected Works*, trans., Elisabeth Koutaissoff and Marilyn Minto (London: Honeyglen, 1990), 34.

38. Ibid., 39.

39. Ibid., 46–51.

40. See Lukashevich, *N. F. Fedorov*, 47, for a translation of Nikolai Fedorovich Fedorov, *Filosofiia Obshchago Dela*, vol. 2 (Moscow: 1913), 264, 265.

41. Lukashevich, *N. F. Fedorov*, 47–48.

42. Nicholas Berdyaev, "N. F. Fedorov," *Russian Review* 9, no. 2 (1950), 125.

43. Lukashevich, *N. F. Fedorov*, 18.

44. Fedorov, *What Was Man Created For*, 99.

45. Ibid., 148–150.

46. For details of the American scientific experiments Fedorov refers to see ibid., 144–158; Koutaissoff, "Introduction," 27–28. On Russia and China's attempts to seed clouds see Daniel Engber, "Can the Russians Control Weather? How Cloud Seeding Works," *Slate*, May 11, 2005; Pallavi Aiyar, "Ready, Aim, Fire and Rain," *Asia Times*, July 13, 2007.

47. Fedorov, *What Was Man Created For*, 95.

48. Ibid., 97.

49. Berdyaev, "N. F. Fedorov," 128.

50. Fedorov, *What Was Man Created For*, 193.

51. Berdyaev, "N. F. Fedorov," 127; Fedorov, *What Was Man Created For*, 193ff.

52. Lukashevich, *N. F. Fedorov*, 25.

53. Boris Leonidovich Pasternak, *Doctor Zhivago* (New York: Pantheon Books, 1991), 10.

54. Nicolas Zernov, *The Russian Religious Renaissance of the Twentieth Century* (London: Darton Longman & Todd, 1963), 293n13.

55. S. V. Utechin, "Bolsheviks and Their Allies after 1917: The Ideological Pattern," *Soviet Studies* 10, no. 2 (1958), 131.

56. Ibid.

57. See especially Kendall E. Bailes, *Science and Russian Culture in an Age of Revolutions: V. I. Vernadsky and His Scientific School, 1863–1945* (Bloomington: Indiana University Press, 1990).

58. Lukashevich, *N. F. Fedorov*, 28–29.

59. Ibid., 30.

60. Richard Stites, *Revolutionary Dreams: Utopian Vision and Experimental Life in the Russian Revolution* (Oxford: Oxford University Press, 1989), 34.

61. Ibid., 30.

62. Ibid., 32.

63. Ibid. For a more detailed analysis of Bellamy's importance in Russia see Alexander Nikoljukin, "A Little Known Story: Bellamy in Russia," in *Edward Bellamy Abroad: An American Prophet's Influence*, ed., Sylvia E. Bowman (New York: Twayne Publishers, 1962).

64. See Stites, *Revolutionary Dreams*, 5; Katerina Clark, "The City versus the Countryside in Soviet Peasant Literature of the Twenties: A Duel of Utopias," in *Bolshevik Culture: Experiment and Order in the Russian Revolution*, ed., Abbott Gleason, Peter Kenez, and Richard Stites (Bloomington: Indiana University Press, 1985).

65. Of course Marx and Engels were both highly critical of utopias, particularly utopian socialism and utopian communism. They were highly suspicious of the possible escapist tendencies of utopia while they emphasised the scientific and material transformation of society for Marxism. But, many have argued that the utopian drive was very evident in Marxism when considered externally. See Ruth Levitas, *The Concept of Utopia* (London: Philip Allan, 1990), 35–68; Ruth Levitas, "Educated Hope: Ernst Bloch on Abstract and Concrete Utopia," in *Not Yet: Reconsidering Ernst Bloch*, ed., Jamie Owen Daniel and Tom Moylan (London: Verso, 1997).
66. Stites, *Revolutionary Dreams*, 3.
67. Lewis Mumford states, 'There is, it is true, one universal and accepted symbol of our period in America: the skyscraper.' in Lewis Mumford, "American Architecture Today," *Architecture* 58 (October 1928), 189. For an appraisal of America's idealism manifest in the skyscraper see Carol Willis, "Skyscraper Utopias: Visionary Urbanism in the 1920s," in *Imagining Tomorrow: History, Technology, and the American Future*, ed., Joseph J. Corn (London: MIT Press, 1986); C. H. Walker, "America's Titanic Strength Expressed in Architecture," *Current History* 25 (January 1925); Joseph Korom, *The American Skyscraper, 1850–1940: A Celebration of Height* (Boston: Branden Books, 2008).
68. For critical essays on the history and ethos of Silicon Valley see Martin Kenney, ed., *Understanding Silicon Valley: The Anatomy of an Entrepreneurial Region* (Stanford: Stanford University Press, 2000).
69. For a strong overview of America's history with technology see Thomas Parke Hughes, *American Genesis: A Century of Invention and Technological Enthusiasm, 1870–1970* (London: University of Chicago Press, 2004).
70. John Winthrop, "We Shall Be as a City Upon a Hill," in *Speeches That Changed the World*, ed., Owen Collins (Louisville: John Knox Press, 1998), 65.
71. For an argument of the utopian underpinnings of New Plymouth and the Massachusetts Bay Colony see Robert Appelbaum, *Literature and Utopian Politics in Seventeenth-Century England* (Cambridge: Cambridge University Press, 2002), 72–79.
72. Ernest Lee Tuveson, *Redeemer Nation: The Idea of America's Millennial Role* (Chicago: University of Chicago Press, 1968), 91.
73. William Earl Weeks, *Building the Continental Empire: American Expansion from the Revolution to the Civil War* (Chicago: Ivan R. Dee, 1996), 61.
74. Michael A. Morrison, *Slavery and the American West: The Eclipse of Manifest Destiny and the Coming of the Civil War* (London: University of North Carolina Press, 1997).
75. Merritt Roe Smith, "Technological Determinism in American Culture," in *Does Technology Drive History?: The Dilemma of Technological Determinism*, ed., Merritt Roe Smith and Leo Marx (London: MIT Press, 1994), 10–11.
76. This 'conquering of space' through technology was central to the American ideal and identity. This is convincingly argued in David E. Nye, *America as Second Creation: Technology and Narratives of New Beginnings* (London: MIT Press, 2003).
77. See John Elwood Clark, *Railroads in the Civil War: The Impact of Management on Victory and Defeat* (Baton Rouge: Louisiana State University Press, 2001); George Edgar Turner, *Victory Rode the Rails: The Strategic Place of the Railroads in the Civil War* (Indianapolis: Bobbs-Merrill, 1953).
78. Clark, *Railroads in the Civil War*, 3.
79. Although these men were responsible for many patents and inventions, Thomas Edison is best known for inventing the light bulb and DC current;

Alexander Graham Bell for the telephone; and Nikola Tesla for AC current. See Hughes, *American Genesis*.
80. Margaret Cheney, *Tesla: Man out of Time* (New York: Touchstone, 1981).
81. Howard P. Segal, *Technological Utopianism in American Culture* (Chicago: University of Chicago Press, 1985), 19.
82. Ibid., 45–47.
83. Ibid., 21.
84. One is reminded of R. Buckminster Fuller's Dymaxion House or geodesic domes. With the success of the Fordian assembly line and the mass-produced automobile, many architects held this same model could and should be applied to the home. So, not only was the home subjected to the visionary rationalisation of an imaginary future, but even the very process by which the home was to be constructed was affected by this movement as well. See Brian Horrigan, "The Home of Tomorrow, 1927–1945," in *Imagining Tomorrow: History, Technology, and the American Future*, ed., Joseph J. Corn (London: MIT Press, 1986); Willis, "Skyscraper Utopias."
85. Edgar Chambless, *Roadtown* (New York: Roadtown Press, 1910), 22–24.
86. Ibid., 30.
87. Ibid., 106.
88. Ibid., 71–72.
89. To consult these construction lists see ibid., 153–154.
90. Matthew Beaumont, "Introduction," in *Looking Backward 2000–1887* (Oxford: Oxford University Press, 2007), vii. As we have seen, it was also a great success in Russia.
91. Arthur Lipow, *Authoritarian Socialism in America: Edward Bellamy and the Nationalist Movement* (Berkeley: University of California Press, 1982), 119–120.
92. Edward Bellamy, *Looking Backward: 2000–1887* (Oxford: Oxford University Press, 2007), 77.
93. Ibid., 37.
94. Ibid., 74–75.
95. Chambless, *Roadtown*, 1–2.
96. Ibid., 169.
97. Bellamy, *Looking Backward*, 169–170.
98. Segal, *Technological Utopianism*, 21–23.
99. Ibid., 22.
100. Val Dusek, *Philosophy of Technology: An Introduction* (Oxford: Blackwell, 2006), 46–47.
101. William E. Akin, *Technocracy and the American Dream: The Technocrat Movement, 1900–1941* (Berkeley: University of California, 1977), 27–45.
102. Ibid., x.
103. Ibid., 112.
104. Ibid., 88.
105. Dusek, *Philosophy of Technology*, 47; Akin, *Technocracy and the American Dream*, 110.
106. Leslie H. Fischel, "The Problem of Social Control," in *Technology in Western Civilization*, ed., Carroll W. Pursell and Melvin Kranzberg (New York: Oxford University Press, 1967), 502–504.
107. See especially Howard P. Segal, "R. Buckminster Fuller: America's Last Genuine Utopian?," in *New Views on R. Buckminster Fuller*, ed., Hsiao-yun Chu and Roberto G. Trujillo (Stanford: Stanford University Press, 2009).
108. Olive Hoogenboom, "Fuller, R. Buckminster," *American National Biography Online* (February 2000), http://www.anb.org/articles/13/13-02560.html.

109. Peter F. Drucker, *Adventures of a Bystander* (New York: Wiley, 1997), 244.
110. Fuller even developed a game later in life called 'World Game' which taught young people to have a global perspective and to work together to remedy the major ills of humanity. See Hoogenboom, "Fuller, R. Buckminster."
111. Horrigan, "The Home of Tomorrow," 140.
112. See Lloyd Steven Sieden, *Buckminster Fuller's Universe* (Cambridge: Perseus, 2000), 143–167.
113. R. Buckminster Fuller, *Utopia or Oblivion: The Prospects for Humanity* (Harmondsworth: Penguin, 1972), 331–335.
114. Hoogenboom, "Fuller, R. Buckminster."
115. Ibid.
116. Ibid.
117. Buckminster Fuller Institute, "Fuller's Influence," http://www.bfi.org/our_pro grams/who_is_buckminster_fuller/fullers_influence (accessed 14 April 2010).
118. Alvin Toffler, ed., *The Futurists* (New York: Random House, 1972).
119. Segal, "R. Buckminster Fuller," 51.
120. Alvin Toffler, *Future Shock* (New York: Bantam, 1971), 25–30.
121. For example, Bill Gates, Nathan Myhrvold, and Peter Rinearson, *The Road Ahead* (New York: Penguin Books, 1996); Nicholas Negroponte, *Being Digital* (New York: Vintage Books, 1996). Both predicted the impact computers would have on society. For contemporary issues on technological prediction see David E. Nye, "Technological Prediction: A Promethean Problem," in *Technological Visions: The Hopes and Fears That Shape New Technologies*, ed., Marita Sturken, Douglas Thomas, and Sandra Ball-Rokeach (Philadelphia: Temple University Press, 2004).
122. I am intentionally creating a dichotomy here. I understand there are Christians who have actively incorporated technology into the Christian future. Indeed, chapters 5 and 6 are devoted to two examples of Christian thinkers who have included technology in the Christian future. But, by way of a history of transhumanism and all technological futurisms today, I wanted to chart how many of these secular technological utopias are historically indebted to an *adventus* type of future and are motivated by tacit religious impulses. I am not unique in arguing this. See David F. Noble, *The Religion of Technology: The Divinity of Man and the Spirit of Invention* (London: Penguin, 1999).
123. TED, "TED: Ideas Worth Spreading," http://www.ted.com (accessed 30 October 2013).
124. Richard Barbrook and Andy Cameron, "The Californian Ideology," *Science as Culture* 6, no. 1 (1996).
125. In the fourth chapter, we will see these hopes and dreams in the Information Revolution taken to new heights with transhumanism.
126. Langdon Winner, "Technology Today: Utopia or Dystopia?," *Social Research* 64, no. 3 (1997), 1001.

REFERENCES

Aiyar, Pallavi. "Ready, Aim, Fire and Rain." *Asia Times*, July 13, 2007.
Akin, William E. *Technocracy and the American Dream: The Technocrat Movement, 1900–1941.* Berkeley: University of California, 1977.
Appelbaum, Robert. *Literature and Utopian Politics in Seventeenth-Century England.* Cambridge: Cambridge University Press, 2002.
Bacon, Francis. *The Advancement of Learning and the New Atlantis.* Oxford: Oxford University Press, 1974.

———. *The New Organon*, edited by Lisa Jardine and Michael Silverthorne. Cambridge: Cambridge University Press, 2000.

Bailes, Kendall E. *Science and Russian Culture in an Age of Revolutions: V. I. Vernadsky and His Scientific School, 1863–1945*. Bloomington: Indiana University Press, 1990.

Barbrook, Richard, and Andy Cameron. "The Californian Ideology." *Science as Culture* 6, no. 1 (1996): 44–72.

Beaumont, Matthew. "Introduction." In *Looking Backward 2000–1887*. Oxford: Oxford University Press, 2007.

Bellamy, Edward. "How and Why I Wrote *Looking Backward*." In *America as Utopia*, edited by Kenneth M. Roemer. New York: B. Franklin, 1981.

———. *Looking Backward: 2000–1887*. Oxford: Oxford University Press, 2007.

Berdyaev, Nicholas. "N. F. Fedorov." *Russian Review* 9, no. 2 (1950): 124–130.

Bloch, Ernst. *The Principle of Hope*. Translated by Neville Plaice, Stephen Plaice, and Paul Knight. Vol. 2. Oxford: Basil Blackwell, 1986.

Bose, Mishtooni. "Introduction." In *Utopia*. Ware: Wordsworth Editions Ltd., 1997.

Buckminster Fuller Institute. "Fuller's Influence." http://www.bfi.org/our_programs/who_is_buckminster_fuller/fullers_influence (accessed 14 April 2010).

Chambless, Edgar. *Roadtown*. New York: Roadtown Press, 1910.

Cheney, Margaret. *Tesla: Man out of Time*. New York: Touchstone, 1981.

Clark, John Elwood. *Railroads in the Civil War: The Impact of Management on Victory and Defeat*. Baton Rouge: Louisiana State University Press, 2001.

Clark, Katerina. "The City versus the Countryside in Soviet Peasant Literature of the Twenties: A Duel of Utopias." In *Bolshevik Culture: Experiment and Order in the Russian Revolution*, edited by Abbott Gleason, Peter Kenez, and Richard Stites. Bloomington: Indiana University Press, 1985.

Dostoyevsky, Fyodor. "Appendix I." In *What Was Man Created For? The Philosophy of the Common Task: Selected Works*. London: Honeyglen, 1990.

Drucker, Peter F. *Adventures of a Bystander*. New York: Wiley, 1997.

Dusek, Val. *Philosophy of Technology: An Introduction*. Oxford: Blackwell, 2006.

Engber, Daniel. "Can the Russians Control Weather? How Cloud Seeding Works." *Slate*, May 11, 2005.

Fedorov, Nikolai Fedorovich. *Filosofiia Obshchago Dela*. Vol. 1. Vernyi, 1906.

———. *Filosofiia Obshchago Dela*. Vol. 2. Moscow, 1913.

———. *What Was Man Created For? The Philosophy of the Common Task: Selected Works*. Translated by Elisabeth Koutaissoff and Marilyn Minto. London: Honeyglen, 1990.

Fischel, Leslie H. "The Problem of Social Control." In *Technology in Western Civilization*, edited by Carroll W. Pursell and Melvin Kranzberg. New York: Oxford University Press, 1967.

Fuller, R. Buckminster. *Utopia or Oblivion: The Prospects for Humanity*. Harmondsworth: Penguin, 1972.

Gates, Bill, Nathan Myhrvold, and Peter Rinearson. *The Road Ahead*. New York: Penguin Books, 1996.

Gleason, Abbott, Peter Kenez, and Richard Stites, eds. *Bolshevik Culture: Experiment and Order in the Russian Revolution*. Bloomington: Indiana University Press, 1985.

Harrison, Peter. *The Fall of Man and the Foundations of Science*. Cambridge: Cambridge University Press, 2007.

Hoogenboom, Olive. "Fuller, R. Buckminster." *American National Biography Online* (February 2000). http://www.anb.org/articles/13/13–02560.html (accessed 14 April 2010).

Horrigan, Brian. "The Home of Tomorrow, 1927–1945." In *Imagining Tomorrow: History, Technology, and the American Future*, edited by Joseph J. Corn. London: MIT Press, 1986.

Hudson, Wayne. *The Reform of Utopia*. Burlington: Ashgate, 2003.
Hughes, Thomas Parke. *American Genesis: A Century of Invention and Technological Enthusiasm, 1870–1970*. London: University of Chicago Press, 2004.
Jameson, Fredric. "Reification and Utopia in Mass Culture." *Social Text* 1 (1979): 130–148.
———. *Archaeologies of the Future: The Desire Called Utopia and Other Science Fictions*. London: Verso, 2005.
Jardine, Lisa. "Introduction." In *The New Organon*, edited by Lisa Jardine and Michael Silverthorne. Cambridge: Cambridge University Press, 2000.
Kenney, Martin, ed. *Understanding Silicon Valley: The Anatomy of an Entrepreneurial Region*. Stanford: Stanford University Press, 2000.
Klein, Jürgen. "Francis Bacon's *Scientia Operativa*, the Tradition of the Workshops, and the Secrets of Nature." In *Philosophies of Technology: Francis Bacon and His Contemporaries*, edited by Claus Zittel. Leiden: Brill, 2008.
Korom, Joseph. *The American Skyscraper, 1850–1940: A Celebration of Height*. Boston: Branden Books, 2008.
Koutaissoff, Elisabeth. "Introduction." In N. F. Federov, *What Was Man Created For? The Philosophy of the Common Task: Selected Works*. London: Honeyglen, 1990.
Kuhn, Thomas S. *The Essential Tension: Selected Studies in Scientific Tradition and Change*. Chicago: University of Chicago Press, 1977.
Levitas, Ruth. *The Concept of Utopia*. London: Philip Allan, 1990.
———. "Educated Hope: Ernst Bloch on Abstract and Concrete Utopia." In *Not Yet: Reconsidering Ernst Bloch*, edited by Jamie Owen Daniel and Tom Moylan. London: Verso, 1997.
Levy, Ze'ev. "Utopia and Reality in the Philosophy of Ernst Bloch." In *Not Yet: Reconsidering Ernst Bloch*, edited by Jamie Owen Daniel and Tom Moylan. London: Verso, 1997.
Lipow, Arthur. *Authoritarian Socialism in America: Edward Bellamy and the Nationalist Movement*. Berkeley: University of California Press, 1982.
Lukashevich, Stephen. *N. F. Fedorov (1828–1903): A Study of Russian Eupsychian and Utopian Thought*. Newark: University of Delaware Press, 1977.
Matthews, Steven. *Theology and Science in the Thought of Francis Bacon*. Aldershot: Ashgate, 2008.
McKnight, Stephen A., ed. *Science, Pseudo-Science, and Utopianism in Early Modern Thought*. London: University of Missouri Press, 1992.
———. "Francis Bacon's God." *The New Atlantis* (2005): 73–100.
———. *The Religious Foundations of Francis Bacon's Thought*. London: University of Missouri Press, 2006.
More, Thomas. *Utopia*. Translated by Ralph Robinson. Ware: Wordsworth Editions Ltd., 1997.
Morrison, Michael A. *Slavery and the American West: The Eclipse of Manifest Destiny and the Coming of the Civil War*. London: University of North Carolina Press, 1997.
Mumford, Lewis. "American Architecture Today." *Architecture* 58 (October 1928).
———. *The Myth of the Machine*. London: Secker & Warburg, 1967.
Nanni, Romano. "Technical Knowledge and the Advancement of Learning: Some Questions About 'Perfectability' and 'Invention'." In *Philosophies of Technology: Francis Bacon and His Contemporaries*, edited by Claus Zittel. Leiden: Brill, 2008.
Negroponte, Nicholas. *Being Digital*. New York: Vintage Books, 1996.
Nikoljukin, Alexander. "A Little Known Story: Bellamy in Russia." In *Edward Bellamy Abroad: An American Prophet's Influence*, edited by Sylvia E. Bowman. New York: Twayne Publishers, 1962.

Noble, David F. *The Religion of Technology: The Divinity of Man and the Spirit of Invention*. London: Penguin, 1999.

Nye, David E. *America as Second Creation: Technology and Narratives of New Beginnings*. London: MIT Press, 2003.

———. "Technological Prediction: A Promethean Problem." In *Technological Visions: The Hopes and Fears That Shape New Technologies*, edited by Marita Sturken, Douglas Thomas, and Sandra Ball-Rokeach. Philadelphia: Temple University Press, 2004.

Pasternak, Boris Leonidovich. *Doctor Zhivago*. New York: Pantheon Books, 1991.

Peltonen, Markku. "Introduction." In *The Cambridge Companion to Francis Bacon*, edited by Markku Peltonen. Cambridge: Cambridge University Press, 1996.

Roemer, Kenneth M. *The Obsolete Necessity: America in Utopian Writings, 1888–1900*. Kent: Kent State University Press, 1976.

———, ed. *America as Utopia*. New York: B. Franklin, 1981.

Rossi, Paolo. *Francis Bacon: From Magic to Science*. Translated by Sacha Rabinovitch. London: Routledge & Kegan Paul, 1968.

Segal, Howard P. *Technological Utopianism in American Culture*. Chicago: University of Chicago Press, 1985.

———. "R. Buckminster Fuller: America's Last Genuine Utopian?" In *New Views on R. Buckminster Fuller*, edited by Hsiao-yun Chu and Roberto G. Trujillo. Stanford: Stanford University Press, 2009.

Sieden, Lloyd Steven. *Buckminster Fuller's Universe*. Cambridge: Perseus, 2000.

Smith, Merritt Roe. "Technological Determinism in American Culture." In *Does Technology Drive History?: The Dilemma of Technological Determinism*, edited by Merritt Roe Smith and Leo Marx. London: MIT Press, 1994.

Smith, Merritt Roe, and Leo Marx, eds. *Does Technology Drive History?: The Dilemma of Technological Determinism*. London: MIT Press, 1994.

Smith, Michael L. "Recourse of Empire: Landscapes of Progress in Technological America." In *Does Technology Drive History?: The Dilemma of Technological Determinism*, edited by Merritt Roe Smith and Leo Marx. London: MIT Press, 1994.

Sprat, Thomas. *The History of the Royal Society of London*. London, 1667.

Stites, Richard. *Revolutionary Dreams: Utopian Vision and Experimental Life in the Russian Revolution*. Oxford: Oxford University Press, 1989.

TED. "TED: Ideas Worth Spreading." http://www.ted.com (accessed 30 October 2013).

Toffler, Alvin. *Future Shock*. New York: Bantam, 1971.

———, ed. *The Futurists*. New York: Random House, 1972.

Turner, George Edgar. *Victory Rode the Rails: The Strategic Place of the Railroads in the Civil War*. Indianapolis: Bobbs-Merrill, 1953.

Tuveson, Ernest Lee. *Redeemer Nation: The Idea of America's Millennial Role*. Chicago: University of Chicago Press, 1968.

Utechin, S. V. "Bolsheviks and Their Allies after 1917: The Ideological Pattern." *Soviet Studies* 10, no. 2 (1958): 113–135.

Walker, C. H. "America's Titanic Strength Expressed in Architecture." *Current History* 25 (January 1925).

Weeks, Sophie. "The Role of Mechanics in Francis Bacon's Great Instauration." In *Philosophies of Technology: Francis Bacon and His Contemporaries*, edited by Claus Zittel. Leiden: Brill, 2008.

Weeks, William Earl. *Building the Continental Empire: American Expansion from the Revolution to the Civil War*. Chicago: Ivan R. Dee, 1996.

Whitney, Charles. *Francis Bacon and Modernity*. London: Yale University Press, 1986.

————. "Francis Bacon's Instauratio: Dominion of and over Humanity." *Journal of the History of Ideas* 50, no. 3 (1989): 371–390.

Willis, Carol. "Skyscraper Utopias: Visionary Urbanism in the 1920s." In *Imagining Tomorrow: History, Technology, and the American Future*, edited by Joseph J. Corn. London: MIT Press, 1986.

Winner, Langdon. "Technology Today: Utopia or Dystopia?" *Social Research* 64, no. 3 (1997): 989–1017.

Winthrop, John. "We Shall Be as a City Upon a Hill." In *Speeches That Changed the World*, edited by Owen Collins. Louisville: John Knox Press, 1998.

Young, George M. *Nikolai F. Fedorov: An Introduction*. Belmont: Nordland, 1979.

Zernov, Nicolas. *The Russian Religious Renaissance of the Twentieth Century*. London: Darton Longman & Todd, 1963.

3   Science Fiction and the Technological Imagination

So far, I have been discussing the role of technology in several utopias. It can be concluded that technology has become a strong force in our consideration of the ideal society and the future. If, however, we want to have a more complete understanding of the current technological imagination, then we must examine the area of science fiction. The sheer pervasiveness and consumption of science fiction today is grounds for asserting that our technological imagination is influenced more by science fiction media than political or social engagements with technology and the future. This invariably leads us deeper into different mediums which include elements of fantasy literature and film rather than strict manifestos and planning tracts.

Referring to science fiction is important for the present work not only because it provides further evidence of how we think of technology and future today in contributing to our current technological imagination, but because of its relation to transhumanism. The transhumanist narrative, which will be the theme of the following chapter, draws upon this history of science fiction and the technological imagination cultivated by science fiction. Indeed, transhumanism has largely been influenced by the questioning of the boundary between humanity and machine carried out in science fiction.

This history of the technological imagination I am proposing in the last chapter and in this one is not of a discrete event or object but of a particular way we today envision things of a technological nature. That is, how they have inhabited our cultural memory and imagination and continue to be the source for our dreaming. This history makes explicit where our culture is currently in thinking about technology and the future. The present chapter, however, is also concerned with a broader and more rampant phenomenon today. Even if the common person rejects or is repulsed by transhumanism as a contemporary movement, even if this particular movement ultimately dies the death of other forgotten trends that have gone this way in the past, it is part of a much larger cultural imagination which is much more resilient and seems to be here to stay. We really can't think about the future today without thinking about technology and the way it is and will continue to shape us directly as human beings.

3.1   SCIENCE FICTION TODAY

It might be suggested that although science fiction and its consumption seem to be increasing it doesn't have any real bearing on the activities of engineers, scientists or the public opinion at large. In other words, science fiction should be treated as a nice imaginative genre, but surely not one which should be taken seriously. There are, however, several reasons why science fiction and the technological imagination are worth thoughtful consideration. First, inasmuch as scientists and technologists might pride themselves on removing human variability from their task, much of contemporary philosophy of science reminds us that human beings still drive the scientific method[1] and are at the front of the creation of technology. Whether it be in the form of the construction of hypotheses, the nature of perception or even the categories of the mind, of which imagination is central, how the world is understood and developed is entirely dependent upon human beings—science cannot be practiced without us, technology cannot be conceived without human ingenuity. Separating the scientific and technological imagination from their respective practices actually damages our understanding of those constitutive practices.

Yet, there is also much empirical evidence which suggests that influential scientists and technologists were, from a very young age, inspired by science fiction in choosing their vocation. In an article in *IEEE Spectrum*, a leading magazine on technology, fourteen top technologists were asked what novel influenced them the most.[2] Most named a piece of fiction with science fiction, in particular the writings of Robert A. Heinlein, being very well represented. The authors of the article note, 'Science fiction probably did as much as anything else in the 20th century to push youngsters into engineering.'[3] Also, according to a survey reported by the National Science Foundation there was a high correlation between reading science fiction books and the number of science and mathematics courses one took, level of education and 'attentiveness to science and technology'.[4] Second, beyond polls and surveys, there seems to be an increasing interest in the exchange between science fact and science fiction suggesting that science fiction lays the groundwork for scientific discovery and technological invention. As attested in the introduction to *Science Fact and Science Fiction: An Encyclopedia*, the growing public awareness that science fiction and science fact are becoming more closely bound requires greater study, elucidation and definition.[5] The rhetoric of science fiction goes beyond public entertainment to affect the imagination of those who are on the edge of technological invention. In fact, the editor of *Technology Review* states:

> I grew out of science fiction—which is to say that I learned to enjoy other, more literary writing and to disguise my passionate fandom. But science fiction continues to influence me. To this day, my tastes and choices as an editor and journalist are bluntly science fictional: I look for

technologies that are in themselves ingenious and that have the potential to change our established ways of doing things. Best of all, I like technologies that expand our sense of what it might mean to be human.[6]

All evidence suggests that the public at large and contemporary technologists are influenced by the narratives of science fiction in their own personal lives and in their vocations as scientists and technologists.

Not giving credit to science fiction's significance to today's world is reflected in its exclusion from academic standing for so long. The scholarly study of science fiction is still only some thirty years old.[7] Since that time one of the most fundamental questions has been: 'What is science fiction?' Despite the many arguments over what constitutes a piece of science fiction, most definitions include two very important elements: technology and the future.

Of course, this isn't surprising. Almost everyone can agree that science fiction is concerned with technology and machines. Whether the technology is at the forefront of the storyline or whether it merely provides the conditions and space in which the story takes place, technology is absolutely central in science fiction. Indeed, the most respected critical text on the study of science fiction, Clute's *Encyclopedia of Science Fiction*, identifies the Industrial Revolution and the force of technology on common life as the major impetus for the creation of science fiction itself.[8] In this section are identified some fourteen other technological items which require individual attention alone in the encyclopaedia including automation, computers, cyborgs, robots and spaceships.

The other central feature of science fiction is in its positing of another world or setting. It is an alternative reality which is distinct from the reader's own environment. Most often this alternative world comes in the form of the future. In fact, a common subgenre of science fiction is called the future history.[9] In this kind of text the author, writing from a time in the distant future, recalls the history from the present to the time of the author. Both Paul Alkon and Darko Suvin agree that the shift in environment moves sometime during the 18th and 19th century from one based upon space to time.[10] The alternative reality is relocated from a location which is either tacit or very far removed from known civilisation to the future. As an example, we have already seen this transition in our discussion of technological utopias. Francis Bacon's utopia, *The New Atlantis*, is set on a distant island whereas Bellamy's *Looking Backward* is set in the future. The difference in environment creates what Darko Suvin calls 'cognitive estrangement' and is an essential aspect of science fiction. Darko Suvin's definition of science fiction is helpful in identifying how this estrangement is achieved. He states:

SF in general—through its long history in different contexts—can be defined as a literary genre whose necessary and sufficient conditions are the presence and interaction of estrangement and cognition, and whose main formal device is an imaginative framework alternative to the author's empirical environment, and . . . it is distinguished by the narrative dominance or hegemony of a fictional 'novum' (novelty, innovation) validated by cognitive logic.[11]

This cognitive estrangement is created through the literary trope of the *novum*.[12] What is interesting to note, according to Roberts, is 'The degree of differentiation (the strangeness of the *novum*, to use Suvin's term) varies from text to text, but more often than not involves instances of technological hardware that have become, to a degree, reified with use: the spaceship, the alien, the robot, the time-machine, and so on.'[13] The *novum* is almost always related to technology in science fiction. One might then say that the alternative reality, which is generally set in the future, is created through the *novum* of a technological environment.

The very core of science fiction is concerned with technology and the future. And, while some have commented that science fiction is not about predicting the future,[14] the very presence of technology and the future being definitive for it is instructive enough for how we think of technology and the future today. Considering its wide consumption, science fiction represents one of the best indicators of our present technological imagination.

3.2   TECHNOLOGY AND THE FUTURE IN SCIENCE FICTION

This next section draws out three distinct themes in the treatment of technology and the future within science fiction.[15] I argue that technology has been depicted in the future in science fiction as: (1) adventurous and transcendent; (2) dystopian and oppressive; and (3) questioning the demarcation between humanity and technology. While I contend that there is an historical trend from the first theme to the latter it does not preclude that certain elements from the final theme cannot be seen in much earlier films or texts. This list does not intend to be exhaustive; it is meant to be general enough to include a wide range of specific ways technology and the future have been represented in science fiction. The examples used to elucidate each theme have been selected because they exemplify these themes well, have wide exposure, are historically seminal or have influenced other science fiction or the field more generally. It may seem that certain texts or films don't fall neatly into a particular category. This does not matter. I merely wish to show that technology and the future have been approached in broadly three different ways in science fiction.

3.2.1   First Trend: Technological Adventure and Awe

The first trend is categorised around the awe-inspiring nature of technology and the possibilities it can provide for the future. This theme represents positive responses to the force of technology in our world. The narratives are often accompanied with a sense of adventure where the boundaries of ordinary life are lifted and the character's potential is allowed to explode unabated. In this sense, technology can be a kind of liberation from the shackles of our own limited faculties or societal structures. Technology is often portrayed as new, innovative and sterile—removed from the commoner and associated with the elite and powerful. It accentuates the transcendent and yet empowering nature of technology.

Jules Verne's works are an early example. He created a new genre which he called the *roman scientifique* (the scientific novel) in which he wrote a number of novels for the French publisher Pierre-Jules Hetzel.[16] Hetzel would be Verne's most important publisher and advocate, creating a periodical, *Magasin d'éducation et de recreation*, in which Verne would figure prominently. The illustrated editions of these magazines would come to be known as *voyages extraordinares*. These extraordinary voyages served to educate the magazine's readers on basic science.[17] For this reason, meticulous detail is given to the science behind the stories and how these voyages are made possible through actual calculation and the construction of advanced machines. Technology is seen as the catalysing element to Verne's novels. For instance, it takes an advanced submarine, the *Nautilus*, to plumb the depths of the ocean in his *Twenty Thousand Leagues under the Sea*. Meanwhile, in *From the Earth to the Moon* we find several characters being shot into space by a massive space gun in a capsule which is bound for the moon. Or one might even recognise the technological advancement of the hot-air balloon in Verne's first work, *Five Weeks in a Balloon*, which does not require the release of gas or dumping sandbags so that long distances can be traversed in a balloon. It is clear for Verne that technology opens up great possibilities for the future and that excitement and adventure are what typify it.

Although H. G. Wells wrote a number of novels and stories which show a more nuanced approach to technology and the future, many contain the adventurous spirit which typifies this first trend. Wells's usage of science and technology in his writings is not primarily didactic as with Verne. Rather, they are the means to access another spellbinding and wondrous world.[18] This is particularly salient in his short stories. For example, Wells's short story 'The Argonauts of the Air'[19] portrays the first human flight.[20] The crux of the story is not upon the dimensions of the flying machine or even upon the mechanics of how the machine might fly as they might be if Verne wrote it—we aren't even given an exhaustive description of the vehicle itself—but the majority of the story centres on the actual flight of the craft and the experience of flying it itself. The story is more about the world within the sky rather than the intricacies of the machine. Similarly, another of Wells's short stories, 'In the Abyss', illuminates this same theme.[21] The protagonist is sealed in an advanced chamber with very thick steel walls and high-tech glass that can withstand the pressures of the deep sea. The beginning of the story focuses on whether the chamber will crumble under the extreme conditions of the bottom of the sea, but quickly it becomes apparent that the core of the story is actually the strange, new world of the deep sea made accessible by this craft. An entire civilisation is found at the bottom of the sea, and they lead the protagonist in his craft to what looks to be an altar and bow down before him.[22] He is then pulled back to the surface where he recalls his tale to his colleagues. This same model is even used for Wells's most important work, *The Time Machine*, only the strange new world is now the future. This adventure is premised upon the Time Traveller crafting a complex machine that takes him to the year 802,701.[23] Once again, there is sparse description of the time machine and the central focus of the narrative is actually on what the piece of technology makes possible. The technical device, for Wells, opens up possibilities to explore the unknown and the reader is to feel awe at the sheer power these machines open up to humanity.

The age of the Pulps (1926–1940) and the Golden Age (1940–1960)[24] in science fiction also maintain this almost heroic and transcendent attitude toward technology. The Pulps were intended for mass appeal and boasted colourful magazines which were filled with outlandish, larger-than-life narratives. The form in which this kind of science fiction was presented—highly visual with opulent illustrations—supported the simple heroic tales found within. For instance, the illustrations of Buck Rogers, a famous Pulp character, might have him fighting monstrous aliens in the future—the 25th century to be precise—while equipped with advanced jet packs and laser guns. Another famous character went under the unoriginal name Captain Future. Clad in a futuristic space suit and the proverbial space gun he roamed the galaxy fighting futuristic alien villains. These were glossy, slick and bare narratives that many aficionados consider the least respectable period in science fiction history.

The adventurous spirit indicative of this first theme is found in the most common subgenre of science fiction: the space opera.[25] Many of the examples listed above fall into the space opera category.[26] Several things typify the space opera. First, it is accompanied by a grand narrative that centres on the adventurous plot of often overconfident and larger-than-life characters. In this way it has often been related to the western. Harrison Ford's brash character Han Solo in the *Star Wars* trilogy is an archetypal example of the kind of character in the space opera. Second, the plot generally involves a spacecraft which traverses the entire cosmos at a rapid speed as easily as if it were one's back garden. Despite the vastness of the entire cosmos the space opera maintains a level of familiarity with the cosmos so that even when entering new and unknown solar systems with possible threatening aliens, the reader or viewer is meant to feel comfortable that everything will turn out well in the end. This level of confidence relies upon the protagonist's faith in technology. Han Solo's response to The Force illuminates this well: 'Hokey religion and ancient weapons are no match for a blaster by your side'. The space opera is the most consumed of all the genres of science fiction precisely because it is meant for general appeal and its main function is to entertain with simplistic and outlandish narratives. Perhaps, then, the disdain felt by science fiction aficionados for this more immature narrative correlates with its unabashed faith in technology and what it might do for humanity and the future. Moreover, the more thoughtful and intriguing sub-genres of science fiction, while not being as widely consumed by the larger society,[27] have an uneasy relationship with the force of technology. Science fiction has been the location not just for a complete acceptance of science and technology, but it has also been suspicious of it.

Before turning to the second theme that depicts this suspicion of technology and the future, it is worth reflecting more deeply on how technology invokes a sense of awe in this kind of literature and film. Technology in this particular theme is depicted as clean and sterile thereby serving to make us think it is advanced and intended for the elite.[28] For instance the robots in the film *The Day the Earth Stood Still* (1951) and the spaceship in *Forbidden Planet* (1956) are depicted as 'sleek, bright, and shiny images bent on evoking progressive technological wonder (and wonder at technological progress)'.[29] There are a multitude of spaceships that are geometric, smooth and predominantly a reflective metallic colour such as silver or gold: *The Flight of the Navigator* (1986), *The War of the Worlds* (1953), *This Island Earth* (1955), *Earth vs. the Flying Saucers* (1956) and *Close Encounters of the Third Kind* (1977). This is even despite the seeming apocalyptic narrative of many of these films where malevolent and technologically advanced aliens terrorise the earth. Indeed, scholars of science fiction film such as Vivian Sobchack suggest that the portrayal of technology operates on two levels. Of course, the primary narrative depicts technology and provides a certain tacit interpretation. This can be anywhere on the spectrum from complete pessimism to naive optimism. But, the secondary depiction of technology is seen in the very medium of film itself known as special effects. The spectacle of special effects in film functions to dazzle the audience so that even when technology is oppressive in the storyline or painted in a negative light the actual medium of special effects reinforces the narrative of progress and wonder.[30]

This sense of wonder at technology has often been associated with the sublime. According to commentators such as David Nye and Bronislaw Szerszynski, technology in the 20th century became the vanguard for our contemporary experience of the sublime.[31] Science fiction makes use of this 'technological sublime'. Science fiction scholars agree that a close parallel can be seen in the gothic novel and science fiction precisely because of this shared experience of the sublime. The science fiction writer, Brian Aldiss, goes so far as to say that science fiction is itself just a sublime or Gothic genre of writing.[32] And, Paul Alkon agrees that contemporary science fiction has sought 'to achieve sublimity without recourse to the supernatural.'[33]

This close correlation between the sublime of the 19th century Gothic novel and science fiction is typified in Mary Shelley's *Frankenstein*. *Frankenstein* is historically seminal in that 'it links science and technology to the sublime, not merely to Gothicism, and does so in a way that is unforgettable.'[34] Mont Blanc, previously the muse for the sublime for Percy Shelley a couple years earlier in his poem 'Mont Blanc', is now the setting where Frankenstein meets his monster. When Frankenstein himself invokes the sublime in the presence of nature and Mont Blanc[35] this is immediately juxtaposed with his own creation such that 'the monster is the sublime personified'.[36] Since the 19th century, there has been a development in experiencing the sublime in relationship to technology and this is reflected in science fiction.

This first theme recognises technology as sublime and invariably interprets it in entirely positive ways. This is especially apparent in the shots of spaceships. For instance, the opening scene of *Star Wars: Episode IV—A New Hope* (1977) focuses on a gargantuan ship flying overhead the viewer which is meant to accentuate the sheer size and power. This extended shot, almost twenty seconds long, reinforces the scale of the technological wonder.[37] Shots like this are ubiquitous in science fiction film—especially those in this particular category.

This experience of the sublime in science fiction literature further accentuates the close relationship between religion and technology. The sublime experience has been the basis for many theories of religion. Besides many of the 19th century religious poets such as Blake and Wordsworth relying upon this sublime experience to inform their understanding of God and the holy, other religious theorists in the mystical tradition invoke the sublime experience to create their theory of religion. For instance, Rudolph Otto's mystical interpretation of religion depends upon an experience which is similar to that found in science fiction. For Otto the kernel of all religions is the experience of the numinous and the *mysterium tremendum*. This experience is typified by dread, awe and an overwhelming desire to both be immersed in and reject this wholly other power which takes hold in extreme immediacy.[38] As seen above with Gothic works like *Frankenstein*, science fiction literature shares the same 19th century sublime heritage that informs these mystical religious theories. But, historical evidence for the close proximity of religious and technological experience aside, there has even been psychological evidence as well. A study by Robert W. Daly suggests that psychologically healthy human beings give supernatural agency and power to technological systems in what he refers to as 'spectres of technology'. He states that these 'spectres of technology' come from a '*sense of domination by mysterious agencies or forces which are, or were, linked to technological enterprises but which are now apprehended as being beyond the control of any particular man or collection of men*'.[39] Technologically advanced machines and systems are beyond the laymen's level of expertise and, hence, are then imbued with supernatural significance. We experience the mystery of machines and the things they can do in the same way that we experience the holy and religion.

This first trend in science fiction highlights the transcendent qualities of technology and promotes its growth and influence on society and each individual within it. The works typical of this strand, such as those found in the space opera and written by Jules Verne and H. G. Wells, are bedazzled with technology and depict the future as a time when technology advances humanity's wildest and most sought-after dreams. This wonder at technology and the avenues it opens up for humankind verge on the religious. Hence, technology is often depicted utilising the sublime to elicit its elite and transcendental qualities that promise to lift each human being to where they desire. The experience of the sublime, however, is more nebulous and multifaceted than a simple positive experience depicted in this trend. As the next theme in science fiction's portrayal of technology and the future shows, the feeling of the sublime is still normative, but now it is entirely negative and horrifying.[40]

3.2.2   Second Trend: Dystopia and Technological Enslavement

The second theme of science fiction's portrayal of technology in the future stands in stark contrast to the first in that it is often taken up in the form of dystopia, apocalypse and general distrust of the machine. It does share a common affection in the form of awe and the sheer power that is felt by the force of technology, but this awe is almost entirely negative and frightening. Technology is often portrayed as sterile, stark, cold, characterless and unfeeling. Thus, the separation between humanity and technology here—signified by 'sterility'—does not accentuate the empowering, transcendent quality of technology, but emphasises its foreignness and oppression.

An early example of this kind of depiction can be found in the German silent film *Metropolis* (1927). In the film, society is divided into two classes. The upper class lives above ground and manages the city while the lower class work massive machines that contribute to the day-to-day functioning of the city. Its eerie silence actually accentuates the senseless feeling depicted in the dystopian society and the portrayal of the machine-ridden underground. The beginning of the film starts with vistas of advanced and sublimely lavish skyscrapers above ground. This scene is then immediately juxtaposed with the proletariat workers, dressed in the same drab uniform in perfect lines, trudging to their posts underground at the announcement of the whistle which calls them to their toil. Here are contrasted two different sublime images. The first is of pristine and clean buildings which tower over the skyline and are not much different from what we would envision from the sublime in the first theme elucidated earlier. But, the viewer is at once shown the expense of making such clean towers possible. The horrifying and debilitating side of the sublime is evoked when the following scene cuts to those proletariats being ordered in sheer numbers to march in perfect block formation to perfect time where the clock watches over their every movement. There are extended scenes in the film which show moving mechanical parts working as a complex machine: pistons, levers and interlocking parts. These scenes help illustrate that society has been both placed at the mercy of the functioning machine which keeps them alive, and it is also a sign that society itself has been ordered like a machine and is completely trapped by it.

A more contemporary example of the harsh and frightening depiction of technology and the future can be sought in the *Terminator* film franchise. The basic plot consists of the future human race fighting against advanced machines that are set on destroying all of humanity because they are seen as a threat. This franchise has contributed significantly to our fear of machines and artificial intelligence. The opening scene of *Terminator 2: Judgment Day* (1991) illustrates this well. The first images are of cars driving on freeways and people walking in populated cities. Then, in slow motion, we see children in this city playing in a playground while laughing. But the laughing is slightly distorted and seems to be quite a long way off. The scene turns from a vibrant colour to a cold blue as ominous music rises to reveal in the next scene a human skeleton at the steering wheel of a dilapidated car in what looks to be a dump of surrounding rubbish. The camera then pans out to disclose that this is the same highway of cars shot earlier. The cars have been utterly destroyed and the freeways have been turned into rubbish heaps. As the camera scans the post-apocalyptic landscape we see human skulls littered on the ground in what looks to be the mangled remnants of the children's playground from before. The text 'Los Angeles 2029 A.D.' appears on the screen and an ominous voice narrates, 'Three billion human lives ended on August 29, 1997. The survivors of the nuclear fire called the war Judgment Day. They lived only to face a new nightmare. The war against the machines.' Then the camera stops on a single human skull slightly buried in rubble where a robotic foot crushes the skull. The camera zooms out to show that this robotic foot belongs to one of the mechanical humanoid Terminators who sports a massive gun and is hunting down humans. This first scene blatantly portrays the oppressive potential of machines and causes trepidation at the prospect of advancing technology and artificial intelligence.

Several other notable dystopias utilise the blunt all-powerful force of technology in their vision of an oppressive regime. The engineering task need not be applied to just the natural world in the form of mechanical devices. Rational ordering can be equally applied to society. Indeed, city planning and the functioning of society can be ordered like a machine.[41] Zamyatin's *We*, Orwell's *1984* and Huxley's *Brave New World* are seminal examples of this *technique* and rationality being applied to society.

Zamyatin's *We* is set in the future where the fictional United State controls all areas of human life. Society is relegated to urban living where the living quarters are built with glass so that the authorities, Guardians, can monitor the activities of all the inhabitants and discipline as necessary. Citizens of the United State, often referred to as Numbers, eat synthetic food and rec-reation consists of marching in fours to the anthem of the state. Romantic relationships have been disbanded and the sexual practices have become controlled by the state as well: 'A Number may obtain a license to use any other Number as a sexual product.'[42] The protagonist claims that this was an eventuality of state control: 'Naturally, having conquered hunger (that is, algebraically speaking, having achieved the total of bodily welfare), the United State directed its attack against the second ruler of the world, against love. At last this element also was conquered, that is, organized and put into a mathematical formula. . . . The rest is only a matter of technique'.[43]

The beginning of the book opens with the protagonist, D-503, who happens to be a mathematician of the state, writing about what prompts the journal entries which make up the text. The Well-Doer,[44] the head of the state, has decreed that any of the Numbers who 'feels capable must consider it his duty to write treatises, poems, manifestos, odes, and other compositions on the greatness and the beauty of the United State'.[45] This text, *We*, is crafted in response to this decree and is to be included with the other Numbers' writings in the spaceship Integral—another reference to mathematics—and is to be used for imperialism in spreading rational-ity throughout the cosmos.[46] Mathematical vernacular is utilised frequently throughout and is used to celebrate the precision and regularity of the soci-ety. Such phrases as 'one sees their wonderful equations',[47] 'the square har-mony of the grayish-blue rows of Numbers'[48] and 'the equation was very complex, with transcendent figures'[49] serve to add an ambience of calcula-bility in society and its veneration by all.[50]

The transcendence of calculability is particularly typified in the depiction of machines. For instance D-503 says in response to viewing the construc-tion of the Integral spaceship—invariably a sublime experience for him:

> I saw the lathes; blindly, with abandon, the balls of the regulators were rotating; the cranks were swinging from side to side with a glimmer; the working beam proudly swung its shoulder; and the mechanical chisels were dancing to the melody of unheard tarantellas. I suddenly perceived all the music, all the beauty, of this colossal, this mechanical ballet, illumined by light blue rays of sunshine. Then the thought came: why beautiful? Why is the dance beautiful? Answer: because it is an *unfree* movement.[51]

The machine is beautiful and to be celebrated not because all the parts nec-essarily work in harmony to fulfil a larger goal, although this might be the case implicitly, but because the movements are regulated and unfree. The machine is rationalisation incarnated. The experienced religious sublime in *We* is always a product of technological regularity.

Worship of the machine is also visible in the 'solemn liturgy of the United State'.[52] This occasion celebrates the 'the victory of *all* over *one*, of the *sum* over the *individual*'.[53] Poets speak of the grandeur of the state and reference great figureheads of the past like Prometheus who 'harnessed fire / With machines and steel / And fettered chaos with Law'.[54] However, the climax of the liturgy is the sacrifice of a madman to the Well-Doer's Machine because he has succumbed to freedom and irrationality. The glorification of this death and its symbolic value cannot be overstated:

> Heavy, stony like fate, the Well-Doer went around the machine, put his enormous hand on the lever
> . . . . Not a whisper, not a breath around; all eyes were upon that hand. . . . What crushing, scorching power one must feel to be the tool, to be the resultant of hundreds of thousands of wills! How great his lot!
> Another second. The hand moved down, switching in the current. The lightning-sharp blade of the electric ray. . . . A faint crack like a shiver, in the tubes of the Machine. . . . The prone body, covered with a light phosphorescent smoke; then, suddenly, under the eyes of all, it began to melt—to melt, to dissolve with terrible speed. And then nothing; just a pool of chemically pure water which only a moment ago had been so red and had pulsated in his heart. . . . [55]

The death is cold and clinical. The image depicted is not like that of Holbein's 'The Body of the Dead Christ in the Tomb' which causes Prince Myshkin to exclaim 'That painting! Some people might lose their faith by looking at that painting!'[56] No, there is no reference to torn flesh and a mangled body. In fact, the only reference to blood is indirect in referencing how the colour changes from red to 'chemically pure water'. It is not even entirely clear that those watching actually ever saw the blood that once pumped in the heart. There is no humanity to the death. We are only given a material and scientific description. The madman is reduced to mere elemental constituents and with it symbolises the triumph of the machine over the human experience.

Of course, Zamyatin portrays all of this as dystopia. The reader is to feel disgust and sorrow for the conditions of the inhabitants. Where the Numbers feel a sense of pride at the sacrifice of the irrational man the reader is not meant to experience pride in these sublime experiences but is to be revolted and in many ways is to feel horrified. This experience of the sublime, for the second theme, is entirely oppressive. It does not empower the individual but weighs him down. Zamyatin's dystopia depicts this sublime within the either/or of rationality and irrationality, oppression and freedom. Certainly, this is not new to Russian literature. One hears echoes of Dostoyevsky's 'Underground Man' who states '. . . what will have become of our wills when everything is graphs and arithmetic, and nothing is valid but two and two make four?'[57] Indeed, this second theme recognises that the values of the machine and science are entirely antithetical to the virtues of genuine humanism.

The language of the text is instructive in creating this dichotomy of irrationality and rationality, freedom and oppression. Where the idioms of mathematics and science are used to represent humanity's enslavement in *We*, more narrative and figurative language affirms human uniqueness and individuality. It becomes apparent that the diction of the author, D-503, changes throughout the novel.[58] He has increasing difficulty formulating his thoughts and experiences in reference to scientific rationalism. He states at one point, 'I am losing the sense for figures'.[59] He relates this degradation of his valued rationalism to the creeping irrational number: the square root of negative one. 'And now I am no longer able to distinguish what is dream from what is actuality; irrational numbers grow through my solid, habitual, tridimensional life; and instead of firm, polished surfaces, there is something shaggy and rough'.[60] This decline in his use of the scientific idiom is often attributed to his romantic relationship with the seductive I-330 but, as Patrick Parrinder argues, this is only the superficial explanation: 'D-503 develops a soul . . . by the act of writing'.[61] Where he sets out first to write this diary in order to recall the events of each day that 'we' experience—'I shall try to record only the things I see, the things I think, or, to be more exact, the things *we* think'.[62]—it quickly becomes apparent that keeping this journal is actually serving to reinforce individuality. These are *his* experiences of the day's events, not *we*. It takes a single person to write this diary. The process of writing is the most determinative element in breaking from rationalism and the hegemony of 'we'. This is the decisive factor in the formation of his unique individuality.

Similar views on humanity's relationship to language and the oppressive nature of ordering society like machines can be found in George Orwell's *1984* and Aldous Huxley's *Brave New World*. Orwell's protagonist, Winston Smith, is part of a totalitarian initiative by the Ministry of Truth to deplete the English language. Often referred to in the novel as Newspeak—in contrast to Oldspeak which is still in fashion—the oppressive government actively reduces the vocabulary of its citizens. Where terms such as 'good' and 'bad' are common in Oldspeak, 'bad' has been replaced with 'ungood' or, for superlatively bad, 'double plus ungood'. The ubiquity of technologically advanced screens everywhere to spy on the inhabitants is just one of the many mediums for oppression. But, language is the ultimate weapon in Big Brother's arsenal. Syme, a friend of Winston's at the Ministry of Truth who works on the Newspeak dictionary, states 'Don't you see that the whole aim of Newspeak is to narrow the range of thought?'[63] The most egregious oppression in *1984* is not necessarily the mechanical and bleak environment nor is it the policed control of all activities—not even that of the dreaded Thought Police—but is the corruption of human thought and experience through the limitation of language. This is a major theme Orwell gives detailed attention to as attested by his appendix on Newspeak. In *1984* Orwell brings to light the importance of language to human individuality, creativity and freedom.[64]

One also sees the degradation of language as oppressive to the human experience in Huxley's *Brave New World* as well. Cheap mantras and slogans are conditioned into the citizens at a very young age. Referred to as hypnopædic wisdom, the text is speckled throughout with such jingoistic phrases as 'one cubic centimeter cures ten gloomy sentiments',[65] 'a gramme is better than a damn',[66] 'when the individual feels, the community reels'[67] and 'ending is better than mending; the more stitches the less riches'[68]. In *Brave New World*, as in the other two dystopias, language is part of the massive 'technology of behaviour'[69] and is the strongest cog in the debilitating machine. Words have lost their force and meaning and instead have been used as a tool for suppression and anesthetisation. Words and language in these situations do not open up possibilities and reveal a particular situation, let alone adequately represent it, but actually obfuscate and stunt them.[70]

One of the many similarities between all three dystopias is that technology or the technocratic state has been imbued with religious value. This has already been illustrated in the sacrifice of the madman to the Machine in *We* referenced above, but Huxley also makes strong allusions to religion in *Brave New World*. When members of the dystopia greet each other they make the sign of the T to each other. It is explicit that this is a transformation of the sign of the cross and now refers to the venerable Henry Ford's Model T.[71] In fact, time is now measured from the invention of the Model T, A.F.: After Ford, and is a play on the Julian and Gregorian calendar, A.D.: *Anno Domini*. The term Lord is often substituted by Ford throughout the text.[72] In Orwell's *1984* the liturgy of the state occurs during the 'Two Minutes Hate', a structured time when people gather to watch inflammatory and explicit images which are to manufacture hate in the gathered viewers. The climax of the programme shows images of Emmanuel Goldstein, the primary enemy of the state. Winston describes Goldstein as having 'the face of a sheep, and the voice, too had a sheeplike quality'.[73] This allusion to sheep carries Christological overtones and is compounded when one considers that Goldstein functions in the state as the scapegoat just as Christ has been likened the last scapegoat in Christianity. There is a certain sacrificial parallelism at work here and the very mood and occurrences in the Two Minutes Hate follows the major themes in the social function of the scapegoat: the inherent primordial violence, the focus of this violence on a single individual, the expulsion of this individual from the community and the subsequent return to harmony.[74]

Perhaps what all these authors are commenting on is that technology has become the new religion for humanity. We are mesmerised by the order, the precision and, ultimately, what technology can provide for us. Zamyatin, Huxley and Orwell recognise the transcendent features of technology but they are reacting against the interpretation of this technological transcendence given by those found in the first trend discussed above. These technological optimists do not recognise the hidden dangers inherent in this pursuit of transcendence. Hidden dangers such as an anaesthetised society whose only goal and veneration is the orderability of the machine—dangers like an oppressed people by a malevolent technocratic government. Cloaking the technologically monitored and structured society in religious terms is meant to both show the explicit connection with religion—the technological state as religion—and reveal that we are bedazzled with technology to the point of losing all orientation. Our almost religious obsession with technology, they might say, is also our greatest weakness.

Of course, much more could be said about these great dystopias of the 20th century and many more could be cited which fall into this category.[75] But, what is important in all of these cases is that they distrust the machine and the mechanisation of society. Their images of the future distrust the influence of the machine on human life and represent it as foreign to the human experience and as potentially life threatening.

3.2.3 Third Trend: Technology and Humanity Become One

The final trend of science fiction's portrayal of technology and the future assumes that humanity and the machine are not as different as we think. Instead of rejecting technology as antithetical to human flourishing, this perspective questions that there is even a valid demarcation between man and machine. What makes this line of thinking even possible invariably begins with the increased ubiquity of technology in our everyday lives. Whereas historically the first theme portrayed technology in the future as something which is sterile and intended for the elite—conveying that technology is foreign to the average person—now in the present theme technology is portrayed as worn, dirty and familiar. This theme's ubiquity obviously presupposes that those who consume science fiction of this type today can identify with the reification of technology. Therefore, one can speculate that this shift in technology's portrayal in science fiction is a product of technology reaching a certain critical mass in our everyday lives. In a sense, this technological *Lebenswelt* is required before we begin to question whether we are distinct from this very technological environment.

There are many films of the 1970s and 1980s which depict this technological *Lebenswelt* as dirty, worn and familiar. The message of the 1972 film *Silent Running* is that technology and the future are 'tarnished and grungy for the first time: dirty, dysfunctional and disappointing.'[76] Other films from this era also display technology as dirty. The armoured cars from the *Mad Max* trilogy (1979–1985) look to be a hodgepodge of parts taken from other broken-down machines despite their apparent speed and performance. This filthy technology is accentuated in the films with the overall dusty Australian environment. One can find a similar depiction in the films *Escape from New York* (1981) and the sequel *Escape from L.A.* (1996). The guns are dark and tarnished along with the buildings and vehicles. And, even the excessive and dirty ducts which seem to be omnipresent in *Brazil* (1985) highlight this change in technology's depiction.

What is important in representing technology as dirty and worn is that this is often coupled with a sense of familiarity with the technology: 'technology becomes tamed and domesticated, either under our control or nicely settled into like old slippers'.[77] A prime example, taken from Sobchack, is the *Millennium Falcon*, Han Solo's spaceship in the *Star Wars* trilogy, and Luke Skywalker's speeder, from the same franchise. These technological objects are portrayed in the films as worn, clunky and familiar, so much so that they seem to take on a character of their own. Adam Roberts explains it this way: 'the *Millennium Falcon* is more than the sum of its parts. This is because the spaceships in an SF film are invested by us with a peculiar, almost human concentration of value, what Marxist theorists call "reification".'[78] This kind of statement can be made today precisely because it is not uncommon to find similar relationships in our everyday life. Consider the phenomenon of people naming their car and, if they don't, they often refer to it as 'he' or 'she'. What I contend is that this portrayal of reified technology—like a set of old slippers—is often connected with anthropomorphizing tendencies.[79] Technology of this sort is comparable to the way we experience our own body.[80] From this point it is merely a step away from blurring the bounds between humanity and our surrounding technology.

This is precisely what is done in much contemporary science fiction as in the film *Blade Runner* (1982), which is based upon Philip K. Dick's work *Do Androids Dream of Electric Sheep?*[81] Here we have depicted cybernetic humanoids which are not meant to primarily instil fear in the viewers, as we saw with the *Terminator* series, but actually to evoke pity and sadness. Cognitively, the viewer is put in a conundrum where drawing the boundary between replicants, bioengineered cyborgs, and human beings is very difficult. The final plot twist in the director's cut is especially disconcerting. We discover that the human protagonist Deckard, who has been killing replicants, is actually a replicant himself. In the end we are removed from that comfortable place where the issue of the ontology of man and machine is finally put to rest in the film and are thrown back onto the question as to what distinguishes humanity from machines. The viewer feels this tension not only cognitively but emotionally as well. The viewer is meant to identify with and feel pity for the replicants and their tragic situation. On one level it is tragic that replicants have a very short lifespan and are relegated to menial tasks. But, of course, the viewer can rationalise that these are just machines. Would I care as much about the lifespan of a toaster? Should I feel empathy for a hammer because all it can ever do is fulfil its function as a hammer? The viewer is torn emotionally and cognitively. This tragedy and emotion is compounded with Rachael, an advanced replicant, because the memories she experiences as her own have been implanted unlike the other replicants. Her memories are in fact real human memories and yet they are not her own. Whereas the other replicants are pitied because their potential as intelligent and sentient beings is crushed and not allowed to flourish, for Rachael we feel pity because she is not her own. The other models, even if they don't seem as advanced, can take solace in that they are their own and the memories they have developed come from their own unique lived experiences. But Rachael, who has come closest to humanity, has lost a central feature of her own unique individual identity. Ultimately, however, the viewer has sympathy for the replicants because they share with us more than an identical physical appearance. They exhibit real human qualities and basic existential questions determine their actions. Indeed, the replicants that have escaped and returned to earth have done so precisely because they are in pursuit of such questions like: What is my origin? What makes me me? How do I deal with moods and emotions? How can I transcend my own limitations?

These kinds of questions are explored as well in the *Star Trek* franchise. In particular, two cybernetic organisms, one an android and the other a cyborg,[82] are the occasion for this exploration. In *Star Trek: The Next Generation* the android Data makes it his goal to become as much like a human as possible. He takes up learning a musical instrument for pleasure, tries to learn the nuance of humour and telling a joke and even participates in productions of Shakespeare and Dickens. In fact, it is hard to find an episode where we don't see Data pursuing this dream to be human. Data is constantly puzzled by emotion and this is the one thing which intrigues him the most. In such episodes as 'Brothers' he is even offered a chip by his creator which would make possible this emotional capacity within him. But, as we see from the plot of this episode and its corresponding episode 'Descent', this addition of emotion is quite dangerous and volatile. In a scene which is reminiscent of the biblical story of Esau and Jacob receiving the blessing from their father, Data's more brash, manipulative and selfish android brother, Lore, tricks their 'father' into installing the chip in himself rather than in the intended Data. Lore then uses the emotion chip he has to control not only Data but also a group of rebellious Borg, the cyborg enemy of Starfleet. With the help of his shipmates Data overthrows Lore and intends to destroy the chip because of the harm it caused so many. Nevertheless, his friends urge him to keep it and wait until the time when he is ready to use it with responsibility.

We see similar tendencies in the cyborg Seven of Nine, a character in *Star Trek: Voyager*. As her name signifies, at an early age she was taken by the hostile collective referred to earlier as the Borg. The Borg are not like any other species in the *Star Trek* universe—if one could even refer to them as a species, for they do not have any stable biological characteristics. Instead of procreating sexually to add to their numbers, they assimilate other species into their own collective by retrofitting their bodies with machinery and injecting them with nanoprobes that transform the body into an organic/mechanical hybrid. Each member becomes part of one Borg consciousness and will. Seven of Nine is rescued from the Borg after many years and during the television show's progression tries to reintegrate back into human society after the majority of her Borg technology has been removed. As with Data, Seven of Nine is in pursuit of humanity, but for her it is remembering and regaining that humanity and individuality that has been lost through her forced assimilation. Unlike Data, she is still definitively human, but her time with the Borg means she is developmentally stunted. She has difficulty being on her own with her own thoughts and has withdrawals from not being directly linked to the collective consciousness. She struggles with human inefficiency and, like Data, has difficulty with emotion. As part of her rehabilitation, she forces herself to take part in recreational activities on the holodeck to cultivate her imagination.

What we learn from these cybernetic beings like Data and Seven of Nine is the seeming complexity of the human situation. What they bring to the fore is the way in which the very pursuit of humanity is itself very human. Trying to successfully integrate emotions and rationality is a human struggle. Trying to develop one's own unique individuality in a group community without succumbing to complete definition by that group is human. Gaining the correct balance between creative imagination and recreation with real planning and pragmatic work is entirely human. So, not only are the virtues they try to gain humanistic but also the very process in trying to achieve these and with the correct balance.

Part of what make androids and cyborgs compelling and interesting besides the way in which they illuminate specifically human virtues is that their very ontology is a question.[83] For the android this demarcation is one of degree rather than a strict ontological category. A machine that has reached human levels of intelligence, looks exactly like a human being to the naked eye and is programmed in many other ways to emulate human beings calls into question the very issue of a definition of personhood and what constitutes a human being at all. It really questions the very notion of our ontological categories themselves because the kinds of attributes we might generally associate with the human ontological category are reflected in the android. What would it take to say that a machine is more than a machine? When should one cease referring to a complex android as an 'it' and instead as a 'thou'?[84] But this issue is even more pronounced when considering the cyborg because it clearly has a foot in two ontological camps: the machine and the biological. The cyborg is an heir of the object because it is machine, but it is also a child of biology. Neither category fully dictates what the cyborg is. It has no distinct quiddity. It really is neither completely a machine nor is it completely human.[85] In more Heideggerian terms, its very existence and ontology is a question to itself and, in this way, shares its ontological predicament with humanity. This unclear ontology is unsettling for humanity. We constantly try to locate and define how we are different from our environment around us and the beings that inhabit it. Yet, this is getting increasingly more difficult. The cyborg and android reveal that perhaps we are no different from a complex machine just as Darwin concluded we are no different from others in the animal kingdom. Part of the struggle in science fiction narratives with androids and cyborgs is this incessant desire for the reader or viewer and the human race to be different—invariably interpreted as more advanced and unique—from these characters which resemble us in every way. It is this shared ontological confusion with cyborgs and androids which strikes at the heart of human uniqueness.

It is precisely this admixture of two ontological categories which is the basis for the tragedy of the cyborg and to a lesser degree the android. In its lack of a clear singular ontology the cyborg and the android are left without orientation. The film *A.I.* (2001) and the television series *Battlestar Galactica* (2004–2009) elucidate this *aporia* well. In *A.I.*, David is an advanced android child whose only programmed desire is to love his owners unconditionally but he is eventually discarded by them. David recognises that he would only be loved in return if he were a real boy and in a climactic scene in the film he screams 'I'm sorry I'm not real, if you let me I'll be so real for you!' The rest of the story is his quest to become human.[86] David's very quest to be a real boy elucidates this tension of ontologies. He is a creation of a human being to be like a human being and to love and yet, not being human himself, is never able to fulfil that desire and is trapped in two worlds. His life is a tragedy.

But what if these machines and cyborgs do not pursue humanity as an ideal to be attained? This kind of situation is dealt with in *Battlestar Galactica*. The cybernetic beings in the series, called Cylons, look exactly like human beings in every way. They have rebelled against their creators and pursue the final remnant of the human race after a debilitating first strike. Throughout the entire series the human race is always on the verge of extinction because not only are the Cylons incredibly powerful but they have even infiltrated human society undetected so that no one can be trusted. In fact, some Cylons do not even know they are Cylons and are programmed to do things at particular times even without themselves knowing. One of the models of Cylons, Number 1, referred to as John Cavil, staunchly rejects trying to become like his human parents whereas many of the others, like the Number 8 model, called Sharon, are more merciful and sympathetic to humanity. In a telling dialogue in the episode 'No Exit' we see the contradiction of the cyborg come to light as John Cavil rejects his human parentage:

John Cavil: In all your travels, have you ever seen a star go supernova?
Ellen Tigh: No.
John Cavil: No? Well, I have. I saw a star explode and send out the building blocks of the Universe. Other stars, other planets and eventually other life. A supernova! Creation itself! I was there. I wanted to see it and be part of the moment. And you know how I perceived one of the most glorious events in the universe? With these ridiculous gelatinous orbs in my skull! With eyes designed to perceive only a tiny fraction of the EM spectrum. With ears designed only to hear vibrations in the air.
Ellen Tigh: The five of us designed you to be as human as possible.
John Cavil: I don't want to be human! I want to see gamma rays! I want to hear X-rays! And I want to—I want to smell dark matter!

> Do you see the absurdity of what I am? I can't even express these things properly because I have to—I have to conceptualize complex ideas in this stupid limiting spoken language! But I know I want to reach out with something other than these prehensile paws! And feel the wind of a supernova flowing over me! I'm a machine! And I can know much more! I can experience so much more. But I'm trapped in this absurd body! And why? Because my five creators thought that God wanted it that way!

It is this possibility of cyborgs and androids rejecting their human virtues, values and origin which is the catalyst for fear in such science fiction narratives. This fear is commonplace in such works as *Battlestar Galactica* and others like the *Terminator* series we have already seen. The very ontological difference inherent in the cyborg is grounds for the fear. Why should a machine care about its human origins if it is not a human and never will be human? Could these human virtues merely be limitations to their own specific intelligent machine self-actualisation? What is the imperative for struggling towards humanity? It might be said that Isaac Asimov's famous 'Three Laws of Robotics' is used precisely to safeguard against such questions.[87] The basis for the creation of these laws and the subsequent dialogue on these laws is that such a relationship between intelligent machines and human beings requires intervention and rules to govern it. These laws presuppose that the machines could wield enough power to bring harm to human beings and are the occasion for artificial intelligence experts to consider such ethical programming. But, Asimov's robotic laws reflect more than a pragmatic decision to moderate the human/machine interaction. They appreciate how we want to infuse our image into what we create. When this image includes creating beings with supposed intelligence and volition, of course this can lead to fear and anxiety about how this intelligent being might respond to its maker.[88]

It is clear from the examples above that the depiction of technology in the future is increasingly coalescing around this theme of humanity and technology becoming one. There are countless other instances of films, books, video games and comics that could be mentioned which utilise characters that are intelligent machines. Besides the mere presence of these characters in the storyline, the narrative is often focused on the interesting and unsettling issues related to androids and cyborgs: personal identity, self-directed freedom, questions of origin and of meaning. What these narratives suggest is that our contemporary technological imagination seems to be obsessed with this problem: Is there any significant difference between a machine and a human being? As we shall see in the coming chapter, this question becomes the basis for the contemporary transhumanism movement where it drives serious reflection outside of fantasy and fiction.

3.3   CONCLUSION

Technology and its role in the future have been instrumentally conditioned by science fiction. The technological imagination of the past two centuries has been fuelled by the many science fiction stories in books, films, comics and video games. The portrayal of technology and the future in it has not been one resounding vision but has taken on a multiplicity of interpretations and perspectives. Science fiction really has become the central site where issues related to technology and future are worked out and argued over. As has been intimated in this chapter, the history of the technological imagination begins with recognising the potential technology can offer humanity in the way of transcendence and adventure. Technology liberates man and extends his faculties. Technology is awe inspiring and often for the elite. In general, technology is portrayed very positively. But then a transition occurs and technology and the future are depicted as oppressive and associated with dystopia. Technology, in these instances, is often frightening and dehumanising. Such visions are a direct response to the pace of technological growth in the late 19th and early 20th centuries and technology's parallel incorporation into society and everyday life. Whereas the flood of technology during this time was the basis for technological utopianism seen in the past chapter and in the orientation of wonder seen in the first theme in this chapter, it also opened up a dark side of the technological imagination. The machine seemed to be at odds with human existence and humanity felt the dizzying effects of being swept along by a force which seemed utterly alien to its way of life.

But, this reflection on technology and future morphed again in response to the ever-deepening technological environment. Indeed, it took an adjacent tack which didn't necessarily leave these positive and negative assessments behind but instead brought a new depth to the issue of technology and future. Our technological dreaming then became increasingly aware of the line which separates man and machine. As biotechnology, artificial intelligence and robotics advance, they fuel our own existential questions about what constitutes human beings and the human situation. Whereas the impact of evolution on our understanding of humanity has caused an erosion of the qualitative separation between man and animal, it is our technologically cluttered environment, our information technologies and our technological imagination which have brought together technology and humanity.

The technological imagination explored in great detail in these past two chapters is the intellectual and imaginary heritage for the transhumanist movement. Transhumanists such as Nick Bostrom make explicit that transhumanism is an heir of science fiction dreaming. Besides citing the work of Aldous Huxley and Mary Shelley as having done more to influence current debates about human technological transformation than any other—for better or for worse, I am sure he might add—Bostrom gives credit to such science fiction authors as Arthur C. Clarke, Isaac Asimov, Robert Heinlein and Stanislaw Lem.[89] Bostrom concludes that contemporary transhumanism owes much to these technological dreamers. And yet, one can't help but notice that science fiction literature is treated like the younger, less serious brother of contemporary transhumanists. Of course science fiction helped nurture transhumanism in its infancy, not to mention those transhumanists who grew up on it, but they refer to it as the work of fantasy, not of sober statistical analysis.[90] In their attempts to legitimise their movement they are often found to actually distance themselves from science fiction. They have to fight an uphill battle precisely because the bulk of the technological imagination today has been constructed out of stories easily dismissed as the work of fiction. But, this dismissal has vast side effects which restrict our understanding of what is really going on in transhumanism.

So often transhumanism, in seeking to distinguish itself from the pure speculation of fiction and imagination, has not recognised how its adherents derive narrative and mythic value from it.[91] What seems to get lost in the transhumanist reception of science fiction is this emphasis on the myth-building function of the technological imagination. As we will see with Nick Bostrom's approach to the future and that of many others like him, they emphasise that transhumanism is a real scientific future and worth scientific and statistical analysis. But what gets sidelined is how, while decrying science fiction for its imaginary and unreal tenets, transhumanism is still dependent upon the force of an already robust and developed inherent technological imagination and myth which serves to do more than objectively plan for the future. These stories transhumanists tell have anthropological and religious value.

Science fiction has long recognised its connections with religion and myth and is unapologetic about its relationship to them. As we have seen, many examples of science fiction often explicitly contain substantial religious elements: *Brave New World*'s 'sign of the T', the 'liturgy of the state' and the sacrifice of the madman in *We* and the altar scene in H. G. Wells's 'In the Abyss'. But, it can also be said with real force that science fiction does more than just depict practices we would classify as religious but that many of the central issues science fiction probes are shared by philosophy and theology. Issues related to how we see ourselves, how we relate to our world, what constitutes the human experience and matters of transcendence and the sublime.

These shared matters might be best labelled 'ultimate concerns'. A neologism taken from Paul Tillich's appraisal of religion, an ultimate concern 'demands the total surrender of him who accepts this claim, and it promises total fulfillment even if all other claims have to be subjected to it or rejected in its name.'[92] These ultimate concerns lay open and manifest the unconditioned existential realities towards which our entire lives are orientated. These ultimate concerns need not be found in just traditional religions. Tillich acknowledges that ultimate concern is a universal feature of humanity and is, therefore, visible outside of traditional religion in what he refers to as 'quasi-religions'. These 'quasi-religions' are 'directed towards objects like nation, science . . . society, or a highest ideal of humanity, which are then considered divine'[93] and he gives contemporary examples such as communism and nationalism. However, it is easy to see how science fiction might function as a 'quasi-religion' for the precise reason that it expresses and uncovers ultimate concerns in a highly techno-scientific environment.

If Tillich is right, that human beings have no choice but to ascribe ultimate concern, then science fiction might be a kind of tacit public myth today—a myth that utilises the content and symbols of our highly technical and scientific societies. We imbue meaning into the world and encode our existential experiences into science-fictional myths that in turn help us to understand, organise and orientate us towards our place in the world. They are meaning-rich and existentially-aware narratives. As one science fiction scholar has said, 'There is nonetheless a religious theme that seems to be widely endorsed by science fiction fans and writers: that humanity . . . will give the world, the universe, significance.'[94] Science fiction is unabashed about its myth building and celebrates it as a central feature of being human. Indeed, there is a burgeoning field of fecund interaction between science fiction and religion that focuses on the myth-building feature of both.[95]

Thus, science fiction can provide a needed corrective to transhumanism because it is unabashed about the mythic status of its narratives and the inherent religious undertones it seeks to explore. Transhumanism is either silent on the mythic proportions of its tenets or decries the religious overtones as only incidental to the movement. They say they are motivated by scientific concerns, not religious or anthropological need. Yet, as we shall in the next chapter, this clearly is not the case.

Why is the recognition of the mythic status of the technological imagination important? Because it shows that those that dream about the technological future and speculate about its conditions do so from a place of tacit religious motivation. For transhumanists, it makes dialogue with religion imperative for, whether they like it or not, their territories do overlap.

But, it also means that traditionally religious people in technological societies ought to give serious thought to whether they are involved in a form of religious syncretism. They need to reflect explicitly on their own participation in narratives of the technological imagination to see where they are drawing implicitly on the religious value of these narratives and whether they can be integrated successfully with their religious faith. More could be said in this regard and more will be said in the final chapters. For now, we move on to transhumanism and its approach to technology and the future.

NOTES

1. The challenge of the history of science and the sociology of knowledge are particularly relevant here. See Thomas S. Kuhn, *The Structure of Scientific Revolutions*, 2nd ed. (Chicago: University of Chicago Press, 1970); Bas van

Fraassen, "The Pragmatics of Explanation," in *Philosophy of Science: Contemporary Readings*, ed., Yuri Balashov and Alexander Rosenberg (London; New York: Routledge, 2002). See also the entirety of section six in this last book.

2. G. Zorpette and P. E. Ross, "The Books That Made a Difference," *IEEE Spectrum* 44, no. 3 (2007), 58.
3. Ibid.
4. National Science Board, *Science and Engineering Indicators—2002*, vol. 1 (Arlington, VA: National Science Foundation, 2002), 7–35.
5. See the introduction of Brian M. Stableford, *Science Fact and Science Fiction: An Encyclopedia* (London: Routledge, 2006); Robert Bly, *The Science in Science Fiction: 83 SF Predictions That Became Scientific Reality* (Dallas: BenBella, 2005).
6. Jason Pontin, "On Science Fiction," *Technology Review* 110, no. 2 (2007), 12.
7. Patrick Parrinder, "Introduction: Learning from Other Worlds," in *Learning from Other Worlds: Estrangement, Cognition, and the Politics of Science Fiction and Utopia*, ed., Patrick Parrinder (Liverpool: Liverpool University Press, 2000), 1–2.
8. *The Encyclopedia of Science Fiction* (New York: St. Martin's Griffin, 1995), s.v. "Technology."
9. See Andy Sawyer, "Future History," in *The Routledge Companion to Science Fiction*, ed., Mark Bould et al. (London: Routledge, 2009).
10. Adam Roberts, "The Copernican Revolution," in *The Routledge Companion to Science Fiction*, ed., Mark Bould et al. (London: Routledge, 2009), 9.
11. Darko Suvin, *Positions and Presuppositions in Science Fiction* (Basingstoke: Macmillan, 1988), 66, quoted in Patrick Parrinder, "Revisiting Suvin's Poetics of Science Fiction," in *Learning from Other Worlds: Estrangement, Cognition, and the Politics of Science Fiction and Utopia*, ed., Patrick Parrinder (Liverpool: Liverpool University Press, 2000), 36.
12. Suvin is a devout follower of Ernst Bloch and appropriates the notion of *novum* from Bloch. 'Suvin adopts the concept of the *novum* from the work of Ernst Bloch, for whom the term refers to those concrete innovations in lived history that awaken human collective consciousness out of a static present to awareness that history can be changed.' See Istvan Csicsery-Ronay Jr., "Marxist Theory and Science Fiction," in *The Cambridge Companion to Science Fiction*, ed., Edward James and Farah Mendlesohn (Cambridge: Cambridge University Press, 2003), 119.
13. Adam Roberts, *The History of Science Fiction* (Basingstoke: Palgrave Macmillan, 2006), 2.
14. Ursula Le Guin says that science fiction is descriptive and meant to describe 'reality, the present world'. See the introduction to Ursula Le Guin, *The Left Hand of Darkness* (New York: Ace Books, 2000).
15. These themes are largely inspired by Vivian Sobchack's commentary in Vivian Sobchack, "Science Fiction Film and Technological Imagination," in *Technological Visions: The Hopes and Fears That Shape New Technologies*, ed., Marita Sturken, Douglas Thomas, and Sandra Ball-Rokeach (Philadelphia: Temple University Press, 2004).
16. Arthur B. Evans, "Nineteenth-Century SF," in *The Routledge Companion to Science Fiction*, ed., Mark Bould et al. (London: Routledge, 2009), 17.
17. Ibid.
18. Ibid., 21. Wells admits that technology, 'scientific patter', is meant to actually replace magic as the means by which the fantastic element is broached. See the Preface to H. G. Wells, *Seven Famous Novels* (New York: Knopf, 1934).

19. H. G. Wells, "The Argonauts of the Air," in *Selected Stories of H.G. Wells*, ed., Ursula Le Guin (New York: Modern Library, 2004).

20. The publication of this short story in 1895 preceded the Wright Brothers' flight at Kitty Hawk by some eight years. See Ursula Le Guinn's historical commentary in H. G. Wells, *Selected Stories of H.G. Wells*, ed., Ursula Le Guin (New York: Modern Library, 2004), 112.

21. H. G. Wells, "In the Abyss," in *Selected Stories of H.G. Wells*, ed., Ursula Le Guin (New York: Modern Library, 2004).

22. Note the religious overtones Wells makes explicit in utilising technology. What Wells is tapping into is the way that technology feels when we use it. The reader vicariously experiences the wonder of the person in the craft who sees amazing things in the deep ocean. Wells connects this shared experience and the technological relationship with transcendence. For Wells, it is a kind of religious experience. Just as the person in the craft feels like a god and is worshipped as one so we feel the same in our relationships with technology. As we will see in the coming pages and as we have seen in the history of technological utopianism technology is often imbued with religious significance.

23. H. G. Wells, *The Time Machine* (London: Penguin Books, 2005), 28.

24. The Pulps refers to the period from 1926 to about 1940 in science fiction history. It gets its name from the cheap magazines championed by Hugo Gernsback's *Amazing Stories*. The Golden Age of Science Fiction runs from 1940 to 1960. For detailed appraisals of these eras in science fiction see Roberts, *The History of Science Fiction*, chs. 9–10; Brian Attebery, "The Magazine Era: 1926–1960," in *The Cambridge Companion to Science Fiction*, ed., Edward James and Farah Mendlesohn (Cambridge: Cambridge University Press, 2003); Farah Mendlesohn, "Fiction, 1926–1949," in *The Routledge Companion to Science Fiction*, ed., Mark Bould et al. (London: Routledge, 2009).

25. See Andy Sawyer, "Space Opera," in *The Routledge Companion to Science Fiction*, ed., Mark Bould et al. (London: Routledge, 2009); Gary Westfahl, "Space Opera," in *The Cambridge Companion to Science Fiction*, ed., Edward James and Farah Mendlesohn (Cambridge: Cambridge University Press, 2003).

26. In fact, the space opera flourished the most during the 1920s and 1930s during the time of the Pulp Fictions and the Golden Age of Science Fiction.

27. Of course, one might argue that this is in fact changing. I would be inclined to agree. There does seem to be a larger range of science fiction subgenres being accepted in popular culture today and this could be grounds for inciting a more nuanced stance towards technology and the future in the public consciousness. This actually strengthens my argument that there is an historical progression in how technology and the future are depicted in science fiction. The popularity of the *Terminator* series (1984–2009) and the *Matrix* trilogy (1999–2003) and most recently *Avatar* (2009) could be indicators of a shifting landscape. But, the popularity of the space opera—think of the ubiquity of the *Star Trek* and *Star Wars* franchises today—and its positive appraisal of technology has historically been the driving force for the populace at large.

28. Whereas this sterility is viewed in a positive way here—it provides the basis for its transcendence from common human life—in the next section it will be completely negative.

29. Sobchack, "Science Fiction Film," 150.

30. Ibid., 146ff.

31. See especially David E. Nye, *American Technological Sublime* (London: MIT Press, 1994); Bronislaw Szerszynski, *Nature, Technology and the Sacred* (Oxford: Blackwell, 2005), 61ff. For Szerszynski this is an adequate basis for

making the conclusion that our sense of the sacred has not been lost in the modern age, as so many secularists might claim, but has merely been relocated and technology figures prominently in our contemporary understanding of the sacred.

32. Brian Wilson Aldiss, *Billion Year Spree: The History of Science Fiction* (London: Weidenfeld & Nicolson, 1973), 18ff.

33. Paul K. Alkon, *Science Fiction before 1900: Imagination Discovers Technology* (London: Routledge, 2002), 2.

34. Bart Thurber, "Toward a Technological Sublime," in *The Intersection of Science Fiction and Philosophy: Critical Studies*, ed., Robert E. Myers (Westport: Greenwood Press, 1983), 215.

35. See Mary Wollstonecraft Shelley, *Frankenstein, or, the Modern Prometheus* (London: Penguin Books, 2003), 100ff.

36. Thurber, "Toward a Technological Sublime," 215.

37. It becomes a source for humour in the spoof *Spaceballs* (1987), where the spaceship extends beyond comfort for almost two minutes of film time.

38. See Rudolf Otto, *The Idea of the Holy*, trans., John W. Harvey (Harmondsworth: Penguin Books, 1959).

39. Robert W. Daly, "The Specters of Technicism," *Psychiatry: Journal for the Study of Interpersonal Processes* 33, no. 4 (1970), 421 (italics in the original). Also, see Szerszynski's commentary on this study along with its implications for our contemporary experience of the religious sublime in contemporary society in Szerszynski, *Nature, Technology and the Sacred*, 63ff.

40. For a greater appraisal of science fiction's relation to the sublime see Thurber, "Toward a Technological Sublime"; Robu Cornel, "A Key to Science Fiction: The Sublime," *Foundation: The International Review of Science Fiction* 42 (Spring 1988); Robu Cornel, "The Sense of Wonder Is Sense Sublime," *Science Fiction Research Association* 211 (May/June 1994).

41. As we will see in the coming chapter on Jacques Ellul, in order to understand technology properly we cannot limit ourselves to studying just physical devices, for the technological phenomenon goes deeper to what Ellul calls *technique*. For Ellul, *technique* refers to the actual process itself and includes as much social engineering and totalitarian government as it does the automobile or the airplane. See chapter 6 and Jacques Ellul, *The Technological System*, trans., Joachim Neugroschel (New York: Continuum, 1980), 23ff.

42. Evgeny Ivanovich Zamyatin, *We*, trans., Gregory Zilboorg (New York: E. P. Dutton, 1959), 22.

43. Ibid.

44. Translated elsewhere as Benefactor (Благодетель).

45. Zamyatin, *We*, 3.

46. Ibid. This image of rationalisation through space travel has already been seen in the writings of N. F. Fedorov and it will be seen again in the transhumanist visions of Kurzweil, Rees and Bostrom. This recurrent theme might be enough to ask how much of space travel today is motivated by an inherent belief in the rationalisation of the cosmos.

47. Ibid., 5.

48. Ibid., 7.

49. Ibid., 32.

50. Heidegger locates the unique modern experience in the representation of the world through mathematics and mathematical physics. A decisive shift occurs in the modern epoch when mathematics is the vanguard for knowing the world. Arendt makes similar observations in relation to scientific language being reduced to mathematics. See Martin Heidegger, *What Is a Thing?*, trans., W. B. Barton Jr. and Vera Deutsch (South Bend: Gateway Editions, 1967), 66ff.; Michael Roubach, *Being and Number in Heidegger's Thought*

(London: Continuum, 2008); Michael Roubach, "Heidegger, Science, and the Mathematical Age," *Science in Context* 10, no. 1 (1997); Hannah Arendt, *The Human Condition* (Chicago: University of Chicago Press, 1958), 3–4.

51. Zamyatin, *We*, 5–6.
52. Ibid., 43.
53. Ibid., 44.
54. Ibid., 45.
55. Ibid., 46.
56. Fyodor Dostoyevsky, *The Idiot*, trans., David McDuff (London: Penguin, 2004), 255.
57. Fyodor Dostoyevsky, *Notes from Underground and the Double*, trans., Jessie Coulson (Harmondsworth: Penguin Classics, 1972), 39. Also see T. R. N. Edwards, *Three Russian Writers and the Irrational: Zamyatin, Pil'nyak and Bulgakov* (Cambridge: Cambridge University Press, 1982).
58. A contemporary translator, Natasha Randall, claims that the Russian grammar and punctuation is quite disjointed but that this is entirely intentional for Zamyatin. Indeed, this gets translated into English where ellipses, colons and hyphens accentuate broken and unfinished phrases by the narrator. This illuminates the psychological and personal turmoil D-503 undergoes in the novel. See WNYC, "Underappreciated Literature: Yevgeny Zamyatin," *The Leonard Lopate Show*, interview, 18 August 2006, http://www.wnyc.org/shows/lopate/2006/aug/18/underappreciated-literature-yevgeny-zamyatin/ (accessed 4 July 2011).
59. Zamyatin, *We*, 58.
60. Ibid., 96.
61. Patrick Parrinder, "Imagining the Future: Zamyatin and Wells," *Science Fiction Studies* 1, no. 1 (1973), 23.
62. Zamyatin, *We*, 4.
63. George Orwell, *Nineteen Eighty-Four* (London: Penguin, 2000), 55.
64. Orwell states, 'But if thought corrupts language, language can also corrupt thought'. See George Orwell, "Politics and the English Language," in *A Collection of Essays* (San Diego: Harcourt, 1953), 167. It is not surprising that Orwell also has his protagonist keep a diary as the ultimate act of defiance against Big Brother. Undoubtedly, this parallels Zamyatin's protagonist keeping a diary and the rebellion which ensues from it.
65. Aldous Huxley, *Brave New World and Brave New World Revisited* (New York: HarperCollins, 2005), 60. This refers to the fabricated drug soma which is used to pacify negative emotions. It is used excessively by all to cure anything from mild discomfort to complete reconditioning. See ibid., 143ff, 296ff.
66. Ibid., 61, 89, 110. Referring to soma again.
67. Ibid., 92.
68. Ibid., 55.
69. A phrase of Skinner. See B. F. Skinner, *Beyond Freedom and Dignity* (Harmondsworth: Penguin, 1976).
70. More will be said about how language relates to possibility in chapter 8. Suffice it to say that what we learn from Zamyatin, Orwell and Huxley is that language is more than a benign representation of its corresponding thought. The human experience is yoked to how it relates to—perhaps better, is in—language.
71. 'All crosses had their tops cut and became T's.' Huxley, *Brave New World*, 58.
72. 'Ford, how I hate them!', ibid., 58; 'Thank Ford!', ibid., 81, 91, 100; 'Ford, we are twelve; oh, make us one,/Like drops within the Social River,/Oh, make us now together run/As swiftly as thy shining Flivver.', ibid., 82; 'Oh, for Ford's sake, be quiet!', ibid., 89.
73. Orwell, *Nineteen Eighty-Four*, 14.

74. René Girard's work is invaluable in understanding the social function of the scapegoat. See René Girard, *The Scapegoat*, trans., Yvonne Freccero (Baltimore: Johns Hopkins University Press, 1986).
75. For instance popular examples might include texts such as E. M. Forster's 'The Machine Stops', Bradbury's *Fahrenheit 451* and Gibson's *Neuromancer*. It could include films such as *Equilibrium* (2002), *Logan's Run* (1976) and *THX 1138* (1971). But, space is limited and entire books could be written on how technology is portrayed in seminal dystopias let alone any one of these themes.
76. Sobchack, "Science Fiction Film," 150.
77. Ibid.
78. Adam Roberts, *Science Fiction*, 2nd ed. (London: Routledge, 2006), 112.
79. This is a significant claim Sherry Turkle also makes regarding modern human-technological relationships. See Sherry Turkle, *Alone Together: Why We Expect More from Technology and Less from Each Other* (New York: Basic Books, 2011). Additionally, the recent animated film *WALL-E* (2008) accentuates this theme as WALL-E, the protagonist robot, is imbued with more human characteristics than the remnant of the human race whilst being portrayed as grungy, dirty and familiar. Indeed, WALL-E's home, a rubbish heap which is a product of human laziness, is juxtaposed with the sterile human colony aboard a pristine and ordered spaceship. Further, he loves selflessly which is counterpoint to the individual selfishness of the human race depicted in the film. In this inversion where the human environment and human virtues are actually applied to a machine we are posed the question as to how much machines can exhibit human qualities even when we do not. Indeed, the very fact of this inversion illuminates the blurring of the machine/human boundary in contemporary science fiction.
80. Don Ihde's work is particularly important in scrutinising the relationship between the body and technology. See Don Ihde, *Bodies in Technology* (Minneapolis: University of Minnesota Press, 2001); Don Ihde, *Technology and the Lifeworld: From Garden to Earth* (Bloomington: Indiana University Press, 1990), 72ff.
81. Philip K. Dick, *Do Androids Dream of Electric Sheep?* (New York: Ballantine Books, 1996).
82. An android is a highly advanced synthetic machine made to look like a human whereas a cyborg is made up of a combination of biological and synthetic parts. The synthetic parts generally enhance the overall biological system of the cyborg.
83. This is very Heideggerian. Heidegger localises human existence in precisely this question. See chapter 7 for more detail.
84. Interestingly enough, the *Star Trek: The Next Generation* episode 'The Measure of a Man' tries to determine whether Data is the property of Starfleet and is to be dismantled and studied or whether he can be a free self-determined entity who is not an object. After invoking many different arguments including appealing to Data as a machine, to which the defence responds human beings are a machine as well but of a different type, that he was created by a human being, to which the defence responds that children are built from the building blocks of the respective parents' DNA, they finally conclude that Data must be given the benefit of the doubt to live as a person because the opposite decision has led to enslavement for other life forms.
85. This ontological synthesis has been a fecund image for recent gender theorists and critical theorists. They find in this image an actual reflection of our contemporary understanding of personhood. These scholars tell us that in the 21st century our modern conceptions of identity have become debunked because they either rely on an outdated and suspect understanding of nature or one which is entirely the creation of the individual or the society and cultural

pressures which also seek to define it. For this reason the image of the cyborg is a positive image for it does not succumb to either ontology but rests—perhaps uneasily!—in a nebulous purgatory of identity. Donna Haraway has done the most to advance the cyborg theory of gender and identity. See Donna Haraway, "A Cyborg Manifesto: Science, Technology, and Socialist-Feminism in the Late Twentieth Century," in *Simians, Cyborgs, and Women: The Reinvention of Nature* (New York: Routledge, 1991). Also, for its relation to science fiction, see Veronica Hollinger, "Posthumanism and Cyborg Theory," in *The Routledge Companion to Science Fiction*, ed., Mark Bould et al. (London: Routledge, 2009). And for a constructive Christian engagement with Haraway's cyborg see Jeanine Thweatt-Bates, *Cyborg Selves: A Theological Anthropology of the Posthuman* (Farnham: Ashgate, 2012).

86. The connection with the story of Pinocchio is made explicit by the director Stanley Kubrick and in the storyline itself.
87. 'First Law: A robot may not injure a human being, or, through inaction, allow a human being to come to harm. Second Law: A robot must obey the orders given it by human beings, except where such orders would conflict with the First Law. Third Law: A robot must protect its own existence as long as such protection does not conflict with the First or Second Law.' See R. Clarke, "Asimov's Laws of Robotics: Implications for Information Technology—Part I," *Computer* 26, no. 12 (1993), 55.
88. This is a fear transhumanists contend is a real possibility and one of the most important areas of concern in developing benevolent artificial intelligences that not only safeguard present human beings' safety but also successfully incorporate the image of man, the *imago homo*. This task and the issues surrounding it have vast religious import. See the next chapter for more detail.
89. Nick Bostrom, "A History of Transhumanist Thought," *Journal of Evolution and Technology* 14 (April 2005), 4ff.
90. The only exception to this seems to be Martin Rees who has on record said time and again that 'first rate science fiction is always better than second rate science' because of its nourishment of the imagination. See Martin Rees and Krista Tippett, "Cosmic Origami and What We Don't Know," *American Public Media*, interview, 2 June 2011, http://being.publicradio.org/programs/2011/cosmic-origami/transcript.shtml (accessed 16 August 2011).
91. In many ways I am making a similar argument to Mary Midgley and Langdon Gilkey. See Langdon Gilkey, *Religion and the Scientific Future: Reflections on Myth, Science and Theology* (London: SCM, 1970); Mary Midgley, *The Myths We Live By* (London: Routledge, 2003).
92. Paul Tillich, *Dynamics of Faith* (New York: Harper & Row, 1957), 1. Also see Paul Tillich, *Ultimate Concern: Tillich in Dialogue* (London: SCM Press, 1965). Of course Tillich himself recognised the religious implications of technology and the impact technology was having on modern society. See, for example, Paul Tillich, *The Spiritual Situation in Our Technical Society*, ed., J. Mark Thomas (Macon: Mercer, 1988).
93. Paul Tillich, *Christianity and the Encounter of the World Religions* (New York: Columbia University Press, 1963), 5.
94. Stephen R. L. Clark, "Science Fiction and Religion," in *A Companion to Science Fiction*, ed., David Seed (Oxford: Blackwell, 2005), 107.
95. See, for example, Michael W. DeLashmutt, "The Technological Imaginary: Bringing Myth and Imagination into Dialogue with Bronislaw Szerszynski's *Nature, Technology and the Sacred*," *Zygon* 41, no. 4 (2006); Bronislaw Szerszynski, "A Reply to Anne Kull, Eduardo Cruz, and Michael DeLashmutt," *Zygon* 41, no. 4 (2006). The American Academy of Religion has recently introduced a research group devoted to studying religion and science fiction as well.

REFERENCES

Aldiss, Brian Wilson. *Billion Year Spree: The History of Science Fiction.* London: Weidenfeld & Nicolson, 1973.

Alkon, Paul K. *Science Fiction before 1900: Imagination Discovers Technology.* London: Routledge, 2002.

Arendt, Hannah. *The Human Condition.* Chicago: University of Chicago Press, 1958.

Attebery, Brian. "The Magazine Era: 1926–1960." In *The Cambridge Companion to Science Fiction,* edited by Edward James and Farah Mendlesohn. Cambridge: Cambridge University Press, 2003.

Bly, Robert. *The Science in Science Fiction: 83 SF Predictions That Became Scientific Reality.* Dallas: BenBella, 2005.

Bostrom, Nick. "A History of Transhumanist Thought." *Journal of Evolution and Technology* 14 (April 2005).

Clark, Stephen R. L. "Science Fiction and Religion." In *A Companion to Science Fiction,* edited by David Seed. Oxford: Blackwell, 2005.

Clarke, R. "Asimov's Laws of Robotics: Implications for Information Technology—Part I." *Computer* 26, no. 12 (1993): 53–61.

Clute, John, and Peter Nicholls, *The Encyclopedia of Science Fiction.* New York: St. Martin's Griffin, 1995.

Cornel, Robu. "A Key to Science Fiction: The Sublime." *Foundation: The International Review of Science Fiction* 42 (Spring 1988): 21–37.

———. "The Sense of Wonder Is Sense Sublime." *Science Fiction Research Association* 211 (May/June 1994): 43–64.

Csicsery-Ronay, Istvan, Jr. "Marxist Theory and Science Fiction." In *The Cambridge Companion to Science Fiction,* edited by Edward James and Farah Mendlesohn. Cambridge: Cambridge University Press, 2003.

Daly, Robert W. "The Specters of Technicism." *Psychiatry: Journal for the Study of Interpersonal Processes* 33, no. 4 (1970): 417–432.

DeLashmutt, Michael W. "The Technological Imaginary: Bringing Myth and Imagination into Dialogue with Bronislaw Szerszynski's *Nature, Technology and the Sacred.*" *Zygon* 41, no. 4 (2006): 801–810.

Dick, Philip K. *Do Androids Dream of Electric Sheep?* New York: Ballantine Books, 1996.

Dostoyevsky, Fyodor. *Notes from Underground and the Double.* Translated by Jessie Coulson. Harmondsworth: Penguin Classics, 1972.

———. *The Idiot.* Translated by David McDuff. London: Penguin, 2004.

Edwards, T. R. N. *Three Russian Writers and the Irrational: Zamyatin, Pil'nyak and Bulgakov.* Cambridge: Cambridge University Press, 1982.

Ellul, Jacques. *The Technological System.* Translated by Joachim Neugroschel. New York: Continuum, 1980.

Evans, Arthur B. "Nineteenth-Century SF." In *The Routledge Companion to Science Fiction,* edited by Mark Bould, Andrew M. Butler, Adam Roberts, and Sherryl Vint. London: Routledge, 2009.

Gilkey, Langdon. *Religion and the Scientific Future: Reflections on Myth, Science and Theology.* London: SCM, 1970.

Girard, René. *The Scapegoat.* Translated by Yvonne Freccero. Baltimore: Johns Hopkins University Press, 1986.

Haraway, Donna. "A Cyborg Manifesto: Science, Technology, and Socialist-Feminism in the Late Twentieth Century." In *Simians, Cyborgs, and Women: The Reinvention of Nature.* New York: Routledge, 1991.

Heidegger, Martin. *What Is a Thing?* Translated by W. B. Barton Jr. and Vera Deutsch. South Bend: Gateway Editions, 1967.

Hollinger, Veronica. "Posthumanism and Cyborg Theory." In *The Routledge Companion to Science Fiction*, edited by Mark Bould, Andrew M. Butler, Adam Roberts, and Sherryl Vint. London: Routledge, 2009.

Huxley, Aldous. *Brave New World and Brave New World Revisited*. New York: HarperCollins, 2005.

Ihde, Don. *Technology and the Lifeworld: From Garden to Earth*. Bloomington: Indiana University Press, 1990.

———. *Bodies in Technology*. Minneapolis: University of Minnesota Press, 2001.

James, Edward, and Farah Mendlesohn, eds. *The Cambridge Companion to Science Fiction*. Cambridge: Cambridge University Press, 2003.

Kuhn, Thomas S. *The Structure of Scientific Revolutions*. 2nd ed. Chicago: University of Chicago Press, 1970.

Le Guin, Ursula. *The Left Hand of Darkness*. New York: Ace Books, 2000.

Mendlesohn, Farah. "Fiction, 1926–1949." In *The Routledge Companion to Science Fiction*, edited by Mark Bould, Andrew M. Butler, Adam Roberts, and Sherryl Vint. London: Routledge, 2009.

Midgley, Mary. *The Myths We Live By*. London: Routledge, 2003.

Mulhall, Stephen. *On Film*. 2nd ed. London: Routledge, 2008.

Myers, Robert E., ed. *The Intersection of Science Fiction and Philosophy: Critical Studies*. Westport: Greenwood Press, 1983.

National Science Board. *Science and Engineering Indicators—2002*. Vol. 1. Arlington, VA: National Science Foundation, 2002.

Nye, David E. *American Technological Sublime*. London: MIT Press, 1994.

Orwell, George. "Freedom and Happiness." *Tribune*, 4 January 1946.

———. "Politics and the English Language." In *A Collection of Essays*. San Diego: Harcourt, 1953.

———. *Nineteen Eighty-Four*. London: Penguin, 2000.

Otto, Rudolf. *The Idea of the Holy*. Translated by John W. Harvey. Harmondsworth: Penguin Books, 1959.

Parrinder, Patrick. "Imagining the Future: Zamyatin and Wells." *Science Fiction Studies* 1, no. 1 (1973): 17–26.

———. "Introduction: Learning from Other Worlds." In *Learning from Other Worlds: Estrangement, Cognition, and the Politics of Science Fiction and Utopia*, edited by Patrick Parrinder. Liverpool: Liverpool University Press, 2000.

———. "Revisiting Suvin's Poetics of Science Fiction." In *Learning from Other Worlds: Estrangement, Cognition, and the Politics of Science Fiction and Utopia*, edited by Patrick Parrinder. Liverpool: Liverpool University Press, 2000.

Pontin, Jason. "On Science Fiction." *Technology Review* 110, no. 2 (2007): 12.

Rees, Martin, and Krista Tippett. "Cosmic Origami and What We Don't Know." *American Public Media*. Interview, 2 June 2011. http://being.publicradio.org/programs/2011/cosmic-origami/transcript.shtml (accessed 16 August 2011).

Roberts, Adam. *The History of Science Fiction*. Basingstoke: Palgrave Macmillan, 2006.

———. *Science Fiction*. 2nd ed. London: Routledge, 2006.

———. "The Copernican Revolution." In *The Routledge Companion to Science Fiction*, edited by Mark Bould, Andrew M. Butler, Adam Roberts, and Sherryl Vint. London: Routledge, 2009.

Roubach, Michael. "Heidegger, Science, and the Mathematical Age." *Science in Context* 10, no. 1 (1997): 199–206.

———. *Being and Number in Heidegger's Thought*. London: Continuum, 2008.

Sawyer, Andy. "Future History." In *The Routledge Companion to Science Fiction*, edited by Mark Bould, Andrew M. Butler, Adam Roberts, and Sherryl Vint. London: Routledge, 2009.

———. "Space Opera." In *The Routledge Companion to Science Fiction*, edited by Mark Bould, Andrew M. Butler, Adam Roberts, and Sherryl Vint. London: Routledge, 2009.

Shelley, Mary Wollstonecraft. *Frankenstein, or, the Modern Prometheus*. London: Penguin Books, 2003.

Skinner, B. F. *Beyond Freedom and Dignity*. Harmondsworth: Penguin, 1976.

Slusser, George. "The Origins of Science Fiction." In *A Companion to Science Fiction*, edited by David Seed. Oxford: Blackwell, 2005.

Sobchack, Vivian. "Science Fiction Film and Technological Imagination." In *Technological Visions: The Hopes and Fears That Shape New Technologies*, edited by Marita Sturken, Douglas Thomas, and Sandra Ball-Rokeach. Philadelphia: Temple University Press, 2004.

Stableford, Brian M. *Science Fact and Science Fiction: An Encyclopedia*. London: Routledge, 2006.

Suvin, Darko. *Positions and Presuppositions in Science Fiction*. Basingstoke: Macmillan, 1988.

Szerszynski, Bronislaw. *Nature, Technology and the Sacred*. Oxford: Blackwell, 2005.

———. "A Reply to Anne Kull, Eduardo Cruz, and Michael DeLashmutt." *Zygon* 41, no. 4 (2006): 811–824.

Thurber, Bart. "Toward a Technological Sublime." In *The Intersection of Science Fiction and Philosophy: Critical Studies*, edited by Robert E. Myers. Westport: Greenwood Press, 1983.

Thweatt-Bates, Jeanine. *Cyborg Selves: A Theological Anthropology of the Posthuman*. Farnham: Ashgate, 2012.

Tillich, Paul. *Dynamics of Faith*. New York: Harper & Row, 1957.

———. *Christianity and the Encounter of the World Religions*. New York: Columbia University Press, 1963.

———. *Ultimate Concern: Tillich in Dialogue*. London: SCM Press, 1965.

———. *The Spiritual Situation in Our Technical Society*, edited by J. Mark Thomas. Macon: Mercer, 1988.

Turkle, Sherry. *Alone Together: Why We Expect More from Technology and Less from Each Other*. New York: Basic Books, 2011.

van Fraassen, Bas. "The Pragmatics of Explanation." In *Philosophy of Science: Contemporary Readings*, edited by Yuri Balashov and Alexander Rosenberg. London: Routledge, 2002.

Verne, Jules. *From the Earth to the Moon and Round the Moon*. New York: A. L. Burt Co., 1889.

———. *Five Weeks in a Balloon*. Translated by William Lackland. New York: Hurst, 1869.

———. *Twenty Thousand Leagues under the Sea*. Translated by William Butcher. Oxford: Oxford University Press, 2009.

Wells, H. G. *Seven Famous Novels*. New York: Knopf, 1934.

———. "The Argonauts of the Air." In *Selected Stories of H. G. Wells*, edited by Ursula Le Guin. New York: Modern Library, 2004.

———. "In the Abyss." In *Selected Stories of H. G. Wells*, edited by Ursula Le Guin. New York: Modern Library, 2004.

———. *Selected Stories of H. G. Wells*, edited by Ursula Le Guin. New York: Modern Library, 2004.

———. *The Time Machine*. London: Penguin Books, 2005.

Westfahl, Gary. "Space Opera." In *The Cambridge Companion to Science Fiction*, edited by Edward James and Farah Mendlesohn. Cambridge: Cambridge University Press, 2003.

WNYC. "Underappreciated Literature: Yevgeny Zamyatin." *The Leonard Lopate Show*. Interview, 18 August 2006. http://www.wnyc.org/shows/lopate/2006/aug/18/underappreciated-literature-yevgeny-zamyatin/ (accessed 4 July 2011).

Zamyatin, Evgeny Ivanovich. *We*. Translated by Gregory Zilboorg. New York: E. P. Dutton, 1959.

Zorpette, G., and P. E. Ross. "The Books That Made a Difference." *IEEE Spectrum* 44, no. 3 (2007): 58–59.

4   Transhumanism and the Future

We have been tracing the history of the technological imagination in utopias and science fiction. It has become evident that there has been a steady secularisation of the millennial goal and an inverting of the future as *adventus* to *futurum*—from a future which comes to us from God to one which is built upon through the present and by human technological means. The writings of Bacon and his followers in the Royal Society as well as the line descending from Fedorov represent this turn from a future crafted by God, to one actualised through more human technological effort—so much so that by the 20th century all remnants of the religious goal are implicit in the idealism of technological hope. This was visible in the American technological utopias of Bellamy and Chambless at the turn of the 20th century and in the writings of Buckminster Fuller and the technocracy movement. By the 20th century technological futurism was released from its religious moorings and a secular humanist hope in technology was able to flourish.

This is nowhere more apparent than in the current movement under consideration, transhumanism. Transhumanism draws upon both of the traditions already assessed: technological utopianism and science fiction. The majority of its adherents draw on the utopian strand taking up the unabashed assertion that technology is the panacea that will cure all ills and will lead humanity into the future.[1] These share with its predecessors a utopian vision made possible through technological progress. The future will be a place of endless growth and transcendence where death and toil are eradicated. It takes a very positive position towards the influence of technology on humanity. Those rare transhumanists who would not see technology as an entirely positive force on society and future, at the very least, take from technological utopianism the future-oriented nature of technological utopianism. Certainly, one cannot think of technology without reference to the future after the technological utopian strand.

Transhumanism also takes up many of the themes in science fiction already discussed. For instance, pessimistic transhumanists inherit a propensity towards the dystopia which was a major theme in science fiction's portrayal of technology and the future and import a sense of apocalypticism characteristic of this genre. But, more importantly, all transhumanists follow on from the latest theme in science fiction already discussed. It asserts that the convergence of humanity with its technology is not something relegated to mere speculation and the imagination, but a real projected reality. As technology has crowded the environment in which humanity dwells, becoming ever more intimate, that technology has literally broken into the skin of humanity and with it blending the boundary between man and machine. Transhumanism builds upon this theme in its construction of the future of humanity. In this way, the previous chapters have been a precursor to transhumanism and lay the groundwork for its inception today.

4.1   INTRODUCING TRANSHUMANISM

Transhumanism has been a growing cultural and intellectual movement in the past several decades. Since the founding of the World Transhumanist Association (now called Humanity+) in 1998 by Nick Bostrom and David Pearce,[2] by 2005 this international organisation had some 3,000 members from all over the world.[3] This number does not include the 46 local chapters that are associated, but independent of the global organisation.[4] Its influence has pervaded into academic and political circles as well and all evidence suggests it will continue to expand in the future.

Nick Bostrom defines transhumanism as:

(1) The intellectual and cultural movement that affirms the possibility and desirability of fundamentally improving the human condition through applied reason, especially by developing and making widely available technologies to eliminate aging and to greatly enhance human intellectual, physical, and psychological capacities.

(2) The study of the ramifications, promises, and potential dangers of technologies that will enable us to overcome fundamental human limitations, and the related study of the ethical matters involved in developing and using such technologies.[5]

Transhumanism draws primarily from science with its reliance upon empiricism and a materialistic approach to reality. It takes evolution to be the central history of mankind and, given humanity's evolutionary history, espouses that humanity is in the very early stages of its development as a species. It does not affirm an essentialist anthropology, but takes from its evolutionary premises that humanity is in a state of flux. Already it is easy to see, from the beginning, how transhumanism is related to the future—evolution provides a trajectory in its narrative which points to the future. The future is at the core of transhumanism itself as it moves beyond mere explanation of the history of the human species, like traditional evolutionary biologists, to where the species is going. Transhumanism is entirely future oriented.[6]

Transhumanism, as the term and definition above suggests, is related to humanism. Transhumanism shares with humanism the common commitment to reason and science, human progress and the value of our present life. Both can be said to affirm the bettering of the human condition through rational and scientific thinking so that humanity, for humanity's sake, might flourish. Transhumanists see themselves on the humanist continuum and consider historical humanist figures—Newton, Hobbes, Locke and Kant, as well as those already discussed—to be figureheads and forerunners of transhumanism.[7]

However, transhumanism differs from traditional humanism in advocating the improvement of humanity through 'applied reason, especially by developing and making widely available technologies that eliminate aging and greatly enhance human intellectual, physical, and psychological capacities'.[8] It is this last feature that typifies transhumanism and is its main thrust in political and social circles. Transhumanism advocates the enhancement of the human species through biotechnology and information technology, moving beyond the utilisation of these technologies for therapeutic purposes alone. Thus, technology and the future are central to the transhumanist project and set it apart from colloquial humanism.

The structure of this chapter focuses upon the proposed future of three notable and influential figures who have shaped the transhumanism movement and are well respected even outside of the transhumanist community. I chose these three because they embody the assertion that transhumanism is not a fringe phenomenon which is out of touch with real technological discovery and scientific advancement. Furthermore, like any social group, those who are involved in transhumanism have minor disagreements over what defines transhumanism exactly. Therefore, I chose three transhumanists whose perspectives represent the spectrum of differing beliefs on the future and who were also very influential in the field. I chose to examine the proposed future of Ray Kurzweil, Martin Rees and Nick Bostrom. More than this, this chapter assesses the form of the future, how it comes to existence and the conditions that influence the future. In the process, it will become apparent that contemporary transhumanism relies upon a future which is entirely humanity's creation through technology which drastically depends upon the present and the decisions made today, *futurum*. Finally, some comments will be made about the religious implications of transhumanism and how this movement's tenets are more than just scientific predictions, but they function more like a modern myth which can be a source of religious hope for its believers.

4.2   RAY KURZWEIL AND THE TECHNOLOGIST'S PERSPECTIVE

Ray Kurzweil is an award-winning inventor and futurist. He made *Foreign Policy* magazine's top 100 global thinkers alongside international acclaimed politicians and figures such as Barack Obama, Bill Clinton and

Pope Benedict XVI.[9] Bill Gates has lauded him 'the best person I know at predicting the future of artificial intelligence'.[10] His biography is speckled with successful inventions and companies at the forefront of technological innovation. His CV boasts of a company called Kurzweil Computer Products which catapulted OCR (optical character recognition) into mainstream usage in the middle of the 1970s and aided the blind in reading printed texts.[11] He sold the company and pursued the advancement of electronic instruments at the request of Stevie Wonder. His new company, Kurzweil Music Systems, produced some of the finest electronic keyboards with the most authentically emulated sounds in the 1980s.[12] He then moved on to speech-recognition technology and founded a company entitled Kurzweil Applied Intelligence which splintered into different areas including medicine and education.[13] He holds 13 honorary degrees and countless high-profile awards and his books on the future of technology have been on the *New York Times* bestseller list.[14] More recently, he helped found a new university called Singularity University which resides in the NASA Ames Research Center in Silicon Valley. Its inception was funded by Google and its mission is 'to assemble, educate and inspire leaders who strive to understand and facilitate the development of exponentially advancing technologies in order to address humanity's Grand Challenges.'[15] Needless to say, Kurzweil has been at the forefront and heart of the development of technology in the past three decades and has the practical experience to comment on the viability of how technology has shaped and will shape the future.

The future is predictable for Kurzweil. Despite his impeccable references, he does not claim to have any special ability himself in predicting the future save what he has gleaned from scientific study. Nor does he claim to know specifics about certain world events like some scientific soothsayer. But, as he claims in an interview:

> If you ask me, will the price of Google be higher or lower than it is today three years from now, that's very hard to say. Will WiMax CDMA G3 be the wireless standard three years from now? That's hard to say. But if you ask me, what will it cost for one MIPS of computing in 2010, or the cost to sequence a base pair of DNA in 2012, or the cost of sending a megabyte of data wirelessly in 2014, it turns out that those are very predictable. . . .[16]

Technological trends, for Kurzweil, are very predictable. Kurzweil has a team of ten people who work on models of technological growth.[17] As will become more apparent in the pages that follow, Kurzweil's future is based upon models and heuristics which trend technological data. As he claims, he is an engineer and likes to meticulously measure things.[18] In this way it is easy to see that, for Kurzweil, the future can be predicted through very complex and scientific modelling which can be used to further forecast what tomorrow will be like. And, his predictions over the past two decades have made him a credible source amongst his fellow futurists as well as experts in the area of technology. However, he himself notes that futuristic predictions in the area of technology in the past century have had a spotty history. He quotes several outlandish technological predictions:

> Heavier-than-air flying machines are not possible.—Lord Kelvin, 1895
> Computers in the future may weigh no more than 1.5 tons.—Popular Mechanics, 1949
> 640,000 bytes of memory ought to be enough for anybody.—Bill Gates, 1981
> The Internet will catastrophically collapse in 1996.—Robert Metcalfe (inventor of Ethernet)[19]

But Kurzweil thinks he is different. After citing these failed predictions he goes on to assess his own predictions in the past decade which, for the most part, have been accurate if not precise. What is important to note here, from the beginning, is that the future relies upon sound statistics taken from the past and present and is a product of our own creation.[20] The future is *futurum* rather than *adventus*.

What does the future entail for Kurzweil? Before this can be assessed it is necessary to follow Kurzweil through the history he creates and the data he gathers because the future depends upon models applied to the past and present.

Kurzweil outlines the six epochs of the universe in the second chapter of his most recent work *The Singularity is Near*. The first four epochs refer to the past whereas the final two outline what he expects will occur in the future. It is clear that Kurzweil, like many other transhumanists, consider time on two different levels. The first level is that of cosmic time. This timescale is on the order of tens of thousands if not hundreds of thousands of years and considers the universe as a whole. Astrophysics and quantum physics tend to be the areas of concern on the cosmic timescale—the infinitesimal and the infinite. The second timescale is more imminent, terrestrial and historical. It is in line with time as it is commonly perceived and is on the order of decades and centuries. This timescale focuses on the history of the earth and humanity specifically. While this distinction isn't mentioned explicitly in any of his works, it is helpful in understanding the form of the future Kurzweil has in mind and will guide the following sections.

4.2.1   The Past on the Cosmic Timescale

Kurzweil gives an account of the cosmic past beginning with the Big Bang. His first epoch is entitled 'Physics and Chemistry', for the Big Bang and the diversification of chemistry are the most important occurrences during this epoch. Kurzweil makes the observation that it is during this epoch that time seems to be slowing down. What he means by this is that the most salient events in the epoch occur in a very short amount of time just following the Big Bang. Within the first few minutes after the Big Bang basic quantum mechanics and the laws of the universe have been established. Gravity is formed 10^{-43} seconds after the Big Bang; 10^{-10} seconds later the strong and weak forces emerge; 10^{-5} seconds later protons and neutrons take shape; and after another minute basic atomic nuclei coalesce.[21] From here the significant events in cosmic history begin to be more spread out. Some 300,000 years later atoms begin taking shape; it takes another billion years for the galaxies to form, and still another two billion years following before stars begin to form and have their own solar systems. It is three billion years later that earth is formed. What Kurzweil observes is that on the cosmic continuum the amount of significant events has decreased over time since the universe's inception. He charts this and notices that the relation is exponential, that is it is taking longer for each salient event to occur. Kurzweil tells us that this is related to the amount of chaos in the universe—which is constantly expanding according to the second law of thermodynamics. He generalises this observation in what he calls the Law of Increasing Chaos. It states: 'As chaos exponentially increases, time exponentially slows down (that is, the time interval between salient events grows longer as time passes).'[22] This Law of Increasing Chaos is manifest in other important processes such as the development of organisms. For instance, during human gestation a significant amount of growth and development occurs within the first nine months.[23] Physically, a child develops all major organs and skills to function outside of the womb within these first few months. Child developmental psychologists agree that the first several years of one's life are crucial and can affect the rest of one's life dramatically. The early part of human development is marked with extensive important events. Significant events then spread out until death. The Law of Increasing Chaos seems to govern the overall pattern of the universe and even our own lives.

However, Kurzweil explains that this isn't the entire story. The ultimate fate of humanity and our individual existence does not need to rest in the Law of Increasing Chaos because there is another force at work in the universe. Kurzweil terms this the Law of Accelerating Returns. This law states: 'As order exponentially increases, time exponentially speeds up (that is, the time interval between salient events grows shorter as time passes).'[24] The Law of Accelerating Returns is based upon the process of evolution. Biological evolution leads to greater complexity and order within a species. Biological evolution is made possible through the development of DNA so that biological information from prior generations can be passed down to subsequent generations. The mechanism which makes evolution advantageous and increase in order is that 'it creates a capability and then uses that capability to evolve to the next stage'[25]—nothing is lost from generation to generation. Given a stable, fixed environment evolution will increase the amount of order in the system at an exponential rate.

Kurzweil claims that evolution is not peculiar to biological species alone, but is taken over by technology in the 19th and 20th centuries. While the next section will go into greater detail, suffice it to say here that Kurzweil sees biological and technological evolution as part of a greater evolutionary law within the universe. Evolution has cosmic extension as will be seen in the final section.

Kurzweil puts both of these laws together in his Law of Time and Chaos which states: 'In a process, the time interval between salient events (that is, events that change the nature of the process, or significantly affect the future of the process) expands or contracts along with the amount of chaos.'[26] Therefore, if chaos decreases in the environment in which the process occurs, like with evolution, the amount of significant events will increase. As Kurzweil says, time will seem to speed up. The opposite is true if chaos increases in the system. The amount of time between important process-altering events increases. Time looks as though it slows down. Both of these situations are at work in very significant processes in the universe and Kurzweil notes that there seems to be a conflict between these two laws: the Law of Increasing Chaos and the Law of Accelerating Returns. One seems to work towards greater chaos in the universe with time increasingly slowing down, whereas the other creates order at an increasingly exponential rate which leads to time speeding up. Kurzweil harmonises this discrepancy by asserting that the second law of thermodynamics applies to a closed system, like the universe. Evolution is not a closed system. In fact, the chaos in which evolution is a part is actually helpful to its overall development. He states:

> The Law of Accelerating Returns as Applied to an Evolutionary Process: An evolutionary process is not a closed system; therefore, evolution draws upon the chaos in the larger system in which it takes place for its options for diversity; and Evolution builds on its own increasing order. Therefore: In an evolutionary process, order increases exponentially. Therefore: Time exponentially speeds up. Therefore: The returns (that is, the valuable products of the process) accelerate.[27]

Both laws are at the heart of the universe and guide its movement into the future.

4.2.2   The Singularity is Near: The Imminent Timescale

The majority of Kurzweil's conjectures gain their merit from and occupy the second timescale. As stated, this timescale is more immediately perceivable and centres on terrestrial history and the fate of man. Kurzweil is interested here in following the history of the Law of Accelerating Returns and it is the central axis in this timescale. Therefore, both biological and technological evolution are the central concerns of Kurzweil and provide the data behind his asserted laws.

Kurzweil declares that two paradigmatic shifts occurred in biological evolution which radically affected the shape of evolution. The first was the introduction of DNA, the main feature which defines Kurzweil's second epoch, and its ability to represent an entire organism and reproduce that very organism from the code in the DNA. DNA's impact on the biological landscape has larger scope than just the reproduction of a particular species. The really novel nature of DNA is that it stores the historical information of a species within DNA. This allowed each generation to build on the innovations of the previous resulting in geometric growth. The second, and more important revolution, was the development of the brain and computation. This represents Kurzweil's third epoch. The brain allowed information from the environment to be processed directly through the senses and almost immediately rather than indirectly and delayed as with DNA. This catalysed the evolution of humanity in particular as the pattern recognition and complex behaviours from lower life forms became more complex in the human species and sentience emerged. Kurzweil states, 'Ultimately, our own species evolved the ability to create abstract mental models of the world we experience and to contemplate the rational implications of these models. We have the ability to redesign the world in our own minds and to put these ideas into action.'[28] The brain is an incredibly complex biological system which is still unrivalled in its computational ability, but, Kurzweil explains, pure biological computation is not the fate of the future. Instead, another important event happens which further compresses and quickens the Law of Accelerating Returns.

Kurzweil explains that technology is this important invention. The development of technology virtually takes over for biological evolution because its rate of progress is considerably faster than biological evolution could ever be. Kurzweil presents countless evidence of the exponential nature of technological advancement. Most of his innumerable lectures and presentations around the globe speak towards the discrepancy many laypersons as well as seasoned professionals make in attributing linear advancement to technology rather than geometric. The famous case brought to attention is Moore's Law. Gordon Moore was the founder of Intel and his observation in the 1970s was that integrated circuits could handle double the amount of transistors every two years. Not only would the addition of these transistors significantly increase the computational power of the integrated circuit, but as the transistors got smaller, the distance the electron had to travel would become shorter so that processing speed would increase even more.[29] Moore's original prediction, one year instead of two years, is accurate and even today we are still experiencing Moore's Law.

The exponential growth rate of technology is not limited to Moore's Law. In fact, Kurzweil claims that Moore's Law is actually the fifth paradigm reflecting this trend in computing systems in the last century. Those prior were electromechanical computation (punch cards), relays, vacuum tubes and single transistors. Moreover, many other areas of communication and information technologies exhibit exponential growth as well.[30]

Kurzweil claims that all evidence predicts that this trend will continue into the future and that even when Moore's Law moves to the end of its life cycle, like so many other of its predecessors, another paradigm will pick up where it left off. As Kurzweil states, 'there really is a theoretical reason why technology develops in an exponential fashion'[31] aside from the experimental data which only provides evidence for that theoretical reason. He states that just like any other evolutionary system, the information gained from the past generations of technological advance go into the creation of new technologies which can become themselves new paradigms for evolutionary progression. Often the new technologies which take over for the old paradigms are waiting in 'niche industries' which have yet to gain full exposure.

Critics of Kurzweil claim that the exponential trend in computation and technology cannot continue on forever and that it is bound to hit a wall. Kurzweil responds to this by asserting that the Law of Accelerating Returns applies equally to the evolutionary process of computing and that 'the growing order of the evolving technology itself and the chaos from which an evolutionary process draws its options for further diversity—are unbounded. Ultimately, the innovation needed for further turns of the screw will come from the machines themselves.'[32] For Kurzweil, new technologies or innovations will always take over for those on the end of their life cycle and breathe life into the exponential trend of technology.

Kurzweil does not leave his predictions here. These models and patterns he has recognised serve to project into the future the impact these new technologies will have on humanity and society. The bulk of Kurzweil's chapters in *The Age of Spiritual Machines* are given the title of a year in the future and each contains his predictions about the advances that will have been developed by that year. For instance, by the year 2019 Kurzweil suggests that the ubiquity of screens will be trumped by the projection of images directly onto our retinas.[33] Keyboards are rare by 2019 as physical gestures and speech control most computer functions. He also says that a $4,000 computer will have the computing capacity of the human brain by the year 2019.[34] Only ten years later, in 2029, $1,000 will be able to buy a computer with the power of 1,000 brains.[35] Major advancements occur in the next century which invariably lead to an even more rapidly changing landscape.

Kurzweil predicts that three areas of technology, now in their infancy, will be the major vanguards for the future: genetics, nanotechnology and robotics. Already the explosion of genetics is visible with the mapping of the human genome and primitive gene therapy. But, the technological potential for genetics is only at the dawn of utilisation. Genetics can be used to slow the aging process and even cause it to cease. He has coauthored a book with Terry Grossman, M.D., entitled *Fantastic Voyage: Live Long Enough to Live Forever*,[36] in which he outlines steps one can take today to extend one's life to what Aubrey de Grey calls 'Longevity Escape Velocity': living long enough until scientists have discovered how to completely eradicate aging.[37] As is expected, Kurzweil sees aging as yet another problem which will be solved through our increasing knowledge of genetics and the applications that will be created to stop it:

> Whereas some of my contemporaries may be satisfied to embrace aging gracefully as part of the cycle of life, that is not my view. It may be 'natural,' but I don't see anything positive in losing my mental agility, sensory acuity, physical limberness, sexual desire, or any other human ability. I view disease and death at any age as a calamity, as problems to be overcome.[38]

Kurzweil does not just write about the potentials of genetic manipulation, but actually takes between 180 and 210 pills a day to reprogramme his biochemistry and to increase longevity.[39] Kurzweil states that gene therapy will be even more direct in the future utilising new technologies such as RNA Interference, Cell Therapy and Gene Chips to cease ageing.[40]

Similarly, nanotechnology promises to be very fruitful as well. Kurzweil quotes a National Science Foundation report on the potential of nanotechnology, 'Nanotechnology has the potential to enhance human performance, to bring sustainable development for materials, water, energy, and food, to protect against unknown bacteria and viruses, and even to diminish the reasons for breaking the peace [by creating universal abundance].'[41] Nanotechnology has the ability to alter the material world at the molecular level which has vast medical implications. Scenarios have been projected which utilise nanotechnology to seek out and destroy maladies in the body.[42] They could also be used to enhance the human body by outfitting nanobots, very small robots, with oxygen which can be directly injected into individual cells. The benefit of nanotechnology is its precision and high statistical yield. This aspect of nanotechnology, Kurzweil explains, has vast affect on the consumption of energy: 'Because of nanotechnology's ability to manipulate matter and energy at the extremely fine scale of atoms and molecular fragments, the efficiency of using energy will be far greater, which will translate into lower energy requirements.'[43]

The final piece of technology with vast potential for the future is robotics. In particular, it is artificial intelligence (AI) which will have the greatest extension in the future. AI has the distinct advantage over human intelligence in being able to recall information with complete accuracy. Furthermore, it is not limited to the weak hardware of the human synapses and neural net which can only process 10^{16} calculations per second (cps).[44] While this might seem like a lot, currently, IBM's Blue Gene/L supercomputer can perform 3.6×10^{14} cps—very close to the human brain. With the exponential advancement of computing it is projected that the computational power of the brain will be reached by computers by the year 2025.[45] Kurzweil is clear that human biological intelligence is reaching the end of its life cycle and AI is more reliable and faster. Hence, he contends that the convergence of biology and electronic computing is inevitable. Thus, according to Kurzweil, the future of humanity is in the cyborg.

These three areas of technology will lead to what Kurzweil terms the Singularity. The Singularity is 'a future period during which the pace of technological change will be so rapid, its impact so deep, that human life will be irreversibly transformed.'[46] The term is taken from mathematics and astronomy and represents a 'value that transcends any finite limitation'[47] as in the function $y = 1/x$ where 0 is the Singularity: The function never reaches it but constantly approaches it.[48]

For our purposes, the technological Singularity is similar in that the growth rate of technology seems to reach an almost vertical line, that is infinite growth at the Singularity. Kurzweil sets the date for Singularity to be 2045. He supports this by appealing to how much $1,000 will be in terms of computational power:

> By the mid-2040s, however, that one thousand dollars' worth of computation will be equal to 10^{26} cps, so the intelligence created per year (at a total cost of about $1012) will be about one billion times more powerful than all human intelligence today. That will indeed represent a profound change . . .[49]

This level of computing is unimaginable today and represents to today's observer a qualitative break in prediction and forecasting.[50] On an intuitive level and from our current perspective the Singularity represents a point at which prediction becomes very difficult if not impossible altogether. Kurzweil himself admits, 'Some would say that we cannot comprehend it, at least with our current level of understanding. For that reason, we cannot look past its event horizon and make complete sense of what lies beyond. This is one reason we call this transformation the Singularity.'[51] The rapid change around the Singularity represents more to transhumanists than ultimate computing power for it begins to take on a religious significance.[52]

The Singularity has been termed by critics as the 'Rapture for Nerds'[53] and reflects the religious images the Singularity evokes. In many ways, the Singularity represents a kind of apocalypse in that one cannot see beyond its horizon. If Kurzweil is right, then history, from our current perspective, seems entirely different after the Singularity. The Singularity marks a qualitatively different epoch.[54] However, it differs from a traditional apocalypse in that it is entirely seamless with the present. As Kurzweil states, 'It's not like we are going to go along and nothing is going to happen and suddenly we are going to take this huge leap to super-intelligent machines. We are going to get from here to there through thousands of little steps.'[55] Indeed, the Singularity is not like an apocalypse in that it originates from outside of history; rather it is entirely something which comes from within the confines of history and is built upon today. It is an apocalypse related to *futurum* rather than *adventus*.[56]

Kurzweil maintains that human history and the Singularity will become the major features in the cosmos. Imminent history will extend into cosmic history as humanity and technology expand and inhabit the entire universe. The Law of Accelerating Returns will overcome the Law of Increasing Chaos. As Kurzweil states, 'Ultimately, the entire universe will become saturated with our intelligence. This is the destiny of the universe. We will determine our own fate rather than have it determined by the current "dumb," simple, machinelike forces that rule celestial mechanics.'[57] Kurzweil maintains an optimistic outlook on the ultimate cosmic fate of the universe, but he disagrees that his position is purely utopian. This is partially due to his construction of the future which entirely depends upon the occurrences of today and the decisions humanity makes towards preparing itself for this radical future. He understands that technology can be used for evil purposes and that the technological future will have many more problems to solve. He is convinced, nevertheless, that 'a planet approaching its pivotal century of computational growth—as the Earth is today—has a better than even chance of making it through'[58] to the ultimate future.

4.3 MARTIN REES AND THE COSMOLOGIST'S PERSPECTIVE

Martin Rees's assessment of the future is not as brazenly optimistic as Kurzweil's appraisal. As an Englishman, his approach to the future and transhumanity seems to be characteristic of an Old World pessimism or realism in juxtaposition to Kurzweil, a product of American optimism.[59] His entire approach stems from his position as a renowned cosmologist and astrophysicist at the University of Cambridge. He has been the president of the Royal Society, was appointed to the House of Lords in 2005, and is the Master of Trinity College, Cambridge.[60] In fact, he was also awarded the esteemed Templeton Prize in 2011 for his contribution to science and the big questions of life.[61] Rees's biography manifests that he is a well-respected scientist, researcher and educator and, likewise, might be more hesitant in speculating about the future—especially speculation of the sensational nature.

Yet, this Old World realism does not keep him from thinking and writing about the future—particularly the possibility of a transhuman future. As a cosmologist and astrophysicist his central area of focus is much broader than Kurzweil's.[62] The content of his invited lectures often spans millions if not billions of years. He will often begin with a review of the events of the Big Bang and then continue on through to speculate about the far-far future of the universe with a short but significant pit stop commenting on the complexity of human beings.[63] This grand timescale Rees focuses on might seem irrelevant to our everyday lives but, according to Rees, it provides a perspective on our current situation which is entirely relevant. He states:

> What happens in far-future aeons may seem blazingly irrelevant to the practicalities of our lives. But I don't think it is. It is widely acknowledged that the Apollo programme's pictures of the island earth, its

fragile beauty contrasted with the stark moonscape, changed the way we see ourselves in space—strengthening the collective ties that bind us to our environment. No new facts were added to the debate; just a new perspective. A new perspective on how we see ourselves in time might do something similar.[64]

Rees's speculation about the future is most well known for its anxious and, at times, sensationally apocalyptic tone. This is nowhere more evident than in his book which reflects this anxiety about the future, *Our Final Century: Will the Human Race Survive the Twenty-First Century?* This book was given an even more imminently nervous and sensational title in the United States: *Our Final Hour: A Scientist's Warning: How Terror, Error, and Environmental Disaster Threaten Humankind's Future in This Century—on Earth and Beyond.* In this text Rees spells out all the reasons for supposing that we, the human race, have no better than a fifty percent chance of making it through the next century.[65]

Rees makes clear that the human race has always been under threat from natural disasters whether they are terrestrial, in the form of volcanoes and earthquakes, or even celestial, coming from asteroids, comets and other NEOs (near-earth objects).[66] Unsurprisingly, it is the threats from space which interest Rees the most. But, this isn't without justification. Depending on size, NEOs have the ability to cause major destruction to humanity and the earth. Rees admits that these kinds of impacts are a relatively low risk considering the size of earth and the frequency with which they have hit earth in the past, but given the amount of destruction possible they should not be neglected or forgotten but must be mitigated against.

These kinds of threats do not seem to be the ultimate catalyst for Rees's claims that we are in our final century. The major threats in the past century have originated with humanity itself. Rees estimates 187 million people died from 'war, persecution, or policy-induced famine' in both world wars and their aftermath, and the 20th century is perhaps the first in which natural disasters did not kill more than 'war and totalitarian regimes'.[67] He focuses the most on the Cold War and uses the Doomsday Clock as a heuristic for the threat level in the latter part of the 20th century. The Doomsday Clock was a feature of the *Bulletin of Atomic Scientists*, an influential journal founded by many of the physicists who worked on the Manhattan Project. On the cover of each journal was found a large clock which illustrated the relative threat level, according to the editorial board, by how close the clock was to midnight. The Doomsday Clock has been making judgements since 1947 and the time when humanity was at the greatest risk was in the 1950s. Initially this might seem to be a poor judgement, but it was during this decade that the United States and the Soviet Union obtained H-bombs and amassed a sizeable number of other nuclear weapons.[68] For Rees, nuclear weapons were the one factor which escalated the threat level in the past century. The arms race between the United States and Soviet Union caused anxiety around the world. Rees details each decade leading to disarmament, pointing out how close humanity came to not only destroying local cities, as actually happened with Hiroshima and Nagasaki, but even to sparking a complete nuclear war; this would have a global impact and would affect the environment for many years to come because of radiation.

The nuclear arms race is especially pertinent for Rees's projection of destruction in the future because the greatest threat for the future will come from advanced technologies. The major threat from these technologies will come from either their abuse from radical extremists or from possible accidents by scientists and technologists—either terror or error. He wrote *Our Final Century* just following the terrorist attack on the World Trade Center in New York on September 11, 2001. Technological terrorism using nuclear weapons is a genuine possibility for which nations around the world are making every effort to stop. In a globalised economy it is becoming possible for a single person with ill intention to wield massive destructive power in the form of an advanced technological weapon—nuclear or otherwise. Besides terror, Rees also cites the destructive possibilities of scientific error. One only needs to consider the nuclear meltdown at Chernobyl in 1986 for such an example. Rees even cites the far-ranging consequences of an accident occurring in places like the Brookhaven National Laboratory or the CERN laboratory in Geneva—where an accident could even open up a black hole![69]

Yet, the threat of nuclear weapons and potential laboratory accidents are dealt with, for the most part, on the public level. One needs uranium or plutonium to build an atomic weapon and they are difficult to come by and are highly regulated. These laboratories that do quantum experiments are monitored as well. Biotechnologies do not have the same level of restrictions precisely because the equipment and ingredients are so common. One would only need a basic microbiology degree and some cheap equipment which is common even in the agriculture industry. It is because of this that Rees is most worried about the prospects for bioterror and bioerror.

Rees cites one situation in Australia where scientists were experimenting with a particular strand of mousepox virus to sterilise mice. Instead, these scientists accidently created a new and deadly strain of mousepox which killed all of the lab mice.[70] For Rees, this kind of example is instructive for how we regulate biotechnology in the future. As biotechnology expands, along with other technologies such as nanotechnology, the possibility for a runaway epidemic is greatly increased. One only needs a minor accident and an aggressive virus or improperly programmed swarm of nanobots to see the real danger lying ahead.[71]

How then do these threats relate to transhumanism and, in particular, the possibility of a transhuman future? Rees suggests in many places that it would be silly to think, after Darwin, that the human species has reached some plateau and will cease to evolve—we are not the culmination of our species.[72] However, human beings are also unique in that they can directly modify what might take natural selection thousands of years. Humanity's own evolution is not subject to waiting for its advancement on the tree of life. Rees asserts that if we do get beyond this next century, it is very likely that we will reach some kind of transhuman state. As Rees states:

> But human character and physique will soon themselves be malleable. Implants into our brain (and perhaps new drugs as well) could vastly enhance some aspects of human intellectual powers. . . . Humans could then transcend biology by merging with computers. . . . If present technical trends proceeded unimpeded, then we should not dismiss Moravec's beliefs that some people now living could attain immortality.[73]

Like Kurzweil, Rees speculates that it is our ability to create super-intelligent machines that will make the most difference in our transhuman future. In fact, he conjectures that as these super-intelligent machines begin replicating themselves and create their own even more advanced super-intelligent machines it might lead to a Singularity, as Kurzweil predicts.[74] Rees wonders how these super-intelligent machines might transform our world and even our current understanding of science: 'Some of the "staples" of speculative science that flummox physicists today—time travel, space warps, and the like—may be harnessed by the new machines, transforming the world physically as well.'[75] It is clear that Rees thinks that technology will not only bring with it the possibility of imminent catastrophe, as suggested, but that it also has the potential to bring astounding areas of enhancement and growth—technology is truly volatile for Rees and is the single factor which affects the future.

What about the far future? Because Rees is a cosmologist and ultimately concerns himself with the distant future, what might be the fate of these transhumans? Rees does predict that humanity and the intelligence derived from human beings, such as super-intelligent machines created by humanity, will not be limited to earth. Recently, Rees has been advocating greater space travel using highly sophisticated robots and is advocating more unmanned spaceflights.[76] According to him, manned spaceflight should be left to adventurers as it is too costly for the public to fund especially when a cheaper alternative exists in robotics. These robotic explorers might be the vanguard for human beings to settle the far limits of our solar system.[77] Rees goes into detail explaining the viability of living on planets such as Mars which could be 'terraformed' to make it more habitable for humans. Rees projects that 'in the second half of the twenty-first century there could be hundreds of people in lunar bases, just as there now are at the South Pole; some pioneers could already be living . . . on small artificial habitats cruising the solar system, attaching themselves to asteroids or comets.'[78]

Rees looks even further into the future and speculates that the different descendents of the human race which would occupy sundry locations across the solar system could be recognisably humanoid, but would be extremely enhanced to adapt to the conditions in which they dwelt. They might not even be made of organic material, according to Rees, but instead 'genetic material, or blueprints downloaded into inorganic memories, could be launched into the cosmos in miniature spacecraft.'[79]

Moving even further taking a gigayear perspective, Rees claims that the years of advancement could lead to a near-infinite future for humanity's progeny. It is at this point in prediction that Rees's place as a cosmologist reveals the ultimate terms of the fate of humanity and the universe. Astronomers and cosmologists over the past fifty years have vacillated on the ultimate fate of the universe without a decisive conclusion. Many cosmologists in the 1960s speculated that the ultimate fate of the universe was that it would turn back in on itself and lead to the Big Crunch. Expansion would cease at some point in the future and would then reverse the process and begin contracting towards the single point out of which the Big Bang originated. They conjectured that this would continue on, *ad infinitum*, with the universe expanding and contracting infinitely like some kind of Classical or Nietzschean eternal return. Yet, this view of the cosmos has fallen out of favour in recent times, according to Rees, and leaves open the possibility of a constantly expanding universe. This seems to be good news for someone like Rees, despite the other dangers inherent in an expanding universe like the decay of atoms and the cooling universe,[80] for it leaves open the possibility of transhumans to transform the universe into a 'living cosmos'[81] without cosmic interference. The misanthropic cosmic forces might not have the final word when it comes to the future so long as we get through the next century.

4.4   NICK BOSTROM AND THE PHILOSOPHER'S PERSPECTIVE

Nick Bostrom is our final figure under consideration. Whereas Kurzweil and Rees seem to have other 'day jobs' which occupy the majority of their professional lives, transhumanism is much more the central concern of Bostrom's academic and professional life. Currently, he is the director of the Future of Humanity Institute at the University of Oxford where he is also associated with the philosophy faculty.[82] In addition to interests in the anthropic principle and scepticism,[83] Bostrom is most well known for championing the transhumanism movement and could be considered the philosophical gatekeeper of contemporary transhumanism. Most of his academic publications on transhumanism usually help define or clarify major themes and issues with which transhumanism is concerned. As mentioned at the beginning of this chapter, Bostrom helped found Humanity+ (formerly known as the World Transhumanist Organisation) and has been active in promoting transhumanism in the public sphere. He has consulted for the President's Council for Bioethics (USA), Central Intelligence Agency (USA), the European Commission, and the European Group on Ethics.[84] Recently, along with Kurzweil, he was named one of *Foreign Policy* magazine's top 100 global thinkers.[85] Needless to say, transhumanism is the one thing that Bostrom devotes himself to the most.

Like Rees, before claiming the possibility of a transhuman future Bostrom asserts that many obstacles stand in humanity's way.[86] Bostrom labels these obstacles existential risks. Bostrom defines an existential risk as 'one where an adverse outcome would either annihilate Earth-originating intelligent life or permanently curtail its potential.'[87] What typifies an existential risk from other hazards is the intensity and scope of the risk. Existential risks are both global and terminal. The population affected is the entire human population along with its potential successors. An existential risk is also terminal in that the initial shock of the event and the fallout from it cannot be endured. For example, the thinning of the ozone layer is not an existential risk because it can be endured without a terminal effect on the entire human population. Similarly, racial genocide is not an existential risk because its scope is limited to a particular group of people.[88]

Bostrom further classifies existential risks into four categories: bangs, crunches, shrieks and whimpers. The first category, bangs, entails an immediate disaster where 'Earth-originating intelligent life'[89] ends suddenly. This could be due to either an accident or from some purposeful act. Bostrom says many scenarios are probable. First, the world could suddenly end in a bang if nanotechnology were to be misused by a malevolent agent or if there was some accident with nanotechnology. Drexler's grey goo scenario falls under the accidental criteria, but it is just as likely that someone could wield nanotechnology at the expense of humanity and its environment. The power of nanotechnology to transform the world at the molecular level has vast risks associated with it. Another scenario which would end 'the human experiment' suddenly is a poorly programmed super-intelligence. An example he uses to illustrate the far-ranging consequences of such poor programming is of a possible super-intelligence which is programmed to only create paper clips and, because of its influence and power, transforms the entire universe into a massive paper clip factory.[90] Others cited in this 'bang' category are physical disasters, naturally occurring disease, a NEO impact and runaway global warming.

Not all existential risks are sudden. Bostrom also wants to include those kinds of events which would permanently hinder the advancement or growth of the human species into some kind of transhuman. These kinds of events are labelled crunches. Possible scenarios include 'resource depletion or ecological destruction', 'misguided world government', 'dysgenic pressures' and 'technological arrest'.[91] But, these scenarios do not seem as probable, according to Bostrom, because of current technological trends.

The third and fourth categories are relatively similar. The third category of existential risks is shrieks. Shrieks typify those possible scenarios where 'some form of posthumanity is attained but it is an extremely narrow band of what is possible and desirable.'[92] The important qualifier here is 'desirable'.

For instance, Bostrom invokes the flawed super-intelligence again. Suppose the transhuman stage has been reached by humanity, but instead of everyone equally enjoying the benefits of transhumanity they are instead under the control of some poorly programmed super-intelligence. This would not be desirable and is considered an existential risk.

The final possible category is the whimper. In this situation 'a posthuman civilization arises but evolves in a direction that leads gradually but irrevocably to either the complete disappearance of the things we value or to a state where those things are realized to only a miniscule degree of what could have been achieved.'[93] Much like the shriek, a transhuman existence is reached, but certain virtues have been lost and the transhuman future does not seem as desirable.[94] There are two states of affairs Bostrom cites as probable for a whimper to occur. First, the mechanisms inherent in evolution bias certain values (aggressive self-replication at the expense of play and art perhaps) over others thus leading to an incomplete and undesirable transhumanity.[95] Second, however improbable it seems that extraterrestrial life exists at present, if they do exist and are more advanced and are aggressive imperialists, then their way of life might eclipse our own.

As one can see, Bostrom goes to great lengths navigating future disaster scenarios. What isn't apparent is that Bostrom then assigns specific probabilities to each of these scenarios using Bayesian statistics amongst other methods. What Bostrom finds is that the greatest existential risks stem from a highly technological civilisation.[96] Like Rees, Bostrom identifies technology as the greatest threat to humanity's ultimate survival. Technology has the potential to lead to disastrous circumstances. Nevertheless, we should not blame civilisation or technology, Bostrom tells us, because failing to advance our current technologies is actually an existential risk itself. He unwaveringly asserts that without technology our chance of survival is close to nil.[97]

Bostrom's ultimate caveat, that we might not survive existential risks, does not keep him from conjecturing about what the possible transhuman future might look like.[98] He claims if we get beyond these kinds of risks what waits for us on the other side is nothing less than utopia. Bostrom has written an article entitled 'Letter from Utopia',[99] which is premised upon a possible future-self writing to the reader and describing all of the amazing advances and what it might be like in a transhuman world. It focuses initially on the feeling of bliss and how each moment in this new place called Utopia is greater than the best of moments now: 'You could say that I am happy, that I feel good. You could say that I feel surpassing bliss. But these are words invented to describe human experience. What I feel is as far beyond human feelings as my thoughts are beyond human thought.'[100] The speaker in the essay, the future self, gives three specific areas where humanity has advanced and where the current self is to place their efforts to make this future, possible self actual. The first is to secure life which means jettisoning one's organic body: 'Your body is a deathtrap.'[101] At first, one is to take control of the biochemical processes within their body, but then to get rid of it altogether when more 'durable media' can be found to house the mind. Second, Bostrom's author suggests focusing directly on upgrading cognition for it is the key to a more robust internal life. This invariably means, for Bostrom, that one begins to merge with the intelligences one creates by expanding one's memory to include silicon-based memory and enhancing other areas of one's cognition becoming a veritable cyborg. The final area is in elevating well-being. The speaker advocates the complete removal of suffering and promotes some kind of hedonistic situation where one finds everything pleasurable.[102] It is implied that directly tampering with one's brain might be necessary: 'The roots of suffering are planted deep in your brain. Weeding them out and replacing them with nutritious crops of well-being will require advanced skills and instruments for the cultivation of your neuronal soil.'[103]

Bostrom's 'Letter from Utopia' is telling, but its figurative language and pseudonymous authorship might be grounds for keeping Bostrom's own personal beliefs at a distance from those asserted in the essay. Luckily, Bostrom speaks elsewhere directly about the future of the human race and its intelligent successors. Much like the others who have already been discussed, Bostrom believes that humanity will not remain confined to its terrestrial moorings but will begin to spill over into its own solar system at first and then into other galaxies and ultimately the entire universe. Like Rees, Bostrom thinks that mind uploading[104] will be a major technological achievement which will both catalyse a transhuman future and will aid in our intellectual children's propagation beyond earth. Bostrom paints a picture of this advancement in the cosmos by describing a technological sphere which first begins to encompass earth, but then, when seen from the outside, will begin to expand from beyond it. Bostrom says:

> I think . . . there will be planet Earth and then there will be a sphere of technological infrastructure that will spread at some significant fraction of the speed of light in all directions. Colonisation of planets that will be transformed into some suitable infrastructure, maybe computing material. After this process has started it will just be more of the same. One million years into the future the sphere will have just grown bigger. Then you come back and look in another 10 million years nothing will have changed from the outside, it will just have grown bigger. Nothing really happens after that. That sounds like a very boring thing because it is a very predictable growth of civilisation in all directions. That will be fairly easy to predict.[105]

But, what excites Bostrom the most is the seemingly qualitative difference this technological infrastructure will seem like from the inside. In other words, it is virtually unknowable what our intellectual children will be like because we don't know how they will evolve exactly, but more than that, we don't have the relative capacity to understand them. He states, 'this sphere of technology contains life forms that are different from us. We might not be able to understand what such lives would be like. What would it be like to be a Jupiter brain? A brain the size of Jupiter. Presumably those could have thoughts, feelings and concerns that are as inaccessible to us as our concerns are to a rat.'[106]

What is clear, for Bostrom, is that this transhuman future is something both desirable and inevitable so long as the human species is not stunted or wiped out entirely. It is our decisions and good planning today which will prove how we are to fare in the future.

4.5   CONCLUSION: TRANSHUMANISM AND RELIGION

Several important observations can be made about how transhumanism approaches the future. First, all transhumanists would agree that the question of the future might be the single most important question for humanity and even for the universe.[107] As Bostrom and his Future of Humanity Institute makes clear, planning for the future is an important task which needs serious thoughtful attention. This kind of planning for the future should not be left to the writings of literature in science fiction, these transhumanists think, but because of the clear empirically verified advances in technology the scientific study of the future is essential for the human species to survive. Indeed, probabilistic and statistical futurology are at the fore of the transhumanist task in approaching the future—so much so that the future literally becomes statistical and its ontology is grounded in its ability to be calculated.[108]

Second, as was stated in the beginning of this chapter, the basic tenet that humanity is not a fixed creature, but one which is in constant transition through the forces of evolution—whether biological or technological—becomes very important for a transhumanist understanding of the future. Of course, this also leads to a particular criticism one might foresee from evolutionary biologists: Evolution does not have a *telos*. Transhumanists seem to import into their narrative an element of progress which is starkly contested and rejected by evolutionary theorists. One might say that despite their claims otherwise, they depend more upon a progressive/ utopian view of history rather than one informed by evolutionary theory.[109] Regardless, it is still important to note that this narrative of evolution begets a particular orientation to the future—one that, as Rees says, presupposes we are not the culmination of intelligent species after Darwin. This then drives the very project of transhumanism, its relation to the future, and even distinguishes it from its humanistic brother.

And, finally, transhumanists advocate that the future is entirely dependent upon the present. The future is an outworking of the causal forces of today and the decisions humans make in planning for their future today.

The speaker in Bostrom's utopia says 'What unites us is that we are all dependent on you to make us real.'[110] Or as Kurzweil quotes from a fellow transhumanist, 'One of the biggest flaws in the common conception of the future is that the future is something that happens to us, not something we create.'[111] The future is an extension of the present for transhumanism and no other force can save intelligence in the universe. It is up to humanity to safeguard its own intelligent creation. The future is defined by *futurum* and present actuality instead of the future being a reality defined beyond pure actuality.

I think it is clear from the transhumanist claims above that what they propose has greater significance to its adherents than a disengaged scientific appraisal of planning for the future. What I want to suggest is that many of the themes in transhumanism bear a remarkable similarity to common religious themes and that there is enough significant area of commonality to make such connections explicit.[112]

First, transhumanism espouses a cessation of death through technology which is indicative of religious salvation. In fact, when Kurzweil was asked by an interviewer about the religious implications of transhumanism he agreed that transhumanism fulfils many of the same functions that religion has in the past.[113] For him this is especially apparent in the shared commitment to ceasing or 'forestalling death'. As with Fedorov, death does not need to be a feature of humanity—it does not need to define humanity in any way.[114] For transhumanists such as Kurzweil and Aubrey de Grey death is seen as a disease or malady which technology can remedy. In this way, technology is a saviour from our own perishing.

Technology offers more than just a cessation of death for transhumanism. Not only does it help us escape from suffering and our demise, but, second, it also promises a kind of transcendence. Technology, from the beginning, has always had an element of transcendence. Technology extends humanity's faculties and sphere of influence. What is technology, from a simple hammer to a nuclear reactor, but an extension of our own abilities? Indeed, anthropologists for decades have often understood technology and tools to be a unique element in distinguishing humanity from other species, *homo faber*. The hope for our primate ancestors, as we will see with Teilhard de Chardin in the coming chapter, was not in the comparatively feeble body we were endowed with—we weren't equipped directly with claws or excessive strength—but our intellect and tools. According to palaeontologists what gave us the advantage, what kept us from dying out, was our mind and technology. Technology allows us to transcend many of our physical and mental limitations and transhumanism puts religious value on this transcendence.

Third, the religious themes of transformation and glorification are central tenets of transhumanism as well. Advancing technologies are applied to the human body and will transform it into anything from a cybernetic being to a bodiless piece of data. But, this transformation is not just physical. There is a complete transformation of the internal experience as well. Bostrom's 'Letter From Utopia' and his comments on the far future are clear that the transhuman inner life will be nothing short of bliss—beyond what we can even fathom today. Transhumanists assert that the transformation is entirely positive and can be likened to a kind of glorification. Transhumanist images often depict this best. One popular picture shows a transhuman towering over its evolutionary ancestors and is depicted in a glorified state. The transhuman ascends from its bestial origins complete with divine aureoles of light beaming from the head and hands referencing works of art that depict various saints or indeed Christ himself. It is clear from images such as this that transhumanism often uses religious imagery explicitly.

The final theme, hope, draws on many of these other areas. What is the transhumanist hope? First, transhumanists derive hope from technology's ability to extend their faculties and sphere of influence. Second, they hope that technology will be able to eradicate death and suffering. However, as we have seen, these are not guaranteed. Despite an ultimate hope in technology it is not without a greater narrative which posits an equal danger which must be overcome. Indeed, the basic anxiety-producing narrative of primitive human beings struggling to survive in a harsh environment with predators lurking around the corner gets extended to the cosmic scale. For transhumanists, this anxiety today stems from two much larger forces in the universe. On the cosmic scale what threatens humanity and causes anxiety are the inhospitable cosmic forces: entropy, the Big Crunch or any major astrophysical phenomenon which drastically alters the conditions of our universe and threatens the human project. But, this is on the order of thousands and millions of years—quite a long way off.

The other event which produces extreme anxiety and is much more imminent is the Singularity. The Singularity evokes both dread and hope for transhumanists. The Singularity causes anxiety because we can't see beyond its horizon. Things will be so different, according to transhumanist philosophy, that it does seem to signal a break with common history as we know it. We will no longer be the most intelligent entities we know of in the galaxy, the one thing which has kept us alive up to this point. How we relate to our super-intelligent machines through the Singularity is of vast importance as Bostrom has intimated. We could be extinguished by the very technology which has given us an advantage in history.

On the other hand, the Singularity is also a source of hope for transhumanists because it is a time of rapid advancement of the human species. It is also a source of salvation. With the technological advances promised in the Singularity, humanity might be equipped to radically alter its dangerous situation on a cosmic scale. It might be able to survive such harsh astrophysical events as the Big Crunch or the extreme cooling indicative of an ever-expanding universe. These transhumanists say that our only hope in this far, far future lies in the very technology which is also the source for our anxiety.

This opens up an entirely new line of questioning. Can this be of any hope to humanity now? If Bostrom himself states that human extinction is inevitable and that 99.99% of all species that ever existed on earth are already extinct, then why should this be of any hope for us as human beings today?[115] What then is being propagated from the human species to the transhuman species that is common and worth protecting and can provide sufficient grounds for hope for individuals living today? Metz's critique of secular utopias can be applied in this situation. As Soskice paraphrases, 'the difference between hope for the coming of God's kingdom and a secular utopian vision is this: the secular utopias envision a time that would be marvellous for those lucky enough to be alive at the time but offer little solace to those whose lives have been a means to this glorious end.'[116] Not only do transhumanists assert that many of us won't be around to reap the ultimate salvific benefits of technology, but our hope is in a species that might not be anything like us—it might not even be a notably human project.

What, then, are transhumanists trying to protect from extinction? What are they trying to safeguard and what, ultimately, is at the core of their hope? For transhumanists, it is clear that the imperative for studying the future so as to insure not only our survival, even if our progeny is not even recognisably humanoid, is to protect intelligence and rationality in the universe. Transhumanists suggest that humanity has a responsibility to intelligent life everywhere. What I think this illustrates is that ultimately the comfort transhumanism offers is that intelligence and order will triumph over disorder and anarchy. This is most apparent in the picture of the far universe that Kurzweil and Rees both put forward where the stark and inhospitable forces of physics are fighting against the development of intelligence in human evolution. The final appeal for hope seems to reside in a cosmic Manichean battle where the virtues of humanity and the people who have gone before are merely 'the means to this glorious end'.[117]

I don't think it should surprise us that a movement like transhumanism is close to religion. We have already seen how the modern technological task has, from its origin, had religious impulses. While there has been an overtly secularising tendency in these technological futurisms on the surface, the ideological and religious underpinnings have remained close at hand. What we see again here with transhumanism is that despite the secularising tendency in technological futurisms in the 19th and 20th centuries, the religious impulse is never far away from the technological impulse.

Yet, this raises the question whether there are more overtly theological narratives in our present age which consider the force of technology on the future. There must be significant theological works in the 20th century which incorporate technology not only into their theology, but also how they understand the future and eschatology. Indeed, this is the case and is the subject of the next two chapters.

NOTES

1. While there are certain variants of transhumanism which maintain a bleak picture of the future these are almost entirely eclipsed by the majority who assert a more optimistic assessment of the future. At the very least, these other pessimistic transhumanists almost always suggest that the key to overcoming these difficulties ahead is, in fact, more thoughtful technology rather than a complete eradication of technology altogether. Because of the disagreement within the transhumanist community over this issue, we will assume a transhumanist, at the very least, ascribes to technovolatility, technology will lead to extreme outcomes, and gives credence to the possibility of a transhuman future made possible through technology. See Nick Bostrom, "Transhumanist Values," *Review of Contemporary Philosophy* 4, no. (May 2005).
2. Nick Bostrom, "A History of Transhumanist Thought," *Journal of Evolution and Technology* 14 (April 2005), 12.
3. James Hughes, *Report on the 2005 Interests and Beliefs Survey of the Members of the World Transhumanist Association* (Willington, CT: World Transhumanist Association, 2005), 2.
4. World Transhumanist Association, "Chapters of Humanity+," http://humani typlus.org/get-involved/chapters-of-humanity/ (accessed 11 August 2010).
5. Nick Bostrom, "The Transhumanist FAQ: A General Introduction," World Transhumanist Organisation, http://www.transhumanism.org/resources/FAQv21.pdf (accessed 22 May 2009).
6. I am not saying that the future takes precedence over the present in transhumanism but that the future is the central theme of transhumanism. See chapters 7 and 8 for discussion on how this makes a difference.
7. Bostrom, "A History of Transhumanist Thought," 2.
8. Ibid.
9. "The *Foreign Policy* 100 Top Global Thinkers," *Foreign Policy* 176 (2009).
10. Ed Pilkington, "Ed Pilkington Meets Ray Kurzweil, the Man Who Predicts Future," *Guardian*, 2 May 2009.
11. Ray Kurzweil, *The Age of Spiritual Machines* (London: Orion, 1999), 174.
12. Ibid., 175–176.
13. Ibid., 177.
14. Kurzweil Technologies, "Ray Kurzweil: Curriculum Vitae," http://www.kurz weiltech.com/raycv.html (accessed 12 August 2010).
15. Singularity University, "History & Founding," http://singularityu.org/about/history/ (accessed 12 August 2010).
16. "Ray Kurzweil on How Technology Will Transform Us," TED (Technology, Entertainment, Design), Online Video Conference Lecture, 2005, http://www.ted.com/talks/ray_kurzweil_on_how_technology_will_transform_us.html (accessed 9 August 2010).
17. "The Future, Just around the Bend," *Economist* 374, no. 8417 (2005).
18. Ibid.
19. Kurzweil, *The Age of Spiritual Machines*, 169–170.
20. Kurzweil quotes a fellow transhumanist, Michael Anissimov: 'One of the biggest flaws in the common conception of the future is that the future is something that happens to us, not something we create.' See Ray Kurzweil, *The Singularity Is Near: When Humans Transcend Biology* (London: Duckworth, 2006), 299.
21. Kurzweil, *The Age of Spiritual Machines*, 9–10.
22. Ibid., 29.
23. Ibid., 28.

24. Ibid., 30.
25. Kurzweil, *The Singularity Is Near*, 15.
26. Kurzweil, *The Age of Spiritual Machines*, 29.
27. Ibid., 32–33.
28. Kurzweil, *The Singularity Is Near*, 16.
29. Ibid., 56–57.
30. See ibid., 66.
31. "Ray Kurzweil on How Technology Will Transform Us."
32. Kurzweil, *The Age of Spiritual Machines*, 35.
33. Ibid., 202.
34. Ibid., 203.
35. Ibid., 220.
36. Ray Kurzweil and Terry Grossman, *Fantastic Voyage: Live Long Enough to Live Forever* (Emmaus: Rodale, 2004).
37. Aubrey D.N.J. de Grey, "Escape Velocity: Why the Prospect of Extreme Human Life Extension Matters Now," *PLoS Biol* 2, no. 6 (2004).
38. Kurzweil and Grossman, *Fantastic Voyage*, 139–140.
39. Gary Wolf, "Futurist Ray Kurzweil Pulls out All the Stops (and Pills) to Live to Witness the Singularity," *Wired*, 24 March 2008.
40. Kurzweil, *The Singularity Is Near*, 214–215.
41. Ibid., 226.
42. See ibid., 254.
43. Ibid., 244.
44. Ibid., 124.
45. Ibid., 125.
46. Ibid., 7.
47. Ibid., 22.
48. For a graphical representation see ibid., 23.
49. Ibid., 135–136.
50. Kurzweil says, 'From a strictly mathematical perspective, the growth rates will still be finite but so extreme that the changes they bring about will appear to rupture the fabric of human history.' Ibid., 9.
51. Ibid., 29.
52. Indeed, Kurzweil is often asked if the Singularity is a religious belief. This relationship will be given greater attention at the end of the chapter. See VBS. TV, "The Singularity of Ray Kurzweil," *Motherboard*, 2009, http://www. vbs.tv/en-gb/watch/motherboard/the-singularity-of-ray-kurzweil (accessed 16 August 2010).
53. Surfdaddy Orca and R.U. Sirius, "Ray Kurzweil: The H+ Interview," *H+ Magazine*, Winter 2009, 43.
54. Perhaps what we are seeing here is a secular transhumanist equivalent to the *chronos* and *kairos* distinction.
55. VBS.TV.
56. Geraci and Tirosh-Samuelson also notice the religiously-motivated apocalyptic tone of transhumanism. See Robert M. Geraci, *Apocalyptic AI: Visions of Heaven in Robotics, Artificial Intelligence, and Virtual Reality* (Oxford: Oxford University Press, 2010); Hava Tirosh-Samuelson, "Transhumanism as a Secularist Faith," *Zygon* 47, no. 4 (2012), 725–726.
57. Kurzweil, *The Singularity Is Near*, 29.
58. Kurzweil, *The Age of Spiritual Machines*, 257.
59. Rees makes this distinction himself when referring to the utopian optimism of American West Coast forecasters. In reference to cryogenics he states, 'Well for my part I'd sooner end my days in an English churchyard rather than in a Californian refrigerator.' See University of Cambridge, "Lord Martin Rees, What Does the Future Hold?," *Darwin Festival 2009*, http://www.sms.cam.ac.uk/

media/667416 (accessed 5 October 2010); Martin Rees, *Our Final Hour: A Scientist's Warning: How Terror, Error, and Environmental Disaster Threaten Humankind's Future in This Century—on Earth and Beyond* (New York: Basic Books, 2003), 21. Rees prefers to use the term 'posthuman' when speaking about the next step in human evolutionary history, and while it is true that his ties with the transhumanist movement are not as clear as with Kurzweil and Bostrom, many of his contentions on the evolutionary future of the cosmos are similar enough to the transhumanist narrative for him to be included here.

60. Martin Rees, "Martin Rees," http://www.ast.cam.ac.uk/~mjr/ (accessed 12 November 2010).
61. Martin Rees, "Templeton Prize 2011: Full Transcript of Martin Rees's Acceptance Speech," *Guardian*, 6 April 2011.
62. This is not to say Kurzweil does not project on the order of thousands if not millions of years, but that, as a technologist, the majority of his speculation is imminent and grounded in current trends and their influence in the next decades and century.
63. See TEDGlobal, "Martin Rees Asks: Is This Our Final Century?," TED. Lecture, January 2007, http://www.ted.com/talks/martin_rees_asks_is_this_our_final_century.html (accessed 14 November 2010).
64. Martin Rees, "The Science of Eternity," *Prospect* 70 (January 2002), http://www.prospectmagazine.co.uk/2002/01/thescienceofeternity/.
65. Rees, *Our Final Hour*, 8.
66. Ibid., 90ff.
67. Ibid., 25.
68. Ibid., 29.
69. Ibid., 120.
70. Ibid., 57.
71. For nanotechnology, this is often called the 'grey goo' threat. The premise is that self-replicating nanobots might malfunction and transform the entire world into a kind of 'grey goo'. See K. Eric Drexler, *Engines of Creation 2.0* (Wowio, 2006).
72. The Long Now Foundation, "Martin Rees: Life's Future in the Cosmos," fora.tv, August 2010, http://fora.tv/2010/08/02/Martin_Rees_Lifes_Future_in_the_Cosmos#fullprogram (accessed 15 November 2010); Martin Rees, "We Are Custodians of a Posthuman Future," in *What Have You Changed Your Mind About?: Today's Leading Minds Rethink Everything*, ed., John Brockman (New York: Harper Perennial, 2009).
73. Rees, *Our Final Hour*, 18–19.
74. Ibid., 19.
75. Ibid.
76. Cian O'Luanaigh, "No Need for Manned Spaceflight, Says Astronomer Royal Martin Rees," *Guardian*, 26 July 2010.
77. Rees, *Our Final Hour*, 177.
78. Ibid., 180.
79. Ibid., 181.
80. Rees, "The Science of Eternity."
81. Rees, *Our Final Hour*, 182.
82. Nick Bostrom, "Nick Bostrom's Home Page," http://www.nickbostrom.com/ (accessed 16 November 2010).
83. Bostrom has written a book on how observation selection affects the anthropic principle in Nick Bostrom, *Anthropic Bias: Observation Selection Effects in Science and Philosophy* (London: Routledge, 2002). Additionally, his other philosophical writings seem to cluster around quantifying the probability that humanity is in a simulation. See Nick Bostrom, "Are You Living in a Computer Simulation?," *Philosophical Quarterly* 53, no. 211 (2003).

84. Institute for Ethics and Emerging Technologies, "Nick Bostrom," http://ieet. org/index.php/IEET/bio/bostrom/ (accessed 16 November 2010).

85. Bostrom, "Nick Bostrom's Home Page."

86. In fact, Rees wrote the foreword to Bostrom's edited volume which considers these obstacles in detail. See Nick Bostrom and Milan M. Ćirković, eds., *Global Catastrophic Risks* (Oxford: Oxford University Press, 2008).

87. Nick Bostrom, "Existential Risks: Analyzing Human Extinction Scenarios and Related Hazards," *Journal of Evolution and Technology* 9, no. 1 (2002), 2.

88. This, and what follows, is taken mostly from Bostrom, "Existential Risks."

89. Ibid., 5.

90. Closer to Truth, "What Is the Far Far Future of Humans in the Universe? (Nick Bostrom)," 2010, http://www.closertotruth.com/video-profile/ What-is-the-Far-Far-Future-of-Humans-in-the-Universe-Nick-Bostrom-/1070 (accessed 17 November 2010).

91. Bostrom, "Existential Risks," 11–12.

92. Ibid., 5.

93. Ibid.

94. This is important because it shows that Bostrom is well aware that a transhuman future does not necessarily entail a positive future or one which is desirable because certain virtues of the human experience have been lost. While he cites this as a risk one of my major criticisms will be that key areas of the human experience are actually lost in all proposed futures transhumanists proclaim.

95. See Nick Bostrom, "The Future of Human Evolution," in *Death and Anti-Death: Two Hundred Years after Kant, Fifty Years after Turing*, ed., Charles Tandy (Palo Alto: Ria University Press, 2004).

96. Bostrom, "Existential Risks," 19.

97. Ibid., 20.

98. In fact, he is accused by an annoyed interviewer of always making this proviso before he launches into what the future of mankind might be like. When asked why he does this he responds, 'Because I think it is an extremely important qualification.' See Closer to Truth, "What Is the Far Far Future of Humans in the Universe?"

99. Nick Bostrom, "Letter from Utopia," *Studies in Ethics, Law, and Technology* 2, no. 1 (2008).

100. Ibid., 3.

101. Ibid.

102. Indeed, it is precisely writings like these which reveal what transhumanists really think is to be safeguarded in the human experience and worth pursuing. What they find most important and worth safeguarding in the human experience is very reductive and overly simplistic.

103. Bostrom, "Letter from Utopia," 5.

104. For a sustained treatment of mind uploading and its consequences see Nick Bostrom, "The Future of Humanity," in *New Waves in Philosophy of Technology*, ed., Jan Kyrre Berg Olsen, Evan Selinger, and Søren Riis (Basingstoke: Palgrave MacMillan, 2009), 206ff.

105. Closer to Truth, "What Is the Far Far Future of Humans in the Universe?"

106. Ibid.

107. I say the universe because, for transhumanism, the ultimate fate of the universe, whether it is transformed into some intelligent cosmos or collapses into greater entropy, seems to hinge upon how humanity today directs its affairs.

108. Rees might be the only one who would allow some amount of mystery in the future universe. But, he would say that it is only mysterious to us because our minds have not been enhanced. The future is still a product of forces inherent in the present but we can't know all of these yet but, he intimates, perhaps our

transhuman children may. See Martin Rees and Krista Tippett, "Cosmic Origami and What We Don't Know," *American Public Media*, interview, 2 June 2011, http://being.publicradio.org/programs/2011/cosmic-origami/transcript.shtml (accessed 16 August 2011).

109. Transhumanists might be happy, at this point, to disassociate themselves with evolutionary biologists and assert that technological evolution is distinct in that it has a greater teleology and an element of progress. But, this might serve my point that they have inherited more from a progressive view of history than from an evolutionary narrative.

110. Bostrom, "Letter from Utopia," 1.

111 Kurzweil, *The Singularity Is Near*, 299.

112. Indeed others have noted this explicit connection as well. See Geraci, *Apocalyptic AI*; Tirosh-Samuelson, "Transhumanism"; Brent Waters, "Whose Salvation? Which Eschatology?: Transhumanism and Christianity as Contending Salvific Religions," in *Transhumanism and Transcendence: Christian Hope in an Age of Technological Enhancement*, ed., Ronald Cole-Turner (Washington, DC: Georgetown University Press, 2011).

113. MemeBox, "Ray Kurzweil: The Singularity Is Not a Religion," interview, 27 October 2008, http://www.youtube.com/watch?v=CLy0tTfw8i0 (accessed 17 May 2012).

114. This is quite a superlative claim especially when, as we will see in chapter 7 on Heidegger, others have proposed that human beings are entirely defined by their own death and that living with this fact is entirely central to their authenticity. And, as we shall see in the final two chapters, a Christian response to death does not deny death but recognises we are freed from it in Christ. We are given a new possibility beyond death.

115. This is because either they die out or are transformed into a new species. See Bostrom, "The Future of Humanity," 194.

116. Janet Martin Soskice, "The Ends of Man and the Future of God," in *The End of the World and the Ends of God: Science and Theology on Eschatology*, ed., J.C. Polkinghorne and Michael Welker (Harrisburg: Trinity Press International, 2000), 78.

117. Chapter 9 will give an extended Christian response to this.

REFERENCES

Bostrom, Nick. *Anthropic Bias: Observation Selection Effects in Science and Philosophy*. London: Routledge, 2002.
———. "Existential Risks: Analyzing Human Extinction Scenarios and Related Hazards." *Journal of Evolution and Technology* 9, no. 1 (2002).
———. "Are You Living in a Computer Simulation?" *Philosophical Quarterly* 53, no. 211 (2003): 243–255.
———. "The Future of Human Evolution." In *Death and Anti-Death: Two Hundred Years after Kant, Fifty Years after Turing*, edited by Charles Tandy. Palo Alto: Ria University Press, 2004.
———. "A History of Transhumanist Thought." *Journal of Evolution and Technology* 14 (April 2005).
———. "Transhumanist Values." *Review of Contemporary Philosophy* 4 (May 2005).
———. "Letter from Utopia." *Studies in Ethics, Law, and Technology* 2, no. 1 (2008): 1–7.
———. "The Future of Humanity." In *New Waves in Philosophy of Technology*, edited by Jan Kyrre Berg Olsen, Evan Selinger, and Søren Riis. Basingstoke: Palgrave MacMillan, 2009.

———. "The Transhumanist FAQ: A General Introduction." World Transhumanist Organisation. http://www.transhumanism.org/resources/FAQv21.pdf (accessed 22 May 2009).

———. "Nick Bostrom's Home Page." http://www.nickbostrom.com/ (accessed 16 November 2010).

Bostrom, Nick, and Ćirković, Milan M., eds. *Global Catastrophic Risks*. Oxford: Oxford University Press, 2008.

Closer to Truth. "What Is the Far Far Future of Humans in the Universe? (Nick Bostrom)." 2010. http://www.closertotruth.com/video-profile/What-is-the-Far-Far-Future-of-Humans-in-the-Universe-Nick-Bostrom-/1070 (accessed 17 November 2010).

de Grey, Aubrey D. N. J. "Escape Velocity: Why the Prospect of Extreme Human Life Extension Matters Now." *PLoS Biol* 2, no. 6 (2004): e187.

Drexler, K. Eric. *Engines of Creation 2.0*. Wowio, 2006.

"The *Foreign Policy* 100 Top Global Thinkers." *Foreign Policy* 176 (2009): 25–76.

"The Future, Just around the Bend." *Economist* 374, no. 8417 (2005): 37–38.

Geraci, Robert M. *Apocalyptic AI: Visions of Heaven in Robotics, Artificial Intelligence, and Virtual Reality*. Oxford: Oxford University Press, 2010.

Hughes, James. *Report on the 2005 Interests and Beliefs Survey of the Members of the World Transhumanist Association*. Willington, CT: World Transhumanist Association, 2005.

Institute for Ethics and Emerging Technologies, "Nick Bostrom." http://ieet.org/index.php/IEET/bio/bostrom/ (accessed 16 November 2010).

Kurzweil, Ray. *The Age of Spiritual Machines*. London: Orion, 1999.

———. *The Singularity Is Near: When Humans Transcend Biology*. London: Duckworth, 2006.

Kurzweil, Ray, and Terry Grossman. *Fantastic Voyage: Live Long Enough to Live Forever*. Emmaus: Rodale, 2004.

Kurzweil Technologies. "Ray Kurzweil: Curriculum Vitae." http://www.kurzweiltech.com/raycv.html (accessed 12 August 2010).

MemeBox. "Ray Kurzweil: The Singularity Is Not a Religion." Interview, 27 October 2008. http://www.youtube.com/watch?v = CLy0tTfw8i0 (accessed 17 May 2012).

O'Luanaigh, Cian. "No Need for Manned Spaceflight, Says Astronomer Royal Martin Rees." *Guardian*, 26 July 2010.

Orca, Surfdaddy, and R. U. Sirius. "Ray Kurzweil: The H+ Interview." *H+ Magazine*, Winter 2009.

Pilkington, Ed. "Ed Pilkington Meets Ray Kurzweil, the Man Who Predicts Future." *Guardian*, 2 May 2009.

"Ray Kurzweil on How Technology Will Transform Us." 2005. TED (Technology, Entertainment, Design). Online Video Conference Lecture. http://www.ted.com/talks/ray_kurzweil_on_how_technology_will_transform_us.html (accessed 9 August 2010).

Rees, Martin. "The Science of Eternity." *Prospect* 70 (January 2002). http://www.prospectmagazine.co.uk/2002/01/thescienceofeternity/ (accessed 12 November 2010).

———. *Our Final Hour: A Scientist's Warning: How Terror, Error, and Environmental Disaster Threaten Humankind's Future in This Century—on Earth and Beyond*. New York: Basic Books, 2003.

———. "We Are Custodians of a Posthuman Future." In *What Have You Changed Your Mind About?: Today's Leading Minds Rethink Everything*, edited by John Brockman. New York: Harper Perennial, 2009.

———. "Martin Rees." http://www.ast.cam.ac.uk/~mjr/ (accessed 12 November 2010).

————. "Templeton Prize 2011: Full Transcript of Martin Rees's Acceptance Speech." *Guardian*, 6 April 2011.

Rees, Martin, and Krista Tippett. "Cosmic Origami and What We Don't Know." *American Public Media*. Interview, 2 June 2011. http://being.publicradio.org/programs/2011/cosmic-origami/transcript.shtml (accessed 16 August 2011).

Singularity University, "History & Founding." http://singularityu.org/about/history/ (accessed 12 August 2010).

Soskice, Janet Martin. "The Ends of Man and the Future of God." In *The End of the World and the Ends of God: Science and Theology on Eschatology*, edited by J. C. Polkinghorne and Michael Welker. Harrisburg: Trinity Press International, 2000.

Tandy, Charles, ed. *Death and Anti-Death: One Hundred Years after N. F. Fedorov (1829–1903)*. Vol. 1. Palo Alto: Ria University Press, 2003.

TEDGlobal. "Martin Rees Asks: Is This Our Final Century?" TED Lecture, January 2007. http://www.ted.com/talks/martin_rees_asks_is_this_our_final_century.html (accessed 14 November 2010).

The Long Now Foundation. "Martin Rees: Life's Future in the Cosmos." fora.tv, August 2010. http://fora.tv/2010/08/02/Martin_Rees_Lifes_Future_in_the_Cosmos#fullprogram (accessed 15 November 2010).

Tirosh-Samuelson, Hava. "Transhumanism as a Secularist Faith." *Zygon* 47, no. 4 (2012): 710–734.

University of Cambridge. "Lord Martin Rees, What Does the Future Hold?" *Darwin Festival 2009*. http://www.sms.cam.ac.uk/media/667416 (accessed 5 October 2010).

VBS.TV. "The Singularity of Ray Kurzweil." *Motherboard*, 2009. http://www.vbs.tv/en-gb/watch/motherboard/the-singularity-of-ray-kurzweil (accessed 16 August 2010).

Verdoux, Philippe. "Transhumanism, Progress and the Future." *Journal of Evolution and Technology* 20, no. 2 (2009).

Waters, Brent. "Whose Salvation? Which Eschatology?: Transhumanism and Christianity as Contending Salvific Religions." In *Transhumanism and Transcendence: Christian Hope in an Age of Technological Enhancement*, edited by Ronald Cole-Turner. Washington, DC: Georgetown University Press, 2011.

Wolf, Gary. "Futurist Ray Kurzweil Pulls out All the Stops (and Pills) to Live to Witness the Singularity." *Wired*, 24 March 2008.

World Transhumanist Association, "Chapters of Humanity+." http://humanityplus.org/get-involved/chapters-of-humanity/ (accessed 11 August 2010).

Part II

Theological Responses to Technology and the Future

5 Pierre Teilhard de Chardin and Eschatology
The Technological Optimist

Pierre Teilhard de Chardin is one of two theological figures in the past century who has reflected seriously on the force of technology in shaping the future. The other is Jacques Ellul, who will be the subject of the next chapter. Both allow technology to figure prominently in their respective eschatologies and can help contextualise, orient and define what a Christian response to technology and the future might look like. And, more specifically, both can also help Christians to respond to transhumanism and the transhumanist future.

While others might have been advantageous to consider,[1] Ellul and Teilhard represent two very distinct and opposing strands within the Christian tradition on eschatology and how technology might be incorporated into it. Both epitomise the boundary responses to the Christian construction of the future and to Christianity's relation to technology. As we shall see in the next chapter, Ellul represents the techno-pessimist who is entirely sceptical of the force of technology on society and is critical of humanity's unreflective acceptance of it. Ellul's eschatology is directed by an apocalyptic narrative where God's kingdom breaks into a world that is enslaved by its own technological creations. Teilhard, while not accepting technology without some reservations, is very positive about its impact on the world and the future. Teilhard prefers a more progressive eschatology where the Christian future is not apocalyptic but dovetails seamlessly with the forces inherent in history and the present. Both are invaluable resources for the present text on technology and the future because their treatment of both the Christian future and technology are not marginal to the rest of their work but a robust and significant portion of it.

Because Teilhard's approach to the future and eschatology is progressive, an account of how he understands history, or the tendencies within history, is absolutely essential to understanding how he envisions the future and the eschaton. For this reason, the first part of the chapter will focus on Teilhard's account of history before turning to his eschatology. As he himself states, '. . . nothing is comprehensible except through its history,'[2] and this is the case with Teilhard's account of the future.

5.1   TEILHARD DE CHARDIN AND HISTORY

Before turning directly to Teilhard's account of history it needs to be understood that, for Teilhard, evolution is the driving force behind history and is the dominant feature in all of Teilhard's contentions. As he states:

> Is evolutionary theory a system or hypothesis? It is much more: it is a general condition to which all theories, all hypotheses, all systems must bow and which they must satisfy henceforward if they are to be thinkable and true. Evolution is a light illuminating all facts, a curve that all lines must follow.[3]

However, for Teilhard, evolution is not solely a feature of biological organisms. He is in agreement with contemporary transhumanists that evolution is a feature of the entire cosmos. In this way, the cosmos and universe, on the most macroscopic level, are in a state of genesis and transformation and this extends to each particular and specific history within the cosmos as well: Cosmogenesis is seamless with biogenesis, which in turn leads to anthropogenesis. What this adherence to evolution shows is Teilhard's more general ontological presupposition of the priority of becoming over static being.[4] Indeed, all that *is* is in process of becoming. This idea is captured in the Teilhardian term ontogenesis. This becoming is not purposeless as contemporary evolutionary biologists might contend, but Teilhard is a firm advocate in the progress of history and advancement toward a particular end. Reality is in a state of flux, but it also has a *telos*. It is because of this directionality that evolution provides the greatest amount of meaning for today.[5]

A second point of clarification before turning to Teilhard's account of history concerns his use of dialectics. His contention that the world is progressing in history can only be expressed in the form of a dialectical relationship. Several dialectics frame Teilhard's contentions and are related to one another. The most far-reaching dialectic follows two distinct strands in the history told by Teilhard. They are the *within* and the *without* of things. Each history, although distinct in its own right, parallels the other and they not only correspond but even interact. Relating very closely to this is Teilhard's dialectic of material and spirit. Science analyses the world of matter, but must find its crown in the working of spirit. Teilhard also maintains a strict dialectic between humanity and the rest of the cosmos. Humanity is, for the first time, able to consciously comprehend the meaning of the universe in thought and yet is also a product of the cosmological evolution itself. It is in the personal that the universal is fully known and realised. Finally, a further dialectic can be found in the impetus in history which comes not only from within the world itself, but is also drawn from the eschaton towards its particular end. The future depends not only upon worldly actuality as it pushes towards the future, but upon God who pulls it towards its completion.[6]

5.1.1   Terrestrial History and Biogenesis

Teilhard's methodology for giving an account of history begins with a strong scientific basis. Rather than interpreting biblical texts as a foundation for informing the beginning of history, he relies upon the various branches of science which seek to reconstruct a naturalistic picture of prehistory.[7] In doing so, Teilhard utilises complexity, rather than immensity, as the key to analyse the world. Rather than viewing the natural world according to pure measure and magnitude, as if scale dictated what is most important in natural history, he chooses to analyse it according to its relative complexity. What this means practically speaking is that, in terms of cosmological history, the history of what happens on the earth seems rather insignificant when compared with the entirety of what happens around the entire universe. But, if the measure of complexity is the standard, then the events on earth are absolutely vital to natural history.

Teilhard observes that the most complex molecular structures are those which are organic and are the building blocks for life on earth. If one wishes to understand history according to complexity then we need to follow this trajectory. Carbon strands combine to form various proteins which in turn become the basis for cellular life. As is common knowledge, life begins with cells. But not enough attention is given to pre-life and the transition to life. Despite this controversial area, it is through this transition that Teilhard begins his story.[8]

One of the most controversial areas in the evolution to life concerns the qualitative jump from nonlife to life—from merely organic mega-molecules to an actual cellular system which is alive. There are several reasons Teilhard gives in explaining the difficulty of transitioning from mega-molecules to cells. First, he suggests the discovery of origins is always difficult. As he states, '. . . when we come to deal with the first appearance of man on the earth, the "beginnings," in every field, are lost to us: the past swallows them up and our eyes can no longer decipher them'.[9] Second, a perspectival bias leads to the problem of taxonomy.[10] Scientists, when considering mega-molecules, classify them amidst the physico-chemical world. In doing so, the molecules are said to behave according to the particular set of forms and laws of the physico-chemical world. The entire premise of classification and the separation of entities by qualitative properties make progressive evolution very difficult. However, as Teilhard claims, this reflects more of our insufficient classifications rather than the actual physical phenomena we wish to classify. Third, there doesn't seem to be evidence of genuine intermediaries between mega-molecules and cells. Teilhard rebuts this accusation by suggesting that certain viruses and bacteria could be the link between protoplasm and mineral, for not only do their molecular weights bridge this gap, but both even behave like cells.[11]

These issues aside, Teilhard states that enough evidence exists to make the claim that life must have arisen out of the physico-chemical world and that organic chemistry naturally flows into biology and the development of cellular life. Teilhard speculates upon three conditions which must have aided the transition from mega-molecules to life and the greater prevalence of cellular life over these massive organic chains. The first is the necessary environmental conditions which must have been present to nurture cellular life over these other molecules. Teilhard states:

> In the first place, its appearance and development must have been narrowly dependent on the transformation of the general conditions, chemical and thermal, prevailing on the surface of the planet. In contrast to life, which seems to have spread with an inherent speed in practically stable materials surroundings, the mega-molecules must have developed according to the earth's *sidereal* rhythm, i.e. incredibly slow.[12]

Second, over countless generations there must have been a sufficient amount of these transitory entities to beget an entire movement towards the more stable cell. In other words, it had to occur with enough numbers to sustain growth. Third, all of these conditions require a very significant portion of time to allow for the small but significant incremental growth towards the cellular revolution. Teilhard speculates that 'the formation of proteins on the surface of the earth was as long as, perhaps longer than, the whole of geological time from the Cambrian period to the present day.'[13] Copious amounts of time are required for any major significant shift in evolutionary history, but things do change and one can trace the qualitative differences if one steps back far enough.

It is with the development and deployment of cellular life that such a universally significant event occurs on the planet. A qualitative leap forward is produced with the advent of the cell as the tree of life and the biosphere are created. Several characteristics of the biosphere and the tree of life aid in this propagation and continual genesis along the line of life. The first major theme is seen at the origin of multicellular organisms. The grouping of several key strands arose out of monocellular, homogenous life.[14] Distinct families which shared similar forms arose out of this dispersed, primordial mass. Plants and animals are the most important of these that grow out of the monocellular organisms. This first birth out of the more simple organisms is enacted in a fan-like matter where a vast multiplicity of organic life adapt to their distinct environments and group together to form similar envelopes on the earth's surface. This cleavage and condensation continues as the biosphere becomes more robust and varied.

Several other characteristics aided in the success and propagation of life across the earth and are important characteristics of the tree of life. The first relates to reproduction and multiplication.[15] At the heart of this propagation is the ability of cells to undergo mitosis. Cells split as particular centres form distinct units. What was once a mechanism for survival becomes 'promptly transformed and used as an instrument for progress and conquest.'[16] This ability to multiply does not seem to reach an asymptotic stability, but persists in its development. In fact, this progression is not linear. As each cell is capable of division, this in turn necessitates geometric growth and an uncanny ability to spread across the surface of the earth very quickly.

Second, the cellular revolution rests upon renovation and conjugation.[17] The genetic mutations inherent in mitosis produce a gamut of offspring which not only propagate their own type, but also renovate and substitute certain phenotypical characteristics which in turn, if advantageous, spread to adapt the phylum to its particular surroundings. Conjugation is the mere extension of multiplication, but at a much more macroscopic level. Just as cells divide and spread, so do much more complex forms of life. This action aids in the diversification of these higher phyla.

The final characteristics of the tree of life, according to Teilhard, are association and controlled additivity.[18] Each respective centre of life, whether it is the simplest cell or even the human being itself, is confined to the mechanical proximity of others who are the same. While not going into spiritual causes for this phenomenon just yet,[19] Teilhard suggests association amongst similar entities provides a distinct advantage against 'innumerable external obstacles . . . which paralyse the microscopic organisms'[20] and also provides a size 'physically necessary for certain movements'.[21]

Teilhard also contends that each phylum exerts a certain ability to add to itself in a controlled manner. Much like a cell's capacity to renovate, each phylum does more than merely substitute certain traits over time without a particular purpose. As Teilhard asserts, 'But when we look deeper and more generally we see that the rejuvenations made possible by each reproduction achieve something more than mere substitution. They *add*, one to the other, and their sum increases in a *pre-determined direction*.'[22] Teilhard, as has been made plain, asserts that a direction exists in the evolutionary process and that increased complexity is visible over time. Yet, however controversial this *telos* is, it remains for Teilhard the most important and trusted phenomenon. Orthogenesis is a reality for Teilhard for without it 'life would only have spread; with it there is an ascent of life that is invincible.'[23]

Teilhard's identification of a leading shoot on the tree of life is entirely dependent upon his avowal of orthogenesis. For, just as life continues the line of progression on the planet so too does a particular strand of life lead the biosphere in its advancement towards the end of history. In identifying this lead shoot, Teilhard goes to great lengths tracing each particular phylum through its advancement in history. From the earliest amphibian and reptile to the more highly developed mammals, Teilhard adapts a new scale for identifying increased complexity in these more advanced creatures. Using the molecular weight and chemical complexity of an organism to place it on the spectrum of complexity is too difficult and tedious a task. Instead, Teilhard observes that analysing the intricacy of the nervous system in these more sophisticated phyla is the way to identify complexity for these higher organisms.[24] Using this measure will aid in discovering the prime phylum which is at the forefront of orthogenesis.

Teilhard notes that the most intricate of nervous systems resides in mammals. Moreover, the brain represents the capstone of the nervous system and is the chief manifestation of a fully mature organism. In this history of the nervous system and the brain the primates are pinpointed as having the most advanced brains. While other phyla had features which gave them a distinct mechanical advantage like pronounced claws, sharpened teeth and greater speed, the primates 'represent a phylum of *pure and direct cerebralisation.*'[25] While not giving an overt advantage in the beginning, it would later become the most important aspect in relation to these other mutations for it created a more malleable species with advanced instincts and a more versatile body. The primates represent the pinnacle of mammalian life and man is the summit of the primates according to the study of the advancement of nervous tissue. Teilhard claims 'that if the mammals form a dominant branch, *the* dominant branch of the tree of life, the primates (i.e. the cerebro-manuals) are its leading shoot, and the anthropoids are the bud in which this shoot ends up.'[26]

Man is the apex of biogenesis and if one desires to understand the progression of the universe further then the main line of inquiry must shift to the phenomenon of man in particular. It is to this that we now turn.

5.1.2   Anthropogenesis to Date

An epochal shift in the history of the universe occurs with the advent of man. It is with man that the standard notion of evolution seems to change and trends which existed prior to man do not seem to hold or at least are masked by the strength of the new trends ushered in by the phenomenon of man. Natural selection and the survival of the fittest are natural laws which seem to govern the tree of life prior to the human phenomenon, but, as Teilhard asserts, these mechanisms are not sufficient in describing the history of this new epoch.[27]

The germination of thought and reflection represent the greatest qualitative leap forward on the surface of the planet and in the universe. In order to fully comprehend this emergence we must turn to Teilhard's more basic dialectic only briefly mentioned until now. For it is with humanity that this dialectic makes the most sense and provides the greatest basis for its acceptance.

Very early on in Teilhard's *The Phenomenon of Man* he draws a distinction between two distinct aspects of the world. The first has already been elucidated in relation to Teilhard's interpretation of history. This history concerns the *without* of things. The *without* is simply that which is external and physical in the world. The *without* is governed by scientific and natural laws. The *without* is based upon the world of matter: Chemical laws and physics are the prime way of understanding the *without*. Teilhard's phenomenology not only includes that which is empirically observable. The opposing side of the dialectic is termed the *within* of things. As implied, the *within* is not something one can observe with one's eyes and ears or other bodily senses, but is just as important and real. The *within* is an aspect of all reality. Indeed, all material contains a *within* and is inherent in everything. Just as all physical matter has a particular mass, density and volume so too does all matter contain a *within*. The *within* is more difficult to visualise when considering more simplistic forms of matter. Therefore, Teilhard suggests that one first analyse the phenomenon of man to best understand the *within*.

When one considers man as a particular phylum on the tree of life one cannot help but recognise a new capacity which could potentially transform life. The *within* is directly related to this new capacity. This new capacity is merely the most complex instantiation of the *within* in history: human consciousness. And with the discovery of this new phenomenon comes the need to make room for a new category in the universe. As Teilhard suggests, 'consciousness is evident in man . . . therefore, half-seen in this one flash of light, it has a cosmic extension, and as such is surrounded by an aura of indefinite spatial and temporal extensions.'[28] Human consciousness does not fit into the general naturalistic view of the world when taken from the perspective of the *without* alone. Something more is implied in human consciousness and, as a scientist, Teilhard aims to be consistent when approaching nature and understands the implications of human consciousness and its manifestation of a new category of reality. Human consciousness implies a *within*. But what rules govern this new sphere and how does it relate to the realm of the *without*?

Teilhard offers three observations which help to define and characterise the *within*. The *within* parallels the structure of the *without* in its atomicity. As Teilhard describes it, 'Looked at from *within* . . . the stuff of the universe thus stands likewise to be resolved backwardly into a test of particles that are perfectly alike among themselves . . . each co-extensive with the whole of the cosmic realm . . . mysteriously connected among themselves, finally, by a global energy.'[29] Similarly, the second observation links this notion of atomicity with time by asserting the increased complexification of the *within* as history advances. It is with the third observation that Teilhard links directly the *within* and *without* of things. He does so by asserting that 'spiritual perfection (or conscious "centreity") and material synthesis (or complexity) are but the two aspects or connected parts of one and the same phenomenon.'[30] This third observation denotes a key element in relating the *within* to the *without* in that each is a separate sphere relating to a common history and evolution. Both realms remain ontically distinct, but share in a common force which is pushing towards a particular end. For example, Teilhard contends that atoms do coalesce to form greater molecules because of physical laws, but he also asserts that this attraction corresponds to the general trend of the *within* towards greater unification. Teilhard states:

> At a lower level than our souls, there are, no doubt, many interconnections that we speak of as material . . . but these vast fundamental links should not be regarded as proceeding from our roots in matter. We should see them as the symptoms of far-reaching pre-spiritual union, effected, before the appearance of thought, by some sort of *formae cosmicae*: these latter being imposed on the Multiple by a breath from on high. . . . We should say that transience is *an effect*, not of *matter*, but Spirit. What binds the monads together is not, properly speaking, the body, but the soul.[31]

In this way, half of the phenomena have been neglected in our account of history because the general topology of history must be seen in light of the *without* and the *within*.

We now have the necessary structure in place to understand why man is so important and unique for Teilhard. Indeed, it is the appearance of thought which necessitates a categorical interruption of a strictly naturalistic view of the world. As has been noted, this interruption is not something which only takes place with the appearance of man, but is even present amongst more primordial forms of matter and act as forerunners for the emergence of thought and consciousness. As Teilhard states, 'The principle I mean is that consciousness is the peculiar and specific property of *organized states* of matter; it is a property that cannot be detected, and may therefore be neglected in practice, with low values of complexity, but that gradually emerges and finally becomes dominant, with high values.'[32] As suggested, something is brought to bear in the world, with the advent of consciousness, which represents more than a mere interruption in the advancement of a contiguous history. An entirely new and qualitatively different earth is created, for what was once the prime factor in shaping the history of the world has been trumped. According to Teilhard, the *without* primarily governed ontogenesis prior to man, but with his arrival the *within* is most efficacious. We now turn to Teilhard's explanation of how a local phenomenon and slight modification on the tree of life has instituted a global and universal phenomenon.

The origin of thought is like other origins Teilhard has sought to elucidate: cloaked in mystery. However, in thinking about the occurrence of consciousness and the history which has resulted from this phenomenon several things can be said with a degree of certainty which aids in this otherwise tacit point in the development of man. The first is that life must have been preparing a series of factors which culminated in thought itself.[33] Although these individual factors, taken on their own, seem at first sight to be unrelated, one observes that as time progresses these differing traits become providentially intertwined. When taken from the perspective of the *within* the ancestor of human consciousness is animal instinct. Teilhard goes to some length tracing the increasing complexity of instinct in each progressive phylum.[34] These instincts, which resemble a kind of prereflection, then become consciousness in man. Similarly, when analysing consciousness in view of the evolution of the brain and other physical characteristics—taken from the *without*—these individual factors seem like stepping stones towards greater complexity.[35]

The second thing one can induce about the origin of thought is that it must have occurred in a single stride.[36] Teilhard recognises that if something radically and categorically new is observed then this must occur in a single crossing: 'If the threshold of reflection is really . . . a critical transformation, a mutation from zero to everything, it is impossible for us to imagine an intermediary individual at this precise level. Either this being has not yet reached, or it has already got beyond, this change of state.'[37] This is not to say that growth within each successive level is impossible or further that a gradient does not exist on either side of the state change, but at a certain point hominids transitioned from merely having complex instincts to simple consciousness. Teilhard makes clear that this switch into new territory does not signal an end for growth in the human phylum, merely a new space.

Moving from the origin of thought, Teilhard defines two terms which represent the furthering of consciousness across space, so that the entire world is covered, and also across time as well. The first concerns the increased complexity of each individual being in the particular phylum as its centricity grows and the *within* becomes more complex. This is referred to as personalisation and will be dealt with more in the following section. The second term Teilhard defines as hominisation. Hominisation is 'the individual and instantaneous leap from instinct to thought, but it is also, in a wider sense, the progressive phyletic spiritualisation in human civilisation of all the forces contained in the animal world.'[38] This signifies the spreading of consciousness as a basic mutation amidst the sundry forms of hominids. Teilhard notes that the prehuman branch behaves like any other variety of the animal kingdom in its speciation and honing of each particular branch.[39] Several factors also distinguish it completely from other species on the tree of life—it is these which aid in the initial planetisation and hominisation of the species.

The first factor is the extraordinary power of expansion. Man has an uncanny ability to expand like no other species. Teilhard points to the discovery of various anthropoids in various regions around the globe.[40] The second aspect concerns the extreme rapidity of differentiation.[41] More specifically, Teilhard analyses the anatomical characteristics of subsequent hominids. In so doing, Teilhard claims the evolution of man is much faster than others. The dimensions of the brain, the flattening of the face and the specialisation of the lower limbs seem to morph at an incredible rate.[42] Third, man differs from other species in his extreme persistence of phyletic germinative power.[43] Other species which branch into a multiplicity of varying types at their origin only last for a very short amount of time while the more dominant phylums stay the course. Their common ancestry gets lost in time while the different families diverge from one another. Man is distinct in that the main shoot from which all other species of man branch off continues to thrive and provides an associative force amongst the sundry branches. The final feature is the coalescence of the human branches.[44] Each respective form of man prior to *Homo sapiens* seems to follow the general trend of other animal species by diverging from one another in greater differentiation and individualisation. Once *Homo sapiens* arrive on the scene the trend shifts from divergence to convergence.

All these factors describe the distinctiveness of the human phylum and its ability to spread physically over the surface of the earth, but Teilhard makes much more of the increasing robustness of the *within* to enact this distribution and coalescence. Teilhard contends that unity and convergence are virtues of the *within* while divergence and separation characterise the *without*. Thus, one must look to the origin of convergence in the psyche and the development of consciousness: 'a convergent mankind is identical with an ultra-reflective mankind: and, conversely, an ultra-reflective mankind is identical with a convergent mankind.'[45] We now make our turn inwards because, according to Teilhard, the crux of human history and orthogenesis in general follows from thought and consciousness.

The spontaneous emergence of thought does not signify merely a local phenomenon on the face of the earth; man 'is more than a branch, more even than the kingdom; he is nothing less than a "sphere"—the Noosphere (or thinking sphere) superimposed on, and co-extensive with (but in so many ways more close-knit and homogeneous) the biosphere.'[46] As man spreads across the world his unique faculties are seen to pervade as well, so much so that it affects more than just the area of man—it institutes 'a transformation affecting the state of the entire planet.'[47] It is for these reasons Teilhard chooses to use the word Noosphere when referring to this phenomenon. The Noosphere is the collective mind of humanity as thought emerges from man. It is looking at the phenomenon of 'psychic energy' from the planetary level.

The anatomy of the Noosphere depends upon three distinct apparatuses for its propagation and structure. The first is the hereditary apparatus.[48] It should not be surprising that one of the elements of the Noosphere is girded by that which caused its deployment—the biological world. It remains a central aspect of the Noosphere as man is as much consciousness and reflection as he is animal and matter. One of the key tenets of the Noosphere depends upon biological reproduction. Eons of history and the accumulated evolutionary advancement that go along with this are housed in the very chromosomes which get passed along to subsequent generations. And yet, Teilhard asserts, heredity moves beyond mere DNA and biology. Heredity becomes externalised and transfers its main thrust to society, culture and the Noosphere. In fact, Teilhard claims that even if no biological advancement had occurred since the prehominids heredity and human progress can still exist because of this transference to cultural inheritance.

This heredity is most noticeable in education and example.[49] Education, according to Teilhard, is 'the transmission by example of an improvement, an action, and its reproduction by imitation.'[50] One can observe education in the lower forms of the animal kingdom inasmuch as one can see it in man. A bird teaches its progeny how to fly or to build a nest and cats and dogs train their offspring how to hunt. The combination of nature and nurture together form a complete animal. Such is the case with man, only on a much larger scale. We not only inherit our parents' genetic structure, but more importantly, we are trained how to live in a particular society, culture and environment. Education is the 'additive zone' where all of the individual experiences of each person is collected and transmitted. As Teilhard says, 'we see heredity pass through education beyond the individual to enter into its collective phase and become social.'[51] It is now evident how the Noosphere depends upon more than just biological heredity as society and culture through education become the natural successor of the gene. In fact, education's specific function is 'to extend and ensure in collective mankind a consciousness which may already have reached its limit in the individual.'[52]

The second apparatus of the Noosphere is related to our main area of inquiry: technology, or as Teilhard calls it the 'mechanical apparatus' of the Noosphere. Man has remained distinct from other animals in not evolving such that his limbs and physical body are turned into merely mechanical devices. His physicality is supple and can manoeuvre with a vast multiplicity of aims. This leaves him free to develop tools which he can grasp and utilise as an extension of his body, but without transforming it. It is this action, that of tool making, which underlies this aspect of the Noosphere. Teilhard recognises that the development of tools seems to have 'a kind of autonomous vitality'.[53] Teilhard likens the evolution of the tool to that of man himself: Machines beget more machines of greater complexity and seem to have an additive quality. Teilhard was awestruck by many of modern man's technical innovations whether they were the automobile, the airplane, the radio or the cyclotron.[54] However, each individual technology taken on its own is not enough to aid in the architecture of the Noosphere. What Teilhard is most interested in 'is the extent to which this process of mechanization is a collective affair, and the way in which it finally creates, on the periphery of the human race, an organism that is collective in its nature and amplitude.'[55] Technology creates a geo-network that represents the inventive core of the Noosphere. This growing technology complements and enmeshes itself in the fibre of human beings 'thus accelerating and multiplying their own growth and forming a single gigantic network girding the earth.'[56] In this way, technology plays a foundational and structural role in the Noosphere.

The final piece of the Noosphere is the cerebral apparatus. Just as each individual person contains a centre of thought so also does the Noosphere, which is made up of these individual minds, contain a specific centre as well—a cerebroid. Teilhard again points to the influence of the machine in being able to link up various minds in common. Although he recognises that nothing like a true thinking centre exists in the Noosphere today in the same way that it does for each individual human being, he does find certain phenomena to be a harbinger of things to come. In particular, he refers to the ability of television and radio to 'syntonise' minds together in a common thought. He also looks to the 'insidious growth' of computers which, 'pulsating with signals at the rate of hundreds of thousands a second, not only relieve our brains of tedious and exhausting work but, because they enhance the essential . . . factor of "speed of thought," are also paving the way for revolution in the sphere of research.'[57] Teilhard also suggests that despite no distinct 'I' in the Noosphere this does not mean, in turn, that the collection of minds which work to achieve a particular end is not the beginning of such a personalisation. For many concrete counterfactuals suggest otherwise: the development of the idea of the atom or even evolution itself—one man alone could have never achieved so much.[58]

And so, we arrive at modern man and a history which is dictated more by the influence of the Noosphere than by any other. Man is observed converging in history since the arrival of *Homo sapiens* and the Noosphere continues to grow over the earth influencing ontogenesis. Contemporary history represents the culmination of this increased complexity and socialisation which are sustained by the Noosphere. What we might call history today is really just a history of the Noosphere for Teilhard.

Teilhard gives little discussion to the social and political history of the world prior to the Renaissance and even then his general area of focus is more on the 18th century and onward. Despite this poor account of history he does not do so unwittingly, for it must be remembered that Teilhard still interprets history through the lens of ontogenesis and gives an account of history only to follow this thread of advancement. For this reason, Teilhard gives sidelong attention to some of the great civilisations in history and instead is ultimately convinced that the rise of the West bears the most significance for the advancement of the world.[59]

Three significant changes in the West mark its distinction and repute for instituting such a serious turn in the Noosphere. First, the economy changed dramatically. Prior to the end of the 18th century, Teilhard claims, most civilisations were agrarian based and money was still tied to property. It is at the end of the 18th century that money becomes much more 'fluid and impersonal'.[60] One no longer receives their main source of subsistence through the family system, but instead the exchange of wealth is more mobile. The second change is industrial. Teilhard notes that the only form of chemical energy available prior to the 18th century was fire, and the only kind of mechanical energy utilised the human body as its source of power.[61] The final shift in this period is major social change. The French Revolution sparked a massive chain reaction across Europe and North America which ended in greater liberty for each individual and would pave the way for societies to function in accord with each person and one another.

Yet, one need not look only at the effects instituted in society to note this epochal shift. One should also consider the change in psyche to gain the full *gravitas*. What is most striking, for Teilhard, is how the perspective of basic categories of reality are affected. Teilhard suggests that prior to modern man space and time are treated as separate containers which were homogenous and independent.[62] It took evolutionary theory in the middle of the 19th century to change this as it combines both together in a common force. As Teilhard says, 'the *distribution, succession and solidarity of objects are born from their concrescence in a common genesis.* Time and space are organically joined again so as to weave, together, the stuff of the universe.'[63] Evolutionary theory brings together categories which prior remained static and stable, but today ebb and flow in the great becoming of the universe.

And so, this is the contemporary perspective by which man views reality—in a state of transition and becoming. The very consciousness which reflects upon history is the very same which has blossomed out of this creation. All past history—natural and cultural—is personal for man, because not only is he a player in its narrative; he is, more importantly, the pinnacle and creation of that same history. As Teilhard often likes to quote of Julian Huxley, 'Man discovers that *he is nothing else than the evolution become conscious of itself . . .'*[64]

What is notable for the thrust of this text is that Teilhard's account of history to the present day ends with the Noosphere as the primary arena in which ontogenesis takes place and that the central framework for this Noosphere is technology. Natural and cosmic history funnel into this moment where technology is a major force in determining the events of history. We wouldn't have a Teilhardian account of human and cultural history without technology. Indeed, our entire cultural history depends upon the ever-growing network of technology. Teilhard recognises the totalising feature of technology across the globe. Where this is met with indignation and fear by, as we will discover, Ellul and Heidegger, Teilhard found this to be an entirely positive phenomenon because without it we wouldn't be able to advance the Noosphere. In this way, Teilhard shares with transhumanists the conviction that technology is one of the prime engines of history and, if we are to understand not only our past, but particularly our future, then we must reference the power of technology to mitigate and transform the events of the world.

We are brought to the present day, by Teilhard, and faced with a momentous imperative. History is replete with an incredible meaning. Man has become the vanguard of the universe's history and ontogenesis and is faced with the greatest of responsibilities: how to proceed from here. What is humanity to do with the apparent trajectory? Teilhard is not silent in regards to this question. For his response, we must turn to his eschatology.

5.2   TEILHARD DE CHARDIN AND ESCHATOLOGY

As has been asserted, Teilhard's eschatological program is premised upon his understanding of the progress of universal history which finds its summit in humanity. His eschatology derives from the gradual processes and forces inherent in the system of history itself which bring about new epochs of existence. New ontic categories spring naturally from one another in the scheme of evolution. This has already been illuminated in the birth of life out of macro-molecules as well as in the origin of consciousness in humanity—each provides a new epoch in history. Teilhard's eschatology is therefore very much a product of forces already at work in the confines of history. And yet, Teilhard also asserts that something is pulling humanity onward. A 'pull from above' beckons humanity onward into the future. The impetus towards the eschaton is both something which is actualised then and present now to us and influences us towards this direction. It is in light of his use of dialectics that one can most appreciate Teilhard's eschatology—for it is both something which is being created in history and something which stands outside of history which brings about the eschaton.[65] The basic dialectic—the *within* and the *without*—which has coalesced in Teilhard's cosmology is a good heuristic in distinguishing these two poles of influence. Each of these two strands will be dealt with in turn. First, let us consider the drive towards the future from factors derived in our observation of history from the *without*.

5.2.1   The Without and Eschatology

As concluded in the previous section, Teilhard's account of history has left humanity with an imperative. At the pinnacle of universal history humanity is faced with a choice: It can choose to uphold and continue the trajectory of cosmic evolution that has led to humanity or it can deny and reject it. The way into the future is laid before man and Teilhard considers the various options between which man must decide.

The first option is one of choosing between either an optimistic or pessimistic view of the future.[66] Teilhard argues that this choice depends upon one's basic metaphysical view of whether existence is inherently a good or bad thing. Humanity is faced with whether it ought to continue in the development of life and Being or move against this in favour of affirming life's utter meaninglessness and non-Being. If one does choose the optimistic view of the future then one must contend with how one achieves this sense of optimism. This optimism can come from an attitude of engagement with the world or, as Teilhard explains of Eastern religions,[67] from a retreat from the physical world. The final choice, if one chooses to engage in the world, is to decide between plurality and unity.[68] Should one pour effort into greater individuality within the human race or into greater unity?

Teilhard rejects the pessimistic view of the world and the choice of non-Being for the precise reason of the past evolutionary history leading to man.[69] Humanity's existence in the world already speaks towards the choice in favour of optimism of being and becoming over nothingness and purposelessness. The second decision between withdrawal and immersion is not as easily made as the first. This is especially difficult because Teilhard does say that humanity will ultimately separate from the material world. He urges, however, that this should not be premature. There is still much to be gleaned from immersion in the material world and the spirit inherent in it. For this reason, Teilhard maintains immersion in the world over withdrawal. The final option, choosing between plurality and unity, is the most difficult because greater differentiation created through evolution creates more robust phyla and has led to the emergence of consciousness itself. This divergence, despite being historically advantageous, only leads to brief moments of flourishing for each individual. If it is to sustain real growth at the special level then convergence and communalisation are preferred. The only viable way forward for humanity, given this gift of consciousness, is to push still further into the development of the Noosphere and its basic direction towards convergence of all of humanity.[70]

If Teilhard advocates not only the complete acceptance, but even the human advancement of the trends toward the future then it behoves one to consider these trends directly. Already spoken of briefly in Teilhard's account of history, he gives three distinct features which will be major aspects in the future and which are the major players in shaping future history's development towards the eschaton.

First, social unification will continue to thrive. Teilhard claims, 'nothing . . . can arrest the progress of social Man toward greater interdependence and cohesion.'[71] The force which makes this trend virtually inevitable is simply the limited space on our planet.[72] As the population of *Homo sapiens* increases across the face of the globe, it leaves less space for others in the species to exist. When the density of the population increases how does man adapt? Teilhard suggests that when this has occurred historically it has led to a restructuring of the species in greater organisation. We see this phenomenon already occurring in major cities around the world. Cities must organise a multiplicity of resources—food, energy, infrastructure—in order for such a dense population to exist and persist. Indeed, man is in the process of being forced to converge because of external forces and his very survival depends upon it. This trend will only increase in the future as the world becomes one unified society which has learned to adapt to a limited space.[73]

Second, the future will continue in its mechanisation and increasing use of technology. As suggested, technology is an important feature of the history of the Noosphere and in the development of man. It is a reality of our present and, more importantly, the future. For Teilhard, technology is more than an unnatural manipulation of the external world. Instead, it represents 'the sum of processes combined reflectively in such a way as to preserve in men the state of consciousness which corresponds to our state of aggregation and conjunction.'[74] As man has evolved from a more simple state his utilisation and creation of technology has developed a cerebral advantage, allowing him not to be imprisoned in his own body like other species, leaving him free to develop cognitively. Technology represents the external counterpart of which consciousness relies upon for its own propagation—it not only creates these technologies, but even relies upon them for its own evolution. Technology and consciousness are in a symbiotic relationship which finds its most simplistic roots in the coherence of the mind and body itself. Technology merely makes the relation between the two more efficient and productive. For Teilhard claims:

> What has really let loose the Machine in the world, and for good, is that it both facilitates and indefinitely multiplies our activities. Not only does it relieve us mechanically of a crushing weight of physical and mental labour, but by the miraculous enhancing of our senses, through the powers of enlargement, penetration and exact measurement, it constantly increases the scope and clarity of our perceptions. It fulfils the dream of all living creatures by satisfying our instinctive craving for *the maximum consciousness* with a minimum of effort![75]

Thus, consciousness is freed from mundane tasks and instead, through the development of technology; actualisation of an intended end happens with the greatest ease. Furthermore, not only does technology indirectly aid human development through reduced effort, but it can also be used to directly enhance humanity. Teilhard recognised this possibility and suggested that biologists would one day be able to manipulate human chromosomes and psychoanalysis could get at basic human instincts and thought.[76] Much like present-day transhumanists, Teilhard recognised that our technologies would change both our world and, more importantly, they could be applied to us directly to change our very bodies and natures. The future of the individual man will not only be aided externally by his creation of technology but even internally as it is applied to individual persons.[77]

Beyond the growth of technology which depends upon human input, Teilhard contends that technology seems to have grown from a single application dependent upon its relation with humanity to a global, autonomous force.[78] It is a distinct phenomenon which is akin to humanity in its ability to spread, add cumulatively to itself and create a network of related technologies over the globe. Technology has reached a point of systemisation and will only become progressively more collective in the future. Therefore, technology will continue to grow because it is inherently yoked to man's growing global consciousness and also because it is an autonomous system with its own identity. It is its own distinct global phenomenon.

The final trend which will lead humanity into the future is a greater heightening of vision.[79] This heightened vision not only refers to the greater advancement in our technologies which reveal more phenomena, but also to our general enhancement of the knowledge of the universe because of this increase in faculty. As man evolves the Noosphere with the aid of technology his conscious life will become freer. The compression of man on earth leads to greater socialisation, unification and technologisation not only for the sake of survival, but it also leads to an increased freedom of respective individuals. As duties are more compartmentalised in society and trivial tasks are made obsolete in a technological world this creates more space for mental effort to be devoted elsewhere. This heightening of vision is exactly what Teilhard suggests humanity does with its surplus psychic energy in the form of greater research, rationalisation of the world and development of technology.

These represent for Teilhard what is on the world's horizon, what is most immediate in the future. But, what lies beyond this? If we go beyond the horizon, how does this relate to the end of history? Where will these tendencies and social forces finally set us down? Where does Teilhard think we will end?

All of these tendencies lead Teilhard to believe that the world is in a state of convergence and unification towards what he refers to as the Omega Point: the climax and end of ontogenesis and the development of humanity. The end of this convergence leads to a spiritual climax which is the subject of the next section.

Before turning towards the spiritual conditions for the Omega Point, however, we must look more closely at the external forces leading to the Omega Point; particularly at convergence. Teilhard notices that some contend that our modern world, in a state of convergence, only depersonalises each individual. For instance, scientific analysis is concerned with removing individual bias from knowledge and as it becomes the *raison d'être* the individual is sacrificed. Furthermore, he comments on a modern philosophical trend in society today that seeks a monism of totality which treats the world according to a single entity, whether that is the Absolute or energy.[80] The Ego and the All seem to be at odds with one another and the inclination of the future seems to swallow up the individual in the mass of population. However, Teilhard claims, increasing globalisation and the propagation of humanity does not lead to a faceless crowd wherein the individual is likened to some cog in a machine. One's identity is not lost in the future as humanity converges, but rather the entirety of humanity becomes more personalised.

Personalisation is a key tenet of Teilhard's contentions. As man grows and evolves he becomes more of an individual person with greater consciousness. This greater consciousness leads to a more defined centre in each person. What is most important to note in Teilhard's description of personalisation is that it is not divorced from the exterior environment in which the person grows. These personal centres are both centres for the individual human and also represent the greater centricity of the entire world and milieu in which it occurs. The personality created in human consciousness is merely the more complex form of atomisation in the world more generally. Therefore, not only are human individuals ontically distinct from their primordial counterparts, but they are also related in the general trend of personalisation.[81]

This distinction is intensified by the formation and enrichment of the Noosphere. As suggested, the cerebral element of the Noosphere not only refers to each individual mind within the Noosphere, but even to the greater centricity which exists in the Noosphere as an entity in its own right. As Teilhard states, 'all our difficulties and repulsions as regards the opposition between the All and the Person would be dissipated if only we understood that, by structure, the Noosphere (and more generally the world) represent a whole that is not only closed but also centred.'[82] In fact, personalisation is occurring to the Noosphere itself. Each individual within the collectivity of the human race is increasing in its own respective personalisation while this very collectivity is converging towards its own person. This is where Teilhard's distinction between personality and individuality makes the most difference. Personalisation differentiates amidst a total union whereas individualisation separates itself at the expense of the whole and leads to greater plurality. Individuality sacrifices the ultra-personal element of humanity at large. Personalisation is the proper way to the future as it cultivates the centricity of the Noosphere whereas individuality leads to separation, divergence and death.

As seen, Teilhard asserts that the Noosphere is the final strand in the progression of the universe and humanity to the end of history. With this in mind, the force of personalisation in the Noosphere begets a culmination in his eschatology. As he states, 'the only air which Reflection can breathe must, of vital necessity, be that of a psychically and physically *convergent* Universe. There must be some peak, some revelation, some vivifying transformation at the end of the journey.'[83] As the Noosphere becomes more centred itself it leads to the creation of a person. The *telos* of ontogenesis converges in the Noosphere to a particular person—what Teilhard refers to as the Ultra-Human or the Trans-Human. Everything immanent within the cosmos is funnelling its energy toward a single point in the end of history. This Omega Point is reached through 'the push' of evolutionary forces and 'the pull' which comes from the conscious consent and catalyst of human thought, throwing itself towards this end. Indeed, the Noosphere culminates in a particular person, an Ultra-Human. This person is Christ.[84]

Many factors inherent in the world contribute to the convergence of man and eschatology. Increasing socialisation on a fixed space which is aided by technology and a heightening vision contribute to the advancement towards the eschaton. Man's action in this sphere to enhance these forces also aids in his consummation to the end of history. Yet, another part of the story is missing, for forced coalescence through compression is not enough to bring man to the eschaton. It is the virtues of the *within* and Christ's role in pulling humanity to the eschaton that are the final pieces which makeup Teilhard's eschatology. We therefore now examine the future from a more spiritual and religious vantage point from the *within*.

5.2.2 The Within and Eschatology

Teilhard was aware of the religious scepticism of his day. In fact, he makes the observation that 'among the most disquieting aspects of the modern world is its general and growing state of dissatisfaction in religious matters. Except in a humanitarian form . . . there is no present sign anywhere of Faith *that is expanding*. . . .'[85] Teilhard devoted himself to this issue and localised it to a conflict of interpretation of transcendence. Modern man's perspective of the world has changed dramatically. Part of the change can be attributed to an increased hope in humanity's own ability to enact greater progress itself without appeal to transcendence from beyond. Teilhard suggests this modern secular world is sceptical of transcendence which seems to have been developed out of a more static worldview which posits another metaphysical plane out of which transcendence refers.[86] Instead, Teilhard suggests, modern society is more open to an immanent 'horizontal' transcendence.[87] It is these varying interpretations which Teilhard refers to when he speaks of the conflict of the Above and the Ahead. A traditional understanding of transcendence refers to the Above while Teilhard's more modern contention refers to the Ahead.[88]

The Above and the Ahead provide a helpful distinction in Teilhard's eschatology. Teilhard seeks to synthesise these two interpretations as each refers to his own dialectic and both lead to these respective interpretations of transcendence. The previous section sought to develop Teilhard's eschatology from analysing the pole of the Ahead. This section probes Teilhard's view of eschatology from the opposite side, the Above.

The sphere of the *within* has been explored to a degree, but its religious overtones have remained tacit. Teilhard's spirituality is observed most predominantly and extensively in this sphere. The history and future of man, as has been suggested, does reside within the purview of science. However, history and the future of man is not complete without the religious aspect of history and the future—for it is just as efficacious, if not more, in sparking this movement towards the eschaton. For this reason, how supernature and Christianity relate to nature is a seminal part of Teilhard's thought. For this reason in constructing a history and future of the *within* several spiritual issues must be addressed. First, we will analyse how the supernatural and the natural relate in the incarnation and then, second, move into how this affects our activities and passivities which then, third, culminates at the end of history.

The historical Christ's appearance on earth enacts a very real change in the ontology of nature. This change is rooted in the very hypostasis of the person of Christ. For, as Christ breaks into the world his divinity ruptures the enclosure of nature and creates a spark which causes a chain reaction. His divinity mingles with the natural and becomes immanent within it. The Eucharist is not only the reflection upon this coupling of divinity and matter, but in a very real sense is the prototype for the divinisation of matter. As Teilhard exclaims, 'through your own incarnation, my God, all matter is henceforth incarnate.'[89] In this way, through the advent of Christ the supernatural becomes an aspect of both man's history and all of creation.[90] This severely changes natural history and provides the incentive for its consideration. The religious becomes important for the scientist because of Christ's incarnation and the flood of the divine into the world.

Teilhard's placement of Christ in his cosmology extends beyond a static inclusion of divinity in the world, for Christ is central to his religious history and theology more generally. Rideau speaks of Christ's predominance in Teilhard's religious writings as he stands as the 'author and creator, animator and mover, director and leader, centre and head, its consistence and consolidation (active unity), its gatherer and assembler, purifier and regenerator, crown and consummation, spearhead and end.'[91] Christ's prime function in Teilhard's theology resides in what is termed the universal or mystical Christ.[92] As Christ enters the world he then becomes its basis and centre so that the world is held together through the mystical body of Christ. The world is indeed yoked to and in Christ. Yet, in stressing the universal nature of Christ and its equation with the world he never loses sight of the importance of Christ coming in history as a person. In referring to Christ Teilhard emphasises not only Christ's historical and physical character, but also his universal role. Both are necessary for a robust Christology and each supports the role of the other. Teilhard states, 'the mystic Christ, the universal Christ of St. Paul, can have neither meaning nor value for us except as an expansion of the Christ born of Mary and dying on the Cross. It is from the latter, that the former derives essentially his fundamental quality of being indisputably concrete.'[93] The historical Christ undergirds the mystical Christ as its advent and beginning. The enfleshed Christ, as an event, is merely the beginning of his influence and propagation into the rest of the world.

This propagation in the world is related directly to Teilhard's notion of creation. Rather than expressing a static occurrence at the beginning of history, creation is a process enacted through the mystical Christ as it transforms the world into greater divinity. Evolution is the biological mechanism by which God is in process of creating the world and moving deeper within it. Teilhard uses the term Christogenesis to signify the advancement of the mystical Christ in history which not only parallels biological evolution, but because of Christ's hypostasis *is also* biological evolution.

With this necessary theological architecture in place, Teilhard discusses the way in which the cosmic Christ cultivates and lies near our everyday activities and passivities in what he refers to as the *milieu divin*. He describes how Christ lies at the foot of every occurrence in the world. It is in this work, *Le Milieu Divin*, that Teilhard outlines how one's activities can be divinised and in accord with Christ's working.

This divinisation of our activities can be affirming of both God and the world in two ways. One stance interprets the actions of an individual according to its eternal value and treats this world as a testing period where one's faithfulness to God is tried. This is only a partial solution and gives value to our activity's intentions, but leaves behind the physical world and our place as bodies, not just souls, on this earth. Teilhard contends that the world actually cultivates the soul and is here to encourage it: 'But all reality, even material reality, around each one of us, exists for our souls. Hence, all sensible reality, around each one of us, exists, through our souls, for God in Our Lord.'[94] To uplift both aspects of human life, the soul and body, we must make the most of this world, for God not only wants to cultivate the soul but also creation through our actions in it. Our works are divinised and sanctified, for Teilhard, because God lies at its foundation. Therefore, our toil on earth is as much a spiritual practice as the receiving of sacraments and personal holiness.

Teilhard also discusses the way in which our lack of action in the world, our passivity, is used by God in the fulfilment of his plan as well. In referring to the 'two hands of God' Teilhard discusses the way in which God is ever active alongside humanity. First, God provides the force within our own will toward action and love.[95] As one plumbs the depths of one's self one is drawn into the enigma of God laying at the basis of our most primordial faculties. The second hand takes leave from one's inner self and recognises the way in which the world, apart from our own direct action, seems to converge in harmony and common purpose.[96] It is these external influences which Teilhard attributes to God working despite us.

Teilhard also brings to light not only our passivities of growth, but even those of diminishment. God does more than work with humanity's own effort. He also works in spite of it. Elements of diminishment include those of the external world such as disease, fire or other natural disasters, but it is also inclusive of things internal like intellectual or moral weakness. How then does God transfigure these diminishments? Teilhard says these have occurred historically in three ways. A trial might merely be the birth pangs of a more fruitful and advantageous state. The biblical story of Job is an example of this type. Second, suffering can lead to less reliance upon things which are more basic and less worthy of our attention and love. Both of these kinds of suffering lead to a stronger, more mature person. The third example is transformative in its anticipation of our final union with God. Some experiences do not seem to have any value whatsoever and it is these which provide a foretaste of the final death of man and his final entrance into God at the end of history. For everyone must die with Christ to finally partake in His glory.[97] But, beyond the effects of individual suffering and evil, one must also consider cosmic death as it is the culmination of all areas of diminishment.[98] God, in Christ, has overcome death and its evil influence in the world. Thus, everything which is subject to death and diminishment is also subject to God's ultimate transformation. In this way, God weaves together not only our passivities of growth, but even those of diminishment.

Both our overtly spiritual and nonspiritual activities and passivities are the building blocks towards the future of humanity and the consummation of the Universal Christ. Love and attraction are the necessary attributes of Christ working himself through humanity towards his completion. He is both a force upon humanity and also a plea for humanity to pour into this mutual affinity for each other and creation. The convergence of humanity is brought about by this love within the Universal Christ as He is the crux, pinnacle and end of human history.

The end of history sees the convergence of humanity into the completed person of the cosmic Christ. This occurs through an escape from the cosmos and separation of the material world at its termination of history. As Noogenesis and Christogenesis reach maturity, the material world is jettisoned and is the final act before the Omega Point and the Ultra-Human is drawn up into the supernatural Christ. This final union speaks to the ontological distinction and priority Teilhard makes between the supernatural and the natural. Naturalistic evolution, while leading to the final consummation with the divine, is not the final move into the divine itself. It is the necessary precondition for its final unity with God. Teilhard states, 'by structural necessity, the two points inevitably coincide—in this sense, that the fulfilment of hominisation by ultra-reflection is seen to be a necessary pre-condition of its "divinisation".'[99] Instead, this final pull is the work of God alone.[100] This last pull into the spiritual is not violent to the personhood of humanity, according to Teilhard, precisely because the centre of humanity, which has arisen from its biology, no longer resides in its material nature, but rather in its psychic and spiritual part—the Noosphere. It is a loss of humanity's dependence upon a once important aspect of itself, but it has morphed into something entirely different and, Teilhard asserts, is even something humanity will desire: 'when the end of time is at hand, a terrifying spiritual pressure will be exerted on the confines of the real, built up by the desperate efforts of souls tense with longing to escape from the earth.'[101] This final moment, in being taken up with the Universal Christ into the Godhead, is the completion of human history and Teilhard's eschatology.

5.3   CONCLUSION

Both aspects of the future, from the *without* and the *within*, have been detailed separately. However, the two strands which lead to the future—religious as well as scientific—are taken up together by Teilhard. How the two influences relate is very important for Teilhard, as much is at stake if it is improperly balanced. Forced coalescence through technological or other means can lead to an impersonal tyranny and destruction. This is most evident in Teilhard's appraisal of totalitarian regimes. He is hesitant to dismiss the failure of certain totalitarian experiments outright, for the final effects of the initiatives had not been allowed to materialise. One could not properly gauge whether it had caused greater enslavement or a greater increase in spiritual energy.[102] If they were a complete failure, Teilhard interjects, it is not the force of totalisation which went amiss. Instead, it was the 'clumsy and incomplete' way in which it was applied. Teilhard claims, 'the first essential is that the human units involved in the process shall draw closer together; not merely under the pressure of *external* forces, or solely by the performance of material acts, but directly, center to center, through *internal* attraction. Not through coercion, or enslavement to a common task, but through *unanimity* in a common spirit.'[103] This convergence must be yoked with the virtue of the *within*, love, for all of mankind and creation. It takes the religious element of Christ in mutual affinity, at the heart of each individual, to truly bring about a positive future for humanity. A balance of both forces is vital to Teilhard's eschatology.

And this is precisely what separates Teilhard from contemporary transhumanism as outlined in chapter 4. His acceptance of technology in his eschatology is not without qualification. For inasmuch as his theological system and eschatology depend upon a convergent humanity, on an Ultra-Human, he asserts that this is only good if it is set within the overall narrative of Christ as the one who is the Ultra-Human—the end and prototype for all of humanity. This transcendence from the *without* is only good if it is accompanied by transcendence signified by Christ—only if the history and virtues of the *within* accompany it. This Ultra-Human is not the amorphous transhuman signified by Kurzweil and Bostrom, but looks much more like Christ. And, this Christ is not just a cosmic Christ, but a real enfleshed person for, as Teilhard asserts, there is no meaning in the cosmic Christ without the specificity of the historical Christ.[104]

What should we take from Teilhard's Christian approach to the future? First, human work and history are valuable and integral to eschatology. We cannot retreat from the events of history, whether they are evolutionary or cultural. Instead, we must affirm that they are genuinely binding and important for the ultimate future. Teilhard recognises that this includes our technological history and creations. If we are to uphold the value of human work in God's creation, it must invariably include technology.

Second, reflection upon the force of technology on society and its influence on shaping the future is an important task for the Christian. While such a response might be expected given the subject of this book, here we have a very influential spiritual and religious figure in the Christian tradition who identifies technology as an important factor to consider for the Christian future. As a visionary Christian thinker, we might say that his reflections on technology to transform not only the external world, but even the human being itself, is quite prescient. How much more should this be a subject of concern for Christians today? Hasn't the globalising nature of technology advanced to an even greater, more visible, level than in Teilhard's time? Of course, Teilhard is often associated with technological optimism, but what we also need to glean from Teilhard's account of technology and the future is that we cannot accept it without great discernment and serious reflection. Technology is important for the future but it is not a good in itself. Teilhard teaches us that we should not be so sceptical that we deny its real role in shaping our present and future for good aims. However, we also shouldn't allow it to bedazzle us out of good discernment grounded in the Christian tradition.

And, finally, this leads into the final item we need to take from Teilhard. In our approach to the future, we cannot lose the specificity of Christ or the Christian narrative in our imaginings of the future. For the Christian, the future is Christ's future or God's future. Christ must be seen as the institutor and the end of the Christian future such that eschatology and the consummation of the world must always relate to Christology. Teilhard localises this within the doctrine of the cosmic Christ such that the future is always seen with Christian eyes.[105] Indeed, just as Christ is the point at which God comes to the world in a particular historical person, he is also the finality when all of creation at the eschaton is redeemed into the life of God.

However, Teilhard isn't the only perspective within the Christian tradition on this matter. Ellul represents this other perspective which is not as optimistic about technology and its contribution to a Christian future. We turn to Ellul for his reflections.

NOTES

1. Many Christian thinkers have reflected on technology such as George Grant, Romano Guardini and even Paul Tillich, but either technology is not a lynchpin of their overall work or it is not reflected in a robust technological eschatology in the same way it is for Teilhard and Ellul.
2. Pierre Teilhard de Chardin, *The Future of Man*, trans., Norman Denny (New York: Image Books/Doubleday, 2004), 3.
3. Pierre Teilhard de Chardin, *The Phenomenon of Man*, trans., Bernard Wall (London: Fontana, 1965), 241.
4. Ontological issues related to the future and technology are dealt with in greater detail in chapters 7 and 8.
5. It is also what makes him unpalatable to these contemporary evolutionary biologists and to postmodernists who proclaim the death of the metanarrative and a progressive account of history. See my comments on this in Michael Burdett, "Teilhard De Chardin: From Nature to Supernature," in *Darwinism and Natural Theology: Evolving Perspectives*, ed., Andrew Robinson (Newcastle: Cambridge Scholars Publishing, 2012).
6. For a further clarification of Teilhard's use of dialectics see Emile Rideau, *Teilhard De Chardin: A Guide to His Thought* (London: Collins, 1967), 45ff.
7. For a further account of how Teilhard deals with the traditional account of Christian creation see ibid., 152–156.

8. Teilhard gives an account of cosmological history as well and asserts the earth is the specific place where the history of the universe progresses. See Teilhard de Chardin, *The Future of Man*, 90–116.
9. Pierre Teilhard de Chardin, *Man's Place in Nature: The Human Zoological Group*, trans., René Hague (London: Collins, 1966), 38.
10. Teilhard de Chardin, *The Phenomenon of Man*, 89–90.
11. Ibid., 91.
12. Ibid., 94.
13. Ibid.
14. Teilhard de Chardin, *Man's Place in Nature*, 42–43.
15. Teilhard de Chardin, *The Phenomenon of Man*, 115–116.
16. Ibid., 115.
17. Ibid., 116–117.
18. Ibid., 118–119.
19. See Teilhard's history as it is related to the *within* below.
20. Teilhard de Chardin, *The Phenomenon of Man*, 119.
21. Ibid.
22. Ibid., 119–120.
23. Ibid., 120.
24. Ibid., 159–160.
25. Ibid., 176.
26. Ibid.
27. Teilhard de Chardin, *Man's Place in Nature*, 35.
28. Teilhard de Chardin, *The Phenomenon of Man*, 61.
29. Ibid., 64.
30. Ibid., 66.
31. Pierre Teilhard de Chardin, *Writings in Time of War*, trans., René Hague (London: Collins, 1968), 168.
32. Teilhard de Chardin, *The Future of Man*, 167.
33. Teilhard de Chardin, *The Phenomenon of Man*, 189.
34. Ibid., 182–185.
35. Ibid., 189.
36. Ibid., 190.
37. Ibid.
38. Ibid., 200.
39. Teilhard de Chardin, *Man's Place in Nature*, 64–72.
40. Ibid., 74.
41. Ibid., 74–75.
42. Ibid., 74.
43. Ibid., 76.
44. Ibid., 77.
45. Pierre Teilhard de Chardin, *Activation of Energy*, trans., René Hague (London: Collins, 1970), 327.
46. Teilhard de Chardin, *Man's Place in Nature*, 80.
47. Teilhard de Chardin, *The Phenomenon of Man*, 201.
48. Teilhard de Chardin, *The Future of Man*, 156–158.
49. Ibid., 157.
50. Ibid., 18.
51. Ibid., 20.
52. Ibid., 24.
53. Ibid., 159.
54. See especially Teilhard's reflections on viewing a cyclotron in Teilhard de Chardin, *Activation of Energy*, 349–357; Pierre Teilhard de Chardin, *Letters from a Traveller*, trans., René Hague (London: Collins, 1962), 331.

55. Teilhard de Chardin, *The Future of Man*, 159.
56. Ibid., 160.
57. Ibid., 162.
58. Ibid., 163.
59. For instance, Teilhard mentions that five civilisations in the earth's history have had the potential to institute a superior state in the Noosphere: the Mayans, Polynesians, Chinese, Indians and Egyptians. But, for various reasons, they failed to do so. See Teilhard de Chardin, *The Phenomenon of Man*, 228–234.
60. Ibid., 235.
61. Ibid., 236.
62. Ibid., 239–240.
63. Ibid., 240.
64. Ibid., 243.
65. See particularly, Teilhard's comments on the 'push' of evolutionary forces and the 'pull' from above, namely God. Teilhard de Chardin, *The Future of Man*, 277ff. He also contends that the Omega Point is not just something built from evolutionary forces but something which influences the present and transcends those evolutionary forces. See Teilhard de Chardin, *Activation of Energy*, 112–113.
66. Teilhard de Chardin, *The Future of Man*, 32.
67. For a further development of how Teilhard engages with the spirituality and philosophy of the East see Pierre Teilhard de Chardin, *Toward the Future*, trans., René Hague (London: Collins, 1975), 134–147.
68. Teilhard de Chardin, *The Future of Man*, 36.
69. Ibid., 40.
70. Teilhard's rebuttal against the accusation of decreased individuality in ever increasing convergence will be dealt with in the following section on Christ and personalisation.
71. Teilhard de Chardin, *The Future of Man*, 226.
72. Ibid.
73. See also Teilhard de Chardin, *Activation of Energy*, 341–346.
74. Ibid., 159.
75. Teilhard de Chardin, *The Future of Man*, 227.
76. Teilhard de Chardin, *Activation of Energy*, 160. Teilhard was quite the visionary in this respect.
77. While Teilhard does find value in the transformative effects of technology he should not be equated wholly with contemporary transhumanists. See the conclusion of this chapter for more detail.
78. Teilhard de Chardin, *The Future of Man*, 160.
79. Ibid., 227–228.
80. Teilhard de Chardin, *The Phenomenon of Man*, 283.
81. See especially Pierre Teilhard de Chardin, *Human Energy*, trans., J. M. Cohen (London: Collins, 1969), 53–60.
82. Teilhard de Chardin, *The Phenomenon of Man*, 285.
83. Teilhard de Chardin, *The Future of Man*, 278.
84. How the cosmic Christ relates to the Ultra-Human of the eschaton will be elucidated in greater detail in the following section which interprets the future from the *within*.
85. Teilhard de Chardin, *The Future of Man*, 259.
86. Jürgen Moltmann also rejects this notion of transcendence as 'eternal presence' rather than something grounded in history itself. See chapter 8 for further discussion of this topic.
87. This 'immanentising' of transcendence is visible in the utopias discussed in chapter 2.

88. For detailed discussion of the Above and the Ahead and how it relates to Teilhard's eschatology see Teilhard de Chardin, *The Future of Man*, 259–269.
89. Pierre Teilhard de Chardin, *Hymn of the Universe*, trans., Simon Bartholomew (London: Collins, 1965), 24.
90. See Rideau, *Teilhard De Chardin*, 163.
91. Ibid., 162.
92. Teilhard is advancing a notion which goes back to Irenaeus, Gregory of Nyssa and Pauline theology in his avowal of a cosmic Christ. See Charles E. Raven, *Teilhard De Chardin: Scientist and Seer* (London: Collins, 1962), 159–173; Henri de Lubac, *The Religion of Teilhard De Chardin*, trans., René Hague (London: Collins, 1967), 56–62.
93. Pierre Teilhard de Chardin, *Le Milieu Divin: An Essay on the Interior Life*, trans., Bernard Wall (London: Collins, 1960), 105.
94. Ibid., 27.
95. Ibid., 55.
96. Ibid., 56.
97. See ibid., 66–69.
98. Teilhard draws on St. Paul here in asserting that sin not only refers to individual actions, but more importantly to a cosmic force which is dealt with by Christ.
99. Teilhard de Chardin, *Toward the Future*, 191.
100. Teilhard de Chardin, *The Phenomenon of Man*, 327n3.
101. Pierre Teilhard de Chardin, *Science and Christ*, trans., René Hague (London: Collins, 1968), 84.
102. Teilhard de Chardin, *The Future of Man*, 112. This example definitely reveals the major weakness in Teilhard's system. His unyielding optimism about convergence and unity makes him blind to grievous evil.
103. Ibid.
104. See my comments on this earlier in the chapter. Cf. Teilhard de Chardin, *Le Milieu Divin*, 105. David Grumett has a much more extended comparison of Teilhard's Ultra-Human and contemporary transhumanism which I, for the most part, agree with. See David Grumett, "Transformation and the End of Enhancement: Insights from Pierre Teilhard De Chardin," in *Transhumanism and Transcendence: Christian Hope in an Age of Technological Enhancement*, ed., Ronald Cole-Turner (Washington, DC: Georgetown University Press, 2011).
105. See especially Brent Waters, *From Human to Posthuman: Christian Theology and Technology in a Postmodern World* (Aldershot: Ashgate, 2006), 123ff.

REFERENCES

Burdett, Michael. "Teilhard De Chardin: From Nature to Supernature." In *Darwinism and Natural Theology: Evolving Perspectives*, edited by Andrew Robinson. Newcastle: Cambridge Scholars Publishing, 2012.

Cousins, Ewert H., Carl E. Braaten, and American Teilhard de Chardin Association. *Hope and the Future of Man*. Teilhard Study Library, Vol. 6. London: Garnstone Press, 1973.

Delio, Ilia. "Transhumanism or Ultrahumanism? Teilhard De Chardin on Technology, Religion and Evolution." *Theology and Science* 10, no. 2 (2012): 153–166.

Grumett, David. *Teilhard De Chardin: Theology, Humanity, and Cosmos*. Leuven: Peeters, 2005.

———. "Transformation and the End of Enhancement: Insights from Pierre Teilhard De Chardin." In *Transhumanism and Transcendence: Christian Hope in an*

Age of Technological Enhancement, edited by Ronald Cole-Turner. Washington, DC: Georgetown University Press, 2011.

King, Ursula. *Spirit of Fire: The Life and Vision of Teilhard De Chardin*. Maryknoll: Orbis Books, 1996.

Laudadio, Leonard. "Teilhard De Chardin on Technological Progress." *Review of Social Economy* 31, no. 2 (1973): 167–178.

Lubac, Henri de. *The Faith of Teilhard De Chardin*. London: Burns & Oates, 1965.

———. *The Religion of Teilhard De Chardin*. Translated by René Hague. London: Collins, 1967.

———. *Teilhard Explained*. New York: Paulist Press, 1968.

Peacocke, A. R. *Science and the Christian Experiment*. London: Oxford University Press, 1971.

———. *Evolution, the Disguised Friend of Faith?: Selected Essays*. London: Templeton Foundation Press, 2004.

Raven, Charles E. *Teilhard De Chardin: Scientist and Seer*. London: Collins, 1962.

Rideau, Emile. *Teilhard De Chardin: A Guide to His Thought*. London: Collins, 1967.

Teilhard de Chardin, Pierre. *Le Milieu Divin: An Essay on the Interior Life*. Translated by Bernard Wall. London: Collins, 1960.

———. *Letters from a Traveller*. Translated by René Hague. London: Collins, 1962.

———. *The Appearance of Man*. Translated by J. M. Cohen. New York: Harper & Row, 1965.

———. *Hymn of the Universe*. Translated by Simon Bartholomew. London: Collins, 1965.

———. *The Phenomenon of Man*. Translated by Bernard Wall. London: Fontana, 1965.

———. *Man's Place in Nature: The Human Zoological Group*. Translated by René Hague. London: Collins, 1966.

———. *Science and Christ*. Translated by René Hague. London: Collins, 1968.

———. *Writings in Time of War*. Translated by René Hague. London: Collins, 1968.

———. *Human Energy*. Translated by J. M. Cohen. London: Collins, 1969.

———. *Activation of Energy*. Translated by René Hague. London: Collins, 1970.

———. *Christianity and Evolution*. Translated by René Hague. London: Collins, 1971.

———. *Toward the Future*. Translated by René Hague. London: Collins, 1975.

———. *The Future of Man*. Translated by Norman Denny. New York: Image Books/ Doubleday, 2004.

Waters, Brent. *From Human to Posthuman: Christian Theology and Technology in a Postmodern World*. Aldershot: Ashgate, 2006.

6   Jacques Ellul and Eschatology
The Technological Pessimist

Jacques Ellul and Teilhard have much in common. Both were Frenchmen who had significant experience in the world wars: Teilhard was a stretcher-bearer in the First World War and Ellul was part of the resistance movement in the Second World War. But, they part company on many issues. This might be attributed to their theological differences. Ellul was a member of the French Reformed tradition and Teilhard a Roman Catholic. Many of their disagreements can be traced back to this difference in theological tradition. This is particularly the case when we look at history, technology and the future.[1]

It is safe to say that Christianity and technology are the two major areas of discourse for Ellul. They are not just subsidiary interests but the prime areas of discussion in his writings and life. Therefore, it should not be surprising that they are the factors that most inform his eschatology. For this reason, Ellul's sociology and his notion of environment will be the first area of inquiry here as it leads to our contemporary discussion of the technological environment. Then we shall look at how Ellul characterises technology as a force in society and as a system leading to social determinism. Ellul then posits a solution to society's bleak future and locates it in the radical revelation of the Christian God. How this revelation relates to Ellul's conception of apocalypticism and hope will then be elucidated. Finally, Ellul's eschatology will be addressed as it relates to technology and it will be asserted that this vision of hope in the future and God's advent in the world is what breaks this determinism which is inherent in humanity's technological obsession.

6.1   ELLUL'S SOCIOLOGY AND THE ENVIRONMENTS

Ellul's approach to history is influenced by his reading of Marx.[2] From Marx he learns, first, that one's account of history must be true to reality. While this might seem obvious for all approaches to history, what Ellul holds is that history must be anchored in the reality of all peoples—especially for those not usually represented. He takes from Marx the radicality of illuminating those aspects of history which are not told, but are closer to the reality of affairs for all peoples. The second is that history is primarily social. Thus, Ellul's history is sociological rather than natural as with Teilhard.[3]

Ellul has two initial problems with the formulation of any history. The first is that history is always an approximation. History is meant to represent reality and events as they occur, but this representation is never identical with the events themselves. History is a construction and interpreted through the ideals and convictions of the observer. The occurrences in reality are always interpretations of certain events as told by a particular people. This notion of created histories is most acute in the establishment of epochs and eras which are meant to represent a snapshot of this movement in time where key traits remain constant and a coherent world is visible. For example, Medievalism gives way to Modernity which is then subsumed by Postmodernity. It is in these transitions that the purely schematic nature of these creations is most pronounced as one tries to delineate between distinct eras. They are mere fabrications which do not represent the seamlessness of time and the true fluidity of history. These disjointed transitions also further Ellul's belief that progress inherent in history is impossible because it is the historian alone who finds this single thread and projects it onto history itself. In this way, any history must be approached with sensitivity and must remain open for further interpretation and criticism.

The second issue that Ellul has with the formulation of history involves knowing which history one is telling. Defining the field of history and the area in which one must make an account—industrial, biological, law—is a difficult and always partial task. One's history will always be inadequate for the precise reason that other histories, which are not the field of purview, constantly inform and connect with the history one is forming. For this reason, one must eliminate the urge to identify one strand throughout all history which guides this history.[4] Ellul claims, 'My most important thesis, then, is that we must eliminate univocal explanations, that is, those which find in one social relation or one phenomenon a guiding thread or a single dominant and determinative factor in human history.'[5]

Taking a sociological perspective on history, Ellul speaks of the notion of 'environment' as the central guiding factor in history. Environment means more to Ellul than the space in which history occurs. Rather, several characteristics condition the environment. For instance, humanity finds in its environment everything humans need to live and not just to survive.[6] For example, the natural environment not only provides air, water and plants for our consumption, but also is the place where we can create meaningful symbols. Therefore, the environment is not simply a given to which we must adapt, but is also supple in our development as we try to adapt it to ourselves through cultivation and symbolisation. However, the environment also seems to contain an opposing force. The environment does house all the resources which are needed for a good life, but it is also hostile and dangerous.[7] The danger can arise through entities such as wild animals and disease or it could be due to the lack of resources we require such as adequate food and water. The final feature, and probably the most important, is that our environment is always immediate.[8] Our environment always interacts directly with us. If something separates us from the environment then it no longer exists as the prime environment in which we live, for we are no longer subject to it in mutuality. Instead, we become the subject and the relation becomes increasingly unilateral as we manipulate and adapt it to our ends.[9]

Ellul contends that, based upon these assumptions and definitions, three major environments exist successively in history. It is through these environments that Ellul frames his account of history and we now turn to them directly in turn.

6.1.1   The Natural Environment: Prehistory

The most basic environment is also the most evident and least contested of the three Ellul suggests: the natural environment. The natural environment is that which is associated with the physical world. It is the environment of plants, animals and the natural elements. It is humanity stripped of all its own creation. This is the environment of prehistory. Human beings, in this environment, 'were lost in an omnipotent nature over which they had no control'[10] and were affected more by the natural world than other people later in history.

Demographic changes slowly altered the relation humanity had with the natural environment. Ellul believes that greater population density led to the development of social and economic phenomena. As the population grew, so did humanity's abilities to deal with the natural environment. This was most prevalent between 8000 and 2500 BC where one observes humanity generating better tools and weapons which represent this growing capacity.[11] The change in the interaction between humanity and the natural environment is also manifest in artists' representations from the Paleolithic era through the Neolithic era. The vast majority of pictures in the Paleolithic era are of animals whereas this shifts to the depiction of humans in the Neolithic era.[12] This signals greater contact amongst individuals and the burgeoning of social forms. These new social groups become more prevalent throughout this period and provided a greater resilience to the environment. These social creations were a conscious development and they differ from location to location with different social rules and customs. Ellul accounts for this difference in that the groups were created out of the need to adapt to different natural features across the globe.

The family unit was the most common and stable of these social forms that existed in this prehistorical period. What is most interesting about the family unit is not that it was premised upon reproduction, although this is definitely a necessary attribute, but rather its symbolic value gave it 'permanence, legitimacy, and meaning'.[13] This meaning insured its propagation from generation to generation and carried a certain power with it. The family was also ritualised and guaranteed the conformity of the distinctive members within the family as well as its continuity. The institution of the family based purely on biological factors does not do justice to the stability of the institution that is created through ritual and symbol. Where natural stability is insufficient in explaining such a resilient social form, when taken together with the social rite of marriage and other family rituals, it ensures it will last beyond the variation of the individuals involved.

Two other factors seem to be at work in these blossoming social structures which aid one another in the progression of the social forms. First, as these units are created they become more complex.[14] As groups become larger and contend with new situations in the natural environment the group is forced to become more complex as it develops more specific roles which adapt to these new conditions. The function of each constitutive member becomes more fragmented and specific as new obstacles are met. This becomes more evident as the study of the prehistorical period advances—we are met not with merely simple social groups which require little elucidation, but societies which were much more complex than we first imagined. The second factor complements complexity. As social forms adapt and grow they also become honed over time, and there is as much a force to simplify as there is to become more complex.[15] For instance, the myth simplifies reality insofar as it organises it. Also, certain rites and roles in society get jettisoned over time, for they can become redundant in a changing environment or because the form in itself has become too oppressive for those involved. Whatever the reason, both of these factors contributed to the trend towards the coalescing of peoples into new societies. This growth reached a threshold, according to Ellul, and necessitates a new environment for a subsequent era. The natural environment gave way to the social environment in the historical period.

6.1.2 The Social Environment: The Historical Period

Ellul has focused his efforts in the prehistorical period upon the development of the social grouping of humanity. Each distinctive group across the globe represents a particular and unique adaptation of the social group to its natural landscape. Despite this distinctiveness and the existence of these young societies in the prehistorical period, several traits separate it from the previous environment and mark something completely new.

First, Ellul claims, there is a transition to greater reliance upon the voluntary. Society becomes an area of conscious deliberation and is more organised as a result. The first groups were formed spontaneously and, consequently, much of the group's power stems from an invocation of deities and taboos. As the creation of societies becomes more prevalent and reflexive, the society's instantiation and functioning rely less on these deities, rites and taboos.[16] Therefore, society becomes an area of direct reflection. As this distrust in deities to uphold the social forms advances humanity becomes aware that the rules which govern society are flexible and can be changed. Reactionaries revolt against this contention, but other factors aid in the deterioration of the family as the main social form. Ellul explains that writing helps decouple the power inherent in this early social form:

> Writing makes possible the universalizing of a decision or insight. It strengthens leadership, since leaders can now make their will known to wider groups. It makes the composing and preserving of records possible. Above all, it makes possible a type of transmission other than what I would call proto-hereditary. It detaches knowledge from that of ancestors and challenges the validity of what is ancient, that is, the idea that things are as they are because oral lore passed down from one generation to another says that this is how they have always been.[17]

This power then gets transferred to the state as reflection on society led to the creation of law. As social groups grew in size it was inevitable that direct reflection upon them was expected, and this in turn lead to the destruction of power through primitive deities and the family into the state as the creator of law.

The second aspect of the historical period which separates it from its predecessor is an increased creation and use of the artificial.[18] Ellul defines artificial as 'human intervention in nature'.[19] What the abundance of artificiality suggests is that human beings no longer interact primarily in the natural environment. As societies grew it became impossible not to be in contact with the state. This transition to the voluntary and artificial brought not only more contact with other individuals, but the influence of one group on another and one society on another. With the aid of writing, institutions and even religions were detachable from one group and could easily be adopted by another. So, the social milieu became much more fluid as differing societies would come into contact with each other and experience different ways of living. This artificiality also brought with it, at first, a newfound freedom. Humanity no longer had to devote as much conscious effort to the harm the natural environment placed on it and was released to develop more complex societies. Artificiality is also recognisable in the increase of new tools, furnishings and especially the house. Indeed, the creation of the town signifies the most overt form of the artificial environment. It represented the place where the natural environment had been conquered and humanity placed it between itself and the physical elements.

The development of social hierarchy arrives on the scene in the historical period.[20] Its genealogy is to be sought first in families who could claim an eponymous ancestor. This claim to a heroic figure gave these families a distinct advantage in society as the power the hero had over the members gets transferred to the families themselves. Stories and legends get passed from one generation to another in these aristocratic families and slowly, an embryonic caste is observable. This social hierarchy provided more than differentiation in society; it also created a history for a particular group. The aristocracy was charged with the task to uphold this history as it provided a sense of identity to all who were members. It provided a sense of stability from generation to generation and this in turn insured the propagation of the structure of society.

The creation of law is also a significant feature of this era.[21] Law arises between the pressures of voluntary artificialism already discussed and this new social hierarchy. It is something entirely created by humanity to contend with its changing circumstances—it is not natural or a reflection of some divinity, but is developed by humanity for practical reasons. Its creation arises out of three distinct challenges humanity faces in this social era. The first challenge concerns space. The creation of artificial space in the form of society necessitates governance and a set of the laws which give shape to this new environment. Just as certain natural laws dictate the structure of nature so also do laws exist in this new social environment. Second, the creation of law also stems from the challenge of time. Unpredictability and rapid change between members of society and other societies in general required an equal stabilising force. Law fulfilled this function. Finally, the third challenge met by law concerns relationships between people. In much smaller groups everyone was acquainted with one another and behavioural expectations were apparent, but with rapid interchange between societies and growing towns these expectations had to be assured elsewhere. Law provided the means by which people could assume others would act in society. Someone entering this new society was obligated to interact with other people in a particular way. It provided a necessary consistency so that society and its members could thrive.

Ellul states that any social group progresses towards infinite growth and totalisation. What begins as a creation that intends to mediate the natural environment then turns into an environment itself—what was meant to aid humanity and relieve it from the sundry dangers inherent in it becomes an area where this freedom begins to diminish. Laws tend to become more abundant and the state's responsibilities and size increase over time. There is, however, another force within society which seeks to balance this totalisation and loss of freedom of the individual. Ellul asserts, 'in a society in which power tends toward absolutism, or the hierarchy is more static and strict, or law proliferates, extending to all human activities and regulating without end, we find increasing means of evasion.'[22] This compensation in society takes several forms. As totality grows, so too does the presence of holidays and sports which provide an area of informality and leisure. It might also take on a religious form as well. Religious participation which is not heavy-handed and dogmatically institutionalised acts as a diversion and creates a place which balances the effects of an increasingly dogmatic political system.

The social body is the main environment of humanity for the historical period. It grew out of a primitive collection of individuals who found that working in tandem aided their individual lives and that of humanity in general. The creation of law and the ever-increasing size of the political body with rules to order a harmonious society became the norm for humanity. Towns and cities, representing the developing society, became the area of this new environment as nations and kingdoms fell only to have others replace them. This continued for many centuries and while this might seem to be a stable process, another force in society was forming which would ultimately cause its subjugation. Below the surface, the force of technology was gaining weight and instituted a transition for humanity and its history.

6.1.3 The Technological Environment: The Posthistorical Period

A tremendous shift has been observable from the time of the Industrial Revolution. It is plain that society has been in an accelerating vortex since that time although, Ellul claims, it only came to fruition at the beginning of the 20th century. This change is so rapid that it quickly becomes the most important force in society and sparks a complete transformation of the very environment in which humanity dwells. But, before tracing the genealogy of technology to its place as the vanguard of history one must first understand Ellul's terminology related to technology.

A common misnomer, Ellul suggests, is that technology refers directly to the world of objects. Ellul writes in both his mother tongue, French, and English and calls attention to a distinction in the French and English usage of the term technology. Ellul maintains that often people refer to technology when they should be referring to *technique*. The English term technology refers to both the process and means of a particular technical activity as well as to the objects inherent in that activity itself.[23] One refers not only to telecommunications as technology when relying upon the English word, but more importantly, to telephones, fax machines and computer modems. This has slowly found its way into French usage as well and Ellul wishes to distinguish the two for the sake of clarity. First, *technique* in French can refer to any particular method in any given trade. For example, carpenters employ countersinking, sawing and nailing with differing *techniques*. *Technique* can refer to more advanced methods such as crop rotation or it can refer to more primitive *techniques* like ploughing. What is most distinct from the English language is that *technologie* in French refers to the science of *technique*. *Technologie* is the study of *techniques* 'in tracing their history and investigating ways of improving them.'[24] It does not refer to the instruments themselves. However, what is important for Ellul's take on the issue is that *technique* soon becomes much more than the sundry means for a particular trade. Instead, *techniques* became the 'processes of constructing and exploiting machines.'[25] Ellul's study does not consider primarily the field of machines and objects that come to mind when the English term technology is invoked; rather he is concerned with how the means themselves, as well as their study, have influenced society at large. This is not to say that machines are not important to the area of *technique*:

> Technique certainly began with the machine. It is quite true that all the rest developed out of mechanics; it is quite true also that without the machine the world of technique would not exist. But to explain the situation in this way does not at all legitimize it. It is a mistake to continue with this confusion of terms, the more so because it leads to the idea that, because the machine is at the origin and center of the technical problem, one is dealing with the whole problem when one deals with the machine.[26]

In this way, the focus of Ellul's work is on something much more broad than the evoked images of robots, cars and the computer. Instead, he probes the conditions and processes which make these creations possible. Modern *technique*, for Ellul, is the 'totality of methods rationally arrived at and having absolute efficiency (for a given stage of development) in every field of human activity.'[27] This working definition lies at the centre of his inquiry of the modern situation and, as we shall see, sculpts the environment in which humanity dwells.

How then did our obsession with rational processes become an environment for humanity and how does it differ from the previous environments? The explosion of *technique* into its modern equivalent was not possible prior to certain conditions being met. Four factors harboured the growth of *technique* in this era. First, *technique* prior to the 18th century was applied to a very limited area.[28] When one probes history one discovers that the study of *technique* was fairly small in scope. The use and belief in magic was much more prevalent in this area, and where *technique* was found it was almost always secondary to other aspects. For instance, Ellul points to workers in New England who worked together not for the prime reason of amassing wealth, but to socialise.[29] Second, the immaturity of technical means and tools which then got applied to a meagre set of areas stunted its growth. The lack of robust tools had to be compensated for by the worker, so rather than improving the tool or making it more specialised the product was dependent upon the labourer. The skill of a good craftsman was legendary, but it was distinct from today in that each craftsman had their own *technique* and the best *technique* was not sought. The *technique* was subservient to the social role of the craftsmen.[30] Third, the means themselves were dependent upon a particular society and not reflected upon or compared with other means from other societies. Each people had their own *techniques* and were generally prideful of their own and sceptical of others. The fourth factor which stunted growth was that each person had no choice in the matter. Insofar as one was a part of a particular civilisation with certain practices, it was generally taboo to blaze one's own trail in the area of *technique*. All of these factors kept *technique* from spreading and it took the fecund soil of Modernity to transform *technique* into its contemporary equivalent.

Technique did not reach its status overnight. Several things made possible the explosion of *technique* in the Modern era. Ellul states that the 18th century was distinct from its predecessors and created a favourable climate which only cultivated the growth of *technique*:

> The fear of evil diminished. There was an improvement in manners; a softening of the conditions of war; an increasing sense of man's responsibility for his fellows; a certain delight in life, which was greatly increased by the improvement of living conditions in nearly all classes except the artisan; the building of fine houses in great numbers.[31]

According to Ellul, this was not enough to account for the complete transformation of humanity's environment. Additionally, there needed to be a long history of technical experience from which the Modern era could derive its growth.[32] A critical mass of technical innovation was clearly present out of which the 18th century could perfect what was already present—all that was required was a mere structuring of prior invention. Population expansion was another clear precursor. According to Ellul, there is a close link between the expansion of *technique* and population growth. This is exactly what occurred in the 18th century as the population reached this threshold where the needs inherent in such a large population could only be met through technical means. Third, the economy needed to be stable enough so as to propagate clear research in technical areas, but at the same time it needed to be flexible so that it could incorporate these changes that were discovered and created through that very research. Fourth, the social environment needed to be plastic enough so as to be moulded by the technical revolution without rejecting its influence. This could only occur with the disappearance of social taboos and natural social groups. Certain social taboos existed until the 17th century which made altering the natural order of things very difficult. The position of the clergy, nobility and especially kings was not to be interfered with and technical advancement was seen as an affront to this natural order.[33] The natural social groups were also deteriorating about this time under 'the guise of a defense of the rights of the individual'.[34] Society became more and more atomised with the individual becoming the main social unit. Despite all these factors, the most important was a clear technical intention. Ellul cites the influence of much of 18th century philosophy bolstered by Hegel and later Marx to coalesce this will, but it was the arrival of special interest which really solidified this intention: 'But it was only when industrial self-interest, for the sake of efficiency, demanded a search for the "one best way to do work" that research was begun by Gilbreth in the field of *technique*, with the amazing results we see today.'[35] It was first found in the state which developed political and industrial *technique* initially, but which later spread to military and judicial *technique*. These special interests were then found in the 18th century *bourgeoisie* and entrepreneurs who discovered the profitability of a good *technique*. No longer would the power which derived from these *techniques* be reserved for the public sector alone, but became a part of the private sphere where capitalistic ventures thrived on these new *techniques*. With this, the transition to the technological environment was complete and all the mechanisms were in place so that only time was needed to transform society into its own environment.

Technology has become the sole mediator of all relations in this new environment and the relation humanity has with this new environment is very different from its previous environments. For instance, this mediation is entirely autonomous.[36] According to Ellul, technology evades any system of values by which one can choose for or against technology. The environment is such that the mediation is *a priori* a reality through which human beings must interact with one another and the world. The technological mediation is also sterile and sterilising according to Ellul. He states:

> . . . technology is essentially sterile and sterilizing, contrary to all previous systems of mediation, which were plurivocal, equivocal, unstable in their applications, and also deeply rooted in a rich and creative unconscious. Technology, on the other hand, is univocal, superficial, but stable. It involves clear and orderly mediation, but without playing or evoking, without remembering or projecting. It is a truly efficient medium, and it has imposed itself in lieu of poetic mediations.[37]

Finally, the mediation between technology and humanity is distinct from other environments in that it is not regulated by anything else. The mediation is not reflected upon so that the thinking individual comes between the individual and technology and furthermore, no culture exists that might preempt the technological milieu and act as an arbitrating force.[38] It is distinct from all other environments in its discrete totality in dealing with humanity.

How then does the technological environment, if it does mediate differently from its predecessors, react and respond to the previous environments of which humanity has been a part? Ellul gives a very strong response to this question. Technology can only become the new environment for humanity by supplanting the old ones. This implies that in order for technology to become the new environment it must destroy the others by exploiting them until there is nothing left. Ellul claims that the recent depletion of natural resources is due to abusive technologies, but, more importantly, it is a necessary feature of subverting the previous environments. It does this by dividing and fragmenting the old natural and social milieus. Technology reduces and simplifies the previous realities by compartmentalising them so that they can be studied and used on their own. The natural and social worlds get used as resources and plundered for technology's aims.[39] These environments are restructured and rearranged so that the simplest of elements can be artificially manipulated. Abstraction and control become the *raison d'être* of the technological environment, and despite its reliance upon the previous environment for resources it will stop at nothing to shut this dependence off. Technology wishes[40] to turn in on itself and enclose humanity so it increasingly has less interaction with other environments: 'there is a trend toward a genuine enclosure in this environment.'[41]

Therefore, because technology becomes the one means by which one interacts with all else, it becomes the sole determining factor for society and the future. Ellul's account of history, which is defined by these three consecutive environments, first in the natural and then the social, focuses in to our present circumstance where technology is the mediating environment of all relations. If we are to understand contemporary history then we must study technology. And, if we want to understand what the future holds we must recognise how technology influences every area of our lives.

How exactly does technology operate on its own? What are the laws that govern its functioning? We have reflected upon this in part, but only with regard to its role as an environment in which humanity dwells. According to Ellul, it is much more than an environment. In fact, Ellul asserts that it is a system. Before turning to Ellul's eschatology where technology and the Christian future meet, we look more deeply at how technology is shaping our present and what this will mean for the future.

6.2   MODERN TECHNOLOGY CHARACTERISED

After publishing his widely successful work on technology, *The Techno-logical Society*, Ellul became increasingly aware that further description and honing was required. *Technique* needed to be explicated on its own terms and could no longer be defined according to its structure in society alone, but had to be characterised in accordance with system theory. His contact with system theory catalysed his efforts to define technology as a system in his later work, *The Technological System*.

What exactly is a system? Ellul says a system 'is a set of elements inter-relating in such a way that any evolution of one triggers a revolution of the whole, and any modification of the whole has repercussions on each element.'[42] A system is characterised by its network of intimate relations that depend upon one another for its survival. It is not a conglomeration of unrelated objects, but an ensemble that has learned to rely upon each constitutive element. Second, all elements within the system will prefer to combine with one another in relation rather than with a foreign unit from outside of this system.[43] A third feature of a system is that it is dynamic. One might analyse the system at a particular moment within its evolution, but this is only ever a partial depiction of the system and misses a crucial aspect of it as a system. Fourth, a system is never closed off entirely to other systems and will enter into relationship with other systems. The final aspect of a system is one which is dangerously absent in the technological system but still worthy of mention: the presence of structures of feedback which balance the system when a mistake is made.[44]

What are some of the features of technology as a system? One of the most elementary aspects is its relation to rationality. By this, Ellul means that wherever *technique* is found all spontaneous and illogical means must be transformed into fine-tuned processes through rational reflection. One can see this most apparently in 'systemization, division of labour, creation of standards, production norms and the like'.[45] This occurs first by getting rid of all human creativity in the process and then by applying logical calculus to the means alone—only the rational in the process is allowed to remain. As rationality is applied directly to the means themselves it becomes apparent that not all methods are equal or even desirable. As Ellul claims, 'The choice is less and less a subjective one among several means which are potentially applicable. It is really a question of finding the best means in the absolute sense, on the basis of numerical calculation.'[46] As the process becomes refined, only the most efficient and rational means to a particular end remains. In this way, technology no longer studies the various *techniques* that might be available, but rather turns into a hunt for the best *technique* possible for a given area of application.

The application of conscious rationality to a gamut of means can only ever lead then to an autonomous process that is deterministic. Ellul claims, 'This means that technology ultimately depends only on itself, it maps its own route, it is a prime and not a secondary factor, it must be regarded as an "organism" tending toward closure and self-determination: it is an end in itself.'[47] This is not to say it doesn't interact with other entities like the state or science, but Ellul contends that it exercises a certain freedom from these and does not depend upon them for its survival. In fact, Ellul would argue that the state and science depend more upon technology for their survival.[48]

Ellul also refers to automatism in his appraisal of technology. Automatism indicates the self-perpetuating nature of technology. It does not rely upon anything outside of it to function or grow. Human choice does not contribute to the technological development because rationality becomes the only factor for deciding which particular means gets taken up and is even allowed to advance. Through the very nature of 'the one' *technique* all other forms are diminished and relegated to secondary status. Its self-propagation does not come without expense. Ellul states that the technological system demands conformity and 'adjustment by the individual, the social structures, the economic factors and the ideologies.'[49] Not only are there not mechanisms in place where man can alter the automatism of technology, but humanity is even forced to adapt to technology itself. Technology becomes a self-sufficient and automated system which progresses under its own conditions while it subjects others to its own laws.

Ellul further characterises the technological system by referring to it as monistic and as comprising a particular unity. By this he means that distinct technologies and *techniques* actually form a cohesive whole which are linked together in a single organism. Ellul points out that technology's characterisation as a system is key to understanding its monistic nature.

Each component part within the system of technology is 'closely united' and dependent upon the other. Each particular technology seems to react to a common *telos* and schema to the point at which treating individual technologies as unrelated would be seriously detrimental to understanding both the whole of technology and even each constitutive technology itself. As Ellul states, 'Technologies do not have a parallel development, they do not array themselves in a "dispersed order" in a different and alien environment. The truth of the matter is that the possibility of achieving each technology demands a certain number of other achieved technologies.'[50] Each technology is irrevocably linked to another and the entire system itself can only function with the proper interaction with other parts. Ellul says this is most manifest in the phenomena of engineers and technicians combining seemingly disparate technologies to see what might come of it.[51] The systemic aspect of ostensibly unrelated technologies is very important to recognising the general trend of technology towards greater unity amidst growing specialisation of distinct technologies.

A further characteristic which is related to the unity of technology is self-augmentation. Self-augmentation signifies the additive nature of technology. The invention or discovery of new technologies necessarily leaves open the possibility for further invention and development of other related technologies. This can be seen in just about any example. The development of the personal computer and the modem led to computer networking, dedicated servers and the Internet. Technology is a cumulative enterprise as can be observed in the resiliency, rise and profitability of the technical sector in general—growth in the technical economic market depends upon the invention and extension of existing technologies. Technological innovation creates a space for more related technological mechanisms as the technical sphere grows and becomes more particularised.[52]

Technology then tends towards universalisation. As technology self-augments and new technologies are created, this tends to creep into areas where rationality has never been applied. Universality refers to this totalising feature of technology as it spreads to every area of human endeavour. Universalisation rests on two forces. First, the self-propagating feature of technology necessarily causes all other nonrational means to fall by the wayside precisely because, in a kind of survival of the fittest scenario, only the most efficient will remain. As Fasching claims, 'The entrance of *technique* into a non-technical milieu forces its transformation into a technical one, since efficiency renders all less efficient means obsolete.'[53] Yet, the second force also helps further this trend towards universalisation: Humanity has been entirely swept away by the technical revolution—it provides no resistance to technology's growth:

> On the other hand, all people in our time are so passionate about technology, so utterly shaped by it, so assured of its superiority, so engulfed in the technological environment, that they are all, without exception,

oriented toward technological progress, all working toward it, no matter what their trade, each individual seeking the best way to use his
instrument or perfect a method, a device etc.[54]

This pervasion into different areas, which is propelled by humanity's support[55] and the natural functioning of technology, is in some ways clandes-
tine. Major advancements in the technological system are not what make
it profoundly universal, although this does help. Rather, it is the numerous
small refinements, based upon rationality and which seek to simplify the
overall system, which make the most difference to its universality.[56] The
technological system is becoming all-encompassing and is doing so silently
and without counterforce.

We now reach the end of Ellul's strictly sociological account of history.
From the natural environment to the social and now our current technological condition, it is not difficult to see that Ellul's analysis is far-reaching and
exhaustive. Indeed, Ellul probes history for the sole purpose of contextual-
ising our current situation which is why the majority of his effort is spent
analysing technology. But, where has Ellul left us in his analysis? One cannot
help but feel that if this were all Ellul offered, it would seem to be a dark analysis without any room for hope or rudder by which we can navigate through
this new force in history—technology. Ellul has not remained silent on this
issue. Despite offering a technological and historical determinism he has not
shut the door on hope. In order to understand Ellul's solution, we must turn
to his religious response found within Christian eschatology. We now turn
from his sociological works to his distinctly religious and Christian writings.

6.3 TECHNOLOGY AND THE CHRISTIAN RESPONSE

Ellul believes that a gross misestimation and appraisal has been made of
religiosity in the past century. Theologians and sociologists alike admit that
something drastic has occurred to the way people relate to religion. They
argue that the Modern era is characterised by its reliance upon rationality
and increasing distrust of religion. Society, they say, has become secularised
and no longer concerns itself with the question of God. In fact, they say it
is this rationality in the form of the scientific endeavour which has been
instrumental in our world come of age. This secularisation has led many to
observe that nothing is sacred in our contemporary society where atheism
is normative and commonplace. Ellul claims that often these critics associate observation and a descriptive analysis with an imperative—that confusion is propounded where observation of secularism slips into an 'ought' of
secularisation.[57] Not only is the death of God declared a fact, but even 'the
Christian . . . tells modern man that he should definitely abandon God if he
would be a man and fulfil his vocation.'[58] This speaks towards more than a
disengaged appraisal towards secularisation, but of the attitude of man who
is confronted by it. Yet, Ellul asserts that a post-Christian society which has

become 'laicized'[59] does not necessarily entail a complete destruction or a complete removal of the sacred or religion. The secular society implies that modern man functions without reference to myth or religion; however, Ellul asserts that despite the absence of what seems to be traditional myth and religion in modern society, they still exist. He says:

> If, after examining everything which those primarily involved agree to call religion or myth, I discover phenomena not expressly called religion or myth but fulfilling the same function, I would be entitled to say that, while the vocabulary has changed, the substantial reality is identical, and I find that I am really in the presence of a religion or of a myth.[60]

Ellul suggests that the category of the religious and the sacred has not been entirely eradicated; rather, it has merely been repositioned.

The sacred, for Ellul, is precisely that which provides ultimate meaning and a fulfilling life to humanity. The sacred provides necessary 'points of reference' which act as guiding marks in how to navigate life. It provides taboos and a general structure to the conditions of living thereby providing the basis for meaning in life and laying its boundaries.[61] Yet, in this demarcation the individual is also challenged and is filled with dread towards the sacred inasmuch as his individual freedom is confronted. The sacred represents that which is advisable, but also distinguishes itself from the profane. It represents this discrimination and separation. The sacred also provides structure in its relation to time.[62] It provides a space where ecstasy and disorder are allowed to come to the fore. The sacred also functions to mediate the way in which the individual is a part of the group. The sacred is sacred for a particular community and its power resides in the deference its members give to it. In this way, it is evident that the sacred provides a consistent structure that humanity abides by and lives in.

What Ellul makes clear is that often the sacred is associated with the natural environment. However, he insists that this is due to its members extrapolating meaning from their particular environment rather than it being definitive for the sacred as such. In other words, it was sacred not because it was natural, but only because it was all-encompassing. As Ellul states, 'he [humanity] has to attribute an ultimate quality to that condition because it is inevitable. He has to place a value on it because it has been imposed upon him. He has to transmute it into the order of the sacred because he cannot conceive of himself outside of that order.'[63] What is more, as a shift in the sacred occurs in connection with a changing environment there also seems to be an equal force desacralising the previous environment. The sacred, yoked to the natural elements, is desacralised by the institution of the Christian church such that natural religion becomes overturned or disenchanted in the face of this new sacred derived from 'higher' religions.[64]

From here it is very easy to see how Ellul's assertion that the sacred is still an important part of our modern condition could be tenable. The sacred is contingent upon humanity's experience in the world and, in a modern society, it only seems reasonable that what is held as sacred should reflect this change in society. Therefore, Ellul claims:

> That is why the sacred now being elaborated in the individual and in the collective consciousness is tied to society and technique, not to nature. . . . Society now becomes the ground and the place of the forces which man discerns or feels as sacred, but it is a society turned technician, because technique has become the life milieu of man.[65]

The technological society and, indeed, *technique* itself becomes sacred.

What does this mean for Ellul? One does not have the option to choose between sacralising something or not. Humanity attributes meaning to its life through this process and whether we do it consciously or not, Ellul asserts, we will continue doing it. The major issue, for our purposes, is that technology has become much more than a set of tools. Ellul stresses that technology is not necessarily, in itself, enslaving. Rather, it is our attitude, our transference of it to the sacred, which makes it enslaving.[66] Therefore, Ellul's characterisation of technology as a system of totality entirely depends upon how society relates to it. Our hallowing of technology feeds into its systemic nature. Some may maintain that the technological society is really a technological system. However, Ellul makes constant reference to the disparity and distinction between the technological society and the technological system. As he states:

> Still one thing seems absolutely certain: the difference and opposition between the development of the technological system on one hand and society and human beings on the other. People have said . . . that our society is a technological society. But this does not mean that it is entirely modelled on or entirely organized in terms of technology. What it does mean is that technology is the dominant factor, the determining factor within society . . .[67]

Seen in this way, his sociological and religious analysis of technology is more of a prophetic message of what society is in process of becoming. If this is the case, how does Ellul think humanity can keep society from becoming a deterministic system? How can humanity remain free in a world which is running in opposition to this freedom?

Ellul maintains that, in part, recognising the conditions of technology and reflecting upon them is already the first step in turning from this future. It is through contemplation that one can exist in defiance of the technological system. Contemplation is a different way of interacting in the world. Rather than being swept away by the propaganda of the technological society and being subjected to its unitary vision, Ellul asserts that contemplation is the 'art of discovering things that science and technology cannot reveal.'[68] Contemplation is the thoughtful action wherein one distinguishes between mere controlled activism and that which is affirming of one's own identity separate from the technological society. Contemplation is the way in which an individual can begin to act in opposition to the moulding of technology.

Yet is individual effort enough? One's identity is fully integrated into the technological society and Ellul, of all people, has shown that individual effort alone mistakenly presupposes that a vantage point can be taken outside of the technological system. Ellul has revealed a situation that makes this very unlikely, if not impossible. If this is only a partial solution to the creep of technology, how then can humanity's future be safeguarded?

This is where Ellul's advocacy of Christian apocalyptic hope and his eschatology comes into play. The desacralisation of the technological society implies that something must take its place. Something must be given to human beings which, in their freedom, they can hope for. Stripping the technological human from that which he hopes for and relies upon in technology without providing an adequate substitute would lead to disorientation. This is where Ellul contends only an apocalyptic hope safeguards the freedom and stability of humanity.

What then is this apocalyptic hope? First, it is not an image of the future. As Ellul clearly states, it should not be seen as just another utopia to be set alongside other utopias: 'If, on the contrary, it is claimed that Jesus at least presented a real view of the future, I would reply that in fact he did no such thing, since his was an eschatological conception, the very opposite of an "image of the future".'[69] It is not mere projection from our current circumstances to the end of time. It is not an entirely immanent perspective on the world in which what is actual in the world—the forms, structures and laws—are then worked out through to the end of history. It is not a future based upon *futurum*. In fact, Christian apocalyptic hope is completely opposed to utopia. According to Ellul, humanity's projection into the future in the form of utopia enslaves humanity in this false hope. Instead, the structure of real hope is to be found in the biblical book of Revelation and in apocalyptic writing.

The book of Revelation is often interpreted as a dark puzzle which paints a bleak future. It seems it would hardly be the kind of narrative which would evoke hope in its readers. But, it is precisely out of this dark future that a real hope arises for Ellul. The book of Revelation is unique, for Ellul, because it marks a revolutionary hope in the face of a real determinism. This is precisely where it becomes evident that apocalyptic hope can respond to our current technological situation, for hope arises in the midst of an enslaving situation. Real hope, which can be found in the apocalyptic writings of Revelation, does not derive from the confidence that tomorrow will be better:

> First of all, hope is, when the human condition is without issue; when there is not, from the human point of view, any means of escape; when

there is not, in a reasonable expectation, any positive result; when there is no longer, apparently, any history still possible; when there is no longer any possibility in any sense; then hope is the affirmation of the 'in spite of'.[70]

True hope can only exist in an apocalyptic situation in opposition to the powers creating the determinism. This hope appears from outside one's expectation and is situated in a place where humanity has nowhere else to turn. It is true *adventus*.

Ellul argues the book of Revelation and apocalyptic writing in general have often been labelled ahistorical and mystical.[71] One of the most pressing criticisms of this genre is that in referring to a separate place it distinguishes itself from this history and reality. Critics say Revelation and apocalyptic writing is too idealistic because it emphasises a major break in continuity between what the Apocalypse posits and this world. The Apocalypse is something that occurs to humanity where humanity is the observer of such events and plays only a minor role. Often, and this is the case for the book of Revelation, apocalyptic writing contains a violent war between the two major players: cosmic good and evil.[72]

In contrast to this is prophetic thought. Humanity's role is much more active in prophetic eschatology as an imperative is issued which is based upon historical events. The prophet focuses upon the past to issue a warning against the peril that is to come if the people do not change. The crux of the prophetic message relies on the intended action of those hearing the message whereas apocalyptic eschatology focuses on the imagery of the scene presented. Apocalypticism is criticised for not paying enough attention to this world and its own immanent history.

Nevertheless, Ellul suggests, while this might seem to be true of apocalyptic thought it is not entirely correct. The Apocalypse, for Ellul, is the point where God breaks into human history and situates humanity within the greater schema of His kingdom. Ellul asserts 'prophecy describes for us a moment of history in showing us its insertion in the totality of the design of God and in calling us to make history. The Apocalypse does not describe a moment of history but reveals for us the permanent depth of the historical.'[73] Thus, the Apocalypse does not refer only to human history, but, more importantly, it reveals God's working in cosmic history. The Apocalypse does not project into the future or even refer to a specific time ahead, but instead works backwards from the fulfilment of God's completed action in His own time:

It is not the 'what must come' that is essential, but the 'soon'. Actually the Apocalypse is a book of imminence, or urgency. . . . It is the imminence of God in time, it is the 'clash' between two irreconcilable and unimaginable dimensions, that of Eternity and Time . . . that of the Wholly Other and the Similar, that of the Not Yet and the Already, that of the Absolute and the Contingent.[74]

The Apocalypse contextualises our human situation and announces that despite the destruction of real human history through technological determinism, a space is created in the penultimate promise and fulfilment.[75] This promise is lived in by hope and gives real weight to human history while asserting its inclusion in God's plan. Furthermore, the Apocalypse does not present itself entirely as a world outside of human history or at the end of time, but something which is lived and enacted within the confines of this world. The Apocalypse is really present and does much more than provide a weak hope which doesn't change one's present situation: 'And these last things are present, actual; it is in terms of them, from now on revealed and so discernable, that we have to read our actuality.'[76] This then becomes the groundwork for Ellul's Christian ethics as radical, apocalyptic hope gives way to a distinct space in which the Christian lives.[77] It is precisely this living in hope in spite of technological determinism which mediates the Apocalypse here and now as it provides the basis for the Christian life. The Apocalypse resides within and through that very hope where the Christian rests in the presence of the Kingdom.[78]

Thus, it is manifest that the Apocalypse and hope provide the perspective outside of the technological society Ellul suggests is required for humanity. He contends that something entirely distinct from the technological society is required from which one can judge the situation and from which one can gain a foothold. This does not come, he says, from religion or the human construct of religion. When he speaks of the Apocalypse, hope and the transcendent God, he does not refer to the phenomenon of religion which, he states, is based upon human feeling and action.[79] The Apocalypse is the pure revelation of God himself in history. Only the Wholly Other who comes to this world can truly save it and provide the adequate perspective from which to escape the creep of the technological system. Ellul asserts, 'thus, we meet this transcendent, *whose sole action is an action of liberating us, a liberation which is always begun anew. This liberation can be guaranteed and certain only if God is this transcendent.*'[80]

It has been maintained that the Apocalypse, mediated by hope, brings a vision of the Kingdom of God. This then provides a space in which the Christian lives despite the hopelessness of the technological situation. Real perspective, from beyond the sway of technological determinism, can be gained by taking an *adventus* outlook on history and the future.

Some might worry that the Kingdom of God represents a break with human history and its creation. A concern might be that this space is merely a parallel existence which is destructive of human creation as God's reign is superimposed over it. If the Christian is meant to live in the world, but in defiance of it, does human history have any value in God's plan?[81]

This revelation which reveals the Kingdom does not act in defiance of human work and creativity. Rather Ellul asserts, 'I am convinced that all the works of humankind will be reintegrated in the work of God, and that each one of us, no matter how sinful, will ultimately be saved. In other words, the situation may be historically dreadful; but it is never desperate on any level.'[82] This conviction is best observed in Ellul's treatment of the city.[83] The city represents for Ellul the epitome of human creation and is most often associated with the technological system.[84] It was the city which separated humanity from the natural world and provided a physical space in which they no longer needed to worry about the threat and variation of the natural world. However, the city has more than a sociological function for Ellul. It carries spiritual and symbolic value as well. In his research into the meaning of the various cities in the Bible, he attributes spiritual significance to their presence in the text. Humanity was originally placed in the Garden of Eden and in this place humanity was satisfied with what it provided. Humanity, once separated from God, is subsequently thrown from the garden. The construction of sundry notable cities in the Bible—Babel, Babylon, Sodom, Nineveh—are meant to contrast with the provision originally sustained in the garden. Ellul says that the city has a negative meaning in the Bible and is the place where humanity has always chosen to be in opposition to God: Babel excludes God through its own seeking of transcendence; Sodom is a city of corruption; Babylon invents its own gods; and Nineveh represents violence and war. It is only with the construction of the temple and of Jerusalem more broadly that we begin to see God's presence and blessing of the city.[85] It is the New Jerusalem, as city, in biblical eschatology that signifies God's action in aligning himself with all of human creation.[86] Ellul states, 'All human history, then, will enter the new Jerusalem. The creation of the final city is the obvious consummation, not the result, of all that we attempt in history. Nothing in history (collective or individual) is lost, but everything is qualitatively transformed.'[87] God's coming does not obliterate human creation, including technology, but rather is transformed and taken up by God's kingdom.[88]

6.4 CONCLUSION

Ellul has provided a very interesting integration of Christianity and technology. He begins with a sociological analysis of our contemporary society and traces the history of how our environment has become dictated entirely by technology. In this study, he outlines the various characteristics of technology in modern society and identifies it as a system of totality which has become deterministic. It is only the Christian response in the form of a transcendent God who comes to the world, *adventus*, which can fully provide a reference point outside of technological determinism. Humanity's liberation from the technological force is dependent upon God's intervention in an apocalyptic present. The Christian then lives in this liberation through hope until the time in which all is transformed into the Kingdom of God.

What should we take from Ellul? First, Ellul is still a seminal figurehead in the study of technology and its effect on society. His sociological work in this area is valuable on its own. Second, the strength of Ellul's contentions related to technology, the future and Christianity is that he preserves the distinction between human creation, which is inclusive of technology, and God's action in this world. One does not collapse into the other through some progression where the identity of each is compromised. God's condescension does not entirely eradicate the human condition, but transforms it in the eschaton. This is distinct from Teilhard in that Ellul advocates an eschatological transformation that is radical and mysterious. If Teilhard favours God's work in tandem with the forces inherent in human history, Ellul complexifies this and emphasises the newness and radical transformative element of our work into the Kingdom of God. Ellul is useful for our purposes because he emphasises in his approach to technology and the future that a Christian account of the technological future must, in the end, appeal to God who transforms everything.[89]

However, Ellul has several weaknesses as well. Ellul is often cited as being too critical of technology. Indeed, this criticism blinds him from citing some of the major strides technology has made in making life better for everyone. He cannot recognise the positive value of certain technologies such as those in the medical industry because he perceives it only in connection to the overall picture of technology as a network of totality and determinism.[90] He does not suggest that all technology itself is bad, but what it has become systemically is a point of concern and all technologies must be seen in this general light. Does his appeal to technological determinism hinder him from seeing the real benefits technology can provide? If we take Ellul's final eschatology into account where he assures us that human effort should be seen within the Kingdom of God, then this should make one less negative about technology itself. Instead of creating such a bifurcated either/or, his eschatology should inform all of his other work. Ellul should see technology through the lens of the New Jerusalem rather than in opposition to God's kingdom. He should observe technology transformed rather than as a separation from God.

As suggested at the beginning of this chapter, both responses to technology, from Ellul and Teilhard, seem to be entirely informed by their respective confessions. If we take technology to be an extension of the created world then it is easy to see how Teilhard's Roman Catholic presuppositions do not hinder the harmonious integration of technology and eschatology. Human creation through technology would not signal a break or a strict separation between the two, for both have worked together since the beginning. On the other hand, Ellul was influenced by Barth and the Reformed tradition, so his understanding of creation and the immanent world is much more suspicious of God's image in the created orders. This makes his approach tend to favour apocalypticism where divine revelation in the Word, in spite of creation, is efficacious to bring about the Kingdom of God. The Kingdom of God, for Teilhard, works from and in continuity with the immanent creation and in human work, but for Ellul, the Kingdom of God is something that comes to us and must be lived in outside of warped human endeavours.

Teilhard and Ellul are much closer in their responses than we might suppose at first. Both consider technology, on its own terms, to be insufficient for a positive human future. Teilhard has reservations about premature convergence and this most necessarily applies to technology. Ellul posits that only the Christian God can save us from the sociological determinism that has been instituted by technology. They both recognise that technology on its own can be hazardous without the influence of the Christian God. It is in this conviction that both share a common view; they merely disagree on how this then gets worked out. Both have offered arguments for why a future or eschatology without some kind of religious aid is very bleak and possibly detrimental. In responding to something like the transhumanism movement or other technological futurisms, this aspect needs to be emphasised in the dialogue. The *telos* of technology needs to consider religious ideals and a religious ethic. Pure technological transcendence apart from the Christocentric mutual love and apocalyptic hope is potentially dehumanising. What we can glean from both authors is the necessity to inform technological transcendence and the future with the Christian God. Imagining the future must not only include our own work in technology, but also God's completion in the eschaton.

In fact, in our response to transhumanism, we should take the lead from Ellul and Teilhard in that Christian eschatology is much more than mere projection into the future, *futurum*. Both Ellul and Teilhard assert the novelty of the eschaton over and against a secular futurist position. Pannenberg is correct in asserting that Christian eschatology differs from secular futurism in that in Christian eschatology 'the future is taken to confront and even to run counter to the present world, including the trends of its development.'[91] On the other hand, secular futurism is projection from what is actual now into the future, *futurum*. This stark contrast is most observable in the theology of hope tradition and, for our purposes, even Ellul. The eschaton for Ellul signifies an event in the future of which technology plays a role and also something which relates as much to the present in the form of hope. Christian eschatology does not wait for some future date to realise its vision, but is something which is efficacious now and reveals God's promise in the present. Christian eschatology comments on the present and makes it bearable in a way that is absent in futurism. As Pannenberg notes, 'the theological assumption that the future is not simply an extrapolation and prolongation of present and past, but a reality in its own right is based upon the idea of God.'[92] This idea is that a separate reality from this world exists, the Kingdom of God, which is entirely distinct from mere extrapolation from the present. It is precisely the hope in this novel future, acting presently, that distinguishes itself from purely secular technological futurisms. Indeed, a Christian distinction should bring to the table the notion of promise and hope which can be lived today and orients one's present.

More will be said on this in the final two chapters. But, before constructing a Christian approach to the technological future, we must turn to another source in the 20th century who has reflected on the technological future from within the philosophical camp. We now turn to Martin Heidegger's appraisal of technology and the future.

NOTES

1. Ellul explicitly condemns Teilhard and often those who bear a mark of totality and progress in their history and future. See Jacques Ellul, *What I Believe*, trans., Geoffrey William Bromiley (London: Eerdmans, 1989), 13, 97.
2. See especially Jacques Ellul, *Jesus and Marx: From Gospel to Ideology*, trans., Joyce Main Hanks (Grand Rapids: Eerdmans, 1988).
3. This isn't to say that society isn't important for Teilhard or even that the natural world isn't a central part of history for Ellul. But, their relative vocations, Ellul the sociologist and Teilhard the palaeontologist, impact their methodology and focus in giving an account of history and the future.
4. Ellul has Teilhard, and others like him, in mind when making such a claim. See note 1 above.
5. Ellul, *What I Believe*, 92.
6. Ibid., 99–100.
7. Ibid.
8. Ibid.
9. It is this last feature which signals a jettisoning of one environment and adopting another.
10. Ellul, *What I Believe*, 104.
11. Ibid., 105.
12. Ibid., 106–107.
13. Ibid., 111.
14. Ibid., 113.
15. Ibid.
16. Ibid., 116.
17. Ibid., 117.
18. For an interesting discussion on how artificiality and nature relate see Jacques Ellul, "Nature, Technique and Artificiality," in *Research in Philosophy and Technology*, ed., Paul Durbin (Greenwich: JAI Press, 1980).
19. Ellul, *What I Believe*, 115.
20. Ibid., 118–119.
21. Ibid., 120–121.
22. Ibid., 125.
23. Jacques Ellul, *The Technological System*, trans., Joachim Neugroschel (New York: Continuum, 1980), 26.
24. Ibid., 24.
25. Ibid.
26. Jacques Ellul, *The Technological Society*, trans., John Wilkinson (New York: Vintage Books, 1964), 3–4.
27. Ibid., xxv.
28. Ibid., 64.
29. Ibid., 65.
30. Ibid., 66–67.
31. Ibid., 47.

32. Ibid.
33. Ibid., 48.
34. Ibid., 51.
35. Ibid., 53.
36. Ellul, *The Technological System*, 36.
37. Ibid., 37.
38. More will be said on the interaction between humanity and the technological system in the next section.
39. This bears remarkable similarity to Heidegger's contention that the essence of technology is *Bestand*—treating everything as 'standing reserve' or as a resource to be utilised. See the next chapter on Heidegger for more details.
40. This kind of personification of technology is not unique to Ellul. A famous contemporary technologist and the editor of *Wired* magazine, Kevin Kelly, has recently written a book entitled *What Technology Wants* where he makes the case that attributing agency to technology should not be dismissed so quickly. See Kevin Kelly, *What Technology Wants* (New York: Viking, 2010).
41. Ellul, *The Technological System*, 49.
42. Ibid., 77.
43. Ibid.
44. For further clarification on how this makes a difference for the technological system see ibid., 117–121.
45. Ellul, *The Technological Society*, 79.
46. Ibid., 21.
47. Ellul, *The Technological System*, 125.
48. Ibid., 130–153.
49. Ibid., 240.
50. Ibid., 159.
51. Ibid.
52. This feature of technology is what makes the transhumanist's future predictions about the growth of technology so plausible. Technology can be easily broken down into component parts and recombined and extended with very little effort. See chapter 4 for more detail.
53. Darrell J. Fasching, *The Thought of Jacques Ellul: A Systematic Exposition* (Lewiston: Edwin Mellen Press, 1981), 17.
54. Ellul, *The Technological System*, 209.
55. Ellul contends that this unabashed support of technological progress is ill-founded. In fact, he proclaims that technology has provided humanity with the greatest of bluffs and seeks to reveal this contention in Jacques Ellul, *The Technological Bluff*, trans., Geoffrey W. Bromiley (Grand Rapids: Eerdmans, 1990).
56. Ellul, *The Technological System*, 226.
57. Jacques Ellul, *The New Demons* (London: Mowbrays, 1975), 39.
58. Ibid.
59. This term relates to the transfer of power from a select real body which ruled over the masses to a virtual collection of individuals. This term connotes, for Ellul, an opposition to the Christian religion, as opposed to revelation and faith, as one of these real bodies. See ibid., 29–30.
60. Ibid., 47.
61. Ibid., 50–51.
62. Ibid., 52.
63. Ibid., 50.
64. Ibid., 58.
65. Ibid., 66.
66. Ibid., 206.

67. Jacques Ellul, *Perspectives on Our Age: Jacques Ellul Speaks on His Life and Work*, trans., Joachim Neugroschel, ed., Willem H. Vanderburg (New York: Seabury Press, 1981), 68–69.
68. Jacques Ellul, *Autopsy of Revolution*, trans., Patricia Wolf (New York: Alfred A. Knopf, 1971), 285. This way of thinking is very reminiscent of Heidegger's response to technology as well. Poetry and true Heideggerean thinking are other helpful methods and forms for existing in and knowing the world which keep technology from completely encapsulating humanity. See the next chapter for further details.
69. Jacques Ellul, "Search for an Image," *The Humanist* 33, no. 6 (1973), 22.
70. Jacques Ellul, *Apocalypse: The Book of Revelation*, trans., George W. Schreiner (New York: Seabury Press, 1977).
71. Ibid., 20–23.
72. Ibid., 21.
73. Ibid., 24.
74. Ibid., 26.
75. Ellul imports this directly from Jürgen Moltmann. A greater appraisal of this approach to the future will be the subject of chapter 8.
76. Ellul, *Apocalypse*, 24.
77. Ellul works out how the Christian is to live in this hope in Jacques Ellul, *The Ethics of Freedom*, trans., Geoffrey William Bromiley (London: Mowbrays, 1976).
78. Ellul states, 'The apocalyptic conception of history results from the apprehension of hope, from life in hope, of which it is the intellectualized expression.' See Ellul, *Apocalypse*, 60; Jacques Ellul, *The Presence of the Kingdom* (Colorado Springs: Helmers & Howard, 1989).
79. Ellul, *Perspectives on Our Age*, 94.
80. Ibid., 103.
81. This question is a central feature of the final two chapters.
82. Ellul, *Perspectives on Our Age*, 104.
83. See especially Jacques Ellul, *The Meaning of the City*, trans., Dennis Pardee (Grand Rapids: Eerdmans, 1970).
84. Ellul, *What I Believe*, 185.
85. Ellul, *The Meaning of the City*, 94–112.
86. Ellul, *What I Believe*, 219ff.
87. Ibid., 42.
88. This transformation signifies the new ways in which our efforts in history and our human creations are attributed with surprising significance in the Kingdom of God. It is this surprising element, a feature which bears much in common with God's new possibilities spoken of in chapter 8 of this thesis, which is absolutely central to Ellul's idea of transformation. We can't calculate or even quantify how our work today, even in technology, will have ultimate value. See ibid., 217–218.
89. I am not saying that Teilhard doesn't allow for God to transform the world but rather that Ellul emphasises God's work in ushering the kingdom in a way that is much more radical than Teilhard.
90. In fact, Ellul shares with transhumanists the conviction that technology determines history and is a feature of our ultimate future. Both uphold a kind of technological and historical determinism. It is how they view this totality and determinism which separates them.
91. Wolfhart Pannenberg, "Future and Unity," in *Hope and the Future of Man*, ed., Ewert H. Cousins (London: Garnstone Press, 1973), 61.
92. Ibid., 62.

REFERENCES

Ellul, Jacques. "Modern Myths." *Diogenes* 6 (1958): 23–40.

———. "Technology and Culture." In *Encyclopaedia Britannica Conference on the Technological Order* 3, 394–421, Autumn 1962.

———. *The Technological Society.* Translated by John Wilkinson. New York: Vintage Books, 1964.

———. *The Meaning of the City.* Translated by Dennis Pardee. Grand Rapids: Eerdmans, 1970.

———. *Autopsy of Revolution.* Translated by Patricia Wolf. New York: Alfred A. Knopf, 1971.

———. "Losing Faith in Technology." *Playboy* 18 (1971): 55–56.

———. *The Politics of God and the Politics of Man.* Grand Rapids: Eerdmans, 1972.

———. "Search for an Image." *The Humanist* 33, no. 6 (1973): 22–25.

———. *The New Demons.* London: Mowbrays, 1975.

———. *The Ethics of Freedom.* Translated by Geoffrey William Bromiley. London: Mowbrays, 1976.

———. *Apocalypse: The Book of Revelation.* Translated by George W. Schreiner. New York: Seabury Press, 1977.

———. "Technology and the Gospel." *International Review of Mission* 66, no. 262 (1977): 109–117.

———. "Karl Barth and Us: The Groundwork for Our Theological Task." *Sojourners* (December 1978): 22–24.

———. "How I Discovered Hope." *The Other Side* 16, no. 102 (March 1980): 28–31.

———. "Nature, Technique and Artificiality." In *Research in Philosophy and Technology,* edited by Paul Durbin, 3. Greenwich: JAI Press, 1980.

———. *The Technological System.* Translated by Joachim Neugroschel. New York: Continuum, 1980.

———. *Perspectives on Our Age: Jacques Ellul Speaks on His Life and Work.* Translated by Joachim Neugroschel, Edited by Willem H. Vanderburg. New York: Seabury Press, 1981.

———. "New Hope for the Technological Society: An Interview with Jacques Ellul." *Et Cetera* 40, no. 2 (Summer 1983): 192–206.

———. "Technique and the Opening Chapters of Genesis." In *Theology and Technology: Essays in Christian Analysis and Exegesis,* edited by Carl Mitcham and Jim Grote, 123–137. New York: University Press of America, 1984.

———. *The Humiliation of the Word.* Translated by Joyce Main Hanks. Grand Rapids: Eerdmans, 1985.

———. "The Global Technological System and the Human Response." *Bulletin of Science, Technology and Society* 8 (April 1988): 139–142.

———. *Jesus and Marx: From Gospel to Ideology.* Translated by Joyce Main Hanks. Grand Rapids: Eerdmans, 1988.

———. *The Presence of the Kingdom.* Colorado Springs: Helmers & Howard, 1989.

———. *What I Believe.* Translated by Geoffrey William Bromiley. London: Eerdmans, 1989.

———. *The Technological Bluff.* Translated by Geoffrey W. Bromiley. Grand Rapids: Eerdmans, 1990.

Ellul, Jacques, and Patrick Chastenet. *Jacques Ellul on Religion, Technology, and Politics.* Atlanta: Scholars Press, 1998.

Fasching, Darrell J. *The Thought of Jacques Ellul: A Systematic Exposition.* Lewiston: Edwin Mellen Press, 1981.

Goddard, Andrew. *Living the Word, Resisting the World: The Life and Thought of Jacques Ellul.* Carlisle: Paternoster, 2002.

Greenman, Jeffrey P., Read Mercer Schuchardt, and Noah Toly. *Understanding Jacques Ellul*. Eugene: Cascade Books.

Holloway, James Y. *Introducing Jacques Ellul*. Grand Rapids: Eerdmans, 1970.

Kelly, Kevin. *What Technology Wants*. New York: Viking, 2010.

McLuhan, Eric, and Frank Zingrone, eds. *Essential McLuhan*. London: Routledge, 1997.

Pannenberg, Wolfhart. "Future and Unity." In *Hope and the Future of Man*, edited by Ewert H. Cousins. London: Garnstone Press, 1973.

Part III

Philosophical and Theological Issues in Technology and the Future

7 Heidegger
Ontology, Technology and Eschatology

'Wie aber, wenn wir die Zukunft als das verstehen, was heute auf uns zukommt?'[1]

—Martin Heidegger (1961)

There are several reasons why it is not only advisable, but even imperative to include Heidegger in our treatment of technology and the future. First, Heidegger is one of the most important figures in the philosophy of technology: 'Most philosophers of technology would probably agree that, for good or for ill, Martin Heidegger's interpretation of technology, its meaning in Western history, and its role in contemporary human affairs is probably the single most influential position in the field.'[2] Second, Heidegger has come to influence some of the most important work on theology and eschatology in the 20th century. Theologians such as Rudolf Bultmann, John Macquarrie, Karl Rahner and even contemporaries such as John Caputo, Jean-Luc Marion and Jean-Yves Lacoste are all indebted to Heidegger. A third reason Heidegger is referenced in this study of technology and the future is that Heidegger himself lays out a particular vision of the future where technology figures strongly. His later writings, after the turn (*Kehre*),[3] on technology and poetry seem to presuppose an inherent eschatology and a look towards the future from within the technological condition. As I argue below, it is this condition—the technological—which provides the impetus in his later writings to prepare for the return of the god(s).

Finally, Heidegger's placement here is strategic because it underscores the need to place the discussion of technology to the ontological rather than the ontic alone and also because it opens up an entire line of questioning as to how the future is related to Being and ontology in general. Heidegger is employed here to open up the theme of technology and the future more broadly and will prepare the discussion in chapter 8 on the theme of possibility and promise. Heidegger is used here not just for preparation, but also to diagnose and gather up the philosophical presuppositions of technological futurism and its culmination in transhumanism. In assessing Heidegger's works it becomes apparent that any ontology which does not consider possibility as a significant theme in its own right is mislead-ing. I propose that contemporary technological futurism has only a partial, and therefore inadequate, understanding of the future precisely because its ontology depends too much upon the actual.

The shape of this chapter will consist, first, of an introduction of Hei-degger's general philosophy and his focus on ontology and the question of Being. Second, Heidegger's appropriation of Christian eschatology, particu-larly in his earlier works, will be recounted and will lay the groundwork and contextualise his later eschatology. Next, his writings on the essence of technology will be examined with particular focus on how they relate to his entire project and metaphysics. Subsequently, his later eschatology, heavily influenced by Hölderlin, will be outlined in reference to his appraisal of technology. Finally, several closing comments will be made about Hei-degger's relation to the notion of possibility and how this approach is criti-cal of an ontology of actuality, indicative of technological futurism.

7.1   HEIDEGGER AND THE QUESTION OF BEING

Being, for Heidegger, is the most important and most neglected area of phi-losophy. The question of the meaning of Being (which would later become the question of the truth of Being and finally the question of the place of Being[4]) occupied the centre of Heidegger's works throughout his lifetime and is the single line of questioning for which he is most remembered.[5] From his early engagement with Duns Scotus to his reflections on thinking and poetry—ontology was the prime focus of Heidegger's life's work.

Heidegger's *magnum opus, Sein und Zeit (Being and Time)*, attests to the primacy of the question of the meaning of Being. The unnumbered page in *Sein und Zeit*—one might call it the foreword—is particularly clear in this regard. The work opens with a quotation from Plato's *Sophist* which is tell-ing of the overall theme of Heidegger's text: 'For manifestly you have long been aware of what you mean when you use the expression "being". We, however, who used to think we understood it, have now become perplexed'.[6] As stated, Heidegger asserts that the question of the meaning of Being has been long neglected in philosophy and that it is with *Sein und Zeit* that he aims to pose the question anew. In quoting Plato, Heidegger is placing him-self in the line of philosophical thought—this is a philosophical issue—and, in going back to the undisputed beginning of philosophy in the Western world, Greece, Heidegger is preparing the scope for his entire work.[7] In utilising Plato, Heidegger means to challenge the entire philosophical tradi-tion since Plato on the question of the meaning of Being. This quotation also suggests, as Heidegger also overtly states later, that despite the term 'being' having almost universal significance—one can hardly craft a sentence or phrase without using the verb 'to be'—we have very little understanding as to its meaning. The content of the quotation is meant to evoke Heidegger's intention that his aim is to throw the reader, or perhaps thinker, back upon himself and open up a new line of questioning: Do I really know what I mean by Being? This quotation functions to elucidate that Heidegger's aim is to call into question that we, philosophers and laymen alike, need to first adopt a disposition of perplexity towards Being before we can even pose the question of the meaning of Being.[8]

Heidegger's introduction to *Being and Time* suggests that understanding Being is not as easy as it might seem *prima facie*. This difficulty is compounded because its positing is clouded by the historical reception of the importance of the question of Being. As Heidegger states, 'On the basis of the Greeks' initial contributions towards and Interpretation of Being, a dogma has been developed which not only declares the question of the meaning of Being to be superfluous, but sanctions its complete neglect.'[9] Heidegger counters these reasons for the question's apparent neglect in turn. First, one might claim that Being is the most universal predicate. Perhaps we can know Being through the entities that bear its conception. Heidegger dismisses this tack, by rejecting the usage of Being as a predicate amongst other predicates. The application of Being to a particular entity is not the same as applying some other predicate such as red, hot or furry precisely because it is universal. If one proceeded by definition through genus or species Being would be at the top and all entities on the tree would have the property Being. The only thing we have learned from this practice is that Being is not an entity and that its universality actually serves to make its definition more opaque rather than making it more comprehensible.[10] Second, some might then claim that Being itself cannot be defined and, thus, any research into the question of Being is useless and foolhardy. Heidegger contends that a premature admission of defeat lacks real 'philosophical imagination' and that a proposed failure of definition does not entail that one cannot venture into greater elucidation of Being itself. As Heidegger states here, 'The indefinability of Being does not eliminate the question of its meaning; it demands that we look that question in the face.'[11] Finally, Heidegger dismisses with the contention that the nature of Being is self-evident. He suggests that just because people constantly utilise Being in everyday language—'I *am* feeling sick', 'There *is* a horse'—does not mean one has exhausted the meaning of Being, for it is the business of philosophers to make explicit what is implicit. Therefore, according to Heidegger, our contemporary, colloquial understanding of Being is insufficient and requires a new path into the question of Being.

It is at this point that Heidegger claims in *Being and Time* that this new way into the question of Being must be through a particular entity, Dasein. Because Being is only expressed through entities—Being is always an aspect of a particular being—then one must interrogate a particular being so that Being might come to the fore. Dasein is this particular entity precisely because it is the one entity whose own Being is an issue for itself. In its existence, lived temporally, Dasein is that entity whose Being is a question.

It is in existing, through the posing of questions and its realisation of possibilities, that its essence is revealed. Heidegger claims that Dasein is unique because in some way it has an understanding of Being—it 'is ontically distinctive in that it *is* ontological'.[12]

Perhaps at this point it would be important to look in greater detail at what Heidegger means by ontology. In any given field of study, say history, there are certain objects or entities which that field studies. In this instance, they would be historical entities, perhaps events like the French Revolution. Heidegger explains that those who deal with a particular field's entities concern themselves with beings like the French Revolution, are ontical scientists and relate to specific entities themselves within the discipline. Heidegger explains that each of these ontic scientists presupposes their own specific regional ontology or those very things which distinguish it from other disciplines. A regional ontology is concerned with beings only in the perspective of a particular discipline rather than relating directly to those beings themselves. In our example, this might be considered the philosophy of history. Ontology is distinct from the ontic in that the ontic is 'concerned with beings, not with their being',[13] as with ontology. Philosophy is a unique discipline in that its responsibility is to mediate between these regional ontologies and ground them in what Heidegger calls fundamental ontology. As Heidegger states:

> The question of Being aims therefore at ascertaining the *a priori* conditions not only for the possibility of the sciences which examine entities as entities of such and such type, and, in so doing, already operate with an understanding of Being, but also for the possibility of those ontologies themselves which are prior to the ontical sciences and which provide their foundation.[14]

Fundamental ontology analyses the being of Dasein and is the central matter of *Being and Time* and is the way in which Heidegger gets at the question of Being in his earlier writings.

If the early Heidegger, the Heidegger of *Being and Time*, analyses the Being of Dasein so as to elucidate Being itself, there is a distinguishable transition in Heidegger's later writings, which give less priority to the existential analytic of the individual and, instead, focus more directly on Being apart from its entry through Dasein. In the later Heidegger we get such phrases as the 'destining of Being' (*Geschickes des Seins*) or the 'history of Being' (*Seinsgeschichte*), in which it seems the individual no longer takes precedence as the sole mediating instrument of Being, but rather Being has been freed from the existential moorings of Dasein. Being seems to have taken on a life of its own in these later writings.

This dethroning of the individual and the transition in relation to the question of Being is evident in Heidegger's essay 'The Letter on Humanism'. Heidegger is often associated with the existentialist movement popularised in France in the mid-20th century. In fact, this very essay by Heidegger is written in response to the figurehead of French existentialism, Jean-Paul Sartre, and his own *Existentialism as Humanism*. Sartre's existentialism, like Heidegger, presupposes an 'ontological homelessness'[15] where the world in which we live is foreign to our existence in it. Whether it is through Heideggerian thrownness or Sartrean facticity the world precedes us and provides the conditions for our existence and even the possibilities given to us. However, Heidegger and Sartre part company when it comes to how the individual is to relate to this facticity. For Sartre, the individual finds his meaning precisely in reaction against this very facticity. Sartre proclaims that the unique kernel of human identity resides in the freedom one has in any circumstance to choose otherwise. For Sartre, the greatest affront to human authenticity is to succumb to 'bad faith'—allowing the forces of the world, natural and through other human beings—to dictate the events of one's life.[16] Heidegger, in the aforementioned letter, is not quite so extreme in pitting one's individual existence against the world it inhabits. It is here that Heidegger says:

> The human being is rather "thrown" by being itself into the truth of being, so that ek-sisting in this fashion he might guard the truth of being, in order that beings might appear in the light of being as the beings they are. Human beings do not decide whether and how beings appear, whether and how God and the gods or history and nature come forward into the clearing of being, come to presence and depart. The advent of beings lies in the destiny of being.[17]

For Heidegger, here we see one's individual existence drawing upon the very Being which is primary and has its own history. Individuals are then seen as 'shepherds of Being' (*Hirten des Seins*) and find their value and meaning in the way in which they cohere with Being itself. What is important for Heidegger, at this point, is Being rather than the human being.

These introductory remarks on the question of Being reveal that ontology and the question of Being were Heidegger's prime inquiry throughout his life. Despite the sundry and seemingly disparate subjects such as poetry, logic and boredom, Heidegger does have a clear trajectory in his writings. The Heideggerian turn does not represent an entirely new line of thinking where he abandons his philosophical beginning for more mystical and aesthetic commentary, but is rather another pathway to understanding and clarifying Being itself. And, as we shall see, Heidegger makes extensive use of eschatology, both its form and content, to interpret ontology. It might be said that he eschatologises ontology. Before moving directly into Heidegger's later works which express his later eschatology, we first turn to his engagement with Christian eschatology and his subsequent development of a secular eschatology in his early writings, for it is out of the young Heidegger's engagement with early Christian eschatology that his own unique eschatological ontology arises.

7.2   HEIDEGGER'S APPROPRIATION OF EARLY CHRISTIAN ESCHATOLOGY[18]

Heidegger's reading of Overbeck, Dilthey and Schweitzer was central to his appropriation of early Christian eschatology. Heidegger's switch to a more philosophical route in his education upon returning to Freiburg in the winter of 1911 opened up the possibility to come into contact with these authors. As Heidegger was no longer pursuing a career in the priesthood he was allowed to attend non-Catholic lectures. It was here in the Freiburg Philosophy Faculty in the early 1910s, through such teachers as Heinrich Rickert, Richard Reitzenstein and Eduard Schwartz, that Heidegger was first introduced to the 'history of religion' school. As Heidegger's relation to Catholicism weakened through to 1919 when he officially broke with the Catholic Church,[19] his reading of Protestant thinkers strengthened a transforming philosophy and theology.

Heidegger became attracted to the interpretation of religious history and imminent eschatological expectation in the writings of Albert Schweitzer and Franz Overbeck. Heidegger began to focus on the primitive Christian experience (*das Urchristliche*) as decisive for true Christianity. From Overbeck he gleaned the apocalypticism of the early Christians and their rejection of any hope for salvation from within the confines of this world and this time. Likewise, from Schweitzer he took up the eschatological expectation of the early Christians. For Schweitzer it had no importance for how Christians might live today, but, for Heidegger, this disposition was vital for understanding the true Christian life. Besides Heidegger's appropriation of the eschatological moment from these authors, he also valued their strict historical contextualisation of Christianity rather than one which relied upon a dreamy spiritualisation which he saw in the medieval metaphysics of his Catholic upbringing. Indeed, Heidegger would also commend Dilthey for the same reason: localising the crux of Christianity with the individual's religious experience. This was a complete change in Heidegger's religious thought which turned from metaphysical speculation inherent in Catholic dogmatism to an individualised and historical human religious experience. From here, Heidegger would increasingly focus on the historical person at the centre of religious life.[20]

This new perspective on Christianity is most evident in Heidegger's recently translated text, *The Phenomenology of Religious Life*, a conglomeration of lectures given in 1920–1921, together with corresponding notes, entitled 'Introduction to the Phenomenology of Religion'. This text gives us a synthesis of Heidegger's appropriation of early Christian eschatology prior to *Being and Time*. In this work, Heidegger brings together his engagement with early Christian eschatology and his advancing usage of the phenomenological method he takes from Husserl. Heidegger criticises such theologians as Ernst Troeltsch who reduce the phenomenon of religion to an object of scientific thought.[21] Heidegger complains that this objectivity already presupposes the context in which religion draws its value as an object amongst other objects which are then analysed by philosophy. Heidegger presents a new way into approaching religious phenomena which relies heavily upon a phenomenology of the primitive religious experience. For Heidegger, this new approach to the religious is to be based upon factical life experience and this invariably means that it must relate to history and temporality—life as it is lived.[22]

What is important is that Heidegger finds this primitive religious experience in the early Christians and their expectation of the imminent Christ. Heidegger wishes to remove all the subsequent dogmatic trappings which bastardise the kernel of Christianity found in the early Christian's orientation to the eschaton.[23] To this end, Heidegger spends much of one lecture expounding upon Pauline passages in Galatians and 1 and 2 Thessalonians which get to the basis of this original Christian orientation in relation to the *parousia*. For instance, Heidegger comments on the letter to the Galatians and focuses on the 'fundamental posture of Paul' in the letter. Heidegger claims the most important thing to be gleaned from Paul's writing to the Galatians is the orientation Paul has towards Christ, not the object-content of the letter.[24] Elsewhere Heidegger comments on the important eschatological theme in 1 Thessalonians and the insecurity Paul feels in relation to it.[25] Indeed, Heidegger intimates that the basic authentic Christian experience is one of distress or affliction (*Bedrängnis*)[26] in relation to God's second coming. The basic religious mood (*Befindlichkeit*) in relation to the eschaton is not hope rooted in God's promise to be fulfilled; rather, for Heidegger, it is hardship and plight.

The years up to and including the early 1920s were central to Heidegger's turn to Protestant theology and his subsequent utilisation of Christian eschatology as formative for authentic Christian experience. His increasing dissatisfaction with Neo-Scholastic metaphysics which were indicative of his upbringing was slowly replaced with a Protestant equivalent. As seen in *The Phenomenology of Religious Life*, Christian eschatology and the eschatological anxiety in Paul's writings was decisive in transforming Heidegger's thought. Heidegger's development of distress (*Bedrängnis*) as a fundamental experience for religious life would become important for Heidegger's atheistic development of Being-towards-death found in *Being and Time*. What we will find in Heidegger's elucidation of the authentic philosophical life in *Being and Time* is very much informed by his appraisal of Christian eschatology: In fact, it seems to be a secularised version of it.

7.3   HEIDEGGER'S SECULARISED ESCHATOLOGY IN BEING-TOWARDS-DEATH

Heidegger's shifting opinion towards theology and the religious life did not end there. What marks the years following the early 1920s is Heidegger's refusal to allow theology to inform the philosophical task. An often-quoted line from Heidegger's lectures on Aristotle manifests well that Heidegger became increasingly dissatisfied with theology as a precursor to or friend of philosophy: 'Philosophy, in its radical, selfposing questionability, must be a-theistic as a matter of principle. Precisely on account of its basic intention, philosophy must not presume to possess or determine God.'[27] Indeed, these lectures on Aristotle are only a year after Heidegger's *Phenomenology of Religious Life* lectures in the winter semester of 1921–1922. What would characterise this decade of Heidegger's philosophical development would be a secularisation of the philosophical task and a decoupling of eschatology from the eschaton, replacing it instead with death.

Much of this development towards an atheistic eschatology is derived from Heidegger's reading of Kierkegaard, Dostoyevsky and Luther. His trajectory away from metaphysical and dogmatic religion found good company in these giants of the Protestant world. What Heidegger was attracted to in these authors was their radical anthropology which pitted a transcendent God against a depraved and sinful humanity. For them, only after taking seriously humanity's actual egregious state could one properly purport to suggest that God could intervene. For instance, in a lecture on Luther's view of sin in 1924 Heidegger states:

> The more one fails to recognize the radicalness of sin, the more redemption is made little of, and the more God's becoming man in the Incarnation loses its necessity. The fundamental tendency in Luther is found in this manner: the *corruptio* [corruption] of the being of man can never be grasped radically enough—and he said this precisely in opposition to Scholasticism, which in speaking of *corruptio* always minimized it.[28]

Heidegger goes on to elucidate Luther's conception of sin as the state of man. The actual state of the world and man is not glorious, as with Roman Catholicism, but adverse and perverse. Elsewhere, Heidegger quotes Luther in saying 'Hope comes not from works but from suffering'.[29] For Luther, we can only know God and be saved when we first acknowledge our actual state of corruption and, in a sense, a true Christian anthropology, on this side of the Fall, is fraught with suffering and affliction. Indeed, it is a *cursus ad mortem*. This Lutheran anthropology of suffering and affliction finds favour in Heidegger's developing philosophy which we have already seen in his reading of the early Christians.[30]

These sources were major contributors to his development of the atheistic eschatology in *Being and Time*: Being-towards-death. Despite Heidegger's theological background, he was already becoming suspicious of theology's ability to elucidate the factical life-experience. His development of phenomenology as a discipline, which sought out the origins of factical life in 'Basic Problems in Phenomenology',[31] would aid him in his ontological/ontic distinction and would lead him, ultimately, to claim that theology was merely an ontic science which sought to give answers to the questions which phenomenology and philosophy cultivated as an ontological discipline.[32] As Heidegger would claim in 1927 in his lecture 'Phenomenology and Theology', 'Our thesis, then, is that *theology is a positive science, and as such, therefore, is absolutely different from philosophy.*'[33]

Heidegger's Being-towards-death, in a sense, ontologises Luther's *cursus ad mortem* and Kierkegaard's sickness unto death,[34] replacing hope as the authentic mood with anxiety. This anxiety is no longer in reaction to the time of an unknown eschaton or the coming God, but is substituted with death. As has been stated previously, *Being and Time* focuses on Dasein, the individual being who ek-sists out of Being and whose being is a question to itself. The horizon of Dasein is death and could be considered an individualised personal eschatology. For Heidegger, it is more than a specific individual's death which then gets extrapolated into a greater common feature of all of humanity. This would still be an ontic enterprise. Rather, death is an ontological phenomenon which provides the conditions for Dasein's existence. Death is something that Dasein cannot experience itself like other things in life—it no longer exists when it comes to death. Rather, it is a basic ontological structure of Dasein itself.[35]

It is probably worth taking a step back, before looking more at the purpose of death, to consider how Heidegger's positing of Dasein is everywhere already eschatological in nature, not just in relation to death. Dasein, or the human being, is distinct from other entities in its relation to its own Being. As mentioned before, its own Being is a question for itself in such a way that in order to understand Dasein, one cannot define it like other entities. Dasein is distinct in that it is historical—one can only know Dasein in relation to its context and the possibilities related to it. Its essence can only be discovered through its existence. What this means is that Dasein's Being can only be sought in relation to what is not present, 'And if existence is definitive for Dasein's Being and if its essence is constituted in part by potentiality-for-Being, then, as long as Dasein exists, it must in each case, as such potentiality, *not yet be* something.'[36] The very Being of Dasein, what defines it from other entities, is a relation to time—specifically the future. As Wolfe states, 'At its simplest, Heidegger's account of human existence in *Being and Time* is "eschatological" because it envisions the possibility of authentic existence as dependent on a certain (existential) relation to one's future.'[37] Moreover, Heidegger's elucidation of Dasein does not focus on the particulars related to the possibilities that are laid before Dasein in each moment, but rather that Dasein is orientated to possibilities in the first place. What is definitive for Dasein in each moment is that it is related to possibility. Dasein's Being is always deferred and its very Being is always futurally related.[38]

Death is unique for Dasein. It is not something that it experiences like other events such as washing the car, taking a test or typing on a computer.

These things are present to Dasein; they are existentially lived. Death cannot be lived like all other events. Similarly, the meaning of death and acknowledging death cannot be done through observation of another Dasein's death. According to Heidegger, experiencing another's death does not provide us with any clue about our own death. Our death must be our own, is nonrelational and cannot be overcome.[39] This is where Heidegger calls death our possible impossibility,[40] for it is not something that we can experience, not something attainable, but it is Dasein's horizon and figures as one of Dasein's possibilities.

If death cannot be experienced by Dasein, how is it important for Dasein? If it isn't something it can ever appropriate or experience why should it even be considered? Because death cannot be grasped by Dasein it must live in each moment acknowledging that it can never be attained—it is a pure possibility, never an actuality. It is here that one can see Heidegger's Protestant influence, from Luther and Kierkegaard especially, welling up again. The mood indicative of living towards one's own death, Being-towards-death, is angst or dread. This fundamental mode of Being for Dasein, Being-towards-death, is important precisely because it is in this mood, angst, that Dasein lives an authentic existence.[41] Death is important for Dasein not only because it is the end or trajectory of Dasein, but living in the acknowledgment that Death surrounds one's being-in-the-world—that Dasein is contingent—leads to an authentic life.

From here it is easy to see how Heidegger's secularised eschatology in Being-towards-death owes much of its form and bears striking resemblance to his Protestant reading of Christian eschatology. Dasein, the human being, is defined according to an individual eschatology. The future and possibility make up what it means to be human. Authentic existence, first Christian in *The Phenomenology of Religious Life* and then philosophical in *Being and Time*, is derived from an eschatological perspective. For the Heidegger of *The Phenomenology of Religious Life* this is oriented towards the *parousia* whereas in *Being and Time* it is death. In both cases this authentic existence is characterised by dread or angst which are derived from his reading of Luther and Kierkegaard.

Heidegger's study of eschatology and his use of eschatology as a form were important for his early works and his more mature philosophy in *Being and Time*. This early engagement with eschatology will be important for the final section of this chapter on his later eschatology for two reasons. First, much of Heidegger's later eschatology spawns from this era in Heidegger's life and will invariably be influential, despite the bifurcation of Heidegger's work, on Heidegger's later eschatology. Second, and probably more important, scholars speculate whether he returns to his Christian origins late in his life. So, thought on what he means by 'God' or 'the gods' must consider both, as we shall see, his reading of Hölderlin and also his earlier Christian writings. But before turning to his later eschatology directly, we must look to his appraisal of the essence of technology, for it is in reaction to this study that his later eschatology rises to the surface.

7.4   HEIDEGGER AND THE ESSENCE OF TECHNOLOGY

Heidegger gave a series of four lectures related to technology in Bremen in 1949 and again in Bühlerhöhe in 1950.[42] The titles of these lectures were 'The Thing' (*Das Ding*), 'Enframing' (*Das Gestell*), 'The Danger' (*Die Gefahr*) and 'The Turning' (*Die Kehre*). The first lecture, 'The Thing', was expanded in June 1950 and given to the Bavarian Academy of Fine Arts. The second lecture, 'Enframing', was reworked and presented again in 1955 with the new title 'The Question Concerning Technology' (*Die Frage nach der Technik*). These texts are at the core of his work on technology and, thus, will be the main focus of my analysis.[43]

Heidegger's most important essay on technology, 'The Question Concerning Technology', does not approach technology in the way many others have. While the force of technology on society or the feedback loop created with a particular individual utilising a piece of equipment are never far away from Heidegger' analysis of technology, they are not the central aim of this essay he writes. In line with his basic philosophical concern with Being, Heidegger's major concern is the essence of technology. This questioning of the essence of technology need not have any relation to the concrete devices themselves, as Heidegger notes:

> Technology is not equivalent to the essence of technology. When we are seeking the essence of "tree," we have to become aware that That which pervades every tree, as tree, is not itself a tree that can be encountered among all the other trees. Likewise, the essence of technology is by no means anything technological. Thus we shall never experience our relationship to the essence of technology so long as we merely conceive and push forward the technological, put up with it, or evade it.[44]

So, one should not be surprised if Heidegger's treatment of technology, at the last, doesn't seem to involve anything which might not make actual reference to specific technologies themselves because Heidegger is concerned with the essence of technology.

In questioning the 'essence of technology', Heidegger uses the German term *Wesen* for 'essence'. The common English meaning of essence is associated with a static quiddity, a 'whatness'. This conception of essence implies universality likened to that of the Platonic Ideas. But, for Heidegger, this conceals the original more primordial meaning. Rather than the quiddity of a thing *Wesen* signifies a tarrying or that which remains over time: that which lasts.[45] There is an inherent historical quality to the notion of *Wesen*. When Heidegger talks about the essence of technology he is concerned with how, throughout history, this concept and indeed this term have mutated to what we know as technology today. The essence of technology can only be seen in light of this history. So, in consulting these histories and in juxtaposing them with the original Greek, Heidegger is trying to discover the essence of technology.

Heidegger turns towards the Greek words themselves. In particular, he looks at the Greek term *techne* or *Technikon*. These terms are used, according to Heidegger, to refer not only to 'the activities and skills of the craftsmen', but also to 'arts of the mind and the fine arts'.[46] This dual use of the term suggests an underlying difference with the current understanding of the term. The contemporary conception of technology, as Heidegger suggests, is treated as a mere means to a particular end. Heidegger questions whether the essence of technology truly lies with it as a human activity or pure instrumentalism.[47] Heidegger, as a philosopher, contends that our modern conception of technology is deficient and that the essence of *techne*, the root of technology, can only be understood in light of how it is related to the much broader terms associated with it: *aletheia* and *poeiesis*. Strictly translated, *aletheia* is truth. But, for a Greek *aletheia* refers to a kind of revealing. As Pattison notes *aletheia* is 'a term composed . . . of the privative prefix "a-" (as in "a-political" or "a-moral") and a form of the verbal stem—*lath*—"to be concealed". The "original" meaning of "truth", then, is "being unconcealed".'[48] Truth is merely the coming to presence or the presencing of something—the revelation of the entity. One might ask how something comes to presence or becomes unconcealed. The term *poeiesis* relates to the action or the process by which *aletheia* can occur. The Greeks, according to Heidegger, saw *techne* as a way or means of *poeiesis* or bringing forth what is not already present or seen.[49] It is understandable that both the artist and the technician employ *techne* in their practices, for both reveal or bring to presence something which was latent or concealed. Michaelangelo's famous maxim concerning a sculptor's work is quite appropriate in this regard: Every block of stone has a statue inside it and it is the task of the sculptor to discover it—what was hidden in the rock has merely been revealed by the sculptor. Similarly, for the technician Heidegger contends:

> Whoever builds a house or a ship or forges a sacrificial chalice reveals what is to be brought forth, according to the perspectives of the four modes of occasioning. This revealing gathers together in advance the aspect and the matter of ship or house, with a view to the finished thing envisioned as completed, and from this gathering determines the manner of its construction.[50]

Through *techne* the material and the vision of the end product work together to bring forth the hiddenness of the vision in the material. In this way, technology, properly defined by the Greeks, is intended to reveal something which had not been present before rather than a particular means or form of causality.

However, modern technology—that of the atom bomb, quantum physics, the automobile—has a more specialised meaning for Heidegger. Modern technology does not reveal by bringing forth what is latent; it does not work with the natural order, rather it confronts and defies it: 'It sets upon it in the sense of challenging it. Agriculture is now the mechanized food industry. Air is now set upon to yield nitrogen, the earth to yield ore, ore to yield uranium, for example; uranium is set upon to yield atomic energy, which can be released either for destruction or for peaceful use.'[51] Heidegger coins this action through the use of the term *Bestand*, translated as 'resource' or 'standing-reserve'.[52] The action is no longer that of mediation—aiding in the revealing of that which is hidden in the object, but rather is meant to manipulate the resources and properties. Modern technology treats objects as resources and this challenging or ordering of an object's self-revealing is called *Gestell*, often translated 'enframing' or 'setting something up as something'.[53] Technological enframing limits the revealedness of the object to merely that of standing-reserve. Enframing is likened to the more colloquial conception of worldview. In technological enframing the revelation of a particular object is limited to a single view. Heidegger elucidates further this idea when referring to the concept of the World Picture:

> Hence world picture, when understood essentially, does not mean a picture of the world but the world is conceived and grasped as picture. What is, in its entirety, is now taken in such a way that it is in being and only is in being to the extent that it is set up by man, who represents and sets forth. Wherever we have the world picture, an essential decision takes place regarding what is, in its entirety. The Being of whatever is, is sought and found in the representedness of the latter.[54]

Whereas for the Greeks the essence of technology is to aid the thing in unconcealing what it is, in modern technology the thing is used as a mere resource. It is in representing the thing, imposing upon it, that conceals its own ability to shine forth its own Being. A thing in modern technology is bland, faceless and in many ways forgotten. A thing is seen in light of its usefulness as a cog in the system of human interactions with the world. A thing is only a function of the humanly created system, the World Picture. The essence of modern technology is found in the orientation of subject over-against the object by the representation of the object—the object *is* in representation.

This orientation to the world, this technological thinking, is not limited to just a specific individual—one person who happens to approach the world this particular way. Technological thinking is a planetary phenomenon for Heidegger. His appropriation of Ernst Jünger is very important in this regard. Jünger's essay entitled 'Total Mobilisation', which Heidegger read with great enthusiasm, spells out in detail how the First World War was paradigmatically different from its predecessors in that entire countries were mobilised for the war effort.[55] War was not limited to just the select few who happened to fight the battle, but production on the home front and propaganda brought everyone into fighting on some level. Jünger's assessment does not just focus on how mobilisation is linked to victories in war alone. Rather, this tendency towards totalisation pervades all areas of life.[56] The First World War merely reflected a larger undercurrent which had been building for generations. Jünger states, 'As a mode of organizational thinking, Total Mobilisation is merely an intimation of that higher mobilisation that the age is discharging upon us.'[57] Total mobilisation is a global current which engrosses and encompasses all of humanity's affairs where humanity is reduced to little more than a worker in the greater *strata* of technological assembly. This is precisely the origin of Heidegger's appraisal of technology. Technology is more than the specific devices that can be represented through their global systemic, interlocking nature;[58] it is a particular way of thinking that is itself totalising and not limited to a portion of the globe—it is the thinking of this era.

This is a problem for Heidegger, and not just because technology seems to be growing at a rapid pace and is swallowing up natural resources which could possibly lead to an ecological crisis.[59] Heidegger's most pressing concern isn't even, as with Jünger, that humanity itself is being reduced to a worker in the sea of enframing.[60] What is most important for Heidegger is how this all relates to Being itself. This is not just an ecological or anthropological condition. Most important of all is that it is an ontological condition.

Technology is integrally related to Being for Heidegger precisely because it is a way that Being itself is revealed. In agreement with the Greek conception of technology, Heidegger explains, Being is unconcealed by technology. This is not just a phenomenon of the past—as if only temples and Greek statues can reveal Being—but a real process related to the present. Modern technology today reveals Being, but it does so in the form of enframing. Heidegger's most pressing problem with modern technology is that it limits this unconcealing of Being to just that of enframing by standing-reserve. The modern condition is such that Being is only ever seen in relation to enframing; it is unitary rather than pluralistic. There is a certain forgetfulness of Being, an inattentive posture to the authentic world given before us. The modern technological condition reduces everything to a single level.[61]

This negative portrayal of modern technology has led many commentators to suggest Heidegger is a technological determinist and nihilist. This is not entirely fair. Heidegger does not think that something has deviated with modern technology such that the danger of enframing is beyond reprieve. Nor does he think that enframing is a bastardisation of Being. Indeed, the later Heidegger often uses the phrase 'destining of Being' (*Geschickes des Seins*) to describe the greater process in which our current technological era is a significant part.[62] Enframing is not the sole responsibility of human activity, but a genuine movement within the course of Being itself. Heidegger says 'Man cannot, of himself, abandon this destining of his modern essence or abolish it by fiat.'[63] Something else is holding sway in our modern technological era which cannot be eradicated through an effort of a single individual's will, for even this might be subject to the modern temperament of enframing.

It is evident that we are beginning to encroach on what will be called Heidegger's later eschatology. We are moving from a single thought on the essence of technology to its broader implications for philosophy and the destiny, and history, of Being itself. Therefore, we now turn directly to Heidegger's later eschatology and examine how it is integrally related to the issue of technology.

7.5   HEIDEGGER'S LATER ESCHATOLOGY

Heidegger's later eschatology is different from his earlier relation to Christian eschatology and even the secularised eschatology of *Being and Time*. It moves away from an individual eschatology indicative of Being-towards-death to a more traditional global and planetary eschatology. As we have already begun to see with Heidegger's interest in Jünger and his conception of 'total mobilisation', the later Heidegger's field of interest takes on a cosmic or transcendental significance. What is distinctive about the later Heidegger's works, and specifically as they relate to the question of Being, is a move away from the individual as the locus of Heidegger's writings (i.e. even history, time and the world are, in Heidegger's earlier writings, always seen in relation to Dasein). The later Heidegger would cast his net wider to Being more generally. Instead of the world being seen in light of Dasein, the history of Being (*Seinsgeschichte*) seems to be the central subject in these later writings. Therefore, it is not surprising that Heidegger's relation towards eschatology, itself closely bound up with history, takes on a more global character.

7.5.1   Heidegger's Critique of Metaphysics and Ontotheology

This turn towards the history of Being is associated with Heidegger's critique of metaphysics as ontotheology. His later eschatology is a product of his commentary on the history of metaphysics. In referencing these texts we are not leaving behind Heidegger's commentary on technology. Rather, the theme of technology is fundamentally related to Heidegger's criticism of metaphysics as ontotheology. Heidegger's later works have been described as fugal, repeated variations on a single melody or theme.[64] Just as one needs to listen to an entire fugue to gain appreciation of, one might even say understand, the variations to gain the most complete picture of the piece, so it is the case that these distinct themes in Heidegger's later works interweave and support each other and need to be taken together.

Heidegger's criticism of metaphysics as ontotheology is addressed directly in his essay 'The Onto-theo-logical Constitution of Metaphysics'.[65] This essay, written in 1957, contends that the history of thought from the Greeks to today has maintained a unilateral approach to Being and how it is related to thinking. In summary, Heidegger explains that the entire history of Western metaphysics has obfuscated the difference between Being and beings. It has done this by interpreting the Being of beings on the basis of ontotheology. In arriving at the essence of a being metaphysics, from Plato to Nietzsche, has had to appeal to 'beings as such, as a whole'.[66] It has had to always assert the grounding quality of Being on beings. In order to arrive at the essence of a being there has always been something foreign which can anchor it, whether through an appeal to a first cause, a primitive substance or even an ultimate aim. Heidegger defines metaphysics, thus, as onto-theo-logical: 'onto- (from the Greek *ontos*, being) because it views the world with regard to its being, theo- (from the Greek *theos*, God) because it deals with the ultimate cause of the world, and "logical" because it offers an account or discourse (from the Greek *logos*, word or discourse) of its subject matter'.[67] Metaphysics has always concerned itself with two questions related to being. Asking 'What is a being?' has historically taken two different routes, according to Heidegger. The question 'asks on the one hand, What are (in general) beings? The question asks on the other hand, What (which one) is the (ultimate) being?'[68] So, questions related to ontology have always been concerned equally with theology, the highest being.[69]

What is important to note is that in assessing the history of western metaphysics Heidegger contends that this ground for beings is always historically mediated and contingent upon the particular epoch within history. As Heidegger states, 'There is Being only in this or that particular historic character: Φύσις, Λόγος, "Εν, 'Ιδέα, Ενέργεια, Substantiality, Objectivity, Subjectivity, the Will, the Will to Power, the Will to Will.'[70] At different times in the West that which grounds beings has changed. What makes a being what it is has presupposed different frames of metaphysics in different epochs. They are what Iain Thomson calls 'epochal constellations of intelligibility' and are 'neither contingent nor free-floating but, rather, are grounded in and reflect a series of historical transformations in our metaphysical understanding of what entities *are*.'[71] Heidegger claims in the beginning of his essay on the world picture that 'metaphysics grounds an age, in that through a specific interpretation of what is and through a specific comprehension of truth it gives to that age the basis upon which it is essentially formed.'[72] Much of Heidegger's later works draws upon this backbone of metaphysical epochs. When he lectures on the pre-Socratics it is always done with the metaphysical project in mind;[73] when he consults Nietzsche's works it is in reference to Nietzsche as representative of the metaphysics of the age.[74] Heidegger has identified some five distinct epochs in the history of Being: the pre-Socratic, Platonic, medieval, modern and late-modern period. Heidegger's later eschatology is taken up from this characterisation of history and, in particular, his writings on technology are related to the final epoch in the history of Being.

Heidegger claims that the essence of modern technology as *Gestell* is just the culmination, the capstone, of metaphysical thinking and this history of metaphysics. This should not be surprising given that the concept of *Gestell* is very similar to Heidegger's rendering of Western metaphysics as ontotheology. *Gestell* invokes the image of a completed frame by which all else is measured and is related. The world is seen in light of a completed picture placed upon it. Heidegger's rendering of ontotheology purports to relate the essence of a single being to the whole: A single entity can only ever be understood in reference to a whole system, a complete picture. Technology, as we have seen, is more than the tools we use in our everyday lives. What Heidegger is illuminating here is that modern technology participates in a much larger history. It is not just a series of tools, but is part of the most basic history for it 'grounds an age' and provides the conditions for interpreting what is.

Heidegger does not speak about the history of metaphysics for purely indifferent didactic purposes—he is critical of it. As we have seen, this history of Western metaphysics is used as a genealogy for the present metaphysical epoch, the totalising technological era. In presenting this history, Heidegger is explaining that the roots of this technological era go much deeper than the crafting of a few tools which can be extirpated at will. No, technology goes as deep as Western metaphysics, and that in order to move on from the detriments of totalising technology nothing less than a complete overhaul of the most basic ontology of the West is required.

If the later Heidegger's single thought revolves around this criticism of western metaphysics and ontotheology such that the history of Being has worked itself into an ontological corner in its present technological era, how does Heidegger propose we move on from this limiting metaphysical technology? It is here that Heidegger's other works in his later period come to the fore as a response to the enframing of modern technology and as a precursor to moving beyond planetary metaphysics that has occupied ontology for so many centuries. The two areas Heidegger claimed would be the source for such an ontological shift would be in the realm of phenomenology[75] and, more importantly, poetry. It is the latter and the themes related to 'the poet of the poet',[76] Friedrich Hölderlin, that concern most his later eschatology. Indeed, it is 'dwelling poetically' during this empty time that Heidegger claims is the proper response to technology.

7.5.2   Hölderlin and Waiting for the Gods to Return

Hölderlin is different from other poets for Heidegger 'because Hölderlin's poetry was borne on by the poetic vocation to write expressly of the essence of poetry.'[77] Whereas Heidegger goes to great lengths distinguishing between the task of the poet and the philosopher,[78] Hölderlin is specifically useful for ontology because of his peculiar relation to the essence of poetry. Heidegger claims that Hölderlin's poetry is important because it most reveals poetry as *poeiēsis*: It unconceals Being in a radical way. Hölderlin's poetry presents for us the way things really are. Poetry, more generally, is suited to present the thing before us because of its unique relation to language: 'Language has the task of making manifest in its work the existent, and of preserving it as such.'[79] Poetry, in its most primordial form, not as a datum in literary history or an aesthetic piece given for criticism, unconceals Being and presents (presences) that which is. Hölderlin's poetry, according to Heidegger, is distinctly aware of this relation between poetry and ontology and is the kernel of his writings.

Heidegger is attracted to Hölderlin because of his candid awareness of what poetry is meant to be and because Hölderlin is situated in the history of Being as a prophet of our contemporary ontological era. If he considers Nietzsche to be the figurehead of the metaphysical era, the spokesman for the late-modern era of ontotheology, then Hölderlin is the prophet who recognises the destitute present, but looks to the future and prepares the way for a new ontological epoch. This new time is precisely what Heidegger suggests Hölderlin is preparing in his poetry and is where we need to look to begin turning from technological metaphysics.

What exactly do we find in Hölderlin's poetry according to Heidegger? The most salient feature is a juxtaposition between an elegiac present where the gods have flown and an expectant waiting for them to return: 'it is the time of the gods that have fled and of the god that is coming'.[80] For instance, we find Heidegger referencing the seventh stanza of Hölderlin's 'Bread and Wine' (*Brot und Wein*) at the conclusion of his essay 'Hölderlin and the Essence of Poetry':

> But friend! we have come too late. Indeed, the gods are living,
> But over our heads above in a different world.
> Endlessly there they act and little they seem to heed it
> Whether we live, so much do the heavenly spare us.[81]

The gods no longer mingle with mere mortals on earth, but are far off and are no longer in direct relation with humanity. However, Heidegger contends that it is the poet's task to remind mortals that the god's absence signifies that they were once present. Furthermore, the poet is to remind humanity of its source in the gods despite not being present. This is particularly clear in Heidegger's interpretation of Hölderlin's use of rivers. Hölderlin's poems often reference rivers—the Rhine, Main, Neckar and especially the Ister, the ancient name of the Danube. The river is important for Hölderlin because of its relation to the source of the river: the mountains where the gods dwell. The river as it winds from its source in the mountains through valleys, meadows to cities is always indebted to its original source. It is as if the river seems to be flowing the opposite direction towards its source: 'there would be much to tell concerning that appearance that makes it appear as though the river . . . were flowing back to the source.'[82] This is precisely what the poet is intended to do in this time when the source, the gods, is no longer present: to remember them,[83] to point to them, to reveal the present indebtedness.

In this way, for Hölderlin as for Heidegger, the rivers and poets share a common vocation as demigods—those who stand in the gap between the gods and humanity. They are both bound up with what Heidegger calls the 'Between' (*das Zwischen*).[84] Heidegger states:

> The poet is the river. And the river is the poet. The two are the same on the grounds of their singular essence, which is to be demigods, to be in the between, between gods and humans. The open realm of this between is open in the direction of the holy that essentially prevails beyond gods and humans. The unity of locality and journeying cannot be conceived in terms of "space" and "time," for the space with which we are familiar and the time to which we are accustomed are themselves offspring of a realm that first lets all openness spring forth from out of it. . . .[85]

This notion of the 'Between' is quite significant for Heidegger. Whereas in times past the poet opened the space—this Between—for mortals and gods to convene in a direct way, now it is a creation of a space which bears a loss. This Between is the edge of the realm of mortals and the kingdom of the gods: 'As such it is also the "Middle" of Being "from out of which the whole realm of beings, gods, men, earth are to be newly brought out into the open" '.[86] The poet, as does the river, stands in the gap between mortals and the divine—on the edge of both—bringing them together. The poet clears a sacred space for both to convene.[87]

The quotation above on 'The Ister' also speaks about the poetic being the ground of all originary experience. We must remember that poetry is a response to the debilitating modern condition of technological thinking. So that, when Heidegger utilises Hölderlin's figurative language he is not doing so that one might treat it as merely a literary flourish which points to a more basic relationship—one cannot further distil the relation in the poetic word. This relates to technology and ontotheology precisely because poetry presents Being in its most primordial form, whereas, as we have seen, technology challenges this Being and obscures it more than it reveals it. When Heidegger, in the quotation, relates the Between to the most basic dimensions of space and time, he is saying nothing less than that all interpretations of space and time—Newtonian, Einsteinian and so forth—find their root in this originary experience of the Between. Thus, poetry leads us back to that primordial experience of the way things are and is the first step in preparing for the time when the gods will return.

How is one to live in this Between time? How is one to live before the coming God and the departure of the last God? We have already seen how the poet and river prepare for the gods to return in opening up this Between in remembrance of the mortals' indebtedness to the gods. Yet, Heidegger also speaks towards two other related and no less central terms which go some way to responding to how we are to properly live and where our home really is: dwelling (*wohnen*) and the fourfold (*Geviert*).

Dwelling is used by the later Heidegger in reference to other central terms such as thinking, building, poetry and the fourfold. But, most importantly, it needs to be read in opposition to the stark homelessness caused by modern technology. In a memorial address in his hometown of Messkirch in honour of its 700th birthday Heidegger reflects on this issue of homelessness and the homeland[88] in relation to technology: 'One of those signs is, for example, the T.V. and radio antennae that we can see almost in rows on the house-tops in the towns and villages. What do these signs point to? They point out that men are precisely no longer at home in these places where, from the outside, they seem to "dwell".'[89] Heidegger, in the speech, then explains that this modern technological era stifles humanity's coming to terms with its homelessness in this world. The issue of the homeland and its recovery are not overt issues with which the technological man is concerned—they do not take up his time.

Dwelling is a response to this feeling of homelessness and this restless searching for the homeland. Dwelling is not characterised by its finding of the homeland nor does it eradicate this sense of homelessness entirely. Rather, dwelling is the state Heidegger proposes is the most proper for mortals and how one is to live today in expectation of a more complete dwelling in the future. Rather than being taken up with the technological forgetfulness which always seeks to stave off the boredom[90] which is inherent in our ontology—almost denying it—dwelling is the authentic orientation of mortals yesterday, today and tomorrow. In this way, it can be likened to a Christian eschatology which proposes that one live today in the promise of this better time, as if the time is already upon us.[91]

This notion of dwelling as a kind of orientation is related to Heidegger's other term, *Gelassenheit*, often translated as 'calmness, composure, detachment and releasement'.[92] It signifies the orientation or the way in which one is to be in response to techno-ontotheology. One does not approach an object or the world through *Bestand*, by laying hold of what is before us, but is to actively wait and to be attuned (*Stimmung*) to the world. What is indicative of this dwelling contra the technological orientation is precisely this notion of waiting. Poetry and the poet typify *Gelassenheit* as they wait for Being's givenness and the gods to return. Just as the poet is active in this waiting, in remembering and preparing for the god's return, so too is dwelling active, not passive. Indeed, the activity of dwelling, for Heidegger, is in sparing and preserving (*Schonen*).[93] So while dwelling is related to *Gelassenheit* it is not an idle waiting or merely a passive orientation, but another way to be/act in the world which is not technological. In part, dwelling is a type of orientation to the world. But, the very term itself implies that one dwells somewhere. Dwelling implies a context and a place to dwell. For Heidegger, this place is the fourfold (*Geviert*).

The fourfold is an obscure neologism. The term itself evokes images of a frame or square, a space which is enclosed by four sides. Literally, it is translated as 'fouring' but is also the 'fold' used by shepherds.[94] Simply put, the fourfold refers to its constitutive members: earth, sky, mortals and gods.[95] We have already seen two members of the *Geviert*, mortals and gods, in Heidegger's treatment of Hölderlin's poetry, and the other two are just as derivative of Hölderlin. Succinctly put, the earth is that from which the world is built. It refers to the actual earth—dirt, soil and rock. So, in Heidegger's image of the peasant women's shoes in Van Gogh's painting[96] or that which makes up the Greek temple,[97] the earth is that primitive origin from which each of these find their basis, from what they are created. But, more than this is how mortals are related to earth: They dwell on it. It is where mortals are and find their place. Mortals are between earth and sky as they dwell on earth and below the sky. The sky, just as the earth, includes the literal sky with rain falling on the crops that mortals tend to and the stars and planetary bodies that inhabit it. But, the sky also shows the limit of the earth and is 'the place where the unknown God conceals himself'.[98] The sky and gods together reveal the measure of the mortal who inhabits this fourfold: 'the measure consists in the way in which the god who remains unknown, is revealed *as* such by the sky.'[99] What we are seeing here in the fourfold is not necessarily a cosmogony of sorts—as if Heidegger wishes to draw us back to a purely pagan premodern paradigm—but a different, more originary way that Being comes to the world. As discussed, in instantiating this fourfold he is elucidating another way, a more primordial way, of understanding our relation to Being, time and place.[100]

This notion of place is key to the *Geviert*. The very term implies an active creation of space: 'fouring'. It is at once an event, an action, a happening. Indeed, Heidegger even refers to the fourfold as a round dance, another image which evokes active creation of place.[101] As suggested, mortals are related to the *Geviert* as ones that dwell in it, it is their place. It is in the *Geviert* that mortals find their origin, their home. Jeff Malpas phrases this well:

> Recognizing our being as mortals, then, is not a matter simply of facing up to the fact that we die, but more significantly, it means recognizing the way in which we are already given over to the world, to the Fourfold that also encompasses the gods, earth, and sky—it is a matter of recognizing our own belonging within the sway of being, of our own already being gathered into the opening and presencing of what Heidegger calls *Ereignis*. To say that we dwell is to say that we already belong, as mortals, to the Fourfold. . . .[102]

It is clear from this quotation that the fourfold is home for mortals precisely because it is the origin out of which mortals stand out. Mortals already belong to the fourfold despite the strain of this current epoch in the history of Being. This striving for dwelling today must be resigned to that of remembrance as Malpas suggests precisely because the gods are concealed. In a way, just as with Heidegger's elucidations of Hölderlin's poet we are all to be poets who remember our origin in the fourfold and in the measure of the gods who are concealed as we wait for the return of the gods in greater presence. We are to dwell today in the expectation of dwelling tomorrow.

7.6   CONCLUSION

So, in short, what could we say is Heidegger's later eschatology especially as it relates to technology? In the history of Being the current technological epoch is a destitute time. It is a time when Being is concealed and human beings experience grave homelessness from the source of their origin in the fourfold. The essence of technology as *Bestand* is the pinnacle of onto-theology in our current epoch and is the impetus that drives Heidegger's look towards the future where mortals will enjoy a greater unencumbered relation to Being. Recognising that the present is not as it should be—it is not complete but a mere ghost of its true potential—is the first step in any eschatology. With Heidegger, this present is experienced as a loss, a sense of homelessness.

The most salient feature of any eschatology is that one does not take the *status quo* as definitive in its own right. This experience of loss today cataly-ses the vision of a better time to come. With Heidegger, this means looking towards the time in the future when the gods will return and we will have a free relation with our own technology[103] which does not limit the revela-tion of Being to the inflicted World Picture placed upon it. This time will be characterised by an unhindered exchange between gods and mortals where humanity will experience the homeland and dwell in the fourfold. But, for now, mortals are relegated to mere remembrance. They are to take their cue from the poet, especially that of Hölderlin, who understands this destitute time, and in remembering their rightful place as it once was, begins clearing a place for when this time will come again. In this Between time humanity is to remember their origin and become shepherds of Being who cultivate the present and wait for the coming epoch in the destining of Being.

All of this might sound quite pagan and it stands to reckon how much Heidegger has retreated from a Judeo-Christian view of history, the future and especially God. It has already been abundantly clear that Heidegger's personal life and philosophical methodology in the early and middle part of career reflect this move towards a perspective which staunchly excludes God. And yet, Heidegger seems to, in these later works, affirm some kind deity and our need for them—even if they seem more like the Greek pan-theon than the God of Christianity.[104] In fact, even his seminal interview with the newspaper *Der Spiegel* which, under orders, was only to be pub-lished upon his death—as if they represent his final words to the German public—resound with the title 'Only a God Can Save Us Now!'[105] What can be said of his religious commitment when so much of this later work has actually spawned a gamut of religious interpretations with people such as

Bernard Welte[106] and John Macquarrie?[107] First, a simple concrete judgement can't be made either way here which defines, in exact terms, Heidegger's relation to Christianity at the end of his life. This relationship has been considered extensively by others and need not be elucidated further here.[108] What can be said, and with some force, is that the eschatological trope pervades the lifework of Heidegger and is essential to understanding it.

However, Heidegger's thinking is also constructive in its philosophical criticism of a particular approach to the future, the kind of future that transhumanism posits. Heidegger rejects a relation to the future which entirely depends on the present for its construction. His ontology is not built upon the presence of some substance or essence, but upon how the present is made up entirely by the future possibilities in its own right. This is, first, evident in his conception of Dasein. Dasein is not like other entities in the world which can be defined by certain properties and characteristics present before us. As Heidegger has strongly proclaimed, Dasein is its possibilities. The present actual is subjugated to how Dasein is related to the future. Second, as Richard Kearney has written, the later Heidegger's works have as much to do with possibility as Dasein. He states that possibility for the early Heidegger, Heidegger I, utilises such terms as *Möglichkeit* (possibility), *Seinkönnen* (potentiality-to-be) and *Ermöglichen* (to render possible).[109] But, these are all in relation to how Dasein is related to the possible and the future. According to Kearney, the later Heidegger, Heidegger II, utilises the term *Vermögen* (Possibilisation) taken from his lecture, 'Letter on Humanism', to describe how the possible is a feature of Being itself. This term is used to describe the way in which Being gives itself (*es gibt*) in the event of appropriation (*Ereignis*). The text Kearney draws on states:

> When I speak of the "quiet power of the possible", I do not mean the possible of a merely represented *possibilitas*, nor the potential as *essentia* of an *actus* of the *existentia*, but Being itself, which in its loving potency [*das Mögend*] possibilizes [*vermag*] thought and thus also the essence of man, which means in turn his relationship to Being. To possibilize [*vermögen*] something is to sustain it in its essence, to retain it in its element.[110]

Heidegger is not thinking of possibility in relation to metaphysics or causality—in terms of a substance which has both *potentia* and *actus*—but a prior possibility of Being which, in turn, gives beings their possibilities. Whether in the form of Dasein's being as constituted by its possibilities or in this prior gifting of possibility to all beings, Heidegger's thinking in this regard is entirely critical of a flattened ontology which gives greater weight to the actual and a presence which is not inundated with the possible.[111]

We would do well to heed the advice of Heidegger and recognise that a purely substantial presence is not grounds for an adequate understanding of the future. Philosophers of technology and futurists who rely upon technology as a catalyst for speculation about the future should understand that an ontology which does not give significant weight to possibility with respect to their ontology, as with transhumanism, is deeply misguided.

Heidegger is surely not the final picture for Christian eschatology. While many theologians have made good use of Heidegger's approach to the future there is a decided lack, ultimately, in his approach. This parting of ways is especially compounded when one considers notably Christian hope and its relation to the future and specifically the Christian idea of promise. So, whereas Heidegger can aid us in understanding how technological futurism and its culmination in transhumanism are seriously lacking, the Christian has more to say on the future, where these possibilities arise and from whence hope derives. It is these ideas which are the topic of the next chapter.

NOTES

1. 'But what if we understand the future as that which comes towards us today?' Martin Heidegger, "Messkirch's Seventh Centennial," *Listening* 8, nos. 1–3 (1973), 42–43.
2. Robert C. Scharff and Val Dusek, eds., *Philosophy of Technology: The Technological Condition: An Anthology* (Oxford: Blackwell, 2003), 247. Of course, contemporary philosophy of technology has become more pluriform in recent years even though many modern figureheads are directly indebted to Heidegger: Herbert Marcuse, Hubert Dreyfus, Andrew Feenberg and Albert Borgmann. The essentialist interpretation of technology has become replaced by an empirical turn. Regardless, Heidegger and his followers still hold a significant position in the field of philosophy of technology. See David Lewin, *Technology and the Philosophy of Religion* (Newcastle: Cambridge Scholars Press, 2011); Carl Mitcham, *Thinking through Technology: The Path between Engineering and Philosophy* (Chicago: University of Chicago Press, 1994).
3. On Heidegger's 'turn' see Laurence Paul Hemming, *Heidegger's Atheism: The Refusal of a Theological Voice* (Notre Dame: University of Notre Dame Press, 2002), 75ff.
4. Thomas Sheehan, "Introduction: Heidegger, the Project and the Fulfillment," in *Heidegger: The Man and the Thinker*, ed., Thomas Sheehan (New Brunswick: Transaction, 2010), vii.
5. Indeed, some of Heidegger's last words on his life's works found in notes to an unfinished preface to his *Gesamtausgabe* state: 'An on-the-way in the field of paths for the changing questioning of the manifold question of Being'. See Dorothea Frede, "The Question of Being: Heidegger's Project," in *The Cambridge Companion to Heidegger*, ed., Charles B. Guignon (Cambridge: Cambridge University Press, 1993), 42, 66.
6. Martin Heidegger, *Being and Time*, trans., John Macquarrie and Edward Robinson (New York: Harper & Row, 1962), 1.
7. This section on the initial quotation of Plato and its importance to *Being and Time* (and perhaps even Heidegger's entire ontological project) is taken from Stephen Mulhall's lectures on *Being and Time*. Also see John Sallis, *Delimitations: Phenomenology and the End of Metaphysics*, 2nd ed. (Bloomington: Indiana University Press, 1995), 99ff.
8. In fact, Heidegger might be deemed the philosopher whose main function throughout his philosophy is to pose rigorous questions. Whereas most

philosophy works from perplexity and positing questions to understanding and certainty, this is not the case for Heidegger. Indeed, the opposite is the case.

9. Heidegger, *Being and Time*, 2.
10. See Stephen Mulhall, *Routledge Philosophy Guidebook to Heidegger and Being and Time* (London: Routledge, 1996), 8–9.
11. Heidegger, *Being and Time*, 23.
12. Ibid., 32.
13. M.J. Inwood, *A Heidegger Dictionary* (Oxford: Blackwell, 1999), 147.
14. Heidegger, *Being and Time*, 31.
15. George Pattison, *Routledge Philosophy Guidebook to the Later Heidegger* (London: Routledge, 2000), 9.
16. The famous and often quoted refrain from Sartre's play *No Exit* is 'l'enfer, c'est les autres' ('Hell is other people').
17. Martin Heidegger, "Letter on Humanism," in *Pathmarks* (Cambridge: Cambridge University Press, 1998), 252.
18. Much of this section depends upon Judith Wolfe's work on Heidegger and Christian eschatology. See Judith Wolfe, *Heidegger's Eschatology: Theological Horizons in Martin Heidegger's Early Work* (Oxford: Oxford University Press, 2013).
19. See Thomas Sheehan, "Husserl and Heidegger: The Making and Unmaking of a Relationship," in *Husserl: Psychological and Transcendental Phenomenology and the Confrontation with Heidegger (1927–1931)*, ed., Thomas Sheehan and Richard E. Palmer (Boston: Kluwer Academic Publishers, 1997); Robert Vigliotti, "The Young Heidegger's Ambitions for the Chair of Christian Philosophy and Hugo Ott's Charge of Opportunism," *Studia Phaenomenologica* 1, nos. 3–4 (2001).
20. Heidegger would even give a private lecture on Schleiermacher's Second Speech, 'On the Essence of Religion', in 1917 which focused on religion as a disposition of the individual and a type of experience. These lectures have been lost themselves, but the notes to an undelivered lecture on mysticism, which include sections on Schleiermacher, in 1918–1919 have been recorded in Martin Heidegger, *The Phenomenology of Religious Life* (Bloomington: Indiana University Press, 2004), 241–244, 249–251. See also B.D. Crowe, *Heidegger's Religious Origins: Destruction and Authenticity* (Bloomington: Indiana University Press, 2006), 35ff.; Wolfe, *Heidegger's Eschatology*, 47.
21. Heidegger, *The Phenomenology of Religious Life*, 14ff.
22. Ibid., 23.
23. 'Already at the end of the first century the eschatological was covered up in Christianity. In later times one misjudged all original Christian concepts.' See ibid., 73.
24. Ibid., 51.
25. Ibid., 73–74.
26. 'The experience is an absolute distress (θλῖπις) which belongs to the life of the Christian himself. The acceptance (δέχεσθαι) is an entering-oneself-into anguish. This distress is a fundamental characteristic, it is an absolute concern in the horizon of the παρουσια, of the second coming at the end of time.' Ibid., 67.
27. Martin Heidegger, *Phenomenological Interpretations of Aristotle: Initiation into Phenomenological Research*, trans., Richard Rojcewicz (Bloomington: Indiana University Press, 2001), 148.
28. Martin Heidegger, "The Problem of Sin in Luther," in *Supplements: From the Earliest Essays to Being and Time and Beyond* (Albany: State University of New York Press, 2002), 106.

29. Ibid., 107.
30. See John van Buren, "Martin Heidegger, Martin Luther," in *Reading Heidegger from the Start: Essays in His Earliest Thought*, ed., John van Buren and Theodore J. Kisiel (Albany: State University of New York Press, 1994); 'Luther's *Theologia Crucis*' in Crowe, *Heidegger's Religious Origins*, 44ff.
31. The 1919–1920 Winter Semester lectures in Freiburg, not the lectures of the same name delivered in 1927 in Marburg. See Martin Heidegger, *Grundprobleme der Phänomenologie: (1919/20)* Gesamtausgabe 58 (Frankfurt: Klostermann, 1993), 42ff; Wolfe, *Heidegger's Eschatology*, 92.
32. Wolfe, *Heidegger's Eschatology*, 93.
33. Martin Heidegger, "Phenomenology and Theology," in *Pathmarks*, ed., William McNeill (Cambridge: Cambridge University Press, 1998), 41.
34. See Hubert L. Dreyfus, *Being-in-the-World: A Commentary on Heidegger's Being and Time, Division I* (London: MIT Press, 1991), 299ff; Stephen Mulhall, *Philosophical Myths of the Fall* (Princeton: Princeton University Press, 2005), 47ff; Wolfe, *Heidegger's Eschatology*, 125–126.
35. Just like other fundamental structures of Dasein's existence (*existentielle*) like Being-with or Being-in. For the former see sections 25–27 of *Being and Time*; for the latter, see sections 28–34 and 43–44.
36. Heidegger, *Being and Time*, 276.
37. Wolfe, *Heidegger's Eschatology*, 118.
38. It is precisely the inherence of possibility in the human being which acts as a rejoinder to transhumanism.
39. This is a point many disagree with. See especially Edith Stein, "Martin Heidegger's Existential Philosophy," *Maynooth Philosophical Papers* 4, (2007), 77ff.; Simon Critchley and Reiner Schürmann, *On Heidegger's Being and Time*, ed., Steven Matthew Levine (London: Routledge, 2008), 143ff.
40. Heidegger, *Being and Time*, 294.
41. Much more could be said about authenticity and its relation to Being-towards-death—especially as it relates to the releasement of Dasein from *das Man*, the crowd. For our purposes, it is important to just note that authenticity is a product of an eschatological orientation and Heidegger's secular eschatology is drawing upon this distinction. See ibid., 304ff.
42. For further background to these texts see the preface to Martin Heidegger, *The Question Concerning Technology and Other Essays*, trans., William Lovitt (London: Harper & Row, 1977).
43. Save the third unpublished lecture entitled 'The Danger'. The expanded 1950 lecture entitled 'The Thing', 'The Question Concerning Technology' from 1955 and the original 1949 lecture 'The Turning' are those translated into English and the source for discussion. See Martin Heidegger, "The Thing," in *Poetry, Language, Thought* (London: Harper & Row, 2001); Martin Heidegger, "The Question Concerning Technology," in *The Question Concerning Technology and Other Essays* (London: Harper & Row, 1977); Martin Heidegger, "The Turning," in *The Question Concerning Technology and Other Essays* (London: Harper & Row, 1977).
44. Heidegger, "The Question Concerning Technology," 4.
45. See ibid., 3n1; Inwood, *A Heidegger Dictionary*, 52–54.
46. Heidegger, "The Question Concerning Technology," 13.
47. Ibid., 5.
48. Pattison, *Later Heidegger*, 49.
49. Heidegger, "The Question Concerning Technology," 13.
50. Ibid.
51. Ibid., 15.
52. See Lovitt's translational notes in ibid., 17n16. Of particular nuance is Heidegger's use of *Bestand* to imply the 'orderability and substitutability of objects'.

53. See Lovitt's note on the German term *Gestell* in ibid., 19n17.
54. Martin Heidegger, "The Age of the World Picture," in *The Question Concerning Technology and Other Essays* (London: Harper & Row, 1977), 129–130.
55. Michael Zimmerman, *Heidegger's Confrontation with Modernity: Technology, Politics, and Art* (Bloomington: Indiana University Press, 1990), 66ff.
56. The totalising feature of technology is central to understanding its reception in the 20th century. We have already seen this interpreted in oppressive ways by certain dystopian science fiction writers like Orwell and Zamyatin and in the sociological writings of Jacques Ellul. But, others have interpreted it in a positive light as with many technological utopians referenced in chapter 2 and by Teilhard in chapter 5.
57. Ernst Jünger, "Total Mobilization," in *The Heidegger Controversy: A Critical Reader*, ed., Richard Wolin (London: MIT Press, 1993), 134.
58. For example, the airplane is dependent upon the specific network of technology to build it and sustain it. In its construction it requires advanced computer systems, robotic arc welders and specially designed components which themselves are equally indebted to further manufacturing in factories. Furthermore, in order for this machine to function after its creation it relies upon a global technological network to supply its fuel with intricate drilling equipment; sea, ground or air transportation; and even the mechanism to pump the fuel into the airplane. The technology itself is global.
59. Some have even claimed his writings reflect a kind of deep ecology. See Pattison, *Later Heidegger*, 205ff.; Bruce Foltz, *Inhabiting the Earth: Heidegger, Environmental Ethics and the Metaphysics of Nature* (Atlantic Highlands: Humanities Press, 1995).
60. Heidegger is concerned about how technology is affecting humanity. In fact, humanity has a unique role to play in coming to grips with technology as we shall see. But Heidegger is more concerned about the ontological threat than the anthropological or ecological because it is overlooked.
61. See Martin Heidegger, *What Is Called Thinking?*, trans., J. Glenn Gray (New York: Harper & Row, 1968), 32ff.
62. Heidegger, "The Question Concerning Technology," 24ff.; Heidegger, "The Turning," 37ff.
63. Heidegger, "The Age of the World Picture," 153.
64. Pattison, *Later Heidegger*, 22ff.
65. See Martin Heidegger, "The Onto-theo-logical Constitution of Metaphysics," in *Identity and Difference* (New York: Harper & Row, 1969).
66. Ibid., 58.
67. George Pattison, *God and Being: An Enquiry* (Oxford: Oxford University Press, 2011), 5.
68. Martin Heidegger, "Kant's Thesis about Being," in *Pathmarks*, ed., William McNeill (Cambridge: Cambridge University Press, 1998), 340.
69. The next chapter deals with this type of God in greater detail.
70. Heidegger, "The Onto-theo-logical Constitution of Metaphysics," 66.
71. Iain D. Thomson, *Heidegger on Ontotheology: Technology and the Politics of Education* (Cambridge: Cambridge University Press, 2005), 8–9.
72. Heidegger, "The Age of the World Picture," 115.
73. Pattison, *Later Heidegger*, 129ff.; Heidegger, *What Is Called Thinking?*, 172ff.; Martin Heidegger, *Parmenides*, trans., André Schuwer and Richard Rojcewicz (Bloomington: Indiana University Press, 1992).
74. Pattison, *Later Heidegger*, 105ff.; Martin Heidegger, *Nietzsche*, trans., D. F. Krell, vols. 1–2 (San Francisco: Harper, 1991), 3ff.
75. Heidegger proclaims that nothing less than a leap out of metaphysics is called for and that this begins, in part, with seeing things differently. This is precisely why phenomenology, '*die Sache selbst*', is central to beginning to work out

of metaphysics. We must go back to the beginning; to pure unadulterated experience. See Heidegger, *What Is Called Thinking?*, 40ff.; Pattison, *Later Heidegger*, 85ff.

76. Martin Heidegger, "Hölderlin and the Essence of Poetry," in *Existence and Being* (London: Vision Press, 1956), 295.
77. Ibid., 294–295.
78. Heidegger, *Nietzsche*, 73.
79. Heidegger, "Hölderlin and the Essence of Poetry," 298.
80. Ibid., 313. Of particular interest is Heidegger's essay 'The Last God' in Martin Heidegger, *Contributions to Philosophy: (From Enowning)*, trans., Parvis Emad and Kenneth Maly (Bloomington: Indiana University Press, 1999), 285ff.
81. Friedrich Hölderlin, *Poems of Hölderlin*, trans., Michael Hamburger (Kingsway: Nicholson & Watson, 1943), 171.
82. Martin Heidegger, *Hölderlin's Hymn "The Ister"*, trans., William McNeill and Julia Davis (Bloomington: Indiana University Press, 1996), 144.
83. This is precisely the theme of Heidegger's commentary on Hölderlin's poem 'Remembrance'. See Martin Heidegger, "Remembrance," in *Elucidations of Hölderlin's Poetry* (Amherst: Humanity Books, 2000).
84. For a more in-depth study of this term see Inwood, *A Heidegger Dictionary*, 33. Also, see the related term *Ereignis* in ibid., 54–57; Heidegger, *Contributions to Philosophy*, 17ff.
85. Heidegger, *Hölderlin's Hymn "The Ister"*, 165–166.
86. Pattison, *Later Heidegger*, 176.
87. The function of the poet in Heidegger's writings is priestly. Indeed, the poet has even been likened to a kind of Christ figure. See George Pattison, "Heidegger's Hölderlin and Kierkegaard's Christ," in *Martin Heidegger*, ed., Stephen Mulhall (Aldershot: Ashgate, 2006).
88. This term deserves more attention than can be given here, especially because this term is related directly to Hölderlin whose poetry, Heidegger explains, is inundated with a sense of the German landscape and people and even at times addresses the theme of the homeland or homecoming directly. See Martin Heidegger, "Homecoming / to Kindred Ones," in *Elucidations of Hölderlin's Poetry* (Amherst: Humanity Books, 2000). But, more importantly, the image of the homeland and *das Volk* is associated with Heidegger's ties with the Third Reich. This connection plagues not only the later Heidegger, but specifically these later eschatological tendencies which bear a remarkable similarity to Nazi ideology. This cannot be addressed properly here. Wolfe has noted this connection with Heidegger's eschatology, especially as it relates to Hölderlin, in chapter five of Judith Wolfe, *Heidegger and Theology* (London: Bloomsbury T. & T. Clark, 2014). For a more general appraisal of Heidegger's association with Nazism see Pattison, *Later Heidegger*, 25ff.; Richard Wolin, ed., *The Heidegger Controversy: A Critical Reader* (London: MIT Press, 1993); Manfred Stassen, ed., *Martin Heidegger: Philosophical and Political Writings* (New York: Continuum, 2003).
89. Heidegger, "Messkirch's Seventh Centennial," 43.
90. Boredom and its relation technology is another major theme in ibid., 49ff.
91. Indeed, it seems this is precisely what someone like Albert Borgmann has in mind when referring to focal practices. Our dwelling today relies upon certain moments of communal focus. This moment today is especially prevalent in Heidegger's elucidation of the thing. See Albert Borgmann, *Technology and the Character of Contemporary Life: A Philosophical Inquiry* (Chicago: University of Chicago Press, 1984), 196–210; Heidegger, "The Thing."
92. Inwood, *A Heidegger Dictionary*, 117.

93. Martin Heidegger, "Building Dwelling Thinking," in *Poetry, Language, Thought* (London: Harper & Row, 2001), 147.

94. Jeff Malpas, *Heidegger's Topology: Being, Place, World* (Cambridge: MIT Press, 2006), 226.

95. Of course, the fourfold is a concept of Heidegger's worked out over time and, prior to his more mature conception, was originally made up of man and world rather than mortals and sky. For a genealogy of the fourfold see ibid., 224ff.

96. Martin Heidegger, "The Origin of the Work of Art," in *Poetry, Language, Thought* (London: Harper & Row, 2001), 32ff.

97. Ibid., 40ff.

98. Heidegger, *What Is Called Thinking?*, 194.

99. Martin Heidegger, ". . . Poetically Man Dwells . . . ," in *Poetry, Language, Thought* (London: Harper & Row, 2001), 220.

100. Malpas's distinction between space and place is crucial in this regard. Space implies a universality in which anything can occur, whereas place is specific and local. See chapter one of Malpas, *Heidegger's Topology*.

101. Heidegger, "The Thing," 178.

102. Jeff Malpas, "Heidegger's Topology of Being," in *Transcendental Heidegger*, ed., Steven Galt Crowell and Jeff Malpas (Stanford: Stanford University Press, 2007), 131. *Ereignis* is a very important term in the later Heidegger and is related to the Between already discussed above, but a complete treatment of it is beyond the scope of this chapter. See Heidegger, *Contributions to Philosophy*.

103. Indeed, Heidegger does not think that a complete retreat from technology is even possible. Rather we are to live as beings who can authentically live with technology. See Hubert L. Dreyfus, "Heidegger on Gaining a Free Relation to Technology," in *Heidegger Reexamined*, ed., Hubert L. Dreyfus and Mark A. Wrathall (New York: Routledge, 2002).

104. This could even be considered a false dichotomy. Heidegger might not be thinking specifically of a deity which is either a pagan god or the Judeo-Christian God. My own opinion for this interpretation of Heidegger follows that of Richard Kearney, who takes Heidegger's atheistic methodology seriously in pursuing phenomenology so that any God who comes, from a phenomenological point of view, must look like the gods Heidegger has described. From this phenomenological perspective, according to Kearney, 'Christ and Apollo are brothers'. See Richard Kearney, "Heidegger, the Possible and God," in *Martin Heidegger: Critical Assessments*, ed., Christopher E. Macann (London: Routledge, 1992), 317ff.

105. Martin Heidegger, " 'Only a God Can Save Us': *Der Spiegel*'s Interview with Martin Heidegger," in *The Heidegger Controversy: A Critical Reader*, ed., Richard Wolin (London: MIT Press, 1993).

106. Bernhard Welte, "God in Heidegger's Thought," *Philosophy Today* 26, no. 1 (1982).

107. John Macquarrie, *Heidegger and Christianity* (London: SCM, 1994).

108. See John D. Caputo, "Heidegger and Theology," in *The Cambridge Companion to Heidegger*, ed., Charles B. Guignon (Cambridge: Cambridge University Press, 1993); Hemming, *Heidegger's Atheism*; Welte, "God in Heidegger's Thought."

109. Kearney, 300–308.

110. Ibid., 309. This is Kearney's own translation taken from Heidegger's 'Letter on Humanism'.

111. Of course, more can be said in relation to the philosophical and theological treatment of possibility—especially as it relates to Heidegger. This will be a major theme treated in its own right in the next chapter.

200 *Philosophical and Theological Issues*

REFERENCES

Borgmann, Albert. *Technology and the Character of Contemporary Life: A Philosophical Inquiry.* Chicago: University of Chicago Press, 1984.
Buren, John van. "Martin Heidegger, Martin Luther." In *Reading Heidegger from the Start: Essays in His Earliest Thought*, edited by John van Buren and Theodore J. Kisiel. Albany: State University of New York Press, 1994.
Caputo, John D. "Heidegger and Theology." In *The Cambridge Companion to Heidegger*, edited by Charles B. Guignon. Cambridge: Cambridge University Press, 1993.
Critchley, Simon, and Reiner Schürmann. *On Heidegger's Being and Time*, edited by Steven Matthew Levine. London: Routledge, 2008.
Crowe, B. D. *Heidegger's Religious Origins: Destruction and Authenticity.* Bloomington: Indiana University Press, 2006.
Dreyfus, Hubert L. *Being-in-the-World: A Commentary on Heidegger's Being and Time, Division I.* London: MIT Press, 1991.
———. "Heidegger on Gaining a Free Relation to Technology." In *Heidegger Reexamined*, edited by Hubert L. Dreyfus and Mark A. Wrathall, 3. New York: Routledge, 2002.
Dreyfus, Hubert L., and Charles Spinosa. "Highway Bridges and Feasts: Heidegger and Borgmann on How to Affirm Technology." In *Heidegger Reexamined*, edited by Hubert L. Dreyfus and Mark A. Wrathall, 3. New York: Routledge, 2002.
Foltz, Bruce. *Inhabiting the Earth: Heidegger, Environmental Ethics and the Metaphysics of Nature.* Atlantic Highlands: Humanities Press, 1995.
Frede, Dorothea. "The Question of Being: Heidegger's Project." In *The Cambridge Companion to Heidegger*, edited by Charles B. Guignon. Cambridge: Cambridge University Press, 1993.
Gadamer, Hans-Georg. "Heidegger's Later Philosophy." In *Martin Heidegger*, edited by Stephen Mulhall, xvii, 469. Aldershot: Ashgate, 2006.
Heidegger, Martin. "Hölderlin and the Essence of Poetry." In *Existence and Being*. London: Vision Press, 1956.
———. *Being and Time.* Translated by John Macquarrie and Edward Robinson. New York: Harper & Row, 1962.
———. *What Is Called Thinking?* Translated by J. Glenn Gray. New York: Harper & Row, 1968.
———. "The Onto-theo-logical Constitution of Metaphysics." In *Identity and Difference*. New York: Harper & Row, 1969.
———. "Messkirch's Seventh Centennial." *Listening* 8, nos. 1–3 (1973): 40–57.
———. "The Age of the World Picture." In *The Question Concerning Technology and Other Essays*. London: Harper & Row, 1977.
———. "The Question Concerning Technology." In *The Question Concerning Technology and Other Essays*. London: Harper & Row, 1977.
———. *The Question Concerning Technology and Other Essays.* Translated by William Lovitt. London: Harper & Row, 1977.
———. "The Turning." In *The Question Concerning Technology and Other Essays*. London: Harper & Row, 1977.
———. *Nietzsche.* Translated by D. F. Krell. Vols. 1–2. San Francisco: Harper, 1991.
———. *Parmenides.* Translated by André Schuwer and Richard Rojcewicz. Bloomington: Indiana University Press, 1992.
———. *Grundprobleme der Phänomenologie: (1919/20).* Gesamtausgabe 58. Frankfurt: Klostermann, 1993.
———. "'Only a God Can Save Us': *Der Spiegel*'s Interview with Martin Heidegger." In *The Heidegger Controversy: A Critical Reader*, edited by Richard Wolin. London: MIT Press, 1993.

———. *Hölderlin's Hymn "The Ister"*. Translated by William McNeill and Julia Davis. Bloomington: Indiana University Press, 1996.

———. "Kant's Thesis about Being." In *Pathmarks*, edited by William McNeill. Cambridge: Cambridge University Press, 1998.

———. "Letter on Humanism." In *Pathmarks*, edited by William McNeill. Cambridge: Cambridge University Press, 1998.

———. "Phenomenology and Theology." In *Pathmarks*, edited by William McNeill. Cambridge: Cambridge University Press, 1998.

———. *Contributions to Philosophy: (From Enowning)*. Translated by Parvis Emad and Kenneth Maly. Bloomington: Indiana University Press, 1999.

———. "Homecoming / to Kindred Ones." In *Elucidations of Hölderlin's Poetry*. Amherst: Humanity Books, 2000.

———. "Remembrance." In *Elucidations of Hölderlin's Poetry*. Amherst: Humanity Books, 2000.

———. "Building Dwelling Thinking." In *Poetry, Language, Thought*. London: Harper & Row, 2001.

———. "The Origin of the Work of Art." In *Poetry, Language, Thought*. London: Harper & Row, 2001.

———. *Phenomenological Interpretations of Aristotle: Initiation into Phenomenological Research*. Translated by Richard Rojcewicz. Bloomington: Indiana University Press, 2001.

———. ". . . Poetically Man Dwells . . ." In *Poetry, Language, Thought*. London: Harper & Row, 2001.

———. "The Thing." In *Poetry, Language, Thought*. London: Harper & Row, 2001.

———. "The Problem of Sin in Luther." In *Supplements: From the Earliest Essays to Being and Time and Beyond*. Albany: State University of New York Press, 2002.

———. *The Phenomenology of Religious Life*. Bloomington: Indiana University Press, 2004.

Hemming, Laurence Paul. *Heidegger's Atheism: The Refusal of a Theological Voice*. Notre Dame: University of Notre Dame Press, 2002.

———. "Heidegger's God." In *Heidegger Reexamined*, edited by Hubert L. Dreyfus and Mark A. Wrathall, 3. London: Routledge, 2002.

Hölderlin, Friedrich. *Poems of Hölderlin*. Translated by Michael Hamburger. Kingsway: Nicholson & Watson, 1943.

Inwood, M. J. *A Heidegger Dictionary*. Oxford: Blackwell, 1999.

Jünger, Ernst. "Total Mobilization." In *The Heidegger Controversy: A Critical Reader*, edited by Richard Wolin. London: MIT Press, 1993.

Kearney, Richard. "Heidegger, the Possible and God." In *Martin Heidegger: Critical Assessments*, edited by Christopher E. Macann, 4. London: Routledge, 1992.

Lewin, David. *Technology and the Philosophy of Religion*. Newcastle: Cambridge Scholars Press, 2011.

Macann, Christopher E., ed. *Martin Heidegger: Critical Assessments*. London: Routledge, 1992.

Macquarrie, John. *Heidegger and Christianity*. London: SCM, 1994.

Malpas, Jeff. *Heidegger's Topology: Being, Place, World*. Cambridge: MIT Press, 2006.

———. "Heidegger's Topology of Being." In *Transcendental Heidegger*, edited by Steven Galt Crowell and Jeff Malpas. Stanford: Stanford University Press, 2007.

Mitcham, Carl. "Technology as a Theological Problem in the Christian Tradition." In *Theology and Technology: Essays in Christian Analysis and Exegesis*, edited by Jim Grote and Carl Mitcham. Lanham: University Press of America, 1984.

———. *Thinking through Technology: The Path between Engineering and Philosophy*. Chicago: University of Chicago Press, 1994.

Mulhall, Stephen. *Routledge Philosophy Guidebook to Heidegger and Being and Time*. London: Routledge, 1996.

———. *Philosophical Myths of the Fall*. Princeton: Princeton University Press, 2005.

202 *Philosophical and Theological Issues*

Olsen, Jan-Kyrre Berg, Stig Andur Pedersen, and Vincent F. Hendricks, eds. *A Companion to the Philosophy of Technology*. Oxford: Wiley-Blackwell, 2009.
Ott, Hugo. "Martin Heidegger's Catholic Origins." *American Catholic Philosophical Quarterly* 69, no. 2 (1995): 137–156.
Pattison, George. *Routledge Philosophy Guidebook to the Later Heidegger*. London: Routledge, 2000.
———. "Heidegger's Hölderlin and Kierkegaard's Christ." In *Martin Heidegger*, edited by Stephen Mulhall. Aldershot: Ashgate, 2006.
———. *God and Being: An Enquiry*. Oxford: Oxford University Press, 2011.
Rojcewicz, Richard. *The Gods and Technology: A Reading of Heidegger*. Albany: State University of New York Press, 2006.
Roubach, Michael. "Heidegger, Science, and the Mathematical Age." *Science in Context* 10, no. 1 (1997): 199–206.
———. *Being and Number in Heidegger's Thought*. London: Continuum, 2008.
Sallis, John. *Delimitations: Phenomenology and the End of Metaphysics*. 2nd ed. Bloomington: Indiana University Press, 1995.
———. "Where Does *Being and Time* Begin?" In *Martin Heidegger*, edited by Stephen Mulhall. Aldershot: Ashgate, 2006.
Sartre, Jean-Paul. *Existentialism Is a Humanism*. Translated by Carol Macomber. New Haven: Yale University Press, 2007.
Scharff, Robert C., and Val Dusek, eds. *Philosophy of Technology: The Technological Condition: An Anthology*. Oxford: Blackwell, 2003.
Sheehan, Thomas. "Husserl and Heidegger: The Making and Unmaking of a Relationship." In *Husserl: Psychological and Transcendental Phenomenology and the Confrontation with Heidegger (1927–1931)*, edited by Thomas Sheehan and Richard E. Palmer. Boston: Kluwer Academic Publishers, 1997.
———. "Introduction: Heidegger, the Project and the Fulfillment." In *Heidegger: The Man and the Thinker*, edited by Thomas Sheehan. New Brunswick: Transaction, 2010.
Stassen, Manfred, ed. *Martin Heidegger: Philosophical and Political Writings*. New York: Continuum, 2003.
Stein, Edith. "Martin Heidegger's Existential Philosophy." *Maynooth Philosophical Papers* 4 (2007): 55–98.
Thomson, Iain D. *Heidegger on Ontotheology: Technology and the Politics of Education*. Cambridge: Cambridge University Press, 2005.
Vedder, Ben. *Heidegger's Philosophy of Religion: From God to the Gods*. Pittsburgh: Duquesne University Press, 2007.
Vigliotti, Robert. "The Young Heidegger's Ambitions for the Chair of Christian Philosophy and Hugo Ott's Charge of Opportunism." *Studia Phaenomenologica* 1, nos. 3–4 (2001): 323–350.
Welte, Bernhard. "God in Heidegger's Thought." *Philosophy Today* 26, no. 1 (1982): 85–100.
Wolfe, Judith. *Heidegger's Eschatology: Theological Horizons in Martin Heidegger's Early Work*. Oxford: Oxford University Press, 2013.
———. *Heidegger and Theology*. London: Bloomsbury T. & T. Clark, 2014.
Wolin, Richard, ed. *The Heidegger Controversy: A Critical Reader*. London: MIT Press, 1993.
Zimmerman, Michael. *Heidegger's Confrontation with Modernity: Technology, Politics, and Art*. Bloomington: Indiana University Press, 1990.

8 Possibility and Promise
A Christian Response

In the last chapter on Heidegger we looked at how we understand the future and its relation to ontology. What Heidegger brings to light is the way the present is related to the future and how this is a central topic for ontology. His early works explicitly engaged with early Christian eschatology and the fruit of that labour transmogrified into a particular individual orientation towards the ultimate future of the individual—death. His later works carry a more cosmic dimension when considering ontology and the future. In these texts we do not see the future and the present within the context of only a single individual but, instead, they encompass the entire history of Being itself. Heidegger's major thesis is that ontology does not rely purely on the past or present to define itself but is just as much, if not more, inundated with the future. What is present cannot be defined or understood according to some substance or set of characteristics which help distinguish it from other things, but what is present before us in the moment is somehow definitively related to the future.

It was argued that Heidegger's claims can be used to critique a transhumanist understanding of the future. Specifically, transhumanism falls prey to a stunted ontology. This ontology, as we have seen, depends purely upon the present and the actual to construct the future. Whereas transhumanism is, in one sense, entirely about the future, its construction of that future is ontologically grounded in the past and the present: 'If we can but discover all of the causal mechanisms today we would know the future.' For the transhumanist approach, these trends are sought in the arena of human evolution and, specifically, technological evolution. Technology is the kernel out of which history will blossom. For these transhumanists then the future is an extension of present actuality. It is a technological *futurum*.

The previous chapters have provided the relief and set the stage for the main philosophical and theological issues I shall now address. In the first instance, this chapter is a Christian response to the transhumanist approach to the future. But, it is also constructive in that, given the ubiquity of dreaming about the technological future of which transhumanism is central, I shall ask: How should the Christian understand the future today? In particular, this chapter looks at the philosophical and theological parameters of a Christian approach to the future and argues that the themes of possibility and promise are central.

The first part of the chapter seeks to construct a modern Christian notion of possibility contra the transhumanist approach. To do this, I first analyse the common understanding of possibility as potentiality found in Aristotelian metaphysics and reflected in transhumanism. For this, I rely upon the critical commentary of Eberhard Jüngel and Richard Kearney. In this section, I agree that metaphysics since Aristotle has placed an unwarranted emphasis on the priority of present actuality over possibility. I also relate this model of possibility and actuality to its corresponding conceptions of God. I then propose to construct a more adequate vision of possibility, and God's relation to it, utilising the constructive elements of Kearney and Jüngel's work. It is here that I agree with Kearney that God needs to be thought of in terms of possibility. However, as a rejoinder to transhumanism, Jüngel's emphasis on limit and creaturehood still needs to be equally emphasised.

The final part of the chapter constructs a promissory account of the future utilising the works of Jürgen Moltmann. While Moltmann explicitly engages with issues related to possibility, especially because he receives much of his philosophical heritage from Bloch, his project is not set within the frame of an ontological understanding of the future. Moltmann's future and understanding of possibility is contextualised within a promissory theology. Moltmann claims that for the Jew and for the Christian promise drives history, not ontology. A promissory theology is important as a rejoinder to the transhumanist future. The first part of the chapter provides an alternative to a purely *futurum*-based future with sustained reflections on possibility; the latter portion on promise accentuates the entirely interpersonal nature of the future. Inasmuch as the transhumanist future intends to safeguard a general humanism and human relationships in the future, this is ultimately abandoned because of its narrow anthropology and cosmology which reduces all to information and rational intellect. The future within the economy of promise, on the other hand, can safeguard such virtues and emphasises the interpersonal nature of the future. It relocates the centre of confidence from an expectation of a particular state of affairs to a trust in a person, the triune God who invites us into his aboriginal community. Applying a hermeneutic of promise to the future concretises the way in which those things which make us most human—hope, love, friendship, altruism and so forth—are already a world in which we hope will be. So, this promissory future depends upon our interactions with other persons today—this includes God—and it places this as the pinnacle of the future. The virtues inherent in personal relationships are what is given for the future. Promise brings to light a personal God in relation to this future.

8.1   THE GOD OF POSSIBILITY

What I mean by possibility and how it contrasts with transhumanist possibility is detectable in many 20th century criticisms of traditional perspectives on possibility. What I propose is that the transhumanist agenda falls prey to an ontology of presence which relies on an outdated and inadequate view of possibility which originates with Aristotle. There are many whom I could reference here.[1] But, this reinterpretation of possibility and the future is most evident in two 20th-century thinkers who have much in common but have not often been explicitly linked: Eberhard Jüngel and Richard Kearney.[2] The theme of possibility is the philosophical and theological backbone to both of their projects and both share a critical stance towards this outdated model of possibility, while agreeing that the corresponding view of God and the future are also inadequate. Therefore, my criticism of this kind of possibility, which is apparent in transhumanism, will follow these thinkers.

8.1.1   Against Aristotle: Jüngel and Kearney on Possibility and Actuality

Eberhard Jüngel's most sustained treatment of possibility can be found in his essay entitled 'The World as Actuality and Possibility: The Ontology of the Doctrine of Justification'.[3] In this text Jüngel elucidates his misgivings with metaphysics. As he states, 'From the beginnings of metaphysics, actuality has been given ontological priority over possibility'.[4] This priority, Jüngel claims, begins with Aristotle and has been authoritative ever since. It is in Aristotle's *Metaphysics* that Jüngel takes most interest. In particular, Jüngel focuses on Book Θ where Aristotle strives to define the relation between possibility[5] (*dynamis*) and actuality (*energeia, entelecheia*). In this book, Aristotle concludes that 'On the basis of our elucidations of the variety of accounts of priority, there can be no question but that actuality is prior to potentiality.'[6] On the whole, this might seem to be an intuitive conclusion because, physically, it undergirds a common belief about the world: Something can change or come into existence only if it is acted on by something else which is already in existence. For my cup of coffee to potentially move across my desk it takes my arm, which actually exists, to pick up the cup and move it. A potentiality depends upon that which is actual. Jüngel concludes that this is not just a statement which is effective in the physical world or in ontic domains, but that 'the priority of actuality consists in the fact that the possible is *defined* as the possible by reference to actuality'[7]—it is an issue of the very definition of possibility itself. This becomes clear when Aristotle claims that possibility is defined contra impossibility. A possibility exists if it excludes impossibility: 'The criterion for the possibility of walking is the excluded impossibility of walking.'[8] But, this impossibility can only be contradicted by the presence or act of it actually happening. Aristotle states 'The thing which is capable of doing/being the F is the thing such that there is no impossibility of its engaging in the actuality of which it is said to be the potentiality.'[9] In the case of walking, the impossibility of walking can only be contradicted if something actually walks. Therefore, possibility is entirely dependent upon the actual for its definition and existence.

So, Jüngel claims, Aristotle gives priority to actuality over possibility when defining possibility. But, Jüngel has more difficulty with the way Aristotle defines the relationship between possibility and actuality as one where possibility is just a deficient actuality. Possibility is defined according to actuality, but in a deficient mode of actuality. Something which is possible *is not*. It may become so, but at present it is not, and it will take something which is actual to bring this possibility into existence. Possibility is a spectre, a mere ghost of actuality. Indeed, things which are not certainly *could* be, but they do not exist yet, they have not been actualised. According to Aristotle, true being is accredited to that which is no longer in process of becoming. Something *is* only if it has arrived at completion and is fully realised in actuality: 'There are plenty of non-entities with potential being. Only, not being in entelechy [actuality], they are not.'[10]

In fact, this very term Aristotle uses, *entelecheia*, is a neologism of his own invention and relates to this notion of becoming and fulfilment. It first combines the words *enteles* (complete, perfect or full) with *echein* (referring to *hexis*, meaning to carry on in a certain condition). But it is also a play on words where it substitutes *telos* (completion, end) into the term *endelecheia* (persistence).[11] There is this sense with the term *entelecheia* of arrival at fruition and completion while persisting in this arrival. It has often been translated 'having its end within itself' or 'being-at-an-end'.[12] It is clear that something which lacks this complete arrival, *entelecheia*—as in the quotation above, does not enjoy true being. It is stunted and cut off before it can truly *be* in all its perfection. It is because of this, Jüngel concludes, 'being and actuality are identical'[13] for Aristotle.

On Jüngel's interpretation, Aristotelian possibility is fulfilled in the static arrival or *telos* already inherent in the actual. This kind of becoming or possibility is less than the perfect actuality.[14] It isn't even accredited with being at all. There must be a hint or potential latent within the actual for it to be realized at all. Possibility cannot be seen on its own terms. It must always reference not just what is actual or real, but especially the ideal.

8.1.2   God and Possibility: Against the 'I Am'

How does God relate to possibility? How ought God and possibility be thought together? It might be entirely strange, initially, to think these two together when the discussion of possibility for so many centuries has been about lack of completion or perfection. Surely, when talking about God these qualifiers are entirely inappropriate. Isn't God complete and perfect and this is precisely what makes God God?

The biblical witness and particularly the traditional interpretation of Exodus 3:14 is one of the first places where there seems to be evidence against appropriating possibility to God. In Exodus 3:14 Moses asks God who it is he should name when asked who sent him to Egypt to free the Israelites from bondage. God responds to Moses with what is often translated,

'I am who I am'. This passage has had a tremendous influence on the way God has been thought in relation to Being in Christian history, and here we find in a decisive moment in that history God defining himself in relation to Being itself.[15] In Etienne Gilson's seminal text *The Spirit of Medieval Philosophy* he observes, 'Exodus lays down the principle from which henceforth the whole of Christian philosophy will be suspended. From this moment it is understood once and for all that the proper name of God is Being and that . . . this name denotes his very essence.'[16] For instance, Aquinas cites the Exodus passage in his *Summa Theologiae* and concludes, as Gilson has noticed above, this naming of God in reference to Being is the most appropriate one could ascribe to God: 'This name HE WHO IS is most properly applied to God'.[17] But, it is clear that this reference to Being has God interpreted as pure act. Indeed, Aquinas will argue elsewhere that there can be no potency in God for to do so would be a contradiction in the very notion of God: 'If God is eternal, of necessity there is no potency in Him. The being whose substance has an admixture of potency is liable not to be by as much as it has potency. . . . But, God, being everlasting, in His substance cannot not-be. In God, therefore, there is no potency to being'.[18] In this interpretation, God is equated with the absolute act and is the furthest from possibility for he is the one being to whom we cannot attribute possibility by definition.

This interpretation of Exodus 3:14 is not uncommon and has been definitive in how we understand God to be related to Being and possibility.[19] But others have translated this name of God differently. In fact, there is another tradition which is more amenable to relating God to possibility in this passage. Franz Rosenzweig is an example. Rosenzweig is concerned with the 'Hellenistic' interpretation of this passage and cites others who have attempted to move beyond this type of translation in interpreting God's name as 'The Eternal': Calvin, Luther and Mendelssohn.[20] Despite these scholars' efforts, Rosenzweig still claims there are elements of philosophical thought in this translation unintended in the original.[21] Rosenzweig's own translation reads 'I will be-there howsoever I will be-there'.[22] This translation captures the Jewish promissory element of the text.[23] This type of interpretation does not emphasise the conditionless absolute nature of God but rather how God will be with his people in the future. As Gerhard von Rad argues:

> . . . nothing is farther from what is envisaged in this etymology of the name of Jahweh than a definition of his nature in the sense of a philosophical statement about his being . . . a suggestion of his absoluteness, aseity, etc. Such a thing would be altogether out of keeping with the Old Testament. The whole narrative context leads right away to the expectation that Jahweh intends to impart something—but this is not what he is, but what he will show himself to be to Israel.[24]

Here we see a strong emergent tradition that questions the very interpretation of this seminal biblical text suggesting that the equation of God and static, philosophical Being is a later Hellenistic addition entirely foreign to its original intended audience.

8.1.3 God and Possibility: Kearney and the Eschatological God 'Who May Be'

How then do I propose God is to be understood in relation to possibility? Given these many interpretations and criticisms of possibility and God's relation to it outlined above, what do I propose is the proper relation God takes to possibility? And, how can this, ultimately, be a rejoinder to how transhumanism approaches issues related to possibility and the future?

Interpreting the notion of possibility and God along Aristotelian lines is inadequate. First, this notion of possibility, as others have claimed, relies too much on a future which is only a product of the past and present—the possible is inherent in present actuality alone. This is particularly deficient because it does not take account of the radical unforeseen future in which no appeal to present actuality will satisfy our experience. Second, Aristotelian possibility depends upon too rigid an ontology to be taken seriously by scientists after Darwin, thus making this possibility too limiting. For example, according to Aristotelian possibility, a seed of a particular flower, say a lily, only has the possibility of becoming a lily. Its only possibility is to become a lily, whereas, Darwinian evolution proposes that like doesn't necessarily only produce like. Indeed, the entire mechanism of Darwinian evolution depends upon certain mutations which give rise to certain variability across ontological lines.[25] One might say that, since Darwin, we have had to realise that our ontological categories have been pure construction rather than an actual feature of biology and nature.[26] Third, and most important, the corresponding notion of God in this view is too sterile and removed from the cares of the world to be properly Christian. For theological reasons, the God of pure act doesn't allow God enough of a role to shape the past, present and future.

What I mean by possibility and how God relates to it can best be constructed in dialogue with the perspectives of Kearney and Jüngel on this issue. What will be discovered in these authors is that the notion of possibility is and should be at the centre of our thinking about God and the future. This is particularly the case after Heidegger who places the future and possibility as the defining feature of humanity. If we are human beings precisely because we relate to possibility then our talk of God must enter into this arrangement. And, what we find when we do this is that it is only when we acknowledge the role of possibility in the affairs of the world and God, that both are affirmed in their mutual confluence with each other.

Kearney's thought on God's relation to possibility finds good company in those such as Buber and Rosenzweig cited above. Kearney's text, *The God Who May Be*, gives extensive treatment to Exodus 3:14 and his disapproval of the traditional translation of God's name. It is here that Kearney's proposal on God and possibility comes to the fore. He chooses to translate God's name as 'I am who may be',[27] giving it an uneasy relationship with both the present and ontology. As he claims, his approach seeks to find a third way between an apophatic 'God without Being' and a pantheistic equality of God and Being: 'God neither is nor is not but may be'.[28]

This proposition of a God 'who may be' seeks to find a *via media* between the two extreme poles of God's relation to Being. We have already seen the pole that defines God according to Being above and identified many of the drawbacks that Kearney himself suggests. But, Kearney also explains that the other pole has just as many deficiencies. This other extreme states that God cannot be thought and cannot be inscribed within Being at all. God is without Being and beyond all Being. The very categories of Being are insufficient for God. In this sense, when God comes he never stays. Any worldly ontological resources cannot be used to relate God's having come and gone. Kearney is particularly wary of this approach expressed in the thought of Jacques Derrida and Jean-Luc Marion. According to Kearney, Derrida's atheistic God[29] is 'irreducible to the language and limits of anthropo-theo-morphism' and is represented in Derrida's writings on the 'messianic': 'a non-lieu of absolute passion and passivity, of incessant waiting and welcome, preceding and exceeding every historical revelation of a specific messiah'.[30] Kearney's criticism of Derrida on this matter is that one has no way of distinguishing between the transcendent God breaking into the present or a false prophet or, even worse, some strange devil.[31] The wholly Other without content or identification—without Being—can be a frightening image. Jean Luc Marion's singular thesis that God is without Being also falls under this criticism. For all of Derrida and Marion's disagreements on issues related to God, Being, gift and presence, Kearney concludes that Marion's favouring of the *via negativa* has not sufficiently reflected on the need for some content to be attributed to God.[32] Both Derrida and Marion's positions, according to Kearney, do not recognise the inherent need of human beings to imagine God; to have something by which they can relate to God: 'By releasing the "desire of God" from any particular tradition of revelation and narrative, does deconstruction not make it difficult for us to address the human need to identify divinity, to look for at least some sort of credentials before taking it in.'[33] The complete transcendence of God—God without any relation to Being—is impossible to relate to. Moreover, the Christian tradition is wrought with stories and revelations which tell us of God's graciousness and help us understand God. Indeed, the biblical witness, particularly the Hebrew Bible, constantly establishes the remembrance of God's past actions for trust of him in the future—even in times when it looks doubtful. What makes this God decidedly Judeo-Christian if no content—narratives or revelation—can be attributed to God's self? Can we really say that these narratives and histories are not definitive in any way?

Kearney proposes a mediating position which, he claims, safeguards the transcendence of God and also allows for God's actions and speech in the form of narrative and revelation to be meaningful and binding. But, what precisely does Kearney mean by a God 'who may be'?

It means God aligns himself with possibility. This possibility is a real risk for it is not guaranteed that God will be and it does not preclude that God won't be at all. Kearney states that God needs the world and human beings to be for him. That is, he can't *be* on his own rather we *are* for him. This is related to Kearney's view of 'microtheology' which advances a God who is not an 'emblem of sovereignty, omnipotence, and ecclesiastical triumph',[34] but a God who chooses to work by persuasion and promise. History is not a triumphalistic ever-advancing march until the Kingdom of God is ultimately realised in all that is, but a narrow road not discernible in advance that depends upon the interaction between God and humanity. Kearney's God waits for the world to respond to his promise for the future.[35]

How then does Kearney expect God to come about? How do we know when God is? How is the promise fulfilled? Kearney responds that the promise of God to be in the future comes when we choose to actualise that possibility through 'justice and love'.[36] Our seemingly small acts of charity and love—to aid the orphan and the widow, to love our neighbour—is how God concretely comes to the world. God *is* where we choose to respond to his promise in transforming the world and ourselves according to the image of God in terms of love and justice. Kearney himself states:

> Yes, perhaps if we remain faithful to the promise, one day, some day, we know not when, I-am-who-may-be will at last be. Be what? we ask. Be what is promised as it is promised. And what is that? we ask. A kingdom of justice and love. There and then, to the human 'Here I am,' God may in turn respond, 'Here I am.' But not yet.[37]

Kearney speaks of this kingdom in terms of transfiguration. Christ's transfiguration is an eschatological phenomenon in that it localises the events of a worldly transfiguration intended for all of creation and humanity. Each moment of transfiguration happens in history when humanity seeks and acts upon this eschatological justice: 'The transfiguration thus is as much about us as it is about God, for the transfigured Christ "renews our nature in himself restoring it to the pristine beauty of the image charged with the common visage of humanity". Such a transfiguring mission includes all who seek justice-to-come.'[38] Thus, God *is* here and now when we enact that eschatological transfiguration already found in Christ.

Now Kearney claims that this does not presuppose that God is entirely conditioned by the world despite his comments which intimate the mutual dependence of God and the world: 'God may henceforth be recognized as someone who becomes with us, someone as dependent on us as we are on Him'.[39] For Kearney, God's actualisation in this world does depend upon the choices made by human beings, but he also claims that if God's Being rests upon our actions, his love does not: 'Does all this amount to a conditional God? No. For if God's future being is conditional on our actions in history, God's infinite love is not. As a gift, God is unconditional giving. Divinity is constantly waiting.'[40] God's giftedness to the world is not conditional upon the actions of man. God continues to give even when humanity chooses to not bring God into being. Kearney even goes so far as to conjecture that even if humanity completely turns away from this kingdom of love and justice and completely destroys the earth, even here, Kearney suggests, God will live on as a pure possibility waiting to be actualised.[41] Even if it didn't look probable or even logically possible that God's kingdom would be fulfilled here on earth, Kearney exclaims that 'God would live on as an endless promise of love and justice. This would be so even if we fail or frustrate this covenant by denying its potential for historical fulfilment on earth'.[42] Kearney can claim this because God is ultimately beyond being and is primarily a God of love and justice before a God of being.[43]

These comments on the viability of a realised kingdom of love and justice in the face of certain doubt reveal how Kearney relates possibility to impossibility. Kearney exclaims that the impossible is a false ceiling. It is a product of human calculation and an ontology of actuality and potentiality. He says:

> . . . the God-who-may-be reminds us that what seems impossible to us is only seemingly so. For once transfigured by God all things are made possible again, disclosing the eschatological potentials latently inscribed in the historically im-possible. So that if we continue to look at the same event in the light of God's transfiguring power, we can now see . . . the hitherto impossible as possible.[44]

This reminder of the power of God in relation to possibility, which also finds biblical witness,[45] shares much in common with the Kierkegaardian proclamation that 'God is this—that all things are possible'.[46] Impossibilities are possible with God. Indeed, Kearney holds to a radical view of possibility which doesn't just advocate that possibility is merely an intraworldly phenomenon. Possibilities do not only arise from humanity and the universe. Rather, Kearney is much more interested in how God brings new possibilities to humanity and the world hitherto unseen. For Kearney, this is precisely how God transforms the world: in the gifting of possibilities to it. Even—especially—if these possibilities are actually impossibilities prior to God's gifting.

How then does humanity receive these possibilities? How are God's gifted possibilities for the world and humanity also human and worldly possibilities? What is the content or form this takes? This becomes clear when we turn to Kearney's reinterpretation of the Aristotelian concept of the *nous poetikos*, his image of play and what he terms a 'Poetics of the Possible God'.

In Kearney's final chapter of *The God Who May Be* entitled 'Poetics of the Possible God', he gives some initial thoughts of what he proposes a God-who-may-be might entail. Kearney uses a reinterpreted Aristotelian notion of the *nous poetikos*, the active intellect often associated with the divine, to advocate that God provides the means by which humanity can discover these new possibilities offered it from God. Kearney imagines that God provides something like this *nous poetikos* to illuminate the world anew so that humanity might see the world and themselves transfigured. This reinterpreted *nous poetikos* does not actually cause the thought of human beings to think this way, but provides the capacity to see things recreated: 'My eschatological reading . . . sees the divine Creator as transfiguring our being into a can-be—a being capable of creating and recreating new meanings in our world—without determining the actual content of our creating or doing the actual creating for us.'[47] The *nous poetikos* enables a certain capacity for human beings to see these possibilities and illuminates the world in an eschatological light.

For Kearney, God's gifting of possibilities to the world is visible in this 'creating and recreating new meanings in our world': through hermeneutics and the imagination. This is important because Kearney sees God's interaction with the world as part of a hermeneutical process. One might say that the possibilities gifted to the world by God participate in the hermeneutical play of human beings interpreting and reinterpreting their own narratives and history. Kearney finds a fruitful image in this notion of play to describe the way God relates these possibilities to the world. This image is one of joyful participation in which God chooses to present new possibilities to the world in a creative moment with humanity and world. This playful hermeneutic reveals a God who participates with the world and for the world rather than acting as Pantocrator over the world. Instead of expressing a God of dominion and authority it emphasises mutual love, 'promise and powerlessness, fecundity and fragility'.[48] It is hermeneutical because God's new possibilities help reinterpret not only present realities anew, but how we relate to memories of the past, whether corporate or individual, and how we think of them in the future. God transforms the world through this hermeneutical presentation.

As is apparent, Kearney takes a strong literary position when it comes to issues of religion. He utilises the phrase 'poetics of the possible God' because of this appeal to hermeneutical play and he, it has been argued, utilises the human imagination as the central locus of God's revelation. Although Kearney never explicitly states that God's divine revelation of new possibilities comes to and through human imagination—others have argued that this is precisely what he advocates given his work in the area of imagination.[49] We might say that God gives new possibilities to interpret the world through human imagination. What couldn't be imagined before and without God becomes imaginable with God.[50]

It is clear that the theme of possibility is absolutely central to Kearney's conception of God. Rejecting the traditional notion of God as Pure Act and God as unspeakably transcendent and beyond Being, Kearney prefers to understand God as one who may be. His proposal signals a God who is not necessarily defined by Being. He is prior to Being and beyond Being, and yet he maintains a relation with the world and Being such that he may be, but is not limited to it nor equated with it. Kearney's 'possible God' introduces new possibilities into the world through a hermeneutical engagement with it. Language and imagination act as the locus of that engagement where God is not limited to only human possibilities which might foreclose a certain future as impossible, for Kearney's God makes the impossible possible.

8.1.4   'More Than Necessary' and Limit

How does Kearney contribute to our discussion? First, I agree that, after Heidegger, possibility must be a central and definitive element of our understanding of humanity and that this then, subsequently, needs to be a significant element in our speaking about God. In a contemporary philosophical and theological context, God must relate to possibility precisely because human beings are constituted by it. The human being is not defined like other furniture in the world but by its relation to possibilities. Therefore, I commend Kearney for assigning possibility such a significant role. I also affirm Kearney's continual emphasis on a God who defines himself primarily in relational terms. Kearney's God upholds lived ethical[51] relationships and allows human freedom and flourishing such that a certain mutuality is visible between God and humanity. This God does not eclipse human freedom nor does it denigrate human possibilities. The possibilities which arise from this world, apart from God, are given real significance. I also agree with Kearney that possibilities in the world arise from the imagination and in our relation to language. If God is going to provide new possibilities to the world then it will surely be in the area of human imagination and language.[52]

But, I also have reservations with Kearney—specifically in the area of interpreting God's presence to the world as capricious. Kearney's 'weak God' makes him almost powerless to come into Being on his own such that God seems unessential or merely accidental. Kearney's God is free in his love and offering of possibilities to humanity and the world, but is God free to come to the world and humanity without aid? Kearney seems to give more freedom and power to human beings than to God. Ultimately, can Kearney's weak God inspire hope that someday God 'will wipe every tear from their eyes' (Revelation 21:4)? Can Kearney's God safeguard his and our future? How transformative can God really be in the world? Does he have any direct access to the world besides through human creativity and human choice to actualise the possibilities he presents? Kearney's God seems too weak to inspire a real genuine hope.

I might also add that Kearney's incessant refrain, that God makes all things possible—even the impossible—might actually rely too much on possibility. There is an inherent danger wherein too much possibility can lead to an inauthentic life which denies the conditions which invariably make us human. In fact, if possibility is emphasised too much, it can lead to a kind of transhumanist position. If God is really 'that all things are possible' without any qualification, might this leave open the danger of what 19th-century Russian authors call Mangodhood[53] and is expressed precisely in contemporary transhumanism? Or does God maintain limit inasmuch as he upholds our freedom? To import a famous Barthian phrase, might his 'Yes' to new possibilities also include a 'No' to others?

This is where I think Eberhard Jüngel can act as a very important corrective to both of these limitations. Of course, Jüngel has much in common with Kearney. As we have already seen in the early pages of this chapter, Jüngel concerns himself with relating God to issues of possibility and actuality as Kearney does. They both share a criticism for defining this possibility according to the actual present and give priority to possibility over actuality. They both suggest that God relates to the world through possibility provided by figurative language. Kearney's views have been detailed, but Jüngel also devotes considerable effort towards explicating how metaphor is an ontological surplus to present actuality. These metaphors push the boundaries of what is and 'expand the horizon of being by going beyond fixation upon actuality with that which is possible'.[54] Metaphor offers new possibilities to the ontological actual by incorporating foreign ideas into an existing idiomatic framework. It is precisely for this reason that metaphor is proper for speech about God because it can simultaneously refer to something foreign to itself without it actually belonging to what is known.[55]

But for all of their similarities, Jüngel can help clarify and correct Kearney's accidental God and also safeguard against making too much of possibility. In the beginning of Jüngel's *God as the Mystery of the World* he poses the question whether God is necessary. Jüngel responds that to even pose this question in our present modern age presupposes that we can think or speak of God as other than necessary and presumes we can respond negatively. And, this is precisely the answer of the modern age. God is not needed for the world to function on its own. We need not appeal to a divine basis for all that is. What Jüngel concerns himself with is how this idea of the nonnecessity of God can actually contribute to theological thinking; how can it be a theme for theology itself rather than expressing a more basic secularity or ultimate removal of God and all theological talk?[56] Jüngel contends that speaking about the nonnecessity of God can imply that God is not essential to the world, or that God could either be related to the world or not. This type of nonnecessity of God views God as accidental: 'it could either be this way or that way', in the idiom of Jüngel. God is discerned according to capriciousness and thus is 'less than necessary'.[57] This is an inadequate view of God and a nonnecessary God need not be 'less than necessary'; rather, as Jüngel claims, God is 'more than necessary'. This 'more than necessary' does not mean an extension of the necessary into new territory for such would not uphold the definition of the nonnecessity of God—God would still be necessary but in an expanded, superlative sense. Rather, three things characterise God when he is spoken of as 'more than necessary'.[58] First, it refers to God's utter groundlessness. God is not grounded in worldly necessity. Nor is the relationship between God and the world governed, then, by this notion of necessity or grounding. The world need not be primarily thought as grounded in God nor that God is grounded in the world.[59] Second, God's being 'more than necessary' is such that it is visible through God's event-like coming. When God is not seen according to worldly necessity how is he known except through direct event-like revelation? To the world, this seems contingent because God's coming to the world as an event is not presupposed in any necessary relationship with the world. This leads directly into the third aspect of God's being 'more than necessary': It reveals God's absolute freedom in coming to the world. The relationship holding sway between God and the world is not one of necessity but one dictated by freedom.

Jüngel's 'more than necessary' God can help safeguard against a purely capricious and arbitrary God that Kearney is often accused of proposing. Instead of viewing God as 'less than necessary' or in a weak way which seems to give him less power than even human beings, it relocates God's relation to the world in a no less contingent way, but one which accords God his own freedom in coming to the world. Indeed, Jüngel's God comes to the world precisely because he is free. And, for Jüngel, it is clear that our hope in God is a powerful one because his existence does not depend upon the world and he stands outside of the *aporia* of human existence oriented between being and nonbeing. Jüngel thinks we have a real hope in God because God is not held under the categories of being and nonbeing. God is a hope for us in that he chooses being over nonbeing for us. The perennial philosophical question—'why is there something rather than nothing?'—reveals God's graciousness to the world as a decision of being over nonbeing. As creatures oriented to nothingness—indeed nothingness is the ultimate possibility of humanity for Jüngel and in agreement with Heidegger—yet this is not the final word. Hope for the Christian really does not come from this world nor can appealing to worldly necessity help with the question 'why something rather than nothing?' We are held out before nothingness and God chooses being over nonbeing:

> When God reveals himself, then man experiences his existence and the being of his world as a being which has been plucked from nothingness. To that extent, man has already experienced God himself as a being which is not necessary but more than necessary. For, in the experience of being preserved from nothingness in such a way that gratitude results, God is experienced as the Being who disposes over being and nonbeing.[60]

For Jüngel, the Christian response in the context of nothingness is gratitude and hope whereas without God the appropriate response can only ever be anxiety.

Now these issues of a nonnecessary God are entirely related to Jüngel's construction of God and possibility, and they can help in averting the real danger of ascribing too much weight to possibility. The subtitle to Jüngel's essay 'The World as Actuality and Possibility' points to the origin of his contentions about his decidedly theological appropriation of possibility: 'The Ontology of the Doctrine of Justification'. For it is in reflecting on justification that possibility is given its appropriate relation to God while espousing the importance of limit.

What Jüngel says we are to learn from reflecting on the ontology of the doctrine of justification is the way God creates *ex nihilo*.[61] Jüngel contends, as we saw above, that God stands over being and nonbeing and chooses being for humanity and the world. This choosing of being for the world is always and everywhere oriented to God's crafting new possibilities for the world. Such possibilities cannot arise from the confines of what is actual or from within worldly necessity but are gifted and new. In the doctrine of justification man is oriented towards death, destruction and nothingness. This is the *telos* of man but, according to Jüngel, God, out of his freedom and love to the world, provides a new route, a new possibility for humanity. God orients man and the world anew. Thus, Jüngel shares much in common with Kearney because what was impossible before God's coming, namely life, becomes possible with God. For Kearney, God makes the impossible possible. Jüngel would agree with this. But, he chooses to use the formulation that God 'makes the possible to be possible and the impossible to be impossible',[62] giving the formulation a divine orientation rather than a worldly or anthropological one. Why is this important? Because it suggests that in God coming to the world God's new possibilities are accompanied with impossibilities as well: His new promises are accompanied by judgement. In referencing justification, these impossibilities refer to sin and nothingness. Under this new orientation, God does not just provide new possibilities; he also closes others and makes them impossible. Thus, God really creates out of nothing where 'the Word of God lets the possible become possible and hands over to perish that which has become impossible',[63] for 'When justification takes place, there also occurs a divine "No" which reduces the sinner's actuality to nothingness, a "No" which is for the sake of the creative divine "Yes".'[64]

Therefore, unlike Kearney, Jüngel provides a theological basis for applying limits to God's relation to possibility preferring to orient God to both possibility and impossibility where God is the fulcrum of this distinguishing. What I want to suggest is that this distinguishing between the possible and impossible is an important Christian theme which can have large implications for how Christians understand transhumanism. I have not mentioned yet, but have been entirely aware of, a particular rebuttal to my thesis that transhumanism does not adequately account for possibility. Wouldn't a transhumanist claim that they take with real seriousness the way possibilities are to be thought of today? Indeed, wouldn't they contend they are much more open to a wide variety of possibilities for humanity and the world than others today? Yes, this might be the case. But, as I have shown, transhumanists' conception of possibility looks much more like Aristotelian possibility where the future grows out of the technological present than what we have been discovering through Kearney and Jüngel. Transhumanists don't allow for radical newness or the unforeseeable future and the way God interacts with the world to transform and transfigure it here and in the future. Nor do they recognise the way that the limits which are acknowledged by referring to creatureliness and 'Heideggerian thrownness' actually help us to lead authentic and more fulfilling lives.[65] Limit is important. Certainly, these limitations make us human and, for the Christian, they uphold the conviction that we, too, are part of God's creation: We are creatures, not gods.

From here it is clear, then, how a Christian notion of possibility needs to respond to a transhumanist notion of possibility. Christian possibility recognises and affirms creaturehood and limit. What does this creaturehood mean? It means we are finite and not God. A definitive part of being a creature is death. Death is our ownmost possibility, according to Heidegger. Despite transhumanism's denial of death as an ultimate feature of human life, all it can offer is a prolonged finite existence. But, forestalling death is not the same as eradicating death. Death is still a feature of finite existence even if all of the transhumanist claims to the contrary actually do come true. Nothingness shrouds all of our projects and projections. For God's saving grace—his institution of new possibilities for the world—does not reject death and creatureliness but rather enters into our death so that we might partake of God's life. It is false to presume that God safeguards us from having to live our own personal death. Our finitude and creatureliness remain even after God comes to bring new life. We are still finite but instead of living according to nothingness (instead of being-towards-death), we are then oriented to God's life.[66] And, in acknowledging our limitations we are being true to our actual creaturely existence and, at the same time, free to live a meaningful life. We are not caught in the incessant play of infinite possibilities where boredom reigns but rather, real meaning pervades our entire life because there is real risk.[67]

And, finally, a Christian notion of possibility cannot be limited to what is found only in the worldly present. Any amount of probing the depths of the present or past for absolute understanding of the future will always fail. Possibility for the Christian is not just a projection of the worldly present. God gifts new possibilities to the world where God's possibilities are not deducible from the world's possibilities. In fact, God's possibilities might even seem entirely impossible to us. But, our ultimate hope is not in a future state of worldly affairs derivative from the world, but in God who gifts new possibilities to humanity and the world where we are snatched from nothingness and brought to life.[68]

8.2   THE GOD OF PROMISE

We are now moving towards a new line of thought which has been given much attention in the 20th century and claims to have a more theological focus in relation to the future: the theme of promise. This is not to say that we are leaving issues of possibility behind or even that ontology and philosophy are not important to this new line of inquiry. But, what distinguishes this approach to the future is that it aims to draw more upon biblical and theological resources for talking about the future rather than just philosophical or ontological.[69] In fact, there has been significant cross-pollination between these ideas in the 20th century. We have already seen how Kearney's reference to Exodus 3:14 depends upon a certain reference to God's being in relation to a promise in and for the future. And, Kearney's 'God Who May Be' is constructed out of a dialogue with theologians and religious philosophers, such as Buber and Rosenzweig, who see in the biblical texts not a God of 'I am', but a God who promises to be with his people in the future. One might even argue that it is not surprising that such philosophers as Levinas and Derrida hail from the Jewish tradition when considering their accounts of time and history. A theological account of time and the future has been a prevalent resource for continental philosophers who devote themselves to issues of possibility and the future.

And yet, the influence flows in the opposite direction as well: from philosophy to theology. Such is the case with Jürgen Moltmann, the theologian most famous for developing the theme of promise in the 20th century and the figure we will be drawing on here. Moltmann's intellectual heritage stems from both theological and philosophical resources to develop this theme of promise. Indeed, Karl Barth and Ernst Bloch are the foundation out of which Moltmann's theological construction is built.[70] Moltmann's years following the war were taken up reading Barth's works, and when he was introduced to Bloch he said 'all at once the loose threads of a biblical theology, of the theology of the apostolate and the kingdom of God, and of philosophy, merged into the pattern for a tapestry in which everything matched'.[71] So, as we shall see, even in the case of Moltmann, questions of 'possibility' are never far off.

Before giving an account of Moltmann's development of promise, it is important to remember that what we are seeking here is primarily a response to transhumanist notions of the future. And, what a promissory account of the future brings to bear on our discussion is that the future is entirely interpersonal where we are bound for the first relation, the Trinity. The locus of the future hinges on an interpersonal interaction rooted in trust of another. Inasmuch as transhumanists may try to safeguard these human relationships, ultimately, their future reveals that human relations are eclipsed by a focus on transcendence often taking the form of self-transcendence.

8.2.1 Moltmann on Christ and Eschatology

Our analysis of the technological future has been informed by a distinction Moltmann makes between what he terms the future as *adventus* and the future as *futurum*. Moltmann, on several occasions,[72] recounts the historical difference between these two terms. He claims that the term 'future' in English is derived from the Latin word *futurum* whereas the German, *Zukunft*, comes from the Latin term *adventus*. The former describes a future which is an outworking of present conditions and can be translated 'what will be'. *Adventus*, on the other hand, is not characterised by a reference to ontology or a particular state of affairs derived from the present, but gives priority to that 'which is coming'. The term *adventus* is itself derived from the Greek term *parousia* which, in the Bible, refers to the second coming of Christ. But, in its secular context, and what I want to draw attention to here, is that it is grounded in the arrival of a person: 'In secular Greek, parousia means the coming of persons, or the happening of events, and literally means presence; but the language of the prophets and apostles has brought into the word the messianic note of hope'.[73] It is the 'personal presence' of a person who is coming near. Thus it is both imminent and immanent. What we see in this distinction between *adventus* and *futurum* is that the future is relocated away from a future which is defined according to ontology and is instead indicative of a personal relation with one who comes.

This talk about the arrival of a person as definitive for the future becomes the basis for Moltmann's ultimate characterisation of the future. Yes, whenever Moltmann talks about the future, preferring the Christian *adventus* to *futurum*, he refers to Christ's future. For Moltmann, all talk about the future must converge on Christ and his future. He says:

> Christian eschatology does not speak of the future as such . . . Christian eschatology speaks of Jesus Christ and *his* future. It recognises the reality of the raising of Jesus and proclaims the future of the risen Lord. Hence the question whether all statements about the future are grounded in the person and history of Jesus provides it with the touchstone by which to distinguish the spirit of eschatology from that of utopia.[74]

The biblical *parousia* focuses on Christ's second coming as the defining feature of the Christian future. Moltmann contends that this second coming of Christ is not devoid of form or content. It is not a groundless hope without precedence. Rather, Christ's ultimate future is visible in his historical life and the events of his passion, death and resurrection. The events of the historical Christ are not just past events relegated to a memory waiting to be forgotten, but rather they signify something entirely eschatological. As Moltmann says, 'Christology is no more than the beginning of eschatology; and eschatology, as the Christian faith understands it, is always the consummation of

Christology.'[75] Eschatology must be understood in light of Christ and it is between Christ's death and resurrection that the present and future are to find their grounding.

For Moltmann, Christ's death signifies God's real entry into the world and human experience. It shows that God has taken on the mortality of the lived life. The crucified Christ manifests God's taking on human mortality at its most grave in the suffering of this world. And, in Christ's suffering on the cross, God shows his solidarity with those who suffer in this world. This is a radical theology of the cross because Moltmann does not cordon off the divine from suffering or death.[76] As the title of his most sustained treatment of Christ's death shows, *The Crucified God*, God is really present in this crucifixion. Thus Moltmann challenges the metaphysical God who is removed from the evils of this world and is said to be impassible. The proper response to the 'death of God' for Moltmann is located and discovered in the divinity of Christ which brings God into the suffering and death of this world. 'For this theology, God and suffering are no longer contradictions, as in theism and atheism, but God's being is in suffering and the suffering is in God's being itself, because God is love.'[77] God shows his infinite love to humanity by entering into death and suffering and allowing it to be defini-tive for God. For Moltmann, the theological basis of the crucified Christ on the cross—what the cross tells us—is God's love for humanity.[78]

God does show his complete and ultimate concern for humanity by mov-ing into suffering and death through the cross, but this action cannot be separated from the significance Moltmann attributes to Christ's resurrec-tion. Both are joined together in what Richard Bauckham calls Moltmann's 'dialectical Christology'.[79] By this, Bauckham means that the identity of Christ is 'sustained in contradiction'. God in Christ was really forsaken by God—'My God, why hast thou forsaken me?'[80]—but equally this is the same Christ who was raised in glory. There is a complete disjunction between the humiliated and suffering Christ and the Christ of resurrection. In other words, everything of God in Christ was subjected to suffering and death just as everything of God in Christ was raised.

Christ's death and resurrection are to be seen in the light of eschatology—besides being past events they have present value and are the basis for hope for all of creation and humanity. Christ's suffering shows God's interjection into present suffering, making it entirely relevant for today's world, but his resurrection indicates the new life God brings to creation and the world. The resurrection of Christ sets in motion the res-urrecting of the whole world: 'The resurrection has set in motion an escha-tologically determined process of history, whose goal is the annihilation of death in the victory of the life of the resurrection, and which ends in that righteousness in which God receives in all things his due and the creature thereby finds its salvation'.[81] Christ's resurrection depicts the future of cre-ation and humanity. Thus, the resurrection must be the place we look if we are to understand the future.

The value and meaning of Christ's resurrection must also be understood not only for what it means for the future of humanity and creation but also how it arises from out of the Old Testament understanding of promise. Moltmann is adamant that God's promises to Israel are not abolished in Christ's coming. Talk about Christ as the fulfilment of God's promises in the Old Testament must be understood such that Christ's death and resurrection do not eradicate these promises but rather Christ needs to be seen through the medium of the Old Testament development of promise itself.

What then characterises this Old Testament promise for Moltmann as a guiding theological trope? And, how does it relate to Christ?

Moltmann sets the Judaic view of time and history in contrast to epiphanic religions which stress the 'eternal presence' of God. He argues that this idea of 'eternal presence' is derivative of a Greek philosophical conception going back to Parmenides and has entered into Christian theological circles but needs to be avoided.[82] It needs to be avoided because it can easily fall prey to two problems. First, it can lead to an unhelpful equating of God and the world often by localising the deity, sacralising society or divinising the world. This pitfall makes too much of God's immanence. Or, second, it can place God and the world on two separate tracks (*Zweigleisigkeit*) where God's history and time are distinct from the world's time.[83] This approach emphasises the radical transcendence of God and makes the actions of this world, perhaps even God's own actions in this world, less important than what happens 'in eternity'. World history becomes secondary to eternity. Moltmann contends that this view of God's presence in the world is inadequate and not biblical.

Rather, Moltmann prefers to speak about God's relation to the world in terms of promise. He finds precedence for this in both the Old and New Testaments. In the Old Testament, Moltmann upholds the works Martin Buber and also Victor Maags on the difference between agrarian and nomadic realities in shaping the respective communities' conceptions of time.[84] The nomadic God is one who is on the move with the peoples themselves and isn't bound to a particular locality as with other agrarian-influenced religions. This nomadic God, when he appears, does not hallow the time and place of the occurrence.[85] God's theophanies in time and history are not interpreted as an epiphany of God's eternal presence but intimate God's promises which point away from enclosing God in the here and now and instead point towards a fulfilled future. What Moltmann finds being developed in the Old Testament is a drive towards an eschatological interpretation of God's promises. When God makes a covenant with Israel and vows to be faithful to this promise, the trajectory of this promise is towards the future. And, a significant feature Moltmann identifies in the Old Testament promissory trope is that a fulfilment of a promise does not entail the cessation of that promise. The focus is not on the arrival or even perhaps the completion and closure of that promise. Fulfilment here means 'expositions, confirmations and expansions of the promise'.[86] The promise, in a sense, is renewed and points forward yet again.

This renewal of the promise is particularly salient in Moltmann's inter-pretation of New Testament texts and, in particular, Christ's relation to Old Testament promises. Moltmann cites several Pauline passages which speak of Christ as the fulfilment of the Old Testament promises.[87] Moltmann claims that Christ's fulfilment bears much in common with Old Testament views of the fulfilment of Gods promise. Christ's fulfilment does not eradi-cate God's original promise. There is continuity with the Old Testament promise and Christ. But, it must equally be emphasised that Christ is bring-ing something radically new. Something has happened in Christ which trans-forms and alters the course of that promise. Therefore, Moltmann chooses to explain this fulfilment in terms of Jesus Christ bringing an 'eschatological setting-in-force' (*In-kraft-setzung*) of God's promise to Abraham'.[88] Accord-ing to Christopher Morse:

> The continuity between the testaments is to be found in the way in which the resurrection makes the historical Abrahamic promise opera-tive as an eschatological process. The Old Testament promise is fulfilled in Christ. . .with the result that it is enforced with new power—that is the power of 'the New.' . . . What is new in the resurrection, Moltmann explains, is that the eschatological process which is thereby set in motion is not merely one process among others in world history but rather *the* historical process to which all of world history is finally subject.[89]

We have seen how Moltmann's understanding of the future takes its cue not from a future based upon *futurum* but one which understands the future as *adventus*. This *adventus* future refers to God's coming to the world where eschatology and the future is entirely conditioned by Christ. So that, when Christians speak of the future, it must be Christ's future we talk about. This eschatological future is glimpsed in the resurrection in that it points to the ultimate resurrection of all of humanity and creation.

8.2.2   Moltmann's Promise and the Communal God

Moltmann identifies several definitive facets of a theological account of promise in his text *Theology of Hope*.[90] First, 'a promise is a declaration which announces the coming of a reality that does not yet exist'.[91] A prom-ise does not derive its value or impetus from present realities, nor does it arise from out of the past or present, but rather is an announcement of a coming reality. In agreement with Kearney and Jüngel, Moltmann proclaims that a divine promise does not depend upon the 'possibilities inherent in the present'.[92] Rather, Moltmann claims, 'promise opens up history in the possibilities of God'.[93] In many ways, Moltmann makes the same move that Kearney and Jüngel do in relation to possibility. God's gifting of new pos-sibilities is visible, for Moltmann, precisely in the superabundance of the promise and resurrection.[94] They provide a new avenue out of the 'temporal and transitory' nature of this world. It is only within a promissory theology that this graciousness, this divine gift, can be properly located.[95]

Second, promise, as we have seen already, 'binds man to the future and gives him a sense for history'.[96] The promise points towards the future: 'literally *pro-missio*, a sending-ahead of what is to come'.[97] This history Moltmann speaks of is not 'world history' as we might see it against secular events and a kind of *chronos* time, but rather is a history which arises between the given promise and its fulfilment.[98] This reinterpretation of history is related to Moltmann's claim that Christ's resurrection is historic because it is an event that creates not because it has happened in history.[99]

Third, because promise refers to something which does not yet exist, it stands in tension with present realties by contradicting them.[100] This contradiction is visible in Moltmann's appropriation of the Blochian term *novum*. The 'newness' to which this *novum* refers is ultimately the new reality instituted by Christ's resurrection. Historically, the *novum* indicates where God creates a new future. Here Moltmann refers to events found in the Old Testament and New Testament but its ultimate horizon, the *novum ultimum*, indicates the completely new eschatological future related to Christ's resurrection. Moltmann specifies that *novum* presents something new to the present. It does not grow out of the old, rather it renders 'the old obsolete'.[101] Thus, the *novum* creates out of nothing, *creatio ex nihilo*, and 'announces itself in the judgement on what is old'.[102] This facet of the promise as judgement provides the basis for Moltmann's revolutionary writings which engage with political and economic inequalities.[103] Indeed, in standing against present powers where there is no likelihood of change, the marginalised hope in the promises of God alone.

Fourth, because promise does not coincide with present reality, it instead opens up a space whereby human beings can either obey and respond to this promise and choose to act out of hope or become resigned to the fatalism of only that which is. Thus, the promise is not fate or prophecy which depends upon a deterministic and static understanding of history.[104] Rather, within the framework of promise both God and humanity are reassured in their respective freedom.

Fifth, just because God's promise, in creating its own unique history, does not succumb to secular notions of history, nor can it be defined by it, does not mean that there isn't movement or direction between promise and fulfilment. Moltmann claims there is directionality in the space and time opened up between promise and fulfilment. It is in the direction from a given promise towards that fulfilment. In other words, this forward movement does not appeal to modern notions of progress or to evolution, but finds its basis in the faithfulness of God to bring about fulfilment.

This then leads to the final item and the most important for our purpose. God's promise ultimately depends upon the trustworthiness and faithfulness of a personal God. A promise is not a hope in a particular set of circumstances which might or might not come about in the future; instead a promise is always oriented towards God's faithfulness to the promise. Therefore, one cannot dictate in advance in what way God might fulfil this promise. There can be no historical necessity which governs the promise or the fulfilment. For, ultimately, each must submit to the freedom of God in how this promise might be fulfilled.[105] Thus, promise is always grounded in the personal and, I might argue, the interpersonal.[106]

Moltmann's thorough Trinitarianism helps deepen this claim that the future is to be set within the logic of the interpersonal. For Moltmann, the movement of the events of promise are ultimately located within and find their meaning and source within the aboriginal relations of the Trinity. As Grenz points out of Moltmann, 'God's triunity is integrally connected to the divine engagement with the world, which forms a history centering on Jesus Christ.'[107] As suggested prior, for Moltmann the cross is not just a moment of human suffering but reveals God's suffering because Christ, as God, suffers. It is not only a moment of salvation history but 'is taken up into the "history of God," i.e., into the Trinity, and integrated into the future of "the history of God." '[108] Moltmann follows the Rahnerian maxim that the economic Trinity is the immanent Trinity[109] and all efforts to distinguish the two often succumb to two distinct Trinities rather than 'the same tri-une God as he is in his saving revelation and as he is in himself.'[110] So all moments of history that are driven by a promissory theology find their home in the divine life—God's engagement with the world is but a moment of the intra-Trinitarian relation. Moltmann labels this an 'open Trinity' for it is open to creation and includes it amongst itself.[111]

The origin and end of creation, the primary reality out of which it is formed and that to which it is going, is thoroughly relational, interpersonal and *perichoretic*. Not only does a relational or interpersonal interpretation of promise manifest the ultimate future for the Christian but this is everywhere undergirded by the eschatological nature of the social Trinity—we are bound for community in God who is Himself first community. This community, for Moltmann, is *perichoretic* in that it affirms the 'intimate indwelling and complete interpenetration of the persons in one another',[112] where Father, Son and Holy Spirit each gives way to the other constituting a community that makes space for each typified not by lordly domination or assertion but by deference and mutual love. Indeed, Moltmann goes so far as to say that 'human beings are the *imago trinitatis* and only correspond to the triune God when they are united with one another.'[113] Relationality and the interpersonal are not incidental to the human experience nor are they exhausted by or unique to the human sphere alone. Humanity, and indeed all of creation, is marked by an overwhelming drive towards the relational. Creation coheres with that origin and subsequent return to its source when in relation because it owes its existence to the primary community in the Godhead. Reality is interpersonal all the way down[114] and is our final end in the Trinity as a 'cosmic *perichoresis*', 'a mutual indwelling of the world in God and God in the world.'[115]

8.3 CONCLUSION: THE INTERPERSONAL GOD

It is not within the purview of this book to argue for or against all of Molt-mann's claims concerning promise or his Trinitarian theology. What I want to highlight is how Moltmann seeks to relocate talk about the future in a Christian context away from issues related to just ontology and philosophy and instead utilises this notion of promise to understand time, history and the future.

One of the strengths of Moltmann's promissory theology is that Chris-tology plays such a significant role in eschatology and the future. In trying to identify what is unique or characteristically Christian about a Christian understanding of the future, it seems we can find no better ground than Christ. The resurrection is the kernel of the Christian hope for it reveals God's bringing new life and new possibilities to a world which is fraught with suffering and death. God in Christ does not abandon humanity and creation in this fallen state where it is surrounded and moving towards nothingness, but shows love for this world by entering into those darkest places bringing redemption and resurrection. The hope for the Christian must move through death and this world for that is what Christ has done. Indeed, Christ was not left in the tomb to rot but was instead transfigured and this sets in motion the missional aspect of the resurrection until 'God will be all in all'.[116]

This invariably leads to the question as to how much, then, Christ's future is also our future? If the future is God's future and Christ's death and resurrection reveal what the future holds for the Christian, can we do anything significant to add to this kingdom? This has been a recurrent ques-tion throughout this text. Ellul emphasises the absolute difference between human creation in technology and history and God's salvation of the world from this technological determinism. Despite the significance he attributes to the city, specifically the New Jerusalem, in the Kingdom of God, and does so in such a way as to indicate that God transforms our creation in escha-ton, Ellul is entirely pessimistic of its value on its own. Are our technological creations 'interesting for their own sake'? Teilhard offers a more seamless transition between human creations and their ultimate value in God's future at the Omega Point: God divinises our activities and our passivities alike. Indeed, he finds ultimate theological value in our technological creations accepting them almost naively. But what of Moltmann?

Moltmann tries to mediate between, on the one hand, a God who makes all things new, creates from out of nothing and says that this new thing stands in judgement of the old, and also finds continuity with a God in history and creation. God is not above us interjecting himself from some timeless position, but is actually in these events themselves. God is, in a way, in these actions. Moltmann has gone to great lengths to safeguard human action in creation. In his later works Moltmann suggests an alternative image derived from the kabbalistic doctrine *zimzum*. He has devised a way in which God retreats from God's self, carving out an uninhabited space within God, so that human creativity might flourish in this panenthesitic *khora*.[117] Thus, the world is said to be in God, but God is not entirely in the world in history until the end of time.

Moltmann's constant refrain that a Christian hope is not in abandonment of this world is commendable. This newness that Christ brings transforms the world. It is a promise for this world not for another. Christ's body is transformed from death into life signifying the same type of transformation of this world. If we can extend the controlling image, Christ's glorified, resurrected body still bears the scars which act as a reminder, a constant memory, of his suffering and death. This image reveals that this suffering and death is never forgotten in our resurrection. They are not wiped clean as if they never happened but become transformed in Christ's newness. The significance of his wounds remaining shows a sober glorification. Thus, the eschaton is not tearless, but rather depicts a time when he will wipe away our every tear. Our world matters and is a strong basis for real work today and leads to practical steps for change.

Finally, in utilising promise as a theological trope to structure a Christian understanding of the future, we have seen that promise must appeal to the subjects within the promise. A promise binds people together. It sets persons on a common path where they must trust each other. When promise is used as a hermeneutic to understand the future it means that, in some way, those virtues within the promise are ascribed ultimate value: trust, love and faithfulness. The future is not personless for the Christian. It does not appeal to present circumstances which can be used to work out the future so that we can be in the best situation. Rather, it relocates talk about the future from a particular set of affairs to persons. What I am claiming is distinct about a Christian future is that in order to understand the future we must look to the interaction between persons. A Christian appeal to promise makes interpersonal interactions ultimate as it stresses our ultimate origin and end in the triune God who is first community and hence makes all of reality relational.

The next chapter, the final chapter, will comment on how this Christian future provides a needed rejoinder to the transhumanist future and will address the commensurability of both visions of the future.

NOTES

1. Several others could just as easily be used to construct the theme of possibility: Heidegger, Levinas, Bergson and Derrrida, in addition to Pannenberg, Bloch or Ricoeur. While they might not seem to take centre stage in the pages that follow, many figure prominently in these two figures I have chosen.
2. Kevin Hart may be the only exception, in Kevin Hart, "Mystic Maybes," in *After God: Richard Kearney and the Religious Turn in Continental Philosophy*, ed., John Panteleimon Manoussakis (New York: Fordham University

Press, 2006). This is particularly strange because both have strong ties with Paul Ricoeur and his works on religion and language.

3. Eberhard Jüngel, "The World as Actuality and Possibility: The Ontology of the Doctrine of Justification," in *Theological Essays* (Edinburgh: T. & T. Clark, 1989).

4. Ibid., 97.

5. I prefer the term 'possibility' instead of 'potentiality' because it explicitly connects the notion with our contemporary ideas of possibility.

6. Aristotle, *The Metaphysics*, trans., H. C. Lawson-Tancred (London: Penguin, 1998), 272 (1049b).

7. Jüngel, "The World as Actuality and Possibility," 98. Italicised for emphasis.

8. Ibid., 98–99.

9. Aristotle, *The Metaphysics*, 260 (1047a).

10. Ibid., 260 (1047b). The brackets are my own addition.

11. Stephen Makin, *Aristotle Metaphysics Book Theta* (Oxford: Clarendon, 2006), xxix; Joe Sachs, *Aristotle's Physics: A Guided Study* (New Brunswick: Rutgers University Press, 1995), 245.

12. Makin, *Aristotle Metaphysics Book Theta*, xxix; Sachs, *Aristotle's Physics*, 245.

13. Jüngel, "The World as Actuality and Possibility," 99.

14. As we shall see in the coming pages, this has important theological consequences.

15. Indeed, the lineage of criticisms which aim to separate the 'God of the philosophers' from the 'God of Bible'—Pascal, Buber, Moltmann—have to contend with this very important passage.

16. Etienne Gilson, *The Spirit of Medieval Philosophy*, trans., A. H. C. Downes (New York: Charles Scribner's Sons, 1940), 51.

17. Thomas Aquinas, *Summa Theologiae*, vol. 3 (London: Eyre and Spottiswoode, 1964), 91 (Ia, Q13, A11).

18. Thomas Aquinas, *Summa Contra Gentiles*, vol. 1 (Notre Dame: University of Notre Dame Press, 1975), 100 (I, ch16, A2).

19. Gilson, *The Spirit of Medieval Philosophy*, 51ff; Richard Kearney, *The God Who May Be: A Hermeneutics of Religion* (Bloomington: Indiana University Press, 2001), 20ff; Paul Ricoeur, "From Interpretation to Translation," in *Thinking Biblically: Exegetical and Hermeneutical Studies* (Chicago: University of Chicago Press, 1998).

20. Franz Rosenzweig, "The Eternal: Mendelssohn and the Name of God," in *Scripture and Translation* (Bloomington: Indiana University Press, 1994).

21. George Pattison, *God and Being: An Enquiry* (Oxford: Oxford University Press, 2011), 19–20.

22. Rosenzweig, "The Eternal," 102.

23. The latter part of this chapter will expound upon the second part of the title, 'The God of Promise', and scholars such as Buber, Rosenzweig and von Rad cited here are central to understanding a promissory God and this relation to his name in Exodus 3:14.

24. Gerhard von Rad, *Old Testament Theology*, trans., D. M. G. Stalker, vol. 1 (Edinburgh: Oliver and Boyd, 1962), 180. See Buber's similar comments in Martin Buber, *Moses* (Oxford: East and West Library, 1946), 53.

25. Pattison makes this observation as well in Pattison, *God and Being*, 280.

26. Of course, what I am proposing extends further than just biology. But, as others have noted, the effects of the Darwinian Revolution could be felt beyond biology and the sciences. Darwin crystallised the notion that all of nature was in a constant state of flux. See Ian G. Barbour, *Issues in Science and Religion* (London: SCM Press, 1966), 86ff. Of course, transhumanists adhere to this

rejection of a strict Aristotelian ontology of categories as well. But, one might say, that the transhumanist possibility is still like the Aristotelian notion save for the ontological categories. To use the example, a transhumanist might say that, contra Aristotle, the seed of the flower has the potential to become something other than a flower. But, it is still Aristotelian in that what it becomes is derivative from the present alone. The potency exists in the seed.

27. Kearney, *The God Who May Be*, 22.
28. Ibid., 1.
29. Atheistic because it is never here and can never be spoken of or realised. It is the true wholly Other. See Caputo's sustained reflections on Derrida's relation to religion in John D. Caputo, *The Prayers and Tears of Jacques Derrida: Religion without Religion* (Bloomington: Indiana University Press, 1997).
30. Kearney, *The God Who May Be*, 73.
31. Ibid., 147.
32. Ibid., 145.
33. Ibid., 75.
34. Richard Kearney, "Enabling God," in *After God: Richard Kearney and the Religious Turn in Continental Philosophy*, ed., John Panteleimon Manoussakis (New York: Fordham University Press, 2006), 42.
35. In this way, Kearney can be said to adhere to a kind of weak theology associated with such philosophers as John Caputo and Gianni Vattimo. See John D. Caputo, *The Weakness of God: A Theology of the Event* (Bloomington: Indiana University Press, 2006); Gianni Vattimo, *After Christianity*, trans., Luca D'Isanto (New York: Columbia University Press, 2002). Indeed, it bears striking resemblance with relational theologies such as Process and Open Theology as well.
36. Kearney, *The God Who May Be*, 38.
37. Ibid.
38. Ibid., 46.
39. Ibid., 29–30.
40. Ibid., 37.
41. Kearney, "After God," 50.
42. Ibid.
43. This is one of, if not the, central question in Pattison's text *God and Being* and is perhaps one of the most pressing issues when considering a Christian understanding of God's relation to Being. Is God's primary relation first to love or is it to Being? See Pattison, *God and Being*, 223ff; Stephen H. Webb, "God and Being: An Enquiry—by George Pattison," *Conversations in Religion & Theology* 9, no. 1 (2011), 75.
44. Kearney, *The God Who May Be*, 5.
45. Also spoken of by Christ in the Gospel of Mark: 'For mortals it is impossible, but not for God; for God all things are possible.' Mark 10:27 (New Revised Standard Version).
46. Søren Kierkegaard, *The Sickness unto Death*, trans., Howard V. Hong and Edna H. Hong (Princeton: Princeton University Press, 1980), 40. See Pattison's commentary in Pattison, *God and Being*, 285–290.
47. Kearney, *The God Who May Be*, 102.
48. Ibid., 107.
49. B. Keith Putt, "Theopoetics of the Possible," in *After God: Richard Kearney and the Religious Turn in Continental Philosophy*, ed., John Panteleimon Manoussakis (New York: Fordham University Press, 2006), 247–248.
50. Of course, this isn't to say that Kearney's position on God transfiguring the world is merely about reinterpretation—an abstract perception of the world without any grounding or real affecting of the world. He agrees with Ricoeur

that language and hermeneutics really brings new possibilities into the world. This is primarily done through metaphor, narrative and the imagination. 'The function of semantic innovation—which is most proper to imagination—is therefore, in its most fundamental sense, an ontological event. The innovative power of linguistic imagination is not some "decorative excess or effusion of subjectivity, but the capacity of language to open up new worlds".' Richard Kearney, *On Paul Ricoeur: The Owl of Minerva* (Aldershot: Ashgate, 2004), 41; Paul Ricoeur and Richard Kearney, "Myth as the Bearer of Possible Worlds," *The Crane Bag* 2, nos. 1/2 (1978).

51. I use this term in a Levinasian sense which Kearney himself advocates in relation to God. Kearney, *The God Who May Be*, 9ff.

52. Not least, as well, because of the biblical and theological emphasis on the linguistic nature of God's revelation: God came in Christ as the Word become flesh. There is a biblical and theological precedence for God's relating to the world through language.

53. Represented so well in Dostoyevsky's characters Kirilov, Ivan Karamazov, Raskol'nikov and the Underground Man.

54. Eberhard Jüngel, "Metaphorical Truth: Reflections on the Theological Relevance of Metaphor as a Contribution to the Hermeneutics of Narrative Theology," in *Theological Essays* (Edinburgh: T. & T. Clark, 1989), 61.

55. Eberhard Jüngel, *God as the Mystery of the World: On the Foundation of the Theology of the Crucified One in the Dispute between Theism and Atheism*, trans., Darrell L. Guder (Edinburgh: T. & T. Clark, 1983), 285ff.

56. Jüngel states that one of the positive effects of asserting the nonnecessity of God is that it makes the world and God interesting for their own sake. This is one of the strengths of Kearney's and Jüngel's positions. See ibid., 34.

57. Ibid., 23–24.

58. See Paul J. DeHart, *Beyond the Necessary God: Trinitarian Faith and Philosophy in the Thought of Eberhard Jüngel* (Atlanta: Scholars Press, 1999), 69–95; Jüngel, *God as the Mystery of the World*, 28.

59. Much of Jüngel's critique of the necessary God bears much in common with Heidegger's critique of ontotheology. See the last chapter for details on Heidegger's treatment of ontotheology. And, not grounding God or the world in each other within a necessary relationship shows once again that both the world and God are interesting for their own sake.

60. Jüngel, *God as the Mystery of the World*, 33.

61. Jüngel, "The World as Actuality and Possibility," 109.

62. Ibid., 112.

63. Ibid., 113.

64. Ibid., 114.

65. See chapter five of Hubert L. Dreyfus, *On the Internet* (London: Routledge, 2001).

66. Jüngel is adamant on this point. See chapter six of Eberhard Jüngel, *Death: The Riddle and the Mystery*, trans., Ian and Ute Nicol (Edinburgh: Saint Andrew, 1975).

67. See Dreyfus, *On the Internet*.

68. This is not to say that what happens to humanity and the world in the future is not important for the Christian. Indeed, I am not advocating some retreat from worldly affairs. But, our hope cannot reside in the vision of a purely worldly future precisely because God has come. I am not denigrating the role of human creation for God's future, but the Kingdom of God is distinct from utopia in that the power of our hope comes from God making all things new and in his gifting of new possibilities. The Christian hope cannot be based upon what is worldly alone but on a God who transforms the world. God's

vision for the future encompasses the world but the Christian hope has a referent outside of the world. See Jüngel, "The World as Actuality and Possibility," 114–115.

69. Gerhard Sauter claims that when we want to talk about time, history and the future from a theological perspective we have to talk about God's promise. When this is done from a philosophical perspective it is in the arena of ontology. See Christopher Morse, *The Logic of Promise in Moltmann's Theology* (Philadelphia: Fortress Press, 1979), 4–5; Gerhard Sauter, *Zukunft und Verheissung: Das Problem der Zukunft in der Gegenwärtigen Theologischen und Philosophischen Diskussion* (Zurich: Zwingli Verlag, 1965).

70. M. Douglas Meeks, *Origins of the Theology of Hope* (Philadelphia: Fortress Press, 1974), 15–19; Jürgen Moltmann, *Experiences in Theology: Ways and Forms of Christian Theology* (Minneapolis: Fortress Press, 2000), 92–93.

71. Jürgen Moltmann, "Politics and the Practice of Hope," *The Christian Century* 87 (March 11, 1970), 289.

72. It being an important theme in his writings this shouldn't be a surprise. Indeed, serious discussion of these terms makes its way into Jürgen Moltmann, *God in Creation: An Ecological Doctrine of Creation* (London: SCM, 1985), 132–135; Jürgen Moltmann, *The Coming of God: Christian Eschatology* (London: SCM Press, 1996), 25–26. Indeed, this distinction was noted from very early on in Moltmann's writings. See Timothy Harvie, *Jürgen Moltmann's Ethics of Hope: Eschatological Possibilities for Moral Action* (Farnham: Ashgate, 2009), 46n33.

73. Moltmann, *The Coming of God*, 25.

74. Jürgen Moltmann, *Theology of Hope: On the Ground and the Implications of a Christian Eschatology* (London: SCM, 1967), 17. Also, Moltmann's distinction here between a utopian future and Christ's future is important for it not only signals where he breaks with Bloch but also shows that Christian eschatology is not to be confused with utopia. Of course, the looming question here, then, is how Christ's future is also our future. Or, better, does our striving and creativity in history have any lasting value in Christ's future?

75. Jürgen Moltmann, *The Way of Jesus Christ: Christology in Messianic Dimensions* (London: SCM, 1990), xiv.

76. Jürgen Moltmann, *The Crucified God: The Cross of Christ as the Foundation and Criticism of Christian Theology* (Minneapolis: Fortress Press, 1993), 214ff.

77. Ibid., 227.

78. Also see Fiddes's extension of the passable God in Paul S. Fiddes, *The Creative Suffering of God* (Oxford: Clarendon Press, 1988).

79. Richard Bauckham, *The Theology of Jürgen Moltmann* (Edinburgh: T. & T. Clark, 1995), 33.

80. Moltmann makes extensive usage of this passage from Mark 15:34 in Moltmann, *The Crucified God*, 145–153.

81. Moltmann, *Theology of Hope*, 163.

82. Ibid., 28–29.

83. Morse, *Moltmann's Theology*, 32.

84. Moltmann, *Theology of Hope*, 95ff.

85. Ibid., 100.

86. Ibid., 105.

87. The most salient being 2 Corinthians 1:20. See Moltmann, *Theology of Hope*, 147.

88. Morse, *Moltmann's Theology*, 35. The relation to possibility (an alternative translation of *kraft*) here is striking as well, whether Moltmann intends it or not.

89. Ibid., 35–36.

90. The following come from Moltmann, *Theology of Hope*, 102ff.

91. Ibid., 103.
92. Ibid.
93. Moltmann, *Experiences in Theology*, 102.
94. Ricoeur finds this interpretation of the resurrection particularly fruitful and striking. See Paul Ricoeur, "Freedom in the Light of Hope," in *The Conflict of Interpretations: Essays in Hermeneutics* (London: Continuum, 2004).
95. Moltmann, *Experiences in Theology*, 105.
96. Moltmann, *Theology of Hope*, 103.
97. Moltmann, *Experiences in Theology*, 102.
98. Of course, Moltmann comes very close to succumbing to his criticism of epiphanies of eternal presence cited earlier where he denigrates any notion of time and history which sets time on a two-tiered level. Morse goes to great lengths to understand what Moltmann means by history in Morse, *Moltmann's Theology*, 82–108. Moltmann reflects on this issue and instead of suggesting that God has a transcendental eternal time where he breaks into the world's time, of which he is critical, he states that 'they are two world times of God's one same creation'. See Jürgen Moltmann, "Hope and Reality: Contradiction and Correspondence," in *God Will Be All in All: The Eschatology of Jürgen Moltmann*, ed., Richard Bauckham (Edinburgh: T. & T. Clark, 1999), 83.
99. Moltmann, *Theology of Hope*, 180–181.
100. This was the aspect of Moltmann's thought Ellul stressed and, in many ways, manifests Moltmann's preference for apocalyptic talk about God: 'apocalypse of the promised future'. Ibid., 57.
101. Moltmann, *The Coming of God*, 27.
102. Ibid.
103. Jürgen Moltmann, *Religion, Revolution, and the Future* (New York: Scribner, 1969); Jürgen Moltmann, *The Experiment Hope*, trans., M. Douglas Meeks (London: SCM, 1975).
104. Moltmann, *Experiences in Theology*, 93–96.
105. I might add that how the promise and fulfilment end up are dependent upon both parties, man and God, and their freedom—not just God.
106. Moltmann would want to add that the promise encompasses more than just subjects in the promise. Indeed, he was reacting against a particular interpretation of divine revelation where God's transcendental selfhood (*Ichheit*) is revealed. Moltmann wants to claim that theologians which ascribe to a kind of I-Thou interpretation of divine revelation do not make enough of God's work in history nor how God identifies with this work. Therefore, he claims God's historical faithfulness (*Selbigkeit*) is revealed. But, despite this qualification, the appeal to personhood and the interpersonal nature of promise is undeniable. See Moltmann, *Theology of Hope*, 113–116; Morse, *Moltmann's Theology*, 41ff, 67ff.
107. Stanley Grenz, *Rediscovering the Triune God: The Trinity in Contemporary Theology* (Minneapolis: Fortress Press, 2004), 75.
108. Moltmann, *The Crucified God*, 246.
109. Karl Rahner, *The Trinity*, trans., Joseph Donceel (London: Burns & Oates, 2001), 21ff.
110. Jürgen Moltmann, *The Trinity and the Kingdom: The Doctrine of God* (Minneapolis: Fortress, 1993), 151.
111. Ibid., 94–96. Ted Peters, *God as Trinity: Relationality and Temporality in Divine Life* (Louisville: Westminster John Knox, 1993), 103ff.
112. Jürgen Moltmann, *History and the Triune God: Contributions to Trinitarian Theology* (New York: Crossroad, 1992), 86.
113. Moltmann, *God in Creation*, 216.
114. John Polkinghorne makes a similar observation about the reality of the universe being primarily relational because of its Creator being triune. See

J. C. Polkinghorne, *Science and the Trinity: The Christian Encounter with Reality* (New Haven: Yale University Press, 2004), 73ff.
115. Moltmann, *The Coming of God*, 295, 307.
116. Jürgen Moltmann, "The World in God or God in the World?," in *God Will Be All in All: The Eschatology of Jürgen Moltmann*, ed., Richard Bauckham (Edinburgh: T. & T. Clark, 1999).
117. Moltmann, *The Coming of God*, 296ff.

REFERENCES

Aquinas, Thomas. *Summa Theologiae*. Vol. 3. London: Eyre and Spottiswoode, 1964.
———. *Summa Contra Gentiles*. Vol. 1. Notre Dame: University of Notre Dame Press, 1975.
Aristotle. *The Metaphysics*. Translated by H. C. Lawson-Tancred. London: Penguin, 1998.
Barbour, Ian G. *Issues in Science and Religion*. London: SCM Press, 1966.
Bauckham, Richard. *The Theology of Jürgen Moltmann*. Edinburgh: T. & T. Clark, 1995.
Buber, Martin. *Moses*. Oxford: East and West Library, 1946.
Caputo, John D. *The Prayers and Tears of Jacques Derrida: Religion without Religion*. Bloomington: Indiana University Press, 1997.
———. *The Weakness of God: A Theology of the Event*. Bloomington: Indiana University Press, 2006.
DeHart, Paul J. *Beyond the Necessary God: Trinitarian Faith and Philosophy in the Thought of Eberhard Jüngel*. Atlanta: Scholars Press, 1999.
DeRoo, Neal, and John Panteleimon Manoussakis, eds. *Phenomenology and Eschatology: Not Yet in the Now*. Farnham: Ashgate, 2009.
Dostoyevsky, Fyodor. *Notes from Underground and the Double*. Translated by Jessie Coulson. Harmondsworth: Penguin Classics, 1972.
———. *The Idiot*. Translated by David McDuff. London: Penguin, 2004.
Dreyfus, Hubert L. *On the Internet*. London: Routledge, 2001.
Fiddes, Paul S. *The Creative Suffering of God*. Oxford: Clarendon Press, 1988.
———. *Freedom and Limit: A Dialogue between Literature and Christian Doctrine*. Macon: Mercer University Press, 1999.
———. *The Promised End: Eschatology in Theology and Literature*. Oxford: Blackwells, 2000.
Gilson, Etienne. *The Spirit of Medieval Philosophy*. Translated by A. H. C. Downes. New York: Charles Scribner's Sons, 1940.
Grenz, Stanley. *Rediscovering the Triune God: The Trinity in Contemporary Theology*. Minneapolis: Fortress Press, 2004.
Hart, Kevin. "Mystic Maybes." In *After God: Richard Kearney and the Religious Turn in Continental Philosophy*, edited by John Panteleimon Manoussakis. New York: Fordham University Press, 2006.
Harvie, Timothy. *Jürgen Moltmann's Ethics of Hope: Eschatological Possibilities for Moral Action*. Farnham: Ashgate, 2009.
Jüngel, Eberhard. *Death: The Riddle and the Mystery*. Translated by Ian and Ute Nicol. Edinburgh: Saint Andrew, 1975.
———. *God as the Mystery of the World: On the Foundation of the Theology of the Crucified One in the Dispute between Theism and Atheism*. Translated by Darrell L. Guder. Edinburgh: T. & T. Clark, 1983.
———. "Humanity in Correspondence to God: Remarks on the Image of God as a Basic Concept in Theological Anthropology." In *Theological Essays*, 1. Edinburgh: T. & T. Clark, 1989.

———. "Metaphorical Truth: Reflections on the Theological Relevance of Metaphor as a Contribution to the Hermeneutics of Narrative Theology." In *Theological Essays*, 1. Edinburgh: T. & T. Clark, 1989.

———. "The World as Actuality and Possibility: The Ontology of the Doctrine of Justification." In *Theological Essays*, 1. Edinburgh: T. & T. Clark, 1989.

———. "Life after Death: A Response to Theology's Silence about Eternal Life." *Word and World* 11, no. 1 (1991): 5–8.

———. *God's Being Is in Becoming: The Trinitarian Being of God in the Theology of Karl Barth. A Paraphrase*. Translated by J. B. Webster. Edinburgh: T. & T. Clark, 2001.

Kearney, Richard. *The Wake of Imagination: Ideas of Creativity in Western Culture*. London: Routledge, 1988.

———. *Poetics of Modernity: Toward a Hermeneutic Imagination*. Atlantic Highlands: Humanities Press, 1995.

———. *The God Who May Be: A Hermeneutics of Religion*. Bloomington: Indiana University Press, 2001.

———. *On Paul Ricoeur: The Owl of Minerva*. Aldershot: Ashgate, 2004.

———. "Enabling God." In *After God: Richard Kearney and the Religious Turn in Continental Philosophy*, edited by John Panteleimon Manoussakis. New York: Fordham University Press, 2006.

Kierkegaard, Søren. *The Sickness unto Death*. Translated by Howard V. Hong and Edna H. Hong. Princeton: Princeton University Press, 1980.

Lacoste, Jean-Yves. *Experience and the Absolute: Disputed Questions on the Humanity of Man*. Translated by Mark Raftery-Skehan. Perspectives in Continental Philosophy. New York: Fordham University Press, 2004.

Levinas, Emmanuel. *Totality and Infinity: An Essay on Exteriority*. Translated by Alphonso Lingis. Pittsburgh: Duquesne University Press, 1969.

———. *Time and the Other*. Translated by Richard A. Cohen. Pittsburgh: Duquesne University Press, 1987.

———. *Otherwise Than Being, or, Beyond Essence*. Pittsburgh: Duquesne University Press, 1998.

Lyotard, Jean-François. *The Postmodern Condition: A Report on Knowledge*. Translated by Geoff Bennington and Brian Massumi. Minneapolis: University of Minnesota Press, 1984.

Makin, Stephen. *Aristotle Metaphysics Book Theta*. Oxford: Clarendon, 2006.

Manoussakis, John Panteleimon, ed. *After God: Richard Kearney and the Religious Turn in Continental Philosophy*. New York: Fordham University Press, 2006.

Meeks, M. Douglas. *Origins of the Theology of Hope*. Philadelphia: Fortress Press, 1974.

Moltmann, Jürgen. *Theology of Hope: On the Ground and the Implications of a Christian Eschatology*. London: SCM, 1967.

———. *Religion, Revolution, and the Future*. New York: Scribner, 1969.

———. "Politics and the Practice of Hope." *The Christian Century* 87 (March 11, 1970).

———. *The Experiment Hope*. Translated by M. Douglas Meeks. London: SCM, 1975.

———. *God in Creation: An Ecological Doctrine of Creation*. London: SCM, 1985.

———. *The Way of Jesus Christ: Christology in Messianic Dimensions*. London: SCM, 1990.

———. *History and the Triune God: Contributions to Trinitarian Theology*. New York: Crossroad, 1992.

———. *The Crucified God: The Cross of Christ as the Foundation and Criticism of Christian Theology*. Minneapolis: Fortress Press, 1993.

———. *The Trinity and the Kingdom: The Doctrine of God*. Minneapolis: Fortress, 1993.

————. *The Coming of God: Christian Eschatology*. London: SCM Press, 1996.

————. "Hope and Reality: Contradiction and Correspondence." In *God Will Be All in All: The Eschatology of Jürgen Moltmann*, edited by Richard Bauckham. Edinburgh: T. & T. Clark, 1999.

————. "The World in God or God in the World?" In *God Will Be All in All: The Eschatology of Jürgen Moltmann*, edited by Richard Bauckham. Edinburgh: T. & T. Clark, 1999.

————. *Experiences in Theology: Ways and Forms of Christian Theology*. Minneapolis: Fortress Press, 2000.

Morse, Christopher. *The Logic of Promise in Moltmann's Theology*. Philadelphia: Fortress Press, 1979.

Nietzsche, Friedrich. *The Portable Nietzsche*. Translated by Walter Kaufmann. London: Penguin, 1982.

Palakeel, Joseph. *The Use of Analogy in Theological Discourse: An Investigation in Ecumenical Perspective*. Rome: Editrice Pontificia Università Gregoriana, 1995.

Pannenberg, Wolfhart. "Appearance as the Arrival of the Future." *Journal of the American Academy of Religion* 35, no. 2 (1967): 107–118.

Pattison, George. *The Philosophy of Kierkegaard*. Chesham: Acumen, 2005.

————. *God and Being: An Enquiry*. Oxford: Oxford University Press, 2011.

Peters, Ted. *God as Trinity: Relationality and Temporality in Divine Life*. Louisville: Westminster John Knox, 1993.

Polkinghorne, J. C. *Science and the Trinity: The Christian Encounter with Reality*. New Haven: Yale University Press, 2004.

Putt, B. Keith. "Theopoetics of the Possible." In *After God: Richard Kearney and the Religious Turn in Continental Philosophy*, edited by John Panteleimon Manoussakis. New York: Fordham University Press, 2006.

Rahner, Karl. *The Trinity*. Translated by Joseph Donceel. London: Burns & Oates, 2001.

Ricoeur, Paul. *Time and Narrative*. Translated by Kathleen Blamey and David Pellauer. 3 vols. Chicago: University of Chicago Press, 1984.

————. "From Interpretation to Translation." In *Thinking Biblically: Exegetical and Hermeneutical Studies*. Chicago: University of Chicago Press, 1998.

————. *The Rule of Metaphor: The Creation of Meaning in Language*. Translated by Robert Czerny, Kathleen McLaughlin, and John Costello. London: Routledge, 2003.

————. "Freedom in the Light of Hope." In *The Conflict of Interpretations: Essays in Hermeneutics*. London: Continuum, 2004.

Ricoeur, Paul, and Richard Kearney. "Myth as the Bearer of Possible Worlds." *The Crane Bag* 2, nos. 1/2 (1978): 112–118.

Ricoeur, Paul, and John B. Thompson. *Hermeneutics and the Human Sciences: Essays on Language, Action and Interpretation*. Cambridge: Cambridge University Press, 1981.

Rosenzweig, Franz. "The Eternal: Mendelssohn and the Name of God." In *Scripture and Translation*. Bloomington: Indiana University Press, 1994.

Sachs, Joe. *Aristotle's Physics: A Guided Study*. New Brunswick: Rutgers University Press, 1995.

Sauter, Gerhard. *Zukunft und Verheissung: Das Problem der Zukunft in der Gegenwärtigen Theologischen und Philosophischen Diskussion*. Zurich: Zwingli Verlag, 1965.

Singh, Devin. "Resurrection as Surplus and Possibility: Moltmann and Ricoeur." *Scottish Journal of Theology* 61, no. 3 (2008): 251–269.

Soskice, Janet Martin. *Metaphor and Religious Language*. Oxford: Oxford University Press, 1985.

Stewart, David. "In Quest of Hope: Paul Ricoeur and Jürgen Moltmann." *Restoration Quarterly* 13, no. 1 (1970): 31–52.

Taylor, Charles. *A Secular Age*. Cambridge: Belknap Press of Harvard University Press, 2007.

Vattimo, Gianni. *After Christianity*. Translated by Luca D'Isanto. New York: Columbia University Press, 2002.

von Rad, Gerhard. *Old Testament Theology*. Translated by D. M. G. Stalker. Vol. 1. Edinburgh: Oliver and Boyd, 1962.

Walls, Jerry L., ed. *The Oxford Handbook of Eschatology*. Oxford: Oxford University Press, 2008.

Webb, Stephen H. "God and Being: An Enquiry—by George Pattison." *Conversations in Religion & Theology* 9, no. 1 (2011): 66–76.

Webster, J. B. "Eberhard Jüngel on the Language of Faith." *Modern Theology* 1, no. 4 (1985): 253–276.

———. *Eberhard Jüngel: An Introduction to His Theology*. Cambridge: Cambridge University Press, 1986.

———. "Justification, Analogy and Action. Passivity and Activity in Jüngel's Anthropology." In *The Possibilities of Theology: Studies in the Theology of Eberhard Jüngel in His Sixtieth Year*, edited by J. B. Webster. Edinburgh: T. & T. Clark, 1994.

9 Conclusion
Hope in a Technological World

It is clear from the preceding chapters that the transhumanist narrative and certainly all technological futurisms need to be taken with real seriousness not only by Christians but society at large. As I argued in chapters 2 and 3, transhumanist themes are not relegated to just the contemporary movement identified by the term today. There is an historical precedent where technology catalyses thought about the future and how humanity will relate to that technology in the future. Indeed, it is precisely the ubiquity of technological futurisms in the past several hundred years and the presence of transhumanist narratives which galvanise the contention that the claims of contemporary transhumanism do not rise and fall with just this specific group. These ideas are a central preoccupation of our cultural imagination and in our reflections on the future whether they are the topic of literature and intended for fiction or part of real sober planning in politics, philosophy and the academy. These ideas are here to stay and are fundamental to the fabric of our future dreaming.

Furthermore, this transhumanist and technological cultural imaginary is not without its reference to religion. It has been argued that while certain transhumanists desire to distance themselves from accusations that they smuggle in a tacit religious narrative into their claims, there is real force to these criticisms. Not least because, as was shown in the first section of this text, the modern technological endeavour has been speckled with religious motivations since its inception in Francis Bacon: Wherever we find technological dreaming, religion is never far off. This, then, opens the question as to how Christians have sought to engage with technology as a catalyst for future dreaming and, in some instances, with transhumanist themes themselves. Besides Bacon and Fedorov, others in the past century have equally argued for the necessity of a transhumanist future on Christian grounds. Teilhard takes a very positive position on the impact of technology on the Christian future and even suggests that this Ultra-Human future has spiritual and religious implications; that the cosmic Christ is somehow yoked to the emergence and advancement of the transhuman. But other Christians are wary and sceptical of a future under the influence of technology. Ellul is one example. Yet he does share with transhumanists an apocalyptic view of the future. For transhumanism, this apocalypticism is driven by the radical changes technology will make to society and history such that the Singularity invokes feelings of extreme anxiety; this same technology acts as a saviour and promises nothing less than utopia. This is where Ellul wholeheartedly disagrees. Yes, technology will lead to an extreme outcome, in agreement with transhumanism, but his apocalyptic hope resides in a God who saves us from our technological creations which enslave us. Salvation comes from beyond the confines of terrestrial history and human creation. The Christian tradition is full of examples from both ends of the spectrum on integrating technology and transhumanist themes into the Christian future.

Yet theology is not the only arena in which scholars have reflected on technology and the future. Aside from literary and theological sources, the issue of technology was paramount for Heidegger who also offers his own account of technology and the future. What Heidegger brings to bear on these issues is that how one constructs ontology has vast consequences for what constitutes the future. Heidegger challenges the traditional ontology of presence which serves to construct the future purely out of present actuality. Instead, Heidegger looks to our understanding of possibility to come to grips with the future's relation to the present. The final chapters on Heidegger and the themes of possibility and promise sought to construct a Christian approach to the future different from that put forth by transhumanists. This future does not just depend upon present actuality but upon a robust account of possibility which does not define possibility according to the actual. This possibility is the place in which God can be seen to present unforeseen futures that are not derivable from the past and present. The God 'who makes all things new' brings the new to us and transforms us and the world. The Christian account of the future is built upon the promises of an interpersonal God so that when the Christian speaks of the future they refer first to a coming God, *adventus* rather than *futurum*. Talk about the future in the Christian context derives from the interpersonal originally grounded in the Trinity as the primal community, not from statistical projections.

9.1 PERSONAL FUTURE VERSUS IMPERSONAL FUTURE

It is precisely this last point which is a distinctive feature of the Christian future when compared with the transhumanist future and, broadly speaking, scientific approaches to the future. Gerhard Sauter, in a very interesting volume of collected essays on Christian eschatology and scientific accounts of the future, makes this point in an essay entitled 'Our Reason for Hope':

> The mere idea that one day life on Earth will be brought to an end by some cosmic catastrophe is more terrifying than the traditional ideas of the last judgement—even if one considers the fear of ending up on the wrong side of the final division. What is so terrifying about the new

visions of destruction is that it all happens without someone who faces us, who confronts us. There is no other, there are only those who are left to destruction.[1]

This quotation elucidates a common response to scientific appraisals of the far future where all our human efforts are reduced to destruction in the Big Crunch or seemingly eradicated through a supercooled universe. When these scientific cosmologies involving our ultimate demise are brought to the level of human meaning and are allowed to inform our present 'cultural cosmologies' and the myths which provide ultimate orientation and value, they undermine and are often at odds with these constructed cultural cosmologies. This is precisely the contention of William Stoeger in his essay in the previously mentioned text: 'Our physical cosmology has been used to undermine the cultural cosmologies upon which we have depended, and threatens to replace them, anthropologically and philosophically inadequate as it is'.[2]

Transhumanism grows out of this anxiety at being alone in a meaningless universe, an anxiety that caused Pascal to conjecture 'The eternal silence of these infinite spaces fills me with dread'.[3] So, what transhumanism is really pointing to in their hopes for a transhuman race that might just make it beyond these cosmological catastrophes is that we really desire our work to be ultimately meaningful and that we really hope for a future 'where someone faces us'. Transhumanism, in identifying itself in relation to these scientific cosmologies, endeavours to find a way beyond the ultimate nihilism these scientific cosmologies promulgate instead focusing its narrative on this 'human being writ large' which 'faces us' and, so they tell us, is coming. The transhuman future reveals this aversion to a 'faceless future' and, thus, drives home the powerful hope in a future which derives from *adventus* rather than one which relies upon *futurum*. So that, even when transhumanists rely upon a *futurum* account of the future a tacit desire for the *adventus* is visible when taken alongside the other option they tell us: scientific annihilation. We might say we are given the option of a transhuman who faces us in the future or, for the Christian, a caring God who invites us into fellowship with Himself and is thoroughly interpersonal.

9.2 LIMIT AND CREATURELINESS

But, must these two options be exclusive? Clearly, for someone like Teilhard, they do not have to be.[4] The Christian future which arises out of the interpersonal is not entirely averse to transcendence. The Christian tradition is full of examples which promise redemption, glorification and apotheosis to humanity. But, the important question to consider is whether a Christian approach to transcendence is anything like that of the transhumanist one. To deal with this adequately is beyond the scope of this text, but one area is worthy of attention here. The most blatant area of difference is the Christian's upholding of limit and creatureliness in the face of transcendence.

Transcendence for the transhumanist is an eradication of all limits. It proclaims that limits are nothing more than an illusion that we propagate to rationalise our weakness in coming to terms with our actual anthropology which is to transcend all limitations. It is how we explain the discrepancy between what we want to be and what we are. It then follows, for the transhumanist, that we are our greatest enemy because we are the only ones to blame for not grabbing hold of this transcendent future. What makes up this transcendence for the transhumanist and what are the supposed limits that we construct for ourselves but are not genuine features of who we are?

First, transhumanists deny the reality of death as a feature of human existence. They treat death as a disease to be overcome. They propose that human beings are primarily made up of information; their memories, cognitive faculties and bodies can be represented through numbers such that once neuroscience and artificial intelligence are advanced enough that we can just make copies of ourselves like we would a file on a computer.[5] Death is the biggest hoax and lie of all. Second, human beings' lived bodily life is a secondary, and in most cases expendable, aspect of human experience. Bostrom's mantra, 'your body is a deathtrap',[6] depicts the negative attitude many transhumanists have towards their bodies. Bodies aren't the way in which we are in the world and an essential part of what makes us who we are, but are limitations to be overcome. What really matters is the configuration of information which is enclosed in our neural network. For transhumanists, the self resides in the pattern between neurons. Third, most transhumanists proclaim transcendence in terms of self-transcendence. The appeal they make is based on the faith that our greatest wishes will come true, that nothing will be in the way which can limit our desires and our will and, therefore, it is difficult to see how the gross majority do not actually advocate a kind of hedonism. Is the good life nothing but infinite pleasure, the absence of pain and an infinite will? It seems the transhumanist ideal is that the will is unencumbered from any limitation whether from death, the body and, in some places, other people.[7]

But Christian theology has no problem with limitation and suggests that a real virtuous and fulfilling life can only be lived in the acknowledgement that we aren't God or gods and have genuine limitations in the world. Contra transhumanism, death is a feature of being a creature and living as finite beings. The Christian does not deny death's place but is released from its power through Christ entering into death and overcoming it. It is through our death that God grants new possibilities to humanity so that we don't become nothing. This new possibility is a kind of transcendence as we are invited into God's own internal life as 'children of God'. Moltmann's ruminations on this type of transcendence, often identified in the Eastern Church through theosis, argue against a transhumanist interpretation of transcendence: Theosis is not transhumanism:

> This does not mean that human beings will 'become like God' in the way promised by the serpent in the Garden of Eden story. What the axiom is asserting is the divine sonship and daughterhood which Paul ascribes to believers. If being the child of God is meant in a more than metaphorical sense, it implies kinship to God. The children are of the same nature as their father and mother. Even if they are adopted, they acquire the full rights of inheritance. They become partakers of the divine nature. 'Deification' therefore does not mean that human beings are transformed into gods. It means that they partake of the characteristics and rights of the divine nature through their community with Christ, the God-human being.[8]

We are only allotted transcendence through our relationship with God through Christ who is the incarnate Son of God. We only partake in the divine nature inasmuch as we are related to Christ. Transcendence is a gift given by God through Christ not obtained through self-actualisation without reference to those around us.

What Moltmann's thoughts on theosis manifest is that Christian transcendence only comes through relation. Indeed, the ultimate picture of transcendence is the triune God who is first a community with Himself and subsequently shares His presence and divine life with others and particularly the lowly and marginalised. The Christian God is the kenotic God who empties himself and does not consider his divinity something to be exploited or held onto but instead becomes human in Christ and lives a life of ministry to the rejected, sick and sinful.[9] In so doing, Christ opens the divine *perichoretic* life of Father, Son and Holy Spirit to humanity and the rest of creation. To quote the oft-cited words of Athanasius: 'for He was incarnate that we might be made god'.[10]

Self-transcendence, which is often the impulse behind transhumanism, is entirely rejected by Christianity. For the Christian, glorification of the individual can only come through its relation to God and in relation to others. The way we go about our own projects, trying to fulfil our wishes and desires, is entirely a product of and wrapped up in how we relate to others and their projects.[11] In this way, others set a limit to what I can pursue. If transhumanists are serious about a future race of peoples who live together then there needs to be some talk about the limits others place on us as something which will not be going away unless they propose that this future community never interacts. Does the transhumanist also suggest that others are to be treated as a limit to our self-actualisation? Are other people meant to be 'transcended' along with the rest of our environment?

Furthermore, the Christian message, in acknowledging our finitude and creatureliness, upholds this communal life as it is lived bodily. The human body is not an expendable and spurious medium which gets in the way of the self-actualising will, but is the locus of interacting with the environment and is the arena in which we are with others. There is no world without the body. The body is how we experience a particular locality and time, a present. It is the source of frustration, joy and meaning in the world. We are creatures and contained precisely because we are embodied. True transcendence bears the mark of limit where that limit is both bodily and in the community of others.[12]

A final word on wisdom as it is related to creatureliness, finitude and suffering. The transhumanist agenda emphasises the amassing of knowledge as a good in itself whether as an end to help us understand the 'information bearing universe' or as a means by which we can transcend our own limitations. Knowledge is power for the transhumanist. But, for the Christian, knowledge is not a virtue in itself. What matters is not knowledge but wisdom. The virtuous and good life, the end of wisdom, is tied to how Christians live with others who are weak, marginalised and suffering. Virtues arise from the Christian's response and interaction with those who are the forgotten of society. The Christian narrative and identity is Christian insofar as it includes the stories of the marginalised as we learn that God's story is their story and, indeed, is our story. In the transhumanist pursuit of limitless transcendence are these types of virtues lost which can only arise from within a community of those who suffer and are weak? Is not the Christian message of transcendence different precisely because of its reversal of power, attesting that we are only strong when we are weak and in the company of others? And, is not this precisely what we find in the life of Christ?[13]

9.3 RADICAL HOPE AND REAL PLANNING

One of the conclusions of this text has been that a Christian approach to the future must allow for the radically unforeseen. A Christian future does not depend upon statistical analysis of the mechanisms at play in the present and past. The Christian future depends upon a God who makes all things new and is not hindered by what seems possible through our ruminations on the worldly past and present. God's future is derived from his freedom in relation with himself, his promises and the world. This unforeseen *novum* can be the basis for a radical hope that, despite all odds against the possibility of a particular circumstance, can indeed come about. This type of hope is particularly important for those who can see no way out of an oppressive circumstance where not only the situation does not dictate hope, but even in the conditions of that circumstance getting better. When one cannot hope in this world or in its changing, then one must hope in the unforeseen and trust in God's ultimate goodness. This kind of hope is that of the single mother living in the *vertedero*, of the victim of domestic and sexual abuse and that of the tortured victim under the Third Reich, Pinochet or the Khmer Rouge. This hope is very real.

Does this type of future and hope have any value outside of Christianity? I think it does. This radically unforeseen future is a feature of our everyday existence. We constantly meet situations that are new and unexpected. We are predisposed to have experiences of a sublime nature which evade all processing and expectation. Inasmuch as real projection can have tremendous benefits and value, radical dreaming and radical hoping have their roles as well. The scientific and technological endeavours depend upon radical dreaming and openness to a future for its creativity and continued research. Science fiction is a particularly able location for expanding the horizons of our science and technology. Our imagination allows us to envision this radically new future. The non-Christian should be open to this type of future precisely because it is both a feature of our experience and because it contributes to our pursuits today. But, for the Christian, it might be said that God's newness exists on the fringes between this radical hoping and imagination and in that mysterious newness we could never devise on our own.

Am I suggesting that God only works in apocalyptic ways and that we cannot look for real tendencies in the present? No. But, if we are to find them in world or cosmic history it must not be divorced from God's salvation history. Any tendencies we can devise, whether technological or historical, must find their origin and connection to how God work's in new ways. Practically speaking, it means we can find these pockets of God's promised future, but our trust in this future cannot be in our statistical projections but in God's faithfulness to bring his promises about. So, our planning must always be contingent for, as we see in the biblical witness, God's fulfilment of his promises constantly evades how we expect them to be fulfilled. Our planning must always refer back to God's graciousness and our relationship to God. It must be grounded in a person who is coming, *adventus*, rather than in our projections into the future, *futurum*.

I think Phillip Hefner's contention that human beings are to be 'created co-creators' with God has some significant value here.[14] Creation is not just God's handiwork alone; we help contribute to it. Christian hope is grounded in a transformed world where God is the main initiator of this transformation and salvation. All of our action in the world must be seen within this overarching narrative of God's salvation and creation in history. Our work today does have genuine value; we are God's hands and feet in helping the kingdom today. However, the future is primarily God's future and we are called to participate in this future, and sometimes this looks radically different from our own creations, political systems and utopian dreaming.

Is there a problem with these narratives of the Ultra-Human or the transhuman? I would say there is not, so long as we do not ascribe ultimate value to them. It does show a real human proclivity towards transcendence which can help us to understand that we yearn for someone like Christ. But, the Christian hope, ultimately, does not derive from our own abilities to transcend ourselves. Yes, God can work through these technologies to build his kingdom, but they shouldn't eclipse from whence our hope really derives.

Christians need to cautiously consider these narratives. While they might not be dangerous alone, perhaps it is the way we perceive them, the way the transhumanist vision bedazzles us in a religious way, which is the most dangerous. It is when transhumanism becomes our ultimate narrative, when it becomes religious, that we have real need for concern.

NOTES

1. Gerhard Sauter, "Our Reasons for Hope," in *The End of the World and the Ends of God: Science and Theology on Eschatology*, ed., J. C. Polkinghorne and Michael Welker (Harrisburg: Trinity Press International, 2000), 220.
2. William R. Stoeger, "Cultural Cosmology and the Impact of Natural Sciences on Philosophy and Culture," in *The End of the World and the Ends of God: Science and Theology on Eschatology*, ed., J.C. Polkinghorne and Michael Welker (Harrisburg: Trinity Press International, 2000), 76. Stoeger calls for a fresh reintegration of our cultural cosmologies with the publicly acceptable scientific cosmologies stating that these cultural cosmologies should be given the same level of reflection and public warrant as the scientific ones.
3. Blaise Pascal, *Pensées*, trans., A.J. Krailsheimer (London: Penguin Books, 1995), 66 (XV,201).
4. I am not suggesting Teilhard is just a tacit contemporary transhumanist even though many of his ideas, at most, have had a direct influence on the movement and, at least, bear a remarkable similarity. The major difference between Teilhard and contemporary transhumanists is the way human beings achieve that transcendence. For Teilhard, this transcendence is always a function of love amongst a community of persons that is originally grounded in Christ. For a thorough account of similarities and differences see David Grumett, "Transformation and the End of Enhancement: Insights from Pierre Teilhard De Chardin," in *Transhumanism and Transcendence: Christian Hope in an Age of Technological Enhancement*, ed., Ronald Cole-Turner (Washington, DC: Georgetown University Press, 2011).
5. Kurzweil has storage facilities entirely devoted to housing all of the information related to his dead father: bills, notes he scribbled down, diaries and so forth, with the hope that one day he can bring him back again. See John Berman, "Futurist Ray Kurzweil Says He Can Bring His Dead Father Back to Life through a Computer Avatar," *ABC News* (9 August 2011). http://abc news.go.com/Technology/futurist-ray-kurzweil-bring-dead-father-back-life/ story?id=14267712#.T3lrXjF5GSo (accessed 2 April 2012).
6. Nick Bostrom, "Letter from Utopia," *Studies in Ethics, Law, and Technology* 2, no. 1 (2008), 3.
7. I say 'in some places' because there are pockets of more palatable transhumanism which contend that transcendence does not just entail my transcendence—often at the expense of another—but the transcendence of everyone working together. Democratic transhumanism, with James Hughes as the spokesman, offers such an approach. See James Hughes, *Citizen Cyborg: Why Democratic Societies Must Respond to the Redesigned Human of the Future* (Cambridge: Westview, 2004). Furthermore, Jeanine Thweate-Bates contends other variants of posthumanism, such as is represented by Donna Haraway, would make a more palatable conversation partner with Christianity for precisely the reason that it acknowledges limitation and the centrality of embodied existence. See especially chapter five of Jeanine Thweatt-Bates,

  Cyborg Selves: A Theological Anthropology of the Posthuman (Farnham: Ashgate, 2012).

 8. Jürgen Moltmann, *The Coming of God: Christian Eschatology* (London: SCM Press, 1996), 272.

 9. 'Let the same mind be in you that was in Christ Jesus, who, though he was in the form of God, did not regard equality with God as something to be exploited, but emptied himself, taking the form of a slave, being born in human likeness. And being found in human form, he humbled himself and became obedient to the point of death—even death on a cross.' Philippians 2:5–11 (New Revised Standard Version).

10. Athanasius, *On the Incarnation* (Yonkers: St. Vladimir's Seminary Press, 2011), 167 (54).

11. Much of my own thinking in this area is indebted to the writings of those who propose a relational ontology such as Gabriel Marcel and Martin Buber. For them, transcendence is invariably a product of how I relate to others, including God and the natural world. See Martin Buber, *I and Thou*, trans., Walter Kaufmann, 3rd ed. (Edinburgh: T. & T. Clark, 1970); Gabriel Marcel, *The Mystery of Being: Reflection and Mystery*, trans., G.S. Fraser, 2 vols. (Chicago: Henry Regnery Company, 1950).

12. Of course, one could also conclude that limit is important to living an authentic and meaningful life as Hubert Dreyfus does in his book, Hubert L. Dreyfus, *On the Internet* (London: Routledge, 2001). See especially chapter 3 on embodiment and Internet living.

13. The life and writings of Jean Vanier are invaluable to understanding my contentions here. See, for example, Jean Vanier, *Community and Growth: Our Pilgrimage Together* (New York: Paulist Press, 1979); Jean Vanier, *From Brokenness to Community* (New York: Paulist Press, 1992); Jean Vanier, *Becoming Human* (New York: Paulist Press, 1998).

14. See Philip Hefner, *The Human Factor: Evolution, Culture, and Religion*, Theology and the Sciences (Minneapolis: Fortress Press, 1993); Gregory R. Peterson, "The Created Co-creator: What It Is and Is Not," *Zygon* 39, no. 4 (2004). However, I would be inclined to interpret this within a very strong Trinitarian and Christological theology wherein human work is a part of Christ's work. Therefore, I would prefer to speak of a 'created intra-creator'.

REFERENCES

Athanasius. *On the Incarnation*. Yonkers: St. Vladimir's Seminary Press, 2011.

Bauckham, Richard, and Trevor Hart. *Hope against Hope: Christian Eschatology in Contemporary Context*. London: Darton Longman & Todd, 1999.

Berman, John. "Futurist Ray Kurzweil Says He Can Bring His Dead Father Back to Life through a Computer Avatar." *ABC News* (9 August 2011). http://abc news.go.com/Technology/futurist-ray-kurzweil-bring-dead-father-back-life/ story?id=14267712#.T3lrXjF5GSo (accessed 2 April 2012).

Borgmann, Albert. *Crossing the Postmodern Divide*. Chicago: University of Chicago Press, 1992.

———. *Power Failure: Christianity in the Culture of Technology*. Grand Rapids: Brazos Press, 2003.

Bostrom, Nick. "Letter from Utopia." *Studies in Ethics, Law, and Technology* 2, no. 1 (2008): 1–7.

Buber, Martin. *I and Thou*. Translated by Walter Kaufmann. 3rd ed. Edinburgh: T. & T. Clark, 1970.

Cole-Turner, Ronald. "Technology and Eschatology: Scientific and Religious Perspectives on the Transformation of Human Nature." *The Global Spiral* (September 1, 2011). http://www.metanexus.net/essay/technology-and-eschatology (accessed 10 October 2014).

———, ed. *Transhumanism and Transcendence: Christian Hope in an Age of Technological Enhancement*. Washington, DC: Georgetown University Press, 2011.

DeLashmutt, Michael W. "A Better Life through Information Technology? The Techno-Theological Eschatology of Posthuman Speculative Science." *Zygon* 41, no. 2 (2006): 267–288.

Drees, Willem B. *Beyond the Big Bang: Quantum Cosmologies and God*. La Salle: Open Court, 1990.

———. "Religion in an Age of Technology." *Zygon* 37, no. 3 (2002): 597–604.

———, ed. *Technology, Trust, and Religion: Roles of Religions in Controversies on Ecology and the Modification of Life*. Leiden: Leiden University Press, 2009.

Dreyfus, Hubert L. *On the Internet*. London: Routledge, 2001.

Fromm, Erich. *The Revolution of Hope: Toward a Humanized Technology*. New York: HarperCollins 1981.

Garner, Stephen. "Transhumanism and the Imago Dei: Narratives of Apprehension and Hope." PhD thesis, The University of Auckland, 2006.

———. "The Hopeful Cyborg." In *Transhumanism and Transcendence: Christian Hope in an Age of Technological Enhancement*, edited by Ronald Cole-Turner. Washington, DC: Georgetown University Press, 2011.

Gendreau, Bernard. "Gabriel Marcel's Personalist Ontological Approach to Technology." *The Personalist Forum* 15, no. 2 (1999): 229–246.

Graham, Elaine. " 'Nietzsche Gets a Modem': Transhumanism and the Technological Sublime." *Literature and Theology* 16, no. 1 (2002): 65–80.

Grumett, David. "Transformation and the End of Enhancement: Insights from Pierre Teilhard De Chardin." In *Transhumanism and Transcendence: Christian Hope in an Age of Technological Enhancement*, edited by Ronald Cole-Turner. Washington, DC: Georgetown University Press, 2011.

Hefner, Philip. *The Human Factor: Evolution, Culture, and Religion*. Theology and the Sciences. Minneapolis: Fortress Press, 1993.

———. "Technology and Human Becoming." *Zygon* 37, no. 3 (2002): 655–666.

Hughes, James. *Citizen Cyborg: Why Democratic Societies Must Respond to the Redesigned Human of the Future*. Cambridge: Westview, 2004.

Marcel, Gabriel. *The Mystery of Being: Reflection and Mystery*. Translated by G. S. Fraser. 2 vols. Chicago: Henry Regnery Company, 1950.

———. *Homo Viator: Introduction to a Metaphysic of Hope*. Translated by Emma Craufurd. Chicago: Henry Regnery Company, 1951.

———. *Man against Mass Society*. Translated by G. S. Fraser. South Bend: St. Augustine, 2008.

Moltmann, Jürgen. *The Coming of God: Christian Eschatology*. London: SCM Press, 1996.

Nye, David E. *Technology Matters: Questions to Live With*. London: MIT, 2006.

O'Donovan, Oliver. *Begotten or Made?* Oxford: Oxford University Press, 1984.

Pascal, Blaise. *Pensées*. Translated by A. J. Krailsheimer. London: Penguin Books, 1995.

Pattison, George. *Thinking about God in an Age of Technology*. Oxford: Oxford University Press, 2005.

Peters, Ted. *God—The World's Future: Systematic Theology for a Postmodern Era*. Minneapolis: Fortress Press, 1992.

Peterson, Gregory R. "The Created Co-creator: What It Is and Is Not." *Zygon* 39, no. 4 (2004): 827–840.

Polkinghorne, J. C. *The God of Hope and the End of the World*. London: SPCK, 2002.

Sauter, Gerhard. "Our Reasons for Hope." In *The End of the World and the Ends of God: Science and Theology on Eschatology*, edited by J.C. Polkinghorne and Michael Welker. Harrisburg: Trinity Press International, 2000.

Stoeger, William R. "Cultural Cosmology and the Impact of Natural Sciences on Philosophy and Culture." In *The End of the World and the Ends of God: Science and Theology on Eschatology*, edited by J.C. Polkinghorne and Michael Welker. Harrisburg: Trinity Press International, 2000.

Thweatt-Bates, Jeanine. *Cyborg Selves: A Theological Anthropology of the Posthuman*. Farnham: Ashgate, 2012.

Vanier, Jean. *Community and Growth: Our Pilgrimage Together*. New York: Paulist Press, 1979.

———. *From Brokenness to Community*. New York: Paulist Press, 1992.

———. *Becoming Human*. New York: Paulist Press, 1998.

Waters, Brent. *From Human to Posthuman: Christian Theology and Technology in a Postmodern World*. Aldershot: Ashgate, 2006.

———. *Christian Moral Theology in the Emerging Technoculture: From Posthuman Back to Human*. Farnham: Ashgate, 2014.

Wilkinson, David. *Christian Eschatology and the Physical Universe*. London: T. & T. Clark, 2010.

Index

162, 209, 212, 218, 221,
238–42, 243n4, 243n7,
244n11
transhumanism 2–5, 6n10, 11, 42n125,
80–102; definition of 81–2; and
religion 6n5, 99–102, 107n112;
and science fiction 47, 67–9
Trinity 22, 218, 224–5, 237, 244n14

ultimate concern 3, 68–70
universalisation and totalisation of
technology 3, 6n6, 36, 125,

135, 146–7, 153–4, 184, 187,
197n56
utopian hermeneutic 11–12

Verne, Jules 23, 51, 55
weakness of God 228n35

Wells, H.G. 23, 51–2, 55, 68, 70n18,
71n22
within and *without* of things 114–122
World Transhumanist Association *see*
Humanity+

Made in the USA
Monee, IL
18 August 2021